JOHN'S WONDERFUL GOSPEL

JOHN'S WONDERFUL GOSPEL

by
IVOR POWELL

KREGEL PUBLICATIONS
Grand Rapids, Michigan 49501

John's Wonderful Gospel, by Ivor Powell. Copyright © 1962 by Ivor Powell. Published in 1983 by Kregel Publications, a division of Kregel, Inc. by special arrangements with the copyright owner.
All rights reserved.

Library of Congress Cataloging-in-Publication Data

Powell, Ivor
  John's Wonderful Gospel.

  Includes index.
    1. Bible. N.T. John—Criticism, interpretation, etc.
I. Title.

BS2615.2.P68   1983   226'.506   83–16192

ISBN 0-8254-3514-5

Printed on acid-free paper.

3 4 5 6 7 Printing/year 92 91 90 89 88

Printed in the United States of America

CONTENTS

Contents 7

PREFACE

This book is not just another commentary on John's gospel; it attempts what few other volumes have even tried to do. When I became a Christian I fell in love with the fourth gospel, for John's intimate descriptions of Christ enabled me to believe the Lord was his dearest Friend. John was the disciple whom Jesus loved, and because I also desired to lean upon the Master' bosom, the writings of the ancient author became an irresistible attraction. Over a period of thirty-five years, I have lived with John and his message, and therefore it has not been irksome to sit for long periods producing this volume.

Readers of my earlier Bible books may recognize certain extracts from *Bible Cameos, Bible Pinnacles, Bible Treasures,* and *Bible Highways.* There appeared to be no reason to bypass parts of John's gospel because they had been mentioned in earlier volumes. Students will discover that every chapter has been divided into sections, that every verse has been expounded. Each section has been followed by one or more homilies destined to make sermon preparation an increasing delight. If ministers and laymen become acquainted with the contents of this book, they will never be without sermon material. It is stimulating to know that even before this material was placed in print, it was used by the Lord to lead many souls into the kingdom of God.

I would like to express my indebtedness to other authors. The Rev. A. W. Pink must have been an exceptionally fine Bible teacher, and brief extracts from his writings have been mentioned in various parts of this volume. Paragraphs from the ageless works of Matthew Henry and Bishop Ryle have also been used, but for the most part, the contents of this book represent thirty-five years of Bible research on my own part. Therefore it may be repeated this is not just another commentary on the fourth gospel. This book is *different;* it is the sincere prayer of its author that readers will prove it to be delightfully different.

It only remains to say with John of old: "These things are written, that ye may believe that Jesus is the Christ, the Son of God; and that believing ye might have life through His Name."

IVOR POWELL

Santa Barbara,
California.

INTRODUCTION

Had someone suggested to the youthful fisherman John that he was destined to become one of the world's most famous authors, the son of Zebedee would probably have roared with laughter. Had someone suggested to his colleagues that he would become an apostle of love, they might even have fallen out of the boat! It was most unlikely that the hands made rough by hauling nets would become those of an inspired author. It was even more inconceivable that the quick-tempered, vindictive "Son of Thunder" would become the most loving of all the early Christians. Yet such was the miracle of grace: the fisherman became the father of the churches; the arrogant became the anointed.

It has not been possible to determine accurately the date of John's gospel, but there is reason to believe it belongs late in the first century. There exists the possibility that the other gospels had been completed, and in reviewing these, John decided there was much more to be told about the Lord and His ministry. If this conjecture is correct, it would explain why so much of John's material is not even mentioned in the synoptic records. When he perused the gospels of Matthew, Mark, and Luke, he probably wondered why no mention had been made of *the wedding at Cana* (John 2:1-11); *the healing of the nobleman's son* (John 4:46-54); *the man at the pool* (John 5:1-9); *the man born blind* (John 9:1-7); *the raising of Lazarus* (John 11); *the second draught of fishes* (John 21:1-6). In reviewing the amazing utterances of the Master, John was nonplussed to discover that none of the other writers had mentioned *the talk with Nicodemus* (John 3:1-21); *the discourse with the woman at Sychar's well* (John 4); *the parable of the Good Shepherd* (John 10); *the wonderful sermon concerning the Vine* (John 15). To him then, as to us now, these incidents were of supreme importance, and the possibility that they might be omitted from the sacred record and ultimately forgotten filled him with nameless dread. Something had to be done in the matter, and John picked up his writing materials.

Soon words were flowing from his pen and truth from his heart. The new author not only added details to the record, he supplied new insight into the facts behind the record. He believed and accepted all that the other evangelists had written, and yet remained dissatisfied. Probably the Messianic emphasis of Matthew's gospel filled him with glorious pride. The deep humility and gracious service revealed in Mark's gospel engendered reverence and wonder. Indisputably, the scintillating manhood of Luke's narrative promoted a living faith that Christ was a man's Friend. Yes, all this was superbly true, wonderful, enduring, thrilling, but was it sufficient? Could the picture of a Messianic Ruler alone exhibit the grandeur of One who had inhabited eternity? Could the idea of a ministering servant supplying food to the hungry and health to the sick do justice to the fact that the same hands had placed the stars in the sky? Could the thought of human perfection express all that should be said of One who had helped to create the first human? John's eyes became misty as he looked back over the decades of the first century. He saw his Friend, Jesus of Nazareth, in bold relief against the blue waters of Galilee's lake, and then with magnificent breadth of vision scanned the ages to see the time when the Lord God planted a garden eastward in Eden. Then, with a sigh, he looked back into the obscure ages of eternity and wrote,

> *In the beginning was the Word, and the Word was with God, and the Word was God. The same was in the beginning with God. All things were made by him; and without him was not anything made that was made. In him was life; and the life was the light of men . . . And the Word was made flesh, and dwelt among us, (and we beheld his glory, the glory as of the only begotten of the Father) full of grace and truth* (John 1:1-5; John 1:14).

It was in this manner that the fourth gospel began to make its appearance. It has been justifiably affirmed that Mark was the emanuensis of Simon Peter, that his writings reflected the mind of his hero, that the second gospel is in reality the gospel according to Peter. Similarly it has been stated that what Peter was to Mark, Paul was to Luke. Throughout his long association with Paul, the beloved physician gleaned much knowledge concerning the life and ministry of Jesus, and this, when added to his own personal interviews with the women of the gospels, supplied the material for his writings. Be this as it may; the fact remains irrefutable that John needed none to guide him. These were his own memoirs — he had been there when it happened and he knew what he was talking about!

*That which was from the beginning, which we have heard,
which we have seen with our eyes, which we have looked upon,
and our hands have handled of the Word of Life (for the life was
manifested, and we have seen it, and bear witness, and shew
unto you that eternal life, which was with the Father, and was
manifest unto us). That which we have seen and heard declare
we unto you . . . (I John 1:1-3).*

Yes, he had been there when these things happened. He knew
what he was talking about! Furthermore, the elapse of some thirty,
forty, or even fifty years had not dimmed his sight nor impaired his
memory. Even after many years, the events seemed as if they had
taken place only yesterday. Throughout the record, John supplies
many intimate descriptive details which bear the marks of an eye-
witness. He not only remembered the things which took place; he
still recalled the order in which they happened. Beginning with
Friday of the most memorable week-end of his life, John outlined
the various events of the following days until, on the Tuesday of
the next week, "there was a marriage in Cana of Galilee." The fact
that he could remember so well after nearly half a century suggests
that the early impact made upon his soul by the youthful Carpenter
from Nazareth was likely to remain eternally. During his long life,
John had met innumerable men, but none could compare with Jesus.
He had listened to many discourses on many themes, but none remained word for word in his mind as did the sermons preached by
the Master. Yes, he had indeed been there! He was sure of his
facts, and with the conviction deepening in his soul that the story
should be preserved for posterity, he lifted his pen and addressed
himself to his task.

His action was most timely, for already in John's world, heresy
was lifting an ugly head to challenge the faith once for all delivered
to the saints. Old systems die hard, and oftentimes even sincere people struggle desperately to preserve ideas no longer useful in an
advancing age. The apostle John was the last link between the
ancient and the then modern worlds. He remembered the old Jewish
economy before the advent of Jesus; he had lived through peaceful
and troubled decades. He had endured the initial onslaught of persecution and had lived to see the triumph of the Church. Yet he
now knew the greatest dangers arose from internal strife and not
from outward interference. The enemies of Christ had infiltrated
into the Church and strange new ideas were being announced in
the services. Men who had been unable to shed the garments of
Judaism were now trying hard to reconcile the old faith with the
new. It was said that converts could believe in Christ and at the

same time be obligated to fulfill the requirements of the law. Other leaders sworn to preserve the old systems were the avowed enemies of the Cross, and their fierce challenge to the Incarnation of the Son of God was destined to be heard throughout the centuries. They argued that Jesus was a mere man; He had not "come in the flesh." Others affirmed that He was the Son of God but only in the same sense that all men are sons of God.

As these things were repeated, heresy bred confusion, and confusion paralyzed the doubtful preachers. John was worried. The Lord had entrusted the care of the churches to his hand; the Master depended upon him to fulfill his obligations. The other apostles, one by one, were being called to higher service, and constantly his own responsibilities were increasing. Should heresy be permitted to undermine the life of the assemblies? Should the enemies of Christ be allowed to ruin the testimony? No! People should know the truth, and the truth would make them free.

Beloved . . . In the beginning was the Word . . . and the Word was made flesh and dwelt among us . . . Believe not every spirit, but try the spirits whether they are of God; because many false prophets are gone out into the world. Hereby know ye the Spirit of God: Every spirit that confesseth that Jesus Christ is come in the flesh is of God: And every spirit that confesseth not that Jesus Christ is come in the flesh is not of God . . . (I John 4:1-3). We know that the Son of God is come (I John 5:20). Many other signs truly did Jesus in the presence of his disciples, which are not written in this book: But these are written, that ye might believe that Jesus is the Christ, the Son of God, and that believing ye might have life through his name (John 20:30, 31).

JOHN'S WONDERFUL GOSPEL

The First Chapter of John

THEME: *John's Introduction to an Unprecedented Week-end*

OUTLINE:
    I. Eternity Until a Certain Friday. Verses 1-18.
    II. Friday and Saturday. Verses 19-34.
    III. Sunday and Monday. Verses 35-51.

SECTION ONE

Expository Notes on John's Introduction to the Gospel

In the beginning was the Word, and the Word was with God, and the Word was God. The same was in the beginning with God (vv. 1, 2).

It has already been stated that one of the reasons for the writing of this gospel was the conviction of John that the other writers had not exhausted the theme of the greatness of Christ. The apostle John was a seer, a visionary whose gaze encompassed eternity. To his broad concept, the story of Bethlehem was but a detail in the divine plan for the Ages; his love for the infant Jesus was completely overshadowed by his reverence for the Lord who had been with the Father from eternal ages. *In the beginning . . . Christ.* John made no effort to explain this amazing truth; he was content to proclaim it. John seemed as a small creature looking up at a vast mountain bathed in sunlight. He was not interested in asking whence it came; he saw it, accepted it, proclaimed it. In the beginning Christ; and Christ, the Word, the Logos, was with God, and Christ was God. He proclaimed plurality of persons in the Godhead and this harmonized with the teachings of the sacred writings. "And God said, Let us make man in our image, after our likeness: . . . So God created man in his own image . . ." (Genesis 1:26, 27). This also fulfilled the prediction made by Isaiah the prophet, "For unto us a child is born, unto us a son is given: and the government shall be upon his shoulder: and his name shall be called Wonderful, Counsellor, THE MIGHTY GOD, THE EVERLASTING FATHER, the Prince of Peace" (Isaiah 9:6). Many great mysteries are revealed in the Scripture, but it should always be recognized that man's inability to grasp their true meaning is not evidence that they are false and unreal. The limitations of our intellectual apprehensions should remind us continually that we are too small, and not that God is too large.

It is both thought-provoking and vital to know that in the original Greek Testament, the definite article "the" is missing. Literally, the translation would read, "In beginning, was the Word . . ." To a modern reader this would be provocative and the obvious question would soon be forthcoming — what beginning? The first chapter of Genesis commences in a similar way. There, however, the introductory statement reads, "In the beginning, God created the heaven and the earth." The presence of the definite article suggests a point in time when God did a certain deed. This took place at the beginning of an era. The absence of that qualifying word from John's record suggests that his beginning might be further back — in fact, prior to *any* beginning, the Word was there. All this seems to be faithfully expressed in the fact that John uses two different words, which alas, have been translated by the English word *was*. These Greek words are *ito* and *egeneto*. Arthur W. Pink in his brilliant devotional commentary on John's gospel (pages 19 and 20) has set this forth in a most illuminating manner:

> There are two separate words in the Greek which, in this passage, are both rendered was: the one means *to exist*, the other *to come into being*. The latter word (*egeneto*) is used in 1:3 which, literally rendered, reads, "all things through him *came into being*, and without him *came into being* not even one (thing) which has *come into being*;" and again we have the word *egeneto* in 1:6 where we read, "there *was* (became to be) a man sent from God, whose name was John;" and again in 1:14, "And the word *was made* (became) flesh." But here in 1:1 and 1:2 it is "the word (*ito*) with God." As the Word He did not come into being, or begin *to be*, but He *was* "with God" from all eternity. It is noteworthy that the Holy Spirit uses this word *ito*, which signifies that the Son *personally subsisted*, no less than four times in the first two verses of John 1. Unlike John the Baptist who "*became* (*egeneto*) a man*," the "Word" *was* (*ito*) that is, *existed* with God before time began. (*Exposition of the Gospel of John*, Zondervan Publishing House, 1956).

Through the centuries men and movements have announced Christ was created by God to do the divine will. Yet John maintained that "*all things were created by him.*" If Christ were a created creature, how then could it be said that He created all things?

F. L. Godet, the famous Swiss theologian, in contrasting the beginnings of the book of Genesis and John's gospel, admirably said, ". . . the first words of the two writings manifestly correspond with each other. The beginning of which John here speaks can only be that which Moses had made the starting-point of his narrative. But, immediately afterwards, the two sacred writers separate from each other. Starting from the fact of the creation, Moses descends the stream of time and reaches the creation of man (verse 26). John, having started from the same point, follows the reverse course and ascends from the beginning of things to eternity. It is because his end in view is more remote, and because in order to reach farther, he must start from a point farther back. The Jewish historian had in view only the foundation of the theocratic work in Abraham, while the evangelist would reach the redemption of humanity by Jesus Christ. To find Him who shall be the agent of this second creation, instead of descending the course of things, he must ascend even beyond the beginning of the first creation" (Godet's *Commentary on John's Gospel,* reprint by Kregel Publications, Grand Rapids, Mich. 1978. pages 243, 244).

Thus we stand in awe with God's great servants to gaze at the unknown, unrevealed ages of the past. Here we have a beginning, but farther back, there is no beginning! We measure and date time from some particular moment when something happened, but before anything ever took place, God *WAS.* From everlasting to everlasting, God remains unchanging. He is the eternally present One, and this was beautifully expressed when He commissioned Moses to liberate the captive Israelites: "And Moses said unto God, Behold, when I come unto the children of Israel, and shall say unto them, The God of your fathers hath sent me unto you; and they shall say to me. What is his name? what shall I say unto them? And God said unto Moses, I AM THAT I AM: and he said, Thus shalt thou say unto the children of Israel, I AM hath sent me unto you" (Exodus 3:13, 14). God did not reveal Himself as the "I WAS" nor as the "I WILL BE"; He preferred to remain the eternally present one — the I AM. He never had a beginning; He will never know an end, and if our finite minds reel as they try to grasp the limitless horizons of this amazing truth, let us find refuge and joy in the fact that this great God has become our Heavenly Father. It is wonderful to believe that Almighty God veiled in obscurity watched us; it is infinitely better to know He became dissatisfied with His methods of remote control and decided to come closer to us. "The Word became flesh and dwelt among us."

The Englishman's Greek New Testament, which uses the Greek text of Stephen (1550 A.D.), provides food for thought, for the text reads, "In the beginning was the Word, and the Word was with God — *kai Theos een ho Logos.* AND GOD WAS THE WORD." Young preachers and indeed all Christians should carefully note this fact, for certain door-to-door literature sellers are zealous in stating that in the absence of a definite article, the text should read, "And the Word was a God." This they do to infer that the Word was inferior to the Father. Their distorted conjectures are brought into bold relief when it is seen that the text teaches the exact opposite of what they suggest. It would almost appear as though someone had anticipated their doctrines, for the emphasis is slightly shifted. John seems to be saying "GOD — YES, G-O-D WAS THE WORD."

It is against this background that we must consider again the thrilling prediction of Micah. "But thou, Bethlehem Ephratah, though thou be little among the thousands of Judah, yet out of thee shall he come forth unto me that is to be ruler in Israel, WHOSE GOINGS FORTH HAVE BEEN FROM OF OLD, *from everlasting*" (Micah 5:2). No prophet, not even in moments of extreme imagination, would utter such a fantastic statement. Here then is evidence in support of the inspiration of the Scriptures. He who was destined to walk the streets of Judean towns had walked in eternity with God. "His goings forth had been from eternal ages." There, beyond the reach of all except the eyes of faith, the three members of the divine family had sat — so to speak — around Their conference table, had planned and designed Their worlds, and together had made man. All this, and perhaps much more, John saw clearly, and having considered the other writings of his day, decided "the half had never been told." He reached for his pen, and the fourth gospel was born.

All things were made by him (v. 3).

John saw in Jesus the vehicle of creative expression. The inscrutable, the mystical, the unknown God had decided to reveal Himself, and in order to do so, had chosen the Logos. It must be remembered that in spite of ever recurring denials heard during the centuries, this teaching enunciated by John was the recognized faith of the Early Church. The apostle Paul affirmed, "But to us there is but one God, the Father, of whom are all things, and we in him; and one Lord Jesus Christ, *by whom are all things,* and we in him" (I Corinthians 8:6). " . . . God, who created all things by Jesus Christ . . ." (Ephesians 3:9).

In him was life, and the life was the light of men, and the light shineth in darkness (v. 4).

The germ of life is inexplicable. Within a small acorn lies the mighty oak. Within a tiny seed is the possibility of far-reaching fields of corn. Within a spotted egg is the song of the lark. One moment after decease, a body remains but something has gone. Life defies adequate definition; it remains unchallenged, the most amazing miracle in the universe. Scientists study human tissue, physicians study human ailments, but life remains an inestimable treasure, just out of reach and yet always within our grasp. It can be nourished, preserved, guarded, yet when the time for its departure or cessation arrives, neither vast sums of money nor great accumulations of military strength can prevent its departure. Life is of God, for God is life. John's magnificent breadth of vision swept over the ages spanned by the law and the prophets as he said, "God's life was the light of men, and the light shineth in darkness, and the darkness comprehended it not." Continuing to develop his tremendous theme, the apostle taught that God had revealed himself in (1) creative power; (2) positive commandments; (3) inspired predictions. Alas, the engulfing blackness of human guilt had negated the continuing revelation of God. Then, when the darkness comprehended it not, God did something new.

There was a man sent from God whose name was John (v. 5).

It is worthy of mention that in recent decades the orthodox conception of the deity of Christ has been challenged by the emissaries of certain heretical sects. Stressing the fact that the definite article is not found in the original Greek manuscripts, they affirm that Jesus was a created being, and that the opening statements of John's gospel should read, "In the beginning was the Word and the Word was with God, and the Word was a God." Basing their remarks upon what actually is an absurdity, they teach the inferiority of the Son. However, the same teachers are inconsistent because they do not apply the same rule throughout the entire chapter. By the same standard they should read, "There was a man sent from a God whose name was John" (verse 6). "But as many as received him, to them gave he the power to become the sons of a God" (verse 12).

The same came for a witness to bear witness of the Light, that all men through him might believe (v. 6).

In this and the following verses, three things stand out in bold relief.

(1) *The enduring love of God.* Throughout the Old Testament dispensations, God had often sent angels and prophets to counsel and guide His erring people. Alas, the various missions failed to achieve their purpose; the darkness remained darkness. The commandments were broken, the prophets stoned, and the nation brought to the verge of disaster. Yet God had not abandoned His task. The appearance of John indicated the divine mission had not terminated. God was still trying to reach the unreached.

(2) *The entrancing light of God.* John supplied the standards by which all preachers should estimate the value of their ministry. His primary purpose was not to win souls but to bear witness of the Light. Indeed it is problematical in the final analysis whether

any preacher can win souls. Jesus said, "No man cometh unto me except the Father draw him" (John 6:44). Man's task is to bear witness, to allow God to work through the human instrument. Thus God will have something to use and the influencing of men and women will automatically follow. Ours is the privilege, not to direct, but to be controlled. We are but lamps; God alone supplies the power to make us burn and give light. A God-controlled life leads to a distinguishing ministry.

(3) *The eternal life of God.* "As many as received him, to them gave he the power — the right, the authority — to become the sons of God, even to them which believe on his name. Which were born, not of blood, nor of the will of the flesh, nor of the will of man, but of God" (verses 12 and 13). This is in harmony with Christ's word to Nicodemus, "That which is born of the flesh is flesh; and that which is born of the Spirit is spirit" (John 3:6). Constantly the Lord thought of two families. "But he answered and said, . . . Who is my mother? and who are my brethren? *And he stretched forth his hand toward his disciples,* and said, Behold my mother and my brethren. For whosoever shall do the will of my Father which is in heaven, the same is my brother, and sister, and mother" (Matthew 12:48-50). Intelligent faith in the Person of Christ begets the desire to accept and follow Him, and this opens the door for the incoming of the very life of God. (See notes about Nicodemus, ch. 3).

And the Word was made flesh . . . and we beheld his glory, the glory of the only begotten of the Father, full of grace and truth . . . No man hath seen God at any time; the only begotten Son which is in the bosom of the Father, he hath declared him (vv. 14-18).

Here again, in keeping with his main purpose, John emphasizes the fact that Jesus was the expression of God. In Him we see the glory of the Father; in Him we see the face of the Father. Within the life and testimony of John Baptist, both grace and truth were exhibited. Grace said, "He was preferred before me." Truth said, "For He was before me." That Jesus brought the supreme revelation of the Godhead is indicated by, "For the law was given by Moses, but grace and truth came by Jesus Christ." "Wherefore the law was our schoolmaster to bring us to Christ that we might be justified by faith" (Galatians 3:24). However adequate the law of Moses for the twilight or pre-dawn periods of history, it was totally insufficient to reveal the complete will of God. The Mosaic law was something by which *transgressors might be corrected.* Grace and truth, the twin laws of the Spirit of Life in Christ Jesus, were commandments by which *saints could be perfected.* For example,

Moses said, "Thou shalt not commit adultery," and as long as a man refrained from that gross act of evil, he remained guiltless. Under the new order, the same man could be exceedingly guilty, for Jesus in announcing new standards of morality said, "Ye have heard that it was said by them of old time, Thou shalt not commit adultery: But I say unto you, That whosoever looketh upon a woman to lust after her hath committed adultery with her already in his heart" (Matthew 5:27, 28). This was a new concept of true virtue. It emphasized that ". . . Christ had declared the Father" (John 1:18).

And the Word was made flesh and tabernacled among us (v. 14).

It is most difficult to avoid the feeling that John had in mind the truth that long before, God decided to tabernacle among the children of Israel. In other words, God decided to come down and pitch His tent in the midst of the camp. It is not too difficult to see a progression of thought in the Scripture. At first, God inhabited eternity, but for the sinner in distress, the location seemed so far away. Then God came closer, for in brief moments Jehovah left His dwelling place to walk near Adam in the Garden of Eden. Later, a voice called Abraham, but whence it came, probably even he did not know. Perhaps it was but an ever-deepening conviction within his conscience. Later still, God again drew near, for in speaking with Moses He made it apparent that He had come to stay at least temporarily in the top of Mount Sinai. Yet even this manifestation was not too encouraging, for the overwhelming sense of His holiness made Israel tremble. It is problematical whether any but Moses ever desired to get closer to a God whose very presence filled them with dread. But then came the new revelation. God was not to be feared, for He loved them and desired to live in their midst. This was a new conception of things, and as love begets love, the drawing near of God made it possible for sinners to draw near to Him. "He came down and pitched his tent among them." No longer was there need to climb the lofty cloud-covered mountain; no longer was it necessary to turn in all directions to ask, "Whence came His voice?" God lived in the midst of the camp, and the path which led first to the altar continued into His presence. The life of Israel was soon to revolve around the Tabernacle. Many and varied are the thoughts connected with this truth. It had been suggested that this was a temporary appointment and as such was a definite contrast to Solomon's temple; that beween the two was a great period of time. If this is a type, then it is easily recognized that Christ's coming to tabernacle among us was but for a short time; after a lengthy period known to us as the age of grace, He will return to set up His visible reign on earth.

In comparison with other ornate structures, the Tabernacle in the wilderness would appear to be primitive, insignificant, and humble. It was, with some reservations, but a tent of skins and was erected on a New Year's day (Exodus 40:17). Solomon's temple was costly, elaborate, scintillating, and took many years to erect. There is evidence to support the conclusion that when Christ comes to earth to reign on David's throne, the earth shall be filled with the glory of the Lord as the waters cover the sea. Yet when he came to tabernacle among us, ". . . he hath no form nor comeliness, and when we shall see him, there is no beauty that we shall desire him" (Isaiah 53:2). That does not mean He was plain, ugly, and unattractive. The prophet inferred that judged by the standards of men, He was not great — He had no armies; He had no great wealth; He was born in a stable, not a palace. He was placed in a bed of straw, not one of royal silks and satins. His hands were not soft as velvet; they were hardened by the tools He used every day. He was a Carpenter and not a King, and yet no king was ever born who was worthy to stand in His presence.

Not the least important truth connected with the Tabernacle in the wilderness was the fact that it represented the meeting place between God and man. There was no other common ground. To the mercy seat, God came to forgive; to the same mercy seat, man came to be forgiven. Many years later, the Lord Jesus said, ". . . I am the way, the truth, and the life: no man cometh unto the Father, but by me" (John 14:6). One cannot help but ask if John had these thoughts in his mind when he wrote, "And the Word was made flesh and dwelt — tabernacled — among us."

And of his fulness have all we received, and grace for grace (v. 16).

This is a stimulating verse and begets the question, "What was the fulness of Christ?" Some writers suggested that John was speaking of the fulness of the life of the Godhead, but this interpretation leaves much to be desired. Paul wrote, "For in him dwelleth all the fulness of the Godhead bodily" (Colossians 2:9). It would appear that Paul added something to this conception when he expressed in Ephesians 1:21, 22. ". . . the church, which is his body, the fulness of him that filleth all in all." There is reason to believe that this great term expressed much more than divine life; it also embraces the far reaching purposes of the Godhead. The life, the purposes, the joys, and all that pertains to the divine Family were truly represented in the Word. In these we find redemption for sinners, the creation of the body of Christ, and the eternal determination to bring to full fruition those ideals for which Christ died. This, and probably much more, was included in "the fulness," for continuing his statement in Ephesians 1:22, 23, Paul declares, ". . . the church, which is his body, the fulness of him that filleth all in all . . . till we all come in the unity of the faith, and of the knowledge of the Son of God, unto a perfect man, unto the measure of the stature of *the fulness of Christ*" (Ephesians 4:13). All that God is, all that God says, all that God desires — all is fully expressed in Christ. This was John's conception of the Logos. When a child asked, "What is God like?" the apostle indisputably answered, "Jesus." When the philosophers and theologians debated, argued, and asked, "What does God say?" the same apostle unhesitatingly replied, "Let Jesus tell you." Until the Saviour came, God had been the mysterious One inhabiting eternity, the hidden One whose glory filled the holiest place beyond the veil. It was not given to finite man to behold the Eternal One. Yet when John wrote, "No man hath seen God at any time," he was not unduly worried, for he remembered how Philip said unto Jesus: "Lord, shew us the Father, and it sufficeth us. Jesus saith unto him, Have I been so long time with you and yet hast thou not known me, Philip? He that hath seen me hath seen the Father; and how sayest thou then, Shew us the Father? Believest thou not that I am in the Father, and the Father in me? The words that I speak unto you I speak not of myself: but the Father that dwelleth in me, he doeth the works. Believe me that I am in the Father, and the Father in me: or else believe me for the very works' sake" (John 14:8-11). Thus continuing his statement in John 1:18, he said, "No man hath seen God at any time; the only begotten Son, which is in the bosom of the Father, he hath declared him."

In this way John concluded the prologue to his gospel, and writers of international repute in all ages recognize it to be one of the greatest pieces of literature ever produced.

HOMILIES

Study No. 1

THERE WAS NO OTHER WAY

Perhaps the most effective way to view and to understand the Incarnation is to see it against the background of Levitical law. There were very strict Mosaic laws which governed the redemption of property and persons in Israel.

God's Great Law

"And if a sojourner or stranger wax rich by thee, and thy brother that dwelleth by him wax poor, and sell himself unto the stranger or sojourner by thee, or to the stock of the stranger's family:

After that he is sold he may be redeemed again; *one of his brethren may redeem him.* Either his uncle or his uncle's son may redeem him, *or any that is nigh of kin unto him of his family may redeem him;* or, if he be able, he may redeem himself" (Leviticus 25:47-49). It is clear from the record that for any hungry Israelite bondage was preferable to death. If a man were unable to maintain himself, it was permissible for him to become a bondsman. Once the deed was done, it was irrevocable except in the case of redemption. Unlimited financial resources on the part of some friend would be insufficient to guarantee the emancipation of the slave. For example, even King David could not have enforced legally the liberation of a slave unless David himself were a kinsman of the bondman. Yet, at any time, even five minutes after the servitude commenced, a blood relation, on payment of the necessary redemption money, could demand the release of his kinsman. This was unquestionably the law of God and prevailed throughout the successive generations of Israel. The right to redeem was something exclusively reserved for kinsmen, and when two or more kinsmen were interested, the nearest kinsman had priority of privilege.

This is clearly expressed in Ruth 3:12. "And now it is true that I am thy near kinsman: howbeit there is a kinsman nearer than I." The story continues in Ruth 4:1-8 —

> Then went Boaz up to the gate and sat him down there: and, behold the kinsman of whom Boaz spake came by; unto whom he said, Ho, such an one! turn aside sit down here. And he turned aside and sat down. And he said unto the kinsman, Naomi, that is come again out of the country of Moab, selleth a parcel of land which was our brother Elimelech's: and I thought to advertise thee, saying, Buy it before the inhabitants, and before the elders of my people. If thou wilt redeem it, redeem it: but if thou wilt not redeem it, then tell me, that I may know: for there is none to redeem it beside thee; and I am after thee. And he said, I will redeem it. Then said Boaz, what day thou buyest the field of the hand of Naomi, thou must buy it also of the hand of Ruth the Moabitess, the wife of the dead, to raise up the name of the dead upon his inheritance. And the kinsman said, I cannot redeem it for myself, lest I mar mine own inheritance: redeem thou my right to thyself, for I cannot redeem it. Now this was the manner in former time in Israel concerning redeeming and concerning changing, for to confirm all things, a man plucked off his shoe, and gave it to his neighbour; and this was a testimony in Israel. Therefore the kinsman said unto Boaz, Buy it for thee. So he drew off his shoe.

It has already been stated, redemption referred both to people and property.

God's Great Problem

A judge who deliberately violated his own laws would himself be condemned. A preacher who advocated moral standards he did not observe himself would be a hypocrite. What then would have been said of God had He broken one of His own commandments? In the fullness of time God saw that man was a slave sold under sin (Romans 7:14), and He desired to redeem him. Yet this was impossible, as His own law forbade the operation. The rite of redemption belonged to someone in the slave's family, to someone near of kin. How then could God redeem man when He did not belong to man's family? God was divine, man was human. God was the uncreated, man was the creature, and just as King David under certain circumstances would have been denied the joy of redeeming a slave, so God could not deliver fallen man. Now all this is tremendously interesting and reveals that Christ was indeed the Lamb slain from the foundation of the world. When God enunciated that particular law, He saw what at that time had not been revealed, and within His Word enshrined immortally the glorious fact announced by Abraham, "God will provide himself a lamb for a burnt-offering . . ." (Genesis 22:8). Therefore it seemed for a while that heaven had reached an impasse; the Creator of innumerable worlds had at last found something He could not do. Let me hasten to add, It seemed He had reached an impasse. There can be no doubt that He who sees the end from the beginning knew what would happen.

God's Great Miracle

It was at this time the Eternal Son descended from His throne to undertake the most important mission the world will ever know. Did the law demand that a redeemer belong to the slave's family? Then, the Word would become bone of our bone and flesh of our flesh. He who had never known bondage would enter into the human family and become a servant. Thus would He become eligible to redeem man, and accomplish satisfactorily what otherwise would remain an impossibility. Of this amazing fact, Paul wrote, ". . . Christ Jesus: who, being in the form of God, thought it not robbery to be equal with God: but made Himself of no reputation, and took upon him the form of a servant, and was made in the likeness of men: and being found in fashion as a man, he humbled himself and became obedient unto death, even the death of the cross" (Philippians 2:5-8). "Now all this was done, that it might be fulfilled which was spoken of the Lord by the prophet saying, Behold a virgin shall be with child, and shall bring forth a son, and they shall call his name Emmanuel, which being interpreted is, GOD WITH US" (Matthew 1:22, 23).

> Dying for me, dying for me,
> There on the cross, He was dying for me;
> Now in His death my redemption I see,
> All because Jesus was dying for me.

Study No. 2

IF CHRIST REALLY CAME!

One of man's greatest weaknesses is that he takes too much for granted. That which is often repeated is apt to decrease in importance; familiarity is expert at breeding contempt. In the midst of this space age when even school children discuss freely the problems and possibilities of inter-planetary travel, things have become so commonplace that it no longer makes news when another rocket succeeds in putting a small man-made sphere into orbit around the earth. When the Russian people first put their Sputnik into the sky, newspapers of all nations came out with special editions announcing with glaring headlines the amazing event. This no longer happens. When a man was first sent into outer space, the newspapers had another field-day, but when the event is followed by fifteen or twenty successful flights of a similar nature, it will no longer be news and editors will return to the reporting of horse racing! We live in a strange world, the strangest part of which is the people who live in it!

Possibly the arrival of a flying saucer from a remote planet would supply electrifying material for all journalists, but if our heavenly visitors came in increasing numbers, the possibility exists that before long we would try to arrange inter-planetary baseball matches, and tourist travel would skyrocket! We are all prone to lose sight of the wonder of the miracles about us, and even the supernatural is permitted to pass unnoticed. It is this sad fact that has turned the Christmas season into a gigantic windfall for commercial houses. That the King of angels came to be born in a stable means little except to supply the backdrop for yet another spending spree.

If Christ really came, He must have had great reason for doing so

History reveals that in every world crisis, God has been able to produce the instrument capable of meeting the emergency. Sometimes His choice fell on a judge whose moral integrity commanded national respect. At other times He raised up a military leader to bring liberty to the oppressed. There have been times of spiritual shallowness when God produced a prophet whose fiery denunciations arrested the downward trend in a nation. On rare occasions, when no man was equal to the urgent demands of the moment, God commissioned an angel to do what was necessary. Apparently this has been the outstanding characteristic of all God's dealings with mankind.

The one notable exception occurred when He sent His own Son. This particular thing had never happened before and has never happened since. In all His associations with humanity, there was but one occasion when *something* demanded extreme action on God's part. Neither the best of men nor the best of angels could undertake this special mission. If one might borrow words from our generation, then it would seem as if a state of emergency suddenly existed in heaven. Something had to be done; something of unusual importance had to be done, and only God could do it. It is logical then that we seek for the reason of Christ's coming, and this He Himself supplied when He said, "For the Son of Man is come to seek and to save that which was lost" (Luke 19:10). He came to earth because man needed to be saved. It has been written that "All have sinned and come short of the glory of God," and therefore since even the best of men needed saving, it was obvious that no man could do what had to be done. But why did not God send an angel? The Lord answered this question when He declared, "I am come that they might have life, and that they might have it more abundantly" (John 10:10). It is true that an angel MIGHT have taken away our sin; but no angel could give eternal life and make men partakers of the divine nature. Angels could not do this because they did not have it to give. The purpose of God in Christ was not only to lift us *from* the clutches of evil, but to continue the lifting operation *into* the embrace of God. Who then could do such an enormous thing?

> There was no other good enough
> To pay the price of sin.
> He only could unlock the gate
> Of heaven and let us in.

If Christ really came, how great was His love!

It must never be forgotten that He saw the end from the beginning. He who came to Bethlehem knew that the road would lead to Calvary, and in spite of the threat of forthcoming pain, He turned not back. Again and again throughout His memorable ministry, Christ revealed that He knew what awaited Him at Jerusalem. Often He said, "For the Son of Man must be delivered into the hands of sinful men, and be crucified, and the third day, rise again" (Luke 24:7; Mark 8:31). Yet in spite of the increasing bitterness toward Him, Jesus steadfastly set His face to go to Jerusalem. His overflowing love was manifest in every miracle performed, in every sermon preached, in every word and deed of His never-to-be forgotten ministry. He lifted the children in His arms — and they loved to be lifted. He touched the untouchable lepers, and these unfortunate men never forgot the moment. His touch brought heaven to homes, and the peace of God to troubled hearts. He healed the sick, gave sight to the blind, and banished care from innumerable homes. It was this astounding fact that enabled thousands of people to say as did James Proctor,

> He died, He lives, He reigns, He pleads;
> There's love in all His words and deeds.
> There's all a guilty sinner needs
> Forevermore in Jesus.

If Christ really came, then how great is man's opportunity

A possible objection might be that this was true for the people who lived twenty centuries ago, but for us who are so far removed from the time of His sojourn on earth the opportunity does not exist. Such sentiments are expressed in the lovely lines of the children's hymn:

> I think when I read that sweet story of old
> When Jesus was here among men
> How He called little children as lambs to His fold
> I should like to have been with Him then.
> I wish that His hands had been placed on my head,
> That His arms had been thrown around me,
> And that I might have seen His kind look when He said,
> "Let the little ones come unto Me."

These expressions are not only attractive; they are convincing until we remember that if Christ really came to earth, His teaching would be completely reliable. Surely He had reason to say, "It is expedient for you that I go away: for if I go not away, the Comforter will not come unto you . . ." (John 16:7). Throughout His sojourn on earth, the Master's movements were limited by the restrictions of having to reside within a body. This negated any possibility of being in two places at the same time. Relieved of these limitations, the Comforter would be everywhere, for even the creation is not too large to hold the Divine Presence. Christ promised, "Go ye into all the world and preach the Gospel . . . And lo, I am with you alway" (Mark 16:15; Matthew 28:20). If we believe the teaching of Jesus, we acknowledge that the Incarnate Word is now the omnipresent Saviour. Thus it follows that wherever a man might be, there he can draw near to Christ.

If Christ really came — but how can I know if He came?

Several answers have been given to this question. Some teachers point to the calendar and indicate that even our system of reckoning years points back to the coming of Christ. We specify events as having taken place either before Christ or after Christ. Other men urge the critics to examine the works of the historians and to find there adequate reference to the life and works of Jesus of Nazareth.

However, it is hard to escape the conclusion that any man who asks the question has already considered the answers suggested and, feeling they are insufficient to convince his inquiring soul, is still looking for some tangible proof of the reality of Christ.

The most conclusive evidence in support of the Saviour's coming is the power that changes lives. The only sure way by which to vindicate the veracity of His statements is to put them to the test. I have often looked at a congregation and indicated how foolish it would be if I were to say, "Come unto me, all ye that labour and are heavy laden and I WILL GIVE YOU REST." Were I to issue such an invitation, I would be very frightened that some man might respond. As a preacher, I might offer counsel; if I were a wealthy man, I might offer financial assistance; if I owned vast housing estates, I might offer a home, but no man can offer rest. Rest is something of the soul. It cannot be purchased for money; it is not offered by any manufacturing company. Yet Christ said, "Come . . . and I will give you rest." Obviously, the only way to find out if He is able to honor His promise is to accept His invitation. That is precisely what millions of people have done. They now say,

> I heard the voice of Jesus say
>   Come unto Me and rest:
> Lay down, thou weary one, lay down
>   Thy head upon My breast.
> I came to Jesus as I was —
>   Weary, and worn, and sad.
> I found in Him a resting place
>   And He has made me glad.

Study No. 3

THE WORD — THE NAME THAT LIVES THROUGH THE AGES

It has already been mentioned that John used the name *the Word* because he saw in Jesus the expression of God. By Him, in Him, through Him, the eternal God had spoken. No other evangelist used the term, and this in itself indicates that John aimed to express the majesty of the divine Christ rather than to follow the example of the other writers and dwell at length on the human attributes of the Saviour. It is clear from an examination of John's five books that this central thought never left him. We have no accurate way of deciding over what period of time the apostle continued as an author; we only know that in his gospel, in his epistles, and finally in the book of the Revelation, he continued to call Jesus, *the Word*. This was the name which remained in his mind; indeed, it has continued through the centuries.

The Word in the gospel — The Word took man's place

"And the Word was made flesh and dwelt among us . . ."
(John 1:14). (See the earlier notes on this same topic.) Another
fitting commentary on the wonder of the coming of the Word is
supplied by Paul in II Corinthians 8:9: "For ye know the grace
of our Lord Jesus Christ, that, though he was rich, yet for your
sakes he became poor, that ye through his poverty might become
rich." Link these two verses together and a most admirable commentary is forthcoming.

(1) *His Great Riches* — The Word expressing the Greatness of
God.

"For ye know the grace of our Lord Jesus Christ, that though
he was rich . . ." Rich in glory, rich in power, rich in creative
ability, rich in everything appertaining to the Godhead.

(2) *His Great Reason* — The Word expressing the Grace of God.

". . . yet for your sakes he became poor . . ." He voluntarily
left all that He possessed and became what He had never been
before. Apart from His own unchanging greatness, He became un-
recognizable from what He had hitherto been. And all this He did
for the sake of sinful men. We can only exclaim with the patriarch,
"What is man that thou art mindful of him?"

(3) *His Great Redemption* — The Word expressing the Gospel
of God.

". . . that ye through his poverty might become rich." He came
where we were so that we might return where He belonged. Compare and contrast this revelation with the God whose voice thundered
on Mount Sinai, and ask yourself if these were the same God! The
coming of Christ introduced a new era. He unveiled the face of
Deity and revealed that *God is love.*

The Word in the epistles — The Word supplies man's grace

"For there are three that bear record in heaven, the Father, the
Word, and the Holy Spirit: and these three are one" (John 5:7).
(The following paragraph is taken from *Bible Highways*, page 125.)

"As the church developed and spread through the world, error
began to destroy its unity, and before John went to join his Lord,
he felt constrained to issue stern warnings against those who menaced the Christian faith. Aware of the presence of men who denied
that the Word had come in the flesh, he denounced their teaching
and reaffirmed what he knew to be true . . . The entire passage speaks
of the *truth;* the *witness;* the *record.* And this is the record that God
hath given to us eternal life, and this life is in his Son. He that hath
the Son hath life, and he that hath not the Son of God hath not life

(vv. 11, 12). The Gospel was the truth of God expressed through His Son, and rejection of its message was blasphemy, for it made God to be a liar. Although men denied its teaching, a Triune Witness in heaven eternally vindicated the message. As the Word, in heaven Jesus expressed a threefold fact:

(a) He had indeed been offered, for His hands were scarred.
(b) His sacrifice had been accepted, for God had exalted Him to power.
(c) His ministry at God's right hand was effective, for sinners were being saved.

"His being where He was, proclaimed that He had not died in vain. God acknowledged this; Christ expressed it, and the Holy Spirit came down to earth to proclaim it."

The Word in the Revelation — The Word — the King, who comes from outer space

It should ever be remembered by Bible students that God has not forsaken this planet and left it to be just another sphere in space. If there be any meaning in the declarations of the prophets then, of necessity, Christ must return to earth to establish His kingdom. Long ago, the prophet Daniel announced that, ultimately, the God of heaven would "set up a kingdom" (Daniel 2:44), and God's servants in all ages have repeated the statement. At the end of this dispensation, the Lord Jesus must return to earth in order to reign over His people for, otherwise, a major portion of Scripture will remain unfulfilled. Isaiah 55:11-13 declares, "So shall my word be that goeth forth out of my mouth: it shall not return unto me void, but it shall accomplish that which I please, and it shall prosper in the thing whereto I send it. For ye shall go out with joy, and be led forth with peace; the mountains and hills shall break forth before you into singing, and all the trees of the field shall clap their hands. Instead of the thorn shall come up the fir tree, and instead of the brier shall come up the myrtle tree: and it shall be to the Lord for a name, for an everlasting name that shall not be cut off." These predictions have never been fulfilled. They infer that beneath the millenial reign of the Messiah, the curse will be removed from this earth, and the Garden of the Lord will become what it was meant to be. Much more might be said of this subject, but that is not the purpose of this paragraph. When John was enabled to see and later to describe the triumphant return of the Lord, he said, "And I saw heaven opened, and behold a white horse; and he that sat on him was called Faithful and True, and in righteousness he doth judge and make war. His eyes were as a flame of fire, and on his head were many crowns . . . And he was clothed in a vesture

dipped in blood: and his name is called THE WORD OF GOD . . ."
(Revelation 19:11-13).

Here again, as a great climax to all John had hitherto written,
he reveals the Word as the expression of God, for in His triumphant
return to earth He expressed God's faithfulness (1) to His purposes;
(2) to His promises; (3) to His people.

"And I heard a great voice out of heaven saying, Behold, the
TABERNACLE of God is with men, and he will dwell with them, and
they shall be his people, and God himself shall be with them, and
be their God."

SECTION TWO

Expository Notes on the Ministry of John the Baptist

First, it should be stated categorically that there is no conclusive
evidence that these days may be authentically identified as being
this or that particular day of the week. Furthermore, it may not be
a matter of importance that they be so identified. The division is
suggested because John's own statements lend credence to the sup-
position. He mentions five different days: The first day (verses
19:28): the second day (verses 29-34): the third day (verses 35-42):
the fourth day (verses 43-51): the fifth day (2:1-10). When John
mentioned the fifth day, he referred to it as *the third day* — "And the
third day there was a marriage in Cana of Galilee" (2-1). Now the
fifth day could hardly be called the third day unless that day was
the third day of the week. Rightly or wrongly, we assume this to
be the case and from that point, working backward, come to the
following conclusions: —

Philip found Nathaniel on Monday (verses 43-51).

Andrew and John followed Christ on Sunday (verses 35-42).

John Baptist recognized Christ on the Sabbath (Saturday)
(verses 29-34)

John received his official interrogators on Friday (verses 19-28).

Friday and Saturday (John 1:19-34)

**And this is the record of John, when the Jews sent priests and
Levites from Jerusalem to ask him, Who art thou? (v. 19).**

The rulers of the nation, at last, had been stirred to action. The
revival meetings held in the Jordan valley had become known in all
parts of the country, and the increasing interest of the people demanded action. Possibly the rulers had watched the proceedings
with a measure of disdain, feeling that John was just another fanatical
orator soon to be forgotten. The growing enthusiasm of the audi-

ences, the compelling power of the preacher necessitated that some
enquiry be made, and the official representatives of the hierarchy were
sent to interrogate the evangelist. Throughout the market places
of the cities and towns, people were beginning to whisper that John
Baptist might be Elijah forerunning the coming of that great and
terrible day of the Lord (Malachi 4:5). It was natural and to be
expected that questions should challenge John on this vital point.
"Who art thou?" The famous translator and commentator, Godet,
drawing information from the Byzantine manuscripts, suggests that
John's answer would be more correctly rendered, "I am indeed something — someone, but I am not the Christ." This would suggest that
he clearly anticipated their questions and went on to stress that
neither was he Elijah. "And they asked him, What then, Art thou
Elias? And he saith, I am not. Art thou that prophet? And he
answered, No." It is not too difficult to follow the line of their questioning. Art thou the Christ? Art thou Elias? Art thou *that* prophet?
Probably they here referred to the great prediction made by Moses,
"The Lord thy God will raise up unto thee a Prophet from the midst of
thee, of thy brethren, like unto me; unto him ye shall hearken; . . .
I will raise them up a Prophet from among their brethren, like unto
thee, and will put my words in his mouth; and he shall speak unto
them all that I shall command him" (Deuteronomy 18:15, 18).

There is a point of interest here that should be noted. Malachi,
at the end of his prophecy (4:5), had predicted, "Behold I will
send you Elijah the prophet *before the coming of the great and
terrible day of the Lord.*" The people of Palestine firmly believed
in this prophecy, and the appearance of the wilderness preacher
stirred their imagination and suggested the day of doom was at hand.
We now know that this was false, for the coming of Christ heralded
the age of grace, not judgment. He came to redeem and not to
destroy; to save and not to condemn. This fact was beautifully
revealed when He read the Scripture in the synagogue at Nazareth.
"And he came to Nazareth, where he had been brought up: and
as his custom was, he went into the synagogue on the sabbath day,
and stood up for to read. And there was delivered unto him the
book of the prophet Esaias. And when he had opened the book,
he found where it was written, The Spirit of the Lord is upon me,
because he hath anointed me to preach the gospel to the poor; he
hath sent me to heal the broken hearted, to preach deliverance to
the captives, and recovering of sight to the blind, to set at liberty
them that are bruised, to preach the acceptable year of the Lord.
And he closed the book . . ." It was truly remarkable that the Lord
should cease reading at that particular point for, actually, He had not
completed the quotation from the prophecy of Isaiah 61:1, 2. The

next sentence would have been — *and the day of vengeance of our God*. This was omitted deliberately, for that day had not yet come. Therefore, it follows that John Baptist was *not* the forerunner of the day of judgment. His answer to the official questioners was inspired and correct.

The coming of Elias belongs to another age, and a careful study of Revelation 11:1-13 is recommended. It has been predicted that, prior to the judgment of the nations, two witnesses will appear on earth and the power of their ministry will bring terror to the wicked. Finally, these men will die, be resurrected and received up into heaven in what must be the most sensational events of the age. These witnesses will undoubtedly be Enoch and Elijah, for these are the only two men who have not died! Romans 5:12 declares, "Wherefore, as by one man sin entered into the world, and death by sin; *and so death passed upon all men,* for that all have sinned." This passage has also been rendered, "the sentence of death passed upon all men," but even so, as things stand, the picture is not complete. Even if all men have been sentenced to die, two men have escaped the carrying out of that sentence. That the two prophets must reappear in order to preach and then die, demonstrates how correct John was when he announced directly that he was not Elias, and indirectly that the great and terrible day of the Lord was not yet at hand.

Vv. 19-25:

The three questions, *Who? What? Why?* indicate the trend of the questioning that day. John's answers were truly remarkable and revealed the unquestionable depth of his spirituality. He was one of the most remarkable men of all time, and might have added much to his answer when he was asked to give an account of himself. He had been predicted for centuries; had been filled with the Holy Spirit from his infancy; had been specially trained in the wilderness; his teacher had been the Almighty. His qualifications were second to none, and at that precise moment, his name was upon the lips of every citizen. Yet, when he was asked, "What sayest thou of thyself?" he replied, "*I am the voice of one crying in the wilderness* . . ." His mission was not to advertise his own greatness but to introduce his Lord. It is not without significance that his method of baptism was never questioned. The visitors did not say, "What is this rite of baptism?" They merely asked, "Why baptizest thou then, if thou be not that Christ, nor Elias, neither that prophet?" It would appear that baptism was not a new ordinance. The emissaries only questioned his right to administer the rite. In keeping with the full purpose of his mission, John avoided any reference to his own qualifications and pointed his visitors to Christ.

These things were done in Bethabara beyond Jordan, where John was baptizing (v. 28).

This word has also been translated "Bethany" which by many commentators has been identified as the Bethbara of Judges 7:24. Certain spiritualizing has been attempted by using the two places and the two Scriptures, but of more interest is the fact that John's services were held within easy reach of a certain home in Bethany which, in after days, was destined to become famous. It would be interesting if we could know whether or not Martha, Mary, and Lazarus had ever attended John's preaching services, or had they indeed been present when the evangelist first uttered the cry, "Behold the Lamb of God!"

The next day John seeth Jesus coming unto him, and saith, Behold the Lamb of God, which taketh away the sin of the world (v. 29).

As will be seen in subsequent homilies, the apostle John became a connoisseur of names. Already we have the Word, the Christ, the Lamb of God, and within a few verses we shall find the Son of God. Of all the names and titles which we shall consider, *the Lamb of God* stands co-equal with the Word. Throughout his writing career, and especially toward its end, John spoke of the Lamb increasingly. Here, in this dynamic utterance of the Baptist, is seen the fulfillment of all the typology which preceded that memorable day beside the Jordan. It was said that Christ was "The Lamb slain from before the foundation of the world," but this fact was clearly demonstrated throughout the sacred writings.

The third chapter of Genesis begins the demonstration of Adam's transgression. When Adam and Eve sinned, ". . . the eyes of them both were opened, and they knew that they were naked; and they sewed fig leaves together, and made themselves aprons" (Genesis 3:7). The garments were in all probability very simple, but at least *they were garments*. Adam and his wife were no longer naked. This was their first production and they had reason to be satisfied. Yet when God came to walk in the garden, ". . . Adam and his wife hid themselves from the presence of the Lord God among the trees of the garden. And the Lord God called unto Adam, and said unto him, Where art thou? And he said, I heard thy voice in the garden, and I was afraid, *because I was naked*, and I hid myself" (Genesis 3:8-10). Adam discovered that his clothing was transparent — it was not clothing at all. Indisputably, it represented his best efforts — it was the best he and his wife could produce, yet it was quite useless, and in the presence of the Lord appeared to be as filthy rags! For Adam, as for us, it took the coming of God to reveal the inadequacy of self effort. It was then that God made the coats of skins, and we do well when we seek the source of supply for His material. There had been moments when God spoke the creative word and planets came into being. Yet that had been completed, and He had rested. The first hand to shed blood on this planet was the Creator, for He took an offering; the blood of sacrifice was shed, and from the offering the skins were obtained that ultimately hid the nakedness of the first sinners. Adam received as a gift that which he could not have made in a lifetime. Probably, he taught this truth to his son, for in Genesis 4, Abel in offering to God brought a lamb of the flock. Here, then we see that the slain lamb availed for individuals. There can be no doubt that this idea became firmly implanted in the minds of God's people, for in Genesis 22 is the picture of a helpless man being removed from the place of danger in order that an offering might take his place. Abraham (who rejoiced to see Christ's day and was glad) prophesied, "My Son, God will provide himself a lamb for a burnt offering" (Genesis 22:8).

The circle of effectiveness widened, for when the slaves in Egypt were told to seek refuge from the avenger who would go through the land at midnight, they were instructed that the blood of the Lamb would be effective for an entire household. ". . . they shall take to them every man a lamb, according to the house of their fathers, a lamb for an house" (Exodus 12:3). This important truth is developed still further in Leviticus 16, where it is said the blood of the sacrifice availed for an entire nation. "And this shall be an everlasting statute unto you, to make an atonement for the children of Israel for all their sins once a year . . ." This great truth was never extended until John announced his thrilling message, "Behold the Lamb of God which taketh away *the sin of the world.*" It was then seen that God loved the entire world and not merely a privileged section of it. Even the so-called Gentile dogs could become sons and daughters of the living God.

Yet even this picture did not complete the revelation, for in Revelation 5:8-13 the truth is applied in realms where it becomes a little difficult for finite minds to grasp the implications. There are no means of knowing if and how the taint of evil touched other worlds, or to what degree the fall of Lucifer affected God's domain. Nevertheless, in the afore-mentioned Scripture, ". . . the four living creatures, and the four and twenty elders fell down before the Lamb . . . And they sung a new song saying, Thou art worthy . . . for thou was slain, and hast redeemed us to God by thy blood, out of every kindred, and tongue, and people, and nation . . . And I beheld, and I heard the voice of many angels round about the throne, and the living creatures, and the elders: and the number of them was ten thousand times ten thousand, and thousands of thousands; Saying with a loud voice, Worthy is the Lamb that was slain . . ." It should be noted that the angels did not say, "For thou hast redeemed us." Yet the far reaching powers of Christ's death reached even into the very presence of God, and it is safe to suggest that whatever eternity will be, whatever wonders might be unfolded, all will rest upon the unshakable foundation that we shall owe everything to the Lamb who was slain.

> This is he of whom I said, After me cometh a man which is preferred before me: for he was before me . . . . and I saw and bare record that this is the Son of God (vv. 30, 34).

If we can imagine the wilderness country to be a classroom, God playing the role of Tutor, and John as a special student in a private school; if we can read into this passage a reference to the lessons taught, then we shall grasp fully the wonderful experiences known only by John Baptist. The solitude of the desert had produced choicest fellowship; the locusts and wild honey had been items on heaven's menu; a tree had probably been God's leafy throne, and in its shade John found peace. The student remembered one of his lessons; ". . . he that sent me to baptize with water, the same said unto me, Upon whom thou shalt see the Spirit descending and remaining on him, *the same is he* which baptizeth with the Holy Spirit." When the moment came for John Baptist to begin his ministry, he went forth to preach and to watch. He saw the increasing crowds, but he looked for one Man. He preached his thrilling sermons but he waited for one sign, and when that Man and the sign came together, exultantly he cried,

Behold the Lamb, THE SON OF GOD.

Study No. 4

THE LAMB . . . THE ALPHA AND OMEGA OF GOD'S REVELATION

The Book of Revelation is like a great mountain range . . . . Cut out in the rocks of the upper slopes, one imperishable name defies the ravages of time. That name is: *the Lamb.*

The Lamb's Blood Redeeming

This is a mountain peak of unrivalled beauty. The glades and glens of the lowlands lead to the sunlit pastures beyond. There the air is clear, and the flowers of Paradise nod in the breeze. Against the somber background of Sinai, where the law thundered out to trembling man, this celestial eminence rises far above the fog and smoke of earth. It reaches to the throne of God, and provides a path by which all men can draw near to worship. It is truly a remarkable thing that sinners should ever find an entrance into the presence of God; yet it is far more wonderful that the Son of God should have become personally responsible for getting them there. He entered into the world to save sinners; and since the law stated that without the shedding of blood there could be no remission, He gladly laid down His life for men. Peter said, "You were not redeemed with corruptible things . . . but with the precious blood of Christ" (I Peter 1:18, 19). The saints in heaven reiterated these sentiments and sang a new song, "Thou art worthy . . . for thou hast redeemed us to God by thy blood" (Revelation 5:9). When John enquired concerning the people who were present before the throne of God, he was told, "These are they which . . . have washed their robes and made them white in the blood of the Lamb" (Revelation 7:14).

The Lamb's Book Revealing

"And I saw the dead, small and great, stand before God; and the books were opened: and another book was opened which is the book of life: and the dead were judged out of those things which were written in the books, according to their works . . . And whosoever was not found written in the book of life, was cast into the lake of fire" (Revelation 20:12-15). John wrote of the Holy City, "And there shall in no wise enter into it anything that defileth . . . but they which are written in the *Lamb's book of life*" (Revelation 21:27). The text infers three vital things. (1) *God's records are true.* It may be taken for granted that the account will be accurate. What I am, He will record. (2) *God's appointments are inescapable.* John stresses the fact that all men will stand before God. Their reluctance to do so will not provide a way of escape. This is an appointment no one can avoid. (3) *God's decisions are final.* There is no court of appeal. Whatever is meant by the term, *"the lake of fire"* is something each individual must consider personally. To say the least, any verdict leading to eternal rejection can be nothing short of tragic.

The Lamb's Bride Rejoicing

"And I saw a new heaven and a new earth: for the first heaven and the first earth were passed away . . . And I John saw the holy city, new Jerusalem, coming down from God out of heaven, prepared as a bride adorned for her husband. And I heard a great voice out of heaven saying, Behold the tabernacle of God is with men, and he will dwell with them, and they shall be his people, and God himself shall be with them . . . . And God shall wipe away all tears from their eyes; and there shall be no more death, neither sorrow nor crying, neither shall there be any pain" (Revelation 21:1-4).

". . . Come hither, I will shew thee the bride, the Lamb's wife. And he carried me away in the spirit to a great and high mountain, and shewed me that great city, the holy Jerusalem, descending out of heaven from God, having the glory of God: and her light was like unto a stone most precious, even like a jasper stone, clear as crystal . . ." (Revelation 21:9-11).

It has already been said that John seemed to be a connoisseur of names, and among his great collection, THE LAMB occupied pride of place. He began his writings with THE WORD; he finished with THE LAMB. This appears to be most fitting, for it is as God we see Him in the past eternity; throughout the ages to come we shall know Him as *The Lamb* who redeemed us by His blood. The three divisions suggest:

The Lamb redeems; the Lamb records; the Lamb returns.

(Taken from *Bible Treasures*, p. 163.)

Study No. 5

THE DIAMOND WITH MANY FACETS

When seen as a whole, the first chapter of John's gospel resembles an art gallery in which a master hung his masterpieces. All preachers and students should find the following list of titles suggestive, and ministers, with great advantage to their congregations, might well develop each of these sections as a progressive study for Bible classes.

THE WORD . . . reproducing (1:1 and 14).

THE LIGHT . . . revealing (1:9).

THE CHRIST . . . registering (1:20).

THE LAMB . . . redeeming (1:29).

THE SON OF GOD . . . representing (1:34).

THE MASTER . . . receiving (1:38).

THE KING . . . reigning (1:49).

THE SON OF MAN . . . remaining (1:51).

(For further details, see *Bible Highways*, page 121.)

SECTION THREE

Expository Notes on the Beginning of Christ's Ministry

Sunday and Monday

John loses no time in introducing his readers to the primary purpose of the Lord's coming — the winning of men. This section of the chapter (verses 35-51) deals exclusively with that theme, and lists the three main ways by which souls have always been won for

Christ. John Baptist lit a fire which was destined to spread throughout the world.

> **Again the next day after John stood, and two of his disciples; and looking upon Jesus as he walked, he saith, Behold the Lamb of God. And the two disciples heard him speak, and they followed Jesus (vv. 35-37).**

Thus are we introduced to the first method of soul winning. These men had been attracted to John Baptist and were undoubtedly known as being among his keenest followers. Happy is that minister who is able to preach and immediately detect that his listeners have forgotten him in the quest to follow Christ. We shall consider what this meant in a subsequent homily.

> **One of the two which heard John speak, and followed him, was Andrew, Simon Peter's brother. He first findeth his own brother Simon, and saith unto him, We have found the Messiah . . . And he brought him to Jesus (vv. 40-42).**

This is the second method of winning souls for Christ. Those who had been won went out to win others. This proclaimed that the charm and power of the Christ had so thrilled their hearts they were unable to keep this joy a secret. Other people, beginning with the next of kin, should be evangelized. There is reason to believe that it is at this crucial point the modern church has failed. Evangelism is now something reserved for the coming of a special preacher who will be expected to deliver thrilling orations. The idea of ordinary members witnessing for Christ in factories, dockyards, offices, hospitals, schools, and homes seems to have been relegated to church history.

> **The day following Jesus would go forth into Galilee, and findeth Philip, and saith unto him, Follow me (v. 43).**

It is wonderful to know that even when a dynamic John Baptist cannot be found, when enthusiastic followers are conspicuous by their absence, even then, sinners can be won, for the greatest Soul-Winner is the Lord Himself. He still goes forth to the highways and byways of life seeking for lost souls. When Philip went in search of his brother, the second method of winning souls was repeated, and it could well be that this was duplicated to indicate to the entire Church that in the sight of God this is the supreme task of every believer. Preachers must play their part in world evangelism; the Lord will indisputably play His part, but the major portion of the work has been entrusted to us. If we fail, the entire cause might be in jeopardy.

It is not without significance that the Lord dealt with these converts in varying ways. His was not a stereotyped method to be used unfailingly with every seeker. Assessing the latent attributes of each person, He ministered the Word of Life in the way best fitted to meet the needs of each individual. The first two disciples, Andrew and John, were already attracted to Him; to them He issued the invitation to come closer — "Come and see." When Simon, the son of Jona, was brought to Him, the Lord saw a man turbulent in his emotions, unpredictable in his actions, vacillating and perplexing in all his moods; and yet He promised to solve the innate problems of this quick-firing temperament when He announced, "Thou shalt be called . . . a stone." From the shifting, unreliable man that he then was, Simon by God's grace was to become a rock, stable, permanent, strong. The third man, Philip, was not a follower and probably not even attracted by Jesus. He had no friend to influence him and no guide to lead him; therefore, the Lord went forth seeking him. The initial "Follow me" was all that was required to awaken within Philip's heart the desire to obey Christ. This convert was an apt pupil, for when he confronted his own brother, Nathaniel, he met the arguments of the dubious questioner with the same words the Lord had used earlier (verse 39). Nathaniel, although undoubtedly a fine man, was nevertheless very different from the others. He was hardly the man to be swept off his feet by any emotional impulse, and would not be swayed by brilliant rhetoric. He had doubts and many problems and was a man who liked to see where he was going before he even took a step in any direction. The Lord recognized these things and acted accordingly.

(1) *How wise.* "Jesus saw Nathaniel coming unto him, and saith of him, Behold an Israelite indeed, in whom is no guile!" This one statement of justifiable praise disarmed the critic and opened the way for a new advance. Had the Lord said, "Behold a man who has very little faith except in his own deductions," Nathaniel would have been on the defensive immediately.

(2) *How wonderful.* "Nathaniel saith unto him, Whence knowest thou me? Jesus answered and said unto him, Before that Philip called thee, when thou wast under the fig tree, I saw thee. Nathaniel answered and said unto him, Rabbi, thou art the Son of God; thou art the King of Israel." The spontaneous answer of this convert suggests something sensational. Had the Lord been a few yards away, or even within sight of that tree, Nathaniel's objections would not have been overcome so quickly. The man surely realized from the location to which he had just come that it would have been a physical impossibility for the Lord to have seen around so many corners or through so many buildings. The Lord's answer appeared to be phenomenal and, consequently, Nathaniel was amazed.

(3) *How worshipful.* "Jesus answered and said unto him, Be-

cause I said unto thee, I saw thee under the fig tree, believest thou? Thou shalt see greater things than these . . . . Verily, verily, I say unto you, Hereafter ye shall see heaven open, and the angels of God ascending and descending upon the Son of man." Genesis 28:12 speaks of the experience of Jacob: "And he dreamed, and behold a ladder set up on the earth, and the top of it reached to heaven: and behold the angels of God ascending and descending upon it." A comparison of these two texts supplies food for thought. Both the ladder and Christ were the links between God in heaven and man on earth. The *ascending* and *descending* suggest that traffic was moving in two directions. Earth approached heaven, and heaven came down to earth. The entire operation led to a transformation in human affairs. The deceiver became a "Prince with God." One cannot help but ask if some of these truths were in the mind of Christ when He promised to Nathaniel a vision similar to that known by Jacob centuries earlier.

The chapter began with the vision of God being alone in eternal splendor; it ends with a highway from that same eternal splendor down to a needy world. Something has happened to bridge the enormous gulf between eternity and time, between God and man, between holiness and guilt. The chapter explains the miracle. The Son of God became the Son of Man; the Word became flesh to dwell among us.

Study No. 6

THE THREE-FOLD INVITATION OF JESUS

Come and See (John 1:39).

The Jordan valley was a place filled with excitement; tents and caravans were all over the place, for the preaching of John Baptist had stirred the imagination of the nation. At regular intervals during the day, the evangelist delivered his soul-stirring addresses, and his influence was second to none. Already around him were gathered devout followers and these were not slow in announcing that God was visiting His people. A service had ended, and John Baptist was standing with two of his supporters when Jesus of Nazareth came into view. Obviously, He was going somewhere, but when John whispered, "Behold the Lamb of God," his disciples left him to follow Jesus. Possibly stepping behind a tent, the Saviour allowed the men to overtake him, and when they came near, He asked them, "What are you seeking?" "They said unto him . . . where dwellest thou? He saith unto them, Come and see. They came and saw where he dwelt, and abode with him that day: for it was about the tenth hour" (4 P.M.).

There are so many questions that might be asked of those men. Where *did* He live? What did you have for a meal? Who washed the dishes — if there were dishes? Of what did He talk? What was He like and what did He wear? Perhaps we shall never know the answers to these qustions, but we are already sure that whatever transpired in that home, the two visitors were enthralled, for one of the two was Andrew, who at the earliest possible moment found his brother and said unto him, "We have found the Messiah." This was indeed true conversion.

Come and Drink (John 7:37).

The supply of water in the city of Jerusalem was always a matter of concern and provided one of the reasons why the Roman governors disliked Jewish feasts. When thousands of visitors flocked to the temple services, water was always at a premium. John 7 records the memorable scene when on the last day of a great feast, "Jesus stood and cried, saying, If any man thirst, let him come unto me and drink." The streets were thronged with people — sightseers, tourists, worshipers, citizens, and visitors — and everywhere children asked in vain for water. Then came the electrifying voice inviting people to drink. It was astonishing; it was unbelievable. Instantly the crowds converged on the corner whence came the ringing invitation. Alas, there was no water; the cry had come from the mouth of a Preacher who apparently was trying to illustrate a spiritual truth. Some of the hearers were annoyed; others smiled and listened. But no one at that time understood the implications of the Saviour's message. Long afterward, John remembered and wrote, "But this spake he of the Spirit, which they that believe on him should receive: for the Holy Spirit was not yet given; because that Jesus was not yet glorified" (John 7:39). Christ looked out upon hearts as barren as a desert, and with great deliberation promised that if people came to Him to drink, from their inmost beings would flow rivers of living water. This surely is the secret of real consecration. Miracles are performed "not by might; nor by power, but by my Spirit saith the Lord." Furthermore, even John Baptist had predicted this, for he said, "And I knew him not: but he that sent me to baptize with water, the same said unto me, Upon whom thou shalt see the Spirit descending, and remaining on him, the same is he which baptizeth with the Holy Spirit" (John 1:31). All this seems to be exhibited in the fact that Andrew went to win his brother. The soul is more than a receptacle — it becomes a channel. Living water first flows into the human heart, and then through it to a waiting, thirsty world.

Come and Dine (John 21:12).

The beach was still; the silence was unbroken except for the sound of the waves and the sudden squawk of a bird. The Saviour was about to serve breakfast to His tired guests. They looked at His kind, dignified face and remembered the invitation with which He had welcomed them: "Come and dine." A night's fruitless toil had left them weary and discouraged, but when their task seemed to be completely hopeless, His appearance on the beach turned defeat into triumph. He had kindled a fire and invited them to breakfast. At that fireside they were to discover new strength which would enable them to meet the demands of the future. Long afterward, Peter remembered that morning, and when John was old, he could still recall all that happened. They sat on the beach while the Master healed the wounds in their spirit. Probably they remembered, too, that other occasion when, after a period of intinerant preaching, they had returned to hear the Lord say, "Come ye yourselves apart . . . and rest a while . . ." (Mark 6:31). Service is a great privilege, but to commune with Christ is far better. To be alone with the Master means a new appreciation of: (1) *His power* – He, too, can catch fish – many of them. (2) *His purpose* – it is then that He issues His commands, "Feed my sheep," etc. (3) *His person* – surpassing the joy of service is the glory of His presence. It is heaven to be at His feet. "*Come and See*" is enrollment in God's school. "*Come and Drink*" is proficiency in study. "*Come and Dine*" is to graduate; and only then is the Master truly satisfied with His student.

(From *Bible Highways,* page 130.)

Study No. 7

Three Steps to Glory!

Come and See (refer to preceding study).
Go and See (Mark 6:35-38).
Taste and See (Psalm 34:8).
Go and See

The disciples of Jesus were very worried; the sun was beginning to disappear in the western sky and their great audience was far from home. The people had been with them many hours; they were hungry; the children were restless. Alas, even the disciples themselves were getting tired; their patience was being sorely tried. "Master," they said, "This is a desert place, and now the time is far passed. Send them away, that they may go into the country round about, and into the villages, and buy themselves bread: for they have nothing to eat." The Lord listened, smiled, and replied, "Give ye them to eat . . . How many loaves have ye? *Go and see* . . . ." They found a small boy who was willing to surrender his lunch, and the resultant miracle amazed the world. The lad's example is truly inspiring. What have we to bring to Christ? How much sacrificial giving attends our effort?

Taste and See

David sat in the mouth of a cave and shuddered as he remembered the narrowness of his escape in a foreign land. Only extreme necessity had made him feign madness. In retrospect, it appeared comical and perhaps even David smiled as he remembered how he had allowed the spittle to run down his beard, how he had clawed at the walls as if he had taken leave of his senses. Yet at the time there had been no humor; his life had been in grave danger and only his skill at acting the madman saved him. Now it was all over and the sweet singer said, "This poor man cried, and the Lord heard him, and saved him out of all his troubles . . . . The angel of the Lord encampeth round about them that fear him, and delivereth them. *O taste and see* that the Lord is good: blessed is the man that trusteth in him" (Psalm 34:6-8). David, throughout the trying experiences of life, had mastered the art of drawing near to the throne of God to listen to the songs of the Eternal. When he repeated the melodies, people called him "The sweet singer of Israel." *Happy* indeed is the man who visits Christ to learn of Him. *Privileged* indeed is the man who is able to help in providing food for a hungry world. *Thrilled beyond measure* is the man who climbs the steps to the throne of grace to commune with his Master. Here we have progression. *Come and See* led to conversion; *Go and See* led to consecration; *Taste and See* led to communion. These were three steps to a golden throne.

Study No. 8
ANDREW . . . THE PATRON SAINT OF PERSONAL WORKERS

Andrew was a go-getter; and if some readers are unfamiliar with this questionable terminology, an explanation will be welcome. A go-getter is a man who stops at nothing. In order to attain his ends he will remove mountains, cross oceans, turn the world inside out, laugh at impossibilities, and finally set a city on fire while other people are looking for a match! A go-getter is a man who goes and gets what he desires, and woe betide anyone who stands in the way. Failure is never admitted, for the untiring man continues until his purpose is fully achieved. Andrew was a man of this calibre. He knew what he wanted and always took the short cut to reach it. Other men became the great generals in the holy war; but Andrew planned the campaigns, removed the difficulties, and prepared the way for every fresh advance. He was a great go-getter, the patron saint of all who seek souls for Christ.

Andrew first found Peter

Jesus of Nazareth had been entertaining guests, and one of the privileged visitors was Andrew. He had been standing with John Baptist when the Stranger passed, and hearing John say, "Behold the Lamb of God," Andrew and another disciple had followed Christ. When they received the invitation to accompany the Saviour, they gladly accepted the hospitality of the new Friend, and stayed with him the rest of the day. "And one of them which heard John speak . . . was Andrew, Simon Peter's brother. He first findeth his own brother Simon, and saith unto him, We have found the Messiah . . . . And he brought him to Jesus." There was no fuss about this quiet man. He had been with Jesus and was fully assured that his findings were correct. "*We have found the Messiah*" echoed the certainty of his soul, and that was that! Until this time Andrew took pride of place from his brother Simon. It is interesting to notice that the sacred record says of Bethsaida, "It was the city of Andrew and Peter" (John 1:44). Perhaps he was the elder brother.

Andrew first found the lad with the loaves

When the Lord had gathered together His band of disciples, He separated them into couples in order that their ministry might become more effective. And in the new arrangement it would appear that Andrew's partner was Philip, for their names are not only coupled together in the official list (Mark 3:18), but these men are seen together on later occasions. "When Jesus saw a great company come unto him, he saith unto Philip, Whence shall we buy bread that these may eat? . . . Philip answered him, Two hundred penny worth of bread is not sufficient for them, that every one of them may take a little. One of his disciples, Andrew, Simon Peter's brother, saith unto him, There is a lad which hath five barley loaves, and two small fishes: but what are they among so many?" (John 6:5-9). Were his eyes alight with expectation as he uttered those words? The provisions were so inadequate that to mention them on such an occasion was an act of stupidity — unless Andrew had very strong reasons for so doing. While the other disciples were regretting their inability to feed the crowd, Andrew was investigating the position. He discovered a boy's lunch. The big man and the small boy pooled their resources, and through them the Master fed a multitude.

Andrew first brought the Gentiles to Jesus

"And there were certain Greeks among them that came up to worship at the feast: The same came therefore to Philip which was of Bethsaida of Galilee, and desired him, saying, Sir, we would see Jesus. Philip cometh and telleth Andrew: and again Andrew and

Philip tell Jesus" (John 12:20-22). Philip was puzzled. Let us not blame him, for this marked a new departure in the affairs of disciple-ship. These Greeks were proselytes, but they were still Gentiles. Had they any part in Messianic privileges? Would their inclusion result in troublesome repercussions? "Andrew, what do you think about it?" And when Andrew had shrewdly considered the matter, he replied, "Philip, we'll tell the Master. He'll know what to do." "And Andrew and Philip tell Jesus." And Jesus answered, "The hour is come that the Son of man should be glorified . . . . And I, if I be lifted up from the earth, will draw all men unto me." Andrew reminded the Lord of the great world of seeking Gentiles: the Lord gave to Andrew the privilege of bringing those Gentiles to Him. And, perhaps, that is the reason why this disciple became the patron saint of all personal workers for Christ.

(Reprinted from *Bible Treasures*, p. 111.)

The Second Chapter of John

THEME: *Christ Begins His Ministry*

OUTLINE:

    I. The wedding at Cana. Verses 1-11.
    II. The Cleansing of the Temple. Verses 12-17.
    III. The first Signs of Opposition. Verses 18-25.

A Necessary Introduction to the Study of the Wedding at Cana

As a prelude to the study of Christ's first miracle, it might be beneficial to examine the strange interpretations given of this remarkable event. All the miracles performed by the Lord have, from time to time, been challenged by men who found it impossible to believe in the supernatural. Yet this miracle in Cana has aroused more interest and received more criticism than any other event recorded by the New Testament writers.

Rejection

Let us first consider the viewpoint of those who reject the passage. John wrote: *"And when they wanted wine, the mother of Jesus said unto him, They have no wine . . . . And there were set there six waterpots of stone, after the manner of the purifying of the Jews, containing two or three firkins apiece, Jesus saith unto them, Fill the waterpots with water. And they filled them up to the brim. And he saith unto them, Draw out now and bear unto the governor of the feast. And they bare it. When the ruler of the feast had tasted the water that was made wine . . . he saith unto him . . . . thou hast kept the good wine until now."* It is obvious that this emergency did not arise at the beginning of the wedding, for it may safely be assumed that at least some preparation would have been made to meet the needs of the assembled guests. Indeed, it would be fair to assume that the man in charge of the preparations would have provided what he considered sufficient wine to meet the requirements of the occasion. The suggestion has been made that it was the unexpected arrival of Jesus and His disciples which caused the shortage. Whether or not this was the case, the fact remains this embarrassment would hardly be known until the wedding celebrations were nearing conclusion —

that is, after four or five days. Evidence in support of this fact was provided by the governor who said to the bridegroom, "Thou hast kept the good wine until now." Therefore, the miracle was performed to meet the shortage of wine during the last few hours of the wedding celebrations.

It was this fact which aroused the criticism and rejection of writers, among whom were Strauss and Schweitzer. They contended that the amount of wine said to be miraculously produced by Jesus was utterly fantastic and represented unexcusable waste. Godet says, "The measure which is spoken of was of considerable size; its capacity was 27 litres (Rilliet) or even 38 (Keil) or 39 (Arnaud). The entire contents might, therefore, reach even to about 500 litres." A litre is said to be about equal to two pints, and thus anything up to 1000 pints of wine was suddenly produced to meet the comparatively small needs of the closing celebrations. In modern parlance, one might say that this was equal to two thousand bottles of any soft drink. This fact aroused the critics and fostered their belief that the record was entirely false. In conclusion, it only remains to be said that this idea is ludicrous, for the narrative does not say that Jesus made sufficient wine to fill the six waterpots. Subsequent notes will explain what is inferred by this statement.

Dilution

Some of the more modern, and perhaps more gracious, theologians have endeavored to bridge the gap between the cynic and the devout believer. Among these is the English commentator, the Reverend L. Weatherhead. His comments on this miracle at Cana have found acceptance in ever-widening circles, for he affirms that this was never meant to be regarded as a miracle. Not the least engaging feature of Jesus was His ability to adapt Himself to the circumstances in which he was found. Lack of provision at a wedding was sufficient to cause acute embarrassment to everyone present, and in order to meet the predicament, the Honored Guest produced His most sparkling humor. When frowns were beginning to appear on the faces of responsible officials, the Lord laughed, and said, "Take this to the governor and say, 'It is a new kind of wine' — Adam's Ale." The wedding guests were already extremely happy, and the joke became the highlight of the occasion. It is not too difficult to visualize the host lifting his glass of sparkling water and saying, "Guests, drink up. This is the new brew produced by our friend Jesus." Every guest did as he was told, and the laughter increased as one and all smacked their lips and exclaimed, "Wonderful!" Thus was the situation resolved, and the happiness of a young married couple preserved.

Except for one or two very important details, this interpretation would be truly delightful. It is clever, attractive, and reasonable — at first glance. At the conclusion of the fourth chapter of John's gospel, the apostle describes the heart rending scene as a nobleman desperately hurried to Christ in the hope of preventing the death of his boy. The story, as we shall discover when we reach that part of our studies, was most thrilling, but when the record had been completed, and John had explained how the lad had been healed, he added, "This is again *the second miracle* that Jesus did, when he was come out of Judaea into Galilee" (John 4:54). It is difficult to escape the conclusion that if the miracle in Cana was the joyous joke of an important occasion, then, perhaps this second miracle was also a joke, or maybe the nobleman himself was the victim of acute hallucinations and had only imagined his son's life to be in danger.

Distortion

The United States of America, and the great city of Los Angeles in particular, are great places for sects, cults, and fantastic interpretations of Biblical doctrine. The Mormon church has long taught that Jesus of Nazareth married Martha and Mary, and that a descendant of one of their children founded the church. A strange new extension has now been made to this idea, for it is being taught in some circles that the wedding at Cana was, in actual fact, *the Lord's own wedding*. This of course is the most ingenious explanation of the verses, "When the ruler of the feast had tasted the water that was made wine, and knew not whence it was . . . the governor of the feast *called the bridegroom*, and saith unto him, Every man at the beginning doth set forth good wine; and when men have well drunk, then that which is worse: but *thou* hast kept the good wine until now." This is truly fantastic, for it may be supposed from the text that He who produced the wine was indeed *the bridegroom*. But for one small detail, this interpretation would be both sensational and brilliant. John wrote, "And the third day there was a marriage in Cana of Galilee; and the mother of Jesus was there: And both *Jesus was called*, and his disciples to the marriage." John should have added that someone deserved the Congressional Medal for remembering to invite the Bridegroom to his own wedding!

SECTION ONE

Expository Notes on the Wedding at Cana

And the third day there was a marriage in Cana of Galilee . . . (v. 1).

Various expositors have endeavored to find hidden meanings in the statement, "the third day." Certain dispensational suggestions have been made, but it is the avowed intention of this author to keep the comments within the obvious circle of sanity. Whether or not the marriage took place at the end of a three-day journey, or whether this was the third day of the week, as suggested in chapter 1, does not really matter. What is of importance is the fact that the Lord honored an unknown couple by accepting an invitation to be present at their wedding. Marriage is honorable and was instituted by God. We have no way of knowing the identity of the people about to be joined in wedlock, but it is not too difficult to see them making out the list of those people whose presence they desired at the ceremony. It is stimulating even to think that perhaps the name of Jesus was at the top of the list. Happy indeed are those young people who remember to invite the Lord to their wedding. Most guests bring a wedding present, but *this Guest* brings gifts of unusual quality!

And the mother of Jesus was there . . . . And when they wanted wine, the mother of Jesus saith unto him, They have no wine. Jesus saith unto her, Woman, what have I to do with thee? mine hour is not yet come . . . (vv. 1, 3, 4).

To many writers and preachers this has proved to be a difficult passage of Scripture, and strange things have been said of it. It has been suggested that Mary was completely at fault in all her actions and that this brought from the lips of Jesus a stinging rebuke. *This I do not believe.* Two facts must be kept in their true perspective. (1) We are here dealing with language of a bygone age, and (2) during the passing of time, both words and customs change considerably.

"Jesus saith unto her, *Woman,* what have I to do with thee? mine hour is not yet come." The term "Woman" might sound a little harsh in modern ears, but it must be remembered the Lord used this same word when He spoke from the cross. "When Jesus therefore saw his mother, and the disciple standing by, whom he loved, he saith unto his mother, Woman, behold thy son" (John 19:26). It is extremely difficult to believe that Christ on His cross used any utterance suggesting harshness. History teaches that the term "woman" was used in addressing all females, and that sometimes it was used to express reverence and great respect.

It is very hard to accept the suggestion that Mary had wandered far from the will of God when she immediately expressed superlative faith. Let it be considered that as yet Christ had not performed one miracle. There is no information as to what might have happened in the previous years when He and His family lived in Nazareth. There is every possibility that during her sojourn in that city, Mary witnessed things which thrilled her soul. One could never live in the presence of the Saviour for thirty wonderful years without gaining an insight into the wonder of His being and the exemplary nature of His conduct. There is evidence to support the conclusion that Mary had seen enough to encourage the growth of faith. Even *before* He turned the water into wine, Mary said to the servants, "Whatsoever he saith unto you, *do it*" (verse 5). One might be justified in paraphrasing her statement thus: "Whatever He commands, obey Him. He might order the most fantastic thing, but do not worry — He knows what He is doing. Obey Him and all will be well."

Some writers read into Mary's statement the suggestion of blame. They say the shortage of wine was occasioned by the fact that Jesus and His disciples had imposed unnecessary strain upon the limited resources of an impoverished family, that Mary was making the veiled suggestion that Jesus and His followers should make a hurried excuse for a premature departure. Others declare that Mary was exercising unnecessary parental control, and believing her Son could relieve the situation, was *commanding* Him to do so. It is further suggested that this attitude deserved the rebuke instantly forthcoming from the Saviour. Let it be candidly admitted that all this might well be, but at the same time, let us be warned against the error of permitting preconceived ideas to apportion blame where it does not belong. Throughout the world, the false teachings of the Roman Catholic church have elevated Mary to realms of glory where she was never meant to be. She has been termed *The Mother of God,* and millions of worshipers direct their petitions to her, believing she is able to bring pressure to bear upon her Son, to obtain from Him answers that might not otherwise be forthcoming. This is completely foreign to Biblical teaching, and as a consequence many aggressive Protestant leaders have fallen into error because they seek diligently to find anything which reflects upon the character of this chosen woman. Unquestionably, Mary was a sinner as we are; undoubtedly she made many mistakes as we do, but it is always better to think and speak well of a person, particularly when there is no evidence to prove that person has been wrong. Possibly mixed emotions filled the mind of this woman when she addressed the Lord, but the sparkling expression of faith in her subsequent statement shines as a star in the darkness. Let us watch the star rather than stare at the gloom and lose our way in the shadows.

And there were set there six waterpots of stone, after the manner of the purifying of the Jews, containing two or three firkins apiece (v. 6).

The washing of the hands with water was an integral part of every great religious and domestic event. For example, even today in every Moslem mosque the worshiper as a prelude to his devotions is expected to inhale water through the nostrils into the throat and to expel it again through the mouth. This is done three times. The washing of the hands and feet is also repeated thrice, and to make this possible, special wash rooms are a recognized part of every Moslem mosque. Similarly, the Jews observed the rite of washing their hands with water, and reference is made to this in Matthew 15:1, 2: "Then came to Jesus scribes and Pharisees, which were of Jerusalem, saying, Why do thy disciples transgress the tradition of the elders? for they wash not their hands when they eat bread?"

A firkin equals about nine gallons, and thus each water pot would contain between 18 and 27 gallons. The total capacity of the six waterpots would be somewhere in the region of 140 or 150 gallons. The previous estimate of 1000 pints is well within the limits here suggested. That the waterpots were apparently empty at this particular time seems to suggest a large number of diligent guests and an unknown number of careless servants! Some Bible teachers have made the waterpots to represent many things. For example, they have been said to express the emptiness of the Jewish religion and the need for Christ to fill this system with the new wine of spiritual joy. I candidly confess that I have never graduated in this dubious art, and I refrain from further comments lest I should surprise John by announcing something of which he never even thought!

> Jesus said unto them, Fill the waterpots with water. And they filled them up to the brim. And he said unto them, Draw out now and bear unto the governor of the feast. And they bear it (vv. 7, 8).

I have never been able to understand why the commentators have inferred that, having filled the waterpots with water, the servants immediately began to empty them. There is no conclusive evidence that Jesus turned the water *in the waterpots* into wine. The command was, "Draw out now." The servants had already been drawing water from the well, and it would be more logical to say that having drawn from the well, they continued to draw. The water within the waterpots remained water, and thus was ready for any demand made for it. A thousand or more pints of wine filling every receptacle would, it would seem to me, be a nuisance when the guests wished to wash their hands. It is hard to believe they would waste good wine on ceremonial observances! Yet before that wedding terminated, water would certainly be needed. There is good reason to believe that Christ commanded the servants to fill the waterpots for two reasons. (1) That supplies of water would be available from the stone jars when only wine was coming from the well. (2) That since faith is hardly faith until it has been tested and proved true, even the servants had to exercise this before the miracle became a reality. Six or more times they drew water. Yet they continued to obey the Saviour, and this led to triumph. The well continued to produce wine as long as need remained for wine; then it reverted to pattern, and yielded water. This appears to be the only logical interpretation of the passage, and if it be true, then the conclusions of the critics were both unnecessary and false. One wonders what connection might be made between this verse and its predecessor in Isaiah 12:3: "Therefore with joy shall ye draw water out of the wells of God's salvation."

> When the ruler of the feast had tasted the water that was made wine, and knew not whence it was: (but the servants which drew the water knew) the governor of the feast called the bridegroom, and saith unto him, Every man at the beginning doth set forth good wine; and when men have well drunk, then that which is worse: but thou hast kept the good wine until now (vv. 9, 10).

There is no way of knowing whether or not the governor of the feast was aware of the sudden shortage of wine. It is not my wish to be unduly aggressive in refuting the suggestion of other sincere preachers, but in all honesty it must be said that it requires far more faith to believe the modern interpretations of the story than it requires to believe the story itself. Within these verses I find it impossible to detect evidence of a great joke. I think the ruler of the feast and the governor were probably the most surprised and delighted men in the entire company; I believe their congratulations expressed to the bridegroom were utterly sincere. Here, then, in embryonic form we get our first glimpse of the mighty purpose which brought the Word down to earth. Here, the preacher should find food for thought, for three ideas deserve mention. (1) *The Saviour* desires to meet human need. (2) *The servants* are the instruments used to further the divine purpose. They could do nothing except obey their Master. Yet when they yielded to His control, a miracle was brought a little closer. (3) *The supply* was inexhaustible since the wine came from a well and not from the limited waterpots of stone.

> This beginning of miracles did Jesus in Cana of Galilee, and manifested forth his glory; and his disciples believed on him (v. 11).

". . . and we beheld his glory, the glory as of the only begotten of the Father . . ." (John 1:14). Thus did the Saviour begin His ministry, and a comparison of this passage with the preceding chapter suggests that already the scope of His efforts was beginning to be enlarged. His saving influence was beginning to extend in everwidening circles. Throughout the first chapter, John emphasized Christ's ability to meet the need of various individuals, but here we see His power to meet the need of a complete household. Chapter 1:39 tells how Christ invited strangers to enter His home. Chapter 2:1 reveals that unknown people invited Christ to their home. This surely is a striking sequence of thought. When we come to Him, He saves us, but He does it so effectively that we cannot live happily without Him. To meet Christ is to love Him, and to love Him is to desire increasing fellowship.

John recognized in this phenomenal experience the outshining of the glory of the Father. This was no joke; this was not a fantasy of an old man's mind. This was the initial break-through of the supernatural. The Word had come to earth with a specific purpose, and having whetted the appetite of his readers, John continued to write his memoirs.

HOMILIES

Study No. 9

THE WATER THAT BLUSHED!

It has often been said that John Wesley was once required to pass an examination in which he had to write an essay about the miracle at Cana's wedding. Nonplussed, frustrated, mentally paralyzed, the student sat in his desk motionless. When the time was swiftly running out, desperately, and with a stroke of inspirational genius, he took his pen and wrote, "The water looked at Jesus and blushed." It has also been reported that although this essay was extremely brief, it succeeded in gaining the highest commendation. Coming as it does at the beginning of the public ministry of the Saviour, this miracle supports the old saying, "Coming events cast their shadows before." If the Saviour came into the world to save sinners, this entrancing story teaches three things about the salvation He offered.

He demonstrated His power to save

As far as we know, this was the first time the Master was ever confronted by domestic need. Let it be understood that we are not able to examine the thirty hidden years of the life of Jesus. During His sojourn at Nazareth, on innumerable occasions He might have come face to face with human need and domestic strain. However, this was the first time that He was ever requested to solve the problems in any home. This is the story of an outstanding day which was likely to be ruined, when talkative people could create clouds to darken the sky of two lovable young people. The supply of wine had been exhausted; the wedding celebrations would be marred; the memories would certainly linger. When the Saviour turned the water into wine, He performed His first miracle and saved a family from acute embarrassment. Throughout the years to follow, He was to do this kind of thing many times. Other homes would know the same happiness, the identical joy. Thus did Christ demonstrate His power to save. Before His ministry concluded, He would meet innumerable people for whom the supplies of wine would have become non-existent. The wine of hope would be almost missing from the leper's heart; the wine of comfort from the hearts of two sisters in Bethany; the wine of perfect peace from the conscience of many who, as the publican, beat upon their breasts and exclaimed, "God be merciful to me a sinner." Yet for all these people, Christ would perform that greater miracle of which the event at Cana was but a faint foreshadowing.

He demonstrated His power to satisfy

"When the ruler of the feast had tasted the water that was made wine, and knew not whence it was . . . he called the bridegroom and said, . . . Thou hast kept the best wine until now." It is not too difficult to understand the reasoning which expected the best wine to be served first. When men have "well drunk" they are somewhat incapable of detecting any deterioration in the quality of the vintage. When they first taste the wine, guests are apt to become connoisseurs of the refreshment offered. It is perfectly understandable then why this man of a bygone age was a little amazed by the sparkling qualities of the wine produced by Jesus. Yet for the millions of Christians who have known the saving power of their Lord, it would have seemed incongruous and unbelievable had this product passed unnoticed, for no one can equal the Saviour's ability to supply real satisfaction. When the Samaritan woman was about to offer a drink to Christ, He responded with the startling information He was able to supply a well of water within her soul. For two thousand years men of all types have left their homes and callings to follow the Saviour, and their united testimony endorses the truth expressed in the lines:

> I sighed for rest and happiness:
> I yearned for them, not Thee;
> But when I passed my Saviour by,
> His love laid hold on me.
> Now none but Christ can satisfy:
> None other Name for me.
> There's love, and life, and lasting joy,
> Lord Jesus, found in Thee.

He demonstrated His power to sustain

The expository notes preceding these suggestions have already outlined the possibilities that "Draw out now" was a command to approach the well with new faith. Had the requirements of the occasion necessitated sufficient wine to fill fifty waterpots, Christ would have been equal to the demands of the moment. On the other hand, as soon as the need had been met, the supply of wine ceased. There is wisdom in all God's acts. God's wells can never run dry in an emergency. An interesting and challenging parallel to this story may be found in Genesis 21. When domestic strain ruined the tranquillity of Abraham's home, when the expulsion of the maid, Hagar, appeared to be an unfortunate necessity, ". . . Abraham rose up early in the morning, and took bread, *and a bottle of water*, and gave it unto Hagar, putting it on her shoulder, and the child, and sent her away: and she departed and wandered in the wilderness of Beersheba. And the water was spent in the bottle, and she cast the child under one of the shrubs . . . . And she said, Let me not see the death of the child. And she sat over against him, and lifted up her voice, and wept. And God heard the voice of the lad. And the angel of God called to Hagar out of heaven . . . . And God opened her eyes, and she saw a well of water . . . ." This method seems to be characteristic of all divine dealings with humans. Man tries to exist on bottled pleasures, but when supplies become exhausted, he despairs. Extreme need promotes anxious prayer, and this unlocks heaven's treasure house. God's wells are never far away, but sometimes tears ruin the vision! It is better to look up than to look down. It is better to ask, "What will God do next?" than to think He has ceased to do anything. Experience has taught multitudes that He who is able to save is also able to keep one from falling. The Christ who saves from sin continues to save until every need has been fully supplied.

SECTION TWO

Expository Notes on the Cleansing of the Temple

It is necessary first of all to appreciate the fact that there are two accounts of the cleansing of the temple. This has led to the most lively discussion in theological circles. The synoptic writers place the incident at the end of the Lord's public ministry (Matthew 21:12; Mark 11:15; Luke 19:45). In contrast to this, John places the incident at the beginning of Christ's ministry (John 2:15). Obviously a question is sure to arise, Were there one or two cleansings of the temple? It is not my purpose here to reproduce the arguments which have been made on behalf of both viewpoints; neither do I intend to weary readers with a list of meaningless names — names of the various theologians who championed both causes. The shelves of every theological book shop and the studies of every minister contain many volumes which set forth these facts in great detail. I am content merely to state that whereas the support is more or less equally divided between the two points of view, it is my belief that Christ cleansed the temple on two separate occasions and, furthermore, I am glad that He did!

Before we begin the systematic study of the verses describing this event, there is one prerequisite. It is necessary to gain a mental picture of the scene which Christ saw every day He entered the temple courtyards. Writing of this, Godet said, "The temple had three particularly holy courts: that of the *priests,* which enclosed the edifice of the temple properly so-called *(naos);* more to the eastward, that of the *men;* and finally, to the east of the latter, that of the *women.* Around these courts a vast open space had been arranged, which was enclosed on four sides by colonnades, and which was called, the *court of the Gentiles* because it was the only part of the sacred place *(ieron)* into which proselytes were permitted to enter. In this outermost court there were established, with the tacit consent of the temple authorities, a market and an exchange. Here were sold the different kinds of animals intended for the sacrifices; here Greek or Roman money, brought from foreign regions, was exchanged for the sacred money with which the capitation-tax determined by Exodus 30:13 for the support of the temple . . . was paid" (*Godet's Commentary on Gospel of John,* Vol. I, page 361.)

The Saviour's statement that His Father's house had become a den of thieves is all the evidence we need to conclude that under the guise of religion, things were being done which were utterly disgraceful. It is not difficult to imagine what transpired, for all international travelers face the same difficulty. Small fortunes are sometimes made by rogues in exchanging the foreign currency of inexperienced people. The temple ritual represented the heart of the Jewish nation, and although the Jews of the dispersion had been scattered near and far, all who were able to return periodically did so. Obviously they brought with them the currency of their adopted land, and an offering of any kind could not be purchased until this alien money had been exchanged. The temple courtyard had become the abode of swindlers; the sweet smelling incense had been overcome by the increasing unpleasantness of a mammoth stable. The Lord watched these things on many occasions but because His hour had not yet come, He walked away sorrowfully. Hitherto He had done nothing to interfere with the outrageous practices of these men. As the Son of Man, He had entered the temple to worship; now, as the Son of God, He comes to His Father's house with divine authority to attend to His Father's business. He had the right to act as He did, for He was the representative of the Father. Thus John once again reverts to his earlier statement, "No man hath seen

God at any time; the only begotten Son, which is in the bosom of the Father, *he hath declared him*" (John 1:18).

After this he went down to Capernaum, he, and his mother, and his brethren, and his disciples: and they continued there not many days (v 12).

At the conclusion of the wedding celebration, the Lord and His party went down to Capernaum, and in spite of the comments made by certain early church leaders, the term "brethren" refers to his brothers and not to his cousins. The word here translated is *adelphoi;* it means *brothers.* That the Lord had both brothers and sisters there can be no doubt, for Matthew 13:54-56 reads: "And when he was come into his own country, he taught them in their synagogue, insomuch that they were astonished, and said, Whence hath this man this wisdom and these mighty works? Is not this the carpenter's son? is not his mother called Mary? and his brethren, James and Joses, and Simon, and Judas? And his sisters, are they not also with us? Whence then, hath this man all these things?" The possibility exists that the Lord's stay in Capernaum was necessarily brief as He desired to be in Jerusalem for Passover.

. . . and Jesus went up to Jerusalem. And found in the temple those that sold oxen, and sheep, and doves, and the changers of money sitting: And when he had made a scourge of small cords, he drove them all out of the temple . . . (vv. 13-15).

This striking passage has not found acceptance with liberal interpreters, for they like to believe Christ incapable of any severity. That He should make a whip to strike a fellow man seems incompatible with the compassion revealed throughout His ministry. In estimating the value of their deductions, three vital things must be taken into consideration.

(1) God through His prophet Malachi had foretold: "Behold, I will send my messenger, and he shall prepare the way before me: and the Lord, whom ye seek, shall suddenly come to his temple . . . . But who may abide the day of his coming? and who shall stand when he appeareth? for he is like a refiner's fire . . ." (Malachi 3:1, 2). The prediction that the Lord's presence would test the virtue of individuals, that some might be unable to stand in His presence, hardly suggests the coming of a weakling.

(2) It does not say that the Lord made a scourge of small cords and *thrashed the offenders.* Whether or not He might have done so if the men had decided to resist Him is another matter. It would seem that the righteous indignation emanating from His soul was sufficient to strike terror to their hearts. They did not wait for the whip to fall. Forsaking their money tables, they ran for the exits.

(3) There is reason to wonder if all men are in need of redis-

covering the Bible. Three outstanding facts were evident in all the preaching of the men who established the church: (a) The holiness of God, (b) the sinfulness of sin, and (c) the love of Christ. Somehow, for the most part we seem to have weakened on the first two. Holiness has been superceded by sentiment; sin has been replaced by weakness or undeveloped good. To our modern way of living, vice in its worst forms is but another excuse to speak of mental illness. Offenders ought not to be punished; they must be taught to take pills three times a day!

Unfortunately, this attitude has made its appearance in the pulpit, and the clergy who never hurt the congregations are said to be such lovable men. The preachers who refrain from speaking of sin and judgment are known as the most tactful ministers. Alas, they forget that the Bible also speaks of *the wrath of the Lamb.* "And the kings of the earth, and the great men, and the rich men, and the chief captains, and the mighty men, and every bondman, and every freeman, hid themselves in the dens and in the rocks of the mountains; and said to the mountains and rocks, Fall on us, and hide us from the face of him that sitteth upon the throne, *and from the wrath of the Lamb: For the great day of his wrath is come; and who shall be able to stand?"* (Revelation 6:15-17).

And said unto them that sold doves, Take these things hence; make not my Father's house an house of merchandise. And his disciples remembered that it was written, The zeal of thine house hath eaten me up (vv. 16, 17).

Increasingly throughout His memorable ministry, the Lord identified Himself with His Father. A first-class concordance and a little perseverance yield ample rewards in the minister's study. My Father's business, My Father's house, My Father's will, My Father's word, My Father's pleasure belong to scintillating clusters of gems waiting to be discovered. Much speculating has been done in regard to the moment when Jesus became conscious of His mission. It has been said that if He were truly man, as a babe He would not have appreciated the purpose of His mission. The answers to every question are not easily supplied; we must be content to know that even when He was a lad of twelve years, He already knew *who He was* and *why He came to earth.* "And he said unto them, How is it that ye sought me? wist ye not that I must be about my Father's business?" (Luke 2:49).

Possibly the disciples had never witnessed such a manifestation of righteous indignation, and remembering Psalm 69:9, it was easy to associate their Master with the prophecy of a bygone age. This was Christ's initial attack on the evil practices of His times, and since reformers are never popular with the ruling classes, it was to be expected that opposition would rise in mounting tides. The picture supplied by this text is a haunting one; it lingers and promotes concern. The Lord's action revealed a four-fold relationship with the sanctuary.

(1) *His Presence.* Elsewhere we read that He went into the synagogue on the sabbath day as was His custom (see Luke 4:16). If ever man had excuse to rest, that man was Jesus. A strange contrast may be seen between the Lord and His modern followers. He worked so hard throughout His week that He earnestly went to the place of worship to glean additional strength to meet the demands of the next week. Alas, we labor so hard from Monday to Saturday, we need Sunday's refreshing breezes on the golf course to recharge our overworked system! After the irksome morning service, we go forth in search of an open air heaven!

(2) *His Purity.* The Lord never attempted to drive out the offenders until it was obvious that His own life was above reproach. The world and the Church have known many reformers who have driven out questionable evils because they themselves needed the floor space to erect their own tables!

(3) *His Passion.* "The zeal of thine house hath eaten me up." The quality of His worship was never diluted with indifference. What He did, He did enthusiastically. To Him, the Father's house offered heaven; the Father's fellowship offered joy; the Father's will offered perfect freedom. He carried into the service of God all His talents and all His zest. Do we?

(4) *His Power.* "And the blind and the lame came to him in the temple and he healed them" (Matthew 21:12). It was so easy to believe that God had come to His temple, for that was precisely what had taken place. This is in accord with the entire theme of the fourth gospel. He who was in the beginning with God, *the Word,* had been made flesh to tabernacle among us.

HOMILIES

Study No. 10

SPRING-CLEANING IN THE HOUSE OF GOD

The sanctuary had become a stable, the place of devotion, a den of thieves! We shall never know how often the Lord was deeply disturbed as He beheld the hypocrisy in the temple. Here, there, and everywhere, the money changers had set up their tables and had gone into business. Foreign currency was accepted, but the rate of exchange constituted robbery of the worst type. Pilgrims from distant lands probably knew they were being swindled, but what could they do? The temple offerings were sold at exorbitant prices, and what had been meant to be a means of grace was now so commercialized that God was not even remotely related to the daily routines.

And then Jesus came to the temple. He paused, frowned, made a whip from cords (which in all probability had come from a packing case), and advanced toward the tables of the robbers. The money changers looked up expecting another victim, but recognizing the righteous indignation blazing in the Lord's eyes, they became frightened and ran for the exits. "And when he had made a scourge of small cords, he drove them all out of the temple." This is a perfect picture of conversion.

We might well ask, "What is the true temple?" Is it some ornate cathedral which cost millions of dollars to erect? Is it some ancient shrine visited annually by countless pilgrims? Paul wrote to the Corinthians, "Know ye not that *ye are the temple of God?*" (I Corinthians 3:16). The Bible supplies a strange but suggestive parallel. The first sanctuary was but a tent in the wilderness, yet the glory of the Lord came to fill it. As the years passed, a tragic deterioration set in and when we find the temple on the pages of the New Testament, the glory-filled house had become a market. The same truths are exhibited in the story of the human sanctuary. Man was meant to be the companion of God; in the human breast, the Almighty planned to place His own glory. Yet something went wrong; the human heart has become desperately wicked; we have made it a den of thieves. What is true conversion? Is it not the coming of Christ to the very threshold of that human temple? Is it not the entrance of the Lord Jesus to overturn the tables of the money changers and herald the greatest spring-cleaning the human heart is ever likely to know? "The Lord shall suddenly come to his temple . . . ."

Backsliding

The transformation made by the cleansing power of Christ represented the most dynamic thing that had ever happened in the temple. He made the sanctuary what it was meant to be, for the peace of God filled the building. Alas, after a while, things began to change. One of the expelled men slowly approached the door; he stood for a while debating certain possibilities and, obviously arriving at a decision, went in search of his equipment. Soon he returned to set up his table; soon he was in business again. Obviously the moment came when the custodian of the sanctuary became aware of his return, but the money changer was permitted to remain. Before the day terminated, other money changers were back in their old positions, and within a short time, the temple was as filthy as ever.

This is as neat a picture of backsliding as can be found anywhere in the Bible. Each man is the custodian of his own temple, and experience teaches that after the initial cleansing of the human heart, Satan, with great wisdom and patience, refrains from troubling the convert. Yet, sooner or later, the first money changer — the first evil habit — returns to set up his table. It is at this point that so many Chrisians fail. If at that moment the returning evil were mercilessly thrown out, the temple precincts would continue to be clean. Unfortunately, so many people compromise by permitting the return of something which Jesus drove into the streets. This laxity is the thin end of the wedge of evil; soon the other weaknesses begin to appear, "and the latter end of that man is worse than the beginning."

Restoration

We shall never realize what the Saviour felt when He heard of the deplorable conditions existing again within the precincts of the temple courtyard. Had He denounced the sad declension, had He refused to return, no blame could have been attached to His Name. Yet He did return, and if the suggestion made in the earlier expository notes be correct, His glorious action makes thrilling reading. He stood for a while surveying the scene before Him. He remembered what had transpired years earlier and, because He still loved the place, He prepared to repeat His action. Once again He advanced toward the centers of evil; again, the money changers rushed for the street; and, serenity returned to the sanctuary. Then one of the doors opened to admit "the blind and the lame" (Matthew 21:12-14). And He healed them! This surely is God's delightful way of teaching that when the Lord is permitted to re-enter the temple of the backslider, His cleansing work is but the prelude to a fresh display of healing power. One no longer has to walk in darkness, for the light of the glory of God shines into the soul. A man is no longer dependent upon worldly crutches; the power of God enables him to walk in newness of life. All this, many times over, has been re-enacted in the lives of countless people. The two cleansings of the temple, with the sad lapse which separated them, provide the most wonderful picture of the redemptive work of God in Christ. Here all preachers should find food for thought; such material could well turn sermon preparation into an increasing joy.

SECTION THREE

Expository Notes on the Beginning of a Storm

In order to conserve space and time, let us endeavor to unite, for this occasion at least, both exposition and homiletics into one study.

Study No. 11

His critics

> **Then answered the Jews and said unto him, What sign shewest thou unto us, seeing that thou doest these things? (v. 18).**

Reformers have never been popular! Opposition was to be fully expected from those whose financial gains had been threatened. In any case, one should never attempt to work for God unless one is prepared to do battle with evil. Working to extend the Kingdom of God has never been a picnic! The words spoken by the Jews represented the initial blasts of the storm which would reach hurricane force on a green hill outside the city wall. Dark days were ahead, but the long years of communion in Nazareth had fortified the Saviour; He was ready to press on. All this should mean much to those who follow in His footsteps.

His cross

> **Jesus answered and said unto them, Destroy this temple, and in three days I will raise it up (v. 19).**

Already, even at the commencement of His ministry, the Lord saw clearly its end. This was the first of several predictions concerning the events to take place three years later. He spoke of the raising of His body; it follows then that He knew His body would be nailed to a cross. He spoke of *destroying* His body. This was strictly true, for although His body was raised from the dead, it had been changed; the mortal had put on immortality. The body of the Lord Jesus Christ will never again be as it was during the years of His anointed ministry in Palestine.

His claims

He predicted that *He* would raise it up. Acting on the assumption that dead men can do nothing, it follows that even when He was dead, *He would not be dead!* His body would be cold and still, but His body was but a house in which He had chosen to reside temporarily. The decease of His body did not presuppose the soul-sleep of its illustrious Tenant. Indeed, while His body lay peacefully within Joseph's tomb, ". . . *he went and preached unto the spirits in prison*" (I Peter 3:19). It should also be considered that He predicted, "I shall raise it up." This was an open claim to Deity. The verse must be associated with Acts 3:14, 15. "But ye denied the Holy One and the Just, and desired a murderer to be granted unto you; and killed the Prince of life, *whom God hath raised from the dead;* whereof we are witnesses."

His converts

> Then said the Jews, Forty and six years was this temple in building, and wilt thou rear it up in three days? But he spake of the temple of his body. When therefore he was risen from the dead, his disciples remembered that he had said this unto them; and they believed the Scriptures and the word which Jesus had said. (vv. 20-22).

It becomes increasingly evident that the disciples ultimately believed three vital things.

(1) *God had spoken through His word* — "They believed the scripture." This probably referred to the prophetic utterance in Psalm 16:10: "For thou wilt not leave my soul in hell (Sheol); neither wilt thou suffer thine Holy One to see corruption." The disciples believed firmly that David had spoken by the Divine Spirit of their Lord. The law and the prophets were not a collection of ancient fables but the preserved, inspired record of God's dealings with His children.

(2) *God had spoken through His Son.* It is said that they not only believed the Scripture; they also believed *the word which Jesus had said.* They believed what the writer to the Hebrews affirmed: "God, who at sundry times and in diverse manners spake in time past unto the fathers by the prophets, hath in these last days spoken unto us by his Son, whom he hath appointed heir of all things, by whom also he made the worlds" (Hebrews 1:1, 2). Thus we see at a glance that these men whom God signally honored and used were widening the circle of their theological concept of inspiration. The teachings of Christ were of equal importance to the revered records of bygone ages, for both had been conceived in the mind of God.

(3) *They had found a new foundation for their faith.* In direct contrast to the traditions of the fathers — the flimsy foundation upon which the hopes of Israel rested — these men were placing their confidence in the message proclaimed by their Leader. They believed implicitly that whereas ". . . the law was given by Moses, grace and truth came by Jesus Christ." This was a new idea; this teaching was destined to be revolutionary; it turned the world upside down (Acts 17:6).

His Carefulness

> Now when he was in Jerusalem at the passover, in the feast day, many believed in his name, when they saw the miracles which he did. But Jesus did not commit himself unto them, because he knew all men, and needed not that any should testify of man; for he knew what was in man (vv. 23-25).

The Englishman's Greek Testament translates the Greek word *episteuen,* "But Jesus himself did not *trust* himself to them." Even at this early stage of His ministry the Lord recognized the danger of a false enthusiasm. Loaves and fishes, the prospect of a place on the executive council of the kingdom of God, or as American brethren would say, "A seat on the bandwagon," are not the criterions of real discipleship. He who would preach to multitudes must be prepared to journey through the heat of the day to talk with an outcast woman at Sychar's well. He who would reign from a throne should be prepared to die on a cross. Alas, it was soon to be revealed that many of those who "believed on him" would go back, and would no more be numbered among His followers. The man who walks with God will know how to be patient. Impetuosity and the desire to hurry ahead will be ruthlessly restricted. The right things must be done in the right way at the right time; otherwise God's purposes will be in jeopardy. The Lord was wonderful in all His ways, and we do well to emulate His example. (See also the homily on John 4:1-3.)

The Third Chapter of John

THEME: *The Eternal Giver of Eternal Life*

OUTLINE:

    I. Nicodemus Interviews Christ. Verses 1-21.

    II. John Baptist Testifies of Christ. Verses 22-36.

A *Necessary Introduction on the Study of John's Third Chapter*

Sources of Information

Both sections of this chapter are remarkable in that the actual historical narrative is followed by doctrinal teaching. Verses 1-15 are obviously the record of what transpired when Nicodemus sought and obtained an audience with Jesus. Verses 16-31 might also belong to the actual discourse delivered by the Lord, yet, because even the phraseology is so like that used in the epistles of John, the question has arisen whether or not the writer of this gospel used the event as a platform from which to preach the Gospel. In order to prevent any misunderstanding, let it be clearly understood that even if this proved to be the case, no fault can be attributed to the apostle. This was his gospel. He was writing his memoirs and, to the best of his ability, endeavoring to tell his readers what he knew to be the truth concerning the Logos. It will be recognized that the same pattern prevails throughout the closing part of the chapter. Verses 22-30 are clearly the record of the events which took place in Aenon near to Salim. Again it must be stressed that verses 31-36 might be the continuation of this actual historical record. Yet again a question arises: was this truly the case, or did the author seize the opportunity to amplify or expand what John Baptist had declared? In assessing this possibility, two things must be taken into consideration.

(1) This language is obviously used in the epistles of John. For example, in verses 35 and 36 we read, "The Father loveth the Son, and hath given all things into his hand. He that believeth on the Son hath everlasting life: and he that believeth not the Son shall not see life; but the wrath of God abideth on him." I John 5:11-13 reads: "And this is the record, that God hath given to us eternal

life, and this life is in his Son. He that hath the Son hath life; and
he that hath not the Son of God hath not life. These things have I
written unto you that believe on the name of the Son of God; that
ye may know that ye have eternal life, and that ye may believe on
the name of the Son of God." The similarity of expression is obvious,
and the idea lingers that for this passage we are indebted to the
apostle and not primarily to the wilderness preacher.

(2) If, however, this is not true, then it must be admitted
John Baptist here produces a new type of message. There is hardly
any similarity between the sermon expressed in Matthew 3 and the
discourse recorded in these verses. In order to allay any criticism,
let us also admit the possibility that both Jesus and the Baptist used
these terms, and if such were the case, even John's epistles were
but an echo of that to which he himself had listened many years
previously. Many of the European theologians lean to the idea
that only part of the narrative is actual historic fact; that having
faithfully described the events which took place, John thereupon
emphasized these things should beget an appreciation of the Gospel
as expressed in the terms, "the Father," "the Son," and "eternal life."

These details serve as a background against which readers should
have a clearer understanding of what is to be studied. There is,
however, a fact which is important. The writer of this chapter had
been an eyewitness of the things described. It would hardly be
possible to record so clearly the details of Christ's talk with Nicodemus
unless the apostle had been present during the interview. Even after
many years the details of that talk stood out in bold relief and John
had no difficulty in writing what had been spoken fifty years earlier.
Verses 22-23 read, "After these things came Jesus and his disciples
into the land of Judea; and there he tarried with them and baptized.
And John also was baptizing in Aenon near to Salim, because there
was much water there: and they came and were baptized." Then
follows the description of what happened when some of the Jews
began to question the disciples of John. The details are set forth
so clearly that once more we must concede this writer was present
to hear what was said. The possibility exists that since the Saviour
and His party had now come to a place in close proximity to John
Baptist's meetings, the apostle seized the chance to visit his former
leader. This would be quite natural, and indisputably would have
the commendation of the Saviour. If this were the case, then it is
easy to imagine John's going across to Aenon to have fellowship
with his friend. He arrived in time to be present at an argument.
Probably this was the last time he heard John Baptist preaching,
and he never forgot the stirring declaration, "He must increase, but
I must decrease." These words made a deep impression on the

apostle's mind, and after many years, as he reminisced, it was easy to recall the words: "He that cometh from above, is above all: he that is of the earth is earthly, and speaketh of the earth: he that cometh from heaven is above all. And what he hath seen and heard, that he testifieth; and no man receiveth his testimony." If John added these words, he did so because his daily companionship with Christ and his long experience as a pastor enabled him to express clearly what the Baptist had tried to reveal. Here there are two scenes, two interviews, with certain important conclusions coming from both. Theology and scholarship are united in the decision that this chapter is one of the greatest ever written.

SECTION ONE

Expository Notes on Christ's Talk With Nicodemus

There was a man of the Pharisees, named Nicodemus, a ruler of the Jews (v. 1).

The religious life of Palestine, broadly speaking, was divided into two sections — *Pharisees* and *Sadducees*. The chief difference between them was that of the theological conception of survival. The Pharisees maintained that God was not the God of the dead but of the living, that after life on this earth, the faithful enjoyed a better life beyond the grave (see Acts 24:15, 15). The Sadducees rejected this belief and affirmed that death terminated existence. Someone has said this explained their name — they were *sad-you-see!*

Nicodemus belonged to the more spiritual of the two sects and had attained to a place of importance in national life. He was a ruler of the Jews; by that term it is understood he was a member of the Sanhedrin, the chief Jewish council, the senate. Yet it would seem that he was *more* than most of his colleagues. In the course of the conversation subsequently written by the apostle, the Lord Jesus said, "Art thou a master of Israel, and knowest not these things?" The statement in the original Greek is much stronger: *Su ei ho didaskalos tou Israel* . . . . "Thou art *the* teacher of Israel." That Christ should speak in such commendatory terms suggests His illustrious visitor was one of the most acceptable speakers in the nation. In order to reach this exalted position, Nicodemus must have been a man of great learning, great insight into the Scriptures, and a man capable of imparting knowledge to listeners. Possibly the quality of his ministry had made his name a household word. His presence in any pulpit would have commanded the presence of a large audience.

It is both vital and necessary that we consider this fact, for some commentators may have missed important details in their exposition of this chapter. Most people are concerned with the reason for Nicodemus' coming to Christ under cover of darkness. It is of far greater importance why he came at all. We must proceed slowly, for this is one of the greatest chapters in the entire book.

The same came to Jesus by night (v. 2).

It has already been stated that most commentators emphasize the fact that Nicodemus came to Jesus by night. Within the framework of his gospel, John mentions this man three times, and on each occasion repeats the fact that *"Nicodemus came by night"* to see Jesus (John 3:2; John 7:50; John 19:39). It is inevitable that we ask an old question. Why did Nicodemus come during the hours of darkness? There are three possibilities:

(1) It is generally believed that he was afraid to invite criticism, that he was timid and cowardly, that he waited until his movements would be veiled in darkness, and then secretly sought audience with Jesus. I am not convinced this is true.

(2) Nicodemus himself would be a very busy man. His exalted position within the nation carried heavy responsibilities. It should not be forgotten that possibly he was so busy throughout the day, that he was obliged to come when other people were not visiting him.

(3) Nicodemus would not be content to *see* the new Rabbi; he had no particular desire to hear a sermon. He sought an interview. There were things he wanted to know, and to gain this information he would need to ask questions. There existed the possibility that this interview might last a long time, and to Nicodemus the outcome would be far-reaching. How then could he interfere with the already overcrowded schedule of the Carpenter's day? Great crowds followed Jesus everywhere; sermons were being preached; anxious fathers were bringing their sick children; lepers waited hopefully in the distance. Jesus was the busiest Man in the country, and to expect Him to leave a multitude for an hour, two hours, perhaps three hours, in the midst of His crowded day would be an imposition. Nicodemus had no way of knowing how long the interview would last, but he was determined to see the job through. Is it too much to believe that he came by night not because he was a coward but because he was thoughtful, considerate, sincere? Most of the people would have gone home, the Master would have enjoyed His meal, and in the restful seclusion of some simple home He would be free to answer questions. There would then be the least likelihood of incessant interruptions. I have long believed that if Nicodemus had come at any other time, we should have been denied one of the greatest discourses ever given by the Lord Jesus.

Rabbi, we know that thou art a teacher come from God: for no man can do these miracles that thou doest, except God be with him (v. 2).

At first, this appears to be ludicrous. Had the visitor said, "Rabbi, please pardon this visit. You must be tired, but if you could spare a few moments to answer a few questions, I shall be eternally grateful. Would you mind, Sir, if I put my questions to you?" — had he opened his conversation in this manner, his action would have been logical. However, his strange outburst reminds me of my first boyish effort to recite at a Sunday school anniversary. I had memorized the poem until I could almost say it backward. Yet when I walked on the platform, I forgot every word. Nicodemus knew exactly what he desired to say, but he never said it! He stammered out something that was obvious, and then became silent. What caused the sudden loss of memory? We must not overlook the fact that already this great Jew had accepted the miracles of Jesus and attributed them to God. Some of his colleagues were soon to declare that Christ's power to heal came from His close association with Beelzebub! Faith was appearing in this man's heart, but unless we can find its beginning, we might lose the most thrilling details of this entrancing account.

And what did Jesus do? Probably the Lord smiled, and in the most disarming fashion, He put His guest at ease by referring to *the kingdom of God.* This must have been the crux of the man's problem. He was thinking of the coming kingdom; he was concerned with the identity of the promised King, but how could he reach this point in the interview without appearing to be anxious, without making the issue controversial? He wanted to ask, "Are you the promised King? Is the kingdom of God at hand?" Indisputably these questions were filling his mind, but when he entered into the presence of the Teacher, the transcendent glory, the winsomeness of the Master, the compelling charm of his Host, momentarily paralyzed his mind. It was then, in so many words, that Jesus said, "Friend, you are thinking of the kingdom. Except a man be born again, he cannot see the kingdom of God."

We must seek the reason for this nocturnal visit. Nicodemus was THE TEACHER of Israel; therefore it can be assumed he was acquainted with *the law and the prophets.* Believing as he did that the prophets had spoken accurately of the coming Messiah, he studied their writings, and knew precisely what they foretold. Possibly the scroll of the prophet Daniel lay open upon his desk, and from its message arose the problem to haunt this Jewish leader. Daniel had been very precise in his utterances concerning the Messiah. "Seventy weeks are determined upon thy people, and upon thy holy city, to finish the transgression, and to make an end of sins, and to make reconciliation for iniquity, and to bring in everlasting righteousness, and to seal up the vision and prophecy, and to anoint the most Holy. Know therefore and understand, that from the going forth of the commandment to restore and to build Jerusalem unto Messiah the Prince shall be seven weeks, and threescore and two weeks. The street shall be built again, and the wall, even in troublous times. And after three score and two weeks shall Messiah be cut off, but not for himself . . ." (Daniel 9:24-26).

The fixing of dates with absolute accuracy is a most hazardous undertaking and is fraught with peril. Yet in the case of Nicodemus, who was so much nearer to the historical events described by Daniel, the task of understanding the meaning of the prophecy would not have been too difficult. Nicodemus would have known that *if Daniel had spoken the truth, the time for the coming of the Messiah had already elapsed.* Indeed, if Daniel had predicted accurately, the Messiah would soon be cut off. If the prophecy had been of God, then somewhere within the nation, the Messiah had already made an appearance. That Daniel might have been wrong was quite unthinkable; Nicodemus was a devout believer. Where then was the promised Messiah? It was at this point that Nicodemus failed to prevent his thoughts wandering in the direction of the Carpenter from Nazareth. Already a new Rabbi had commenced to minister; already miracles were flowing from His touch. Throughout the nation and in all the market places people were whispering that Jesus was the promised One. Could this be true? And if not, who else could be the Messiah? John Baptist had flatly denied that he was the King, and apart from the wilderness preacher, Jesus was alone in magnificent isolation. Was He the Messiah? If He were not, then Daniel's prediction left much to be desired. The brain of Israel's greatest teacher seemed to be on fire; his problem haunted him. Jesus alone could answer his questions; to Him, Nicodemus would need to go.

The Saviour smiled, read at a glance all that was in His visitor's mind, and immediately coming to the point, said, "Except a man be born again, he cannot see the kingdom of God."

Nicodemus saith unto him, How can a man be born when he is old? Can he enter the second time into his mother's womb, and be born? (v.4).

Here we have Christian psychology at its best. Israel's keenest mind was temporarily embarrassed; the scholar was off balance! To place him at ease, the Lord did not attempt to speak words of reassuring comfort; instead he challenged his mind. And even before he realized what had happened, the ruler of the Jews was interested, eager, and almost argumentative as he considered something apparently impossible. Obviously, he had never heard such a suggestion. Salvation, or acceptance with God, as he understood it, depended upon a man's conformity to Mosaic law. There were certain rigid requirements and there were no exceptions. A man had to strive to bring his conduct into conformity with all God had revealed. Man only possessed one life, and that had to be well-lived. When Christ suggested that the old life, even at its scintillating best, was unacceptable to God, Nicodemus was nonplussed. When the same Christ intimated the need for a new birth, Nicodemus was out of his theological depth; his mind swirled; he knew nothing! Happy indeed is the man who can learn so much in such a short time.

Jesus answered, Verily, verily, I say unto thee, Except a man be born of water and of the Spirit, he cannot enter into the kingdom of God. That which is born of the flesh is flesh; and that which is born of the Spirit is spirit. Marvel not that I said unto thee, Ye must be born again (v. 5-7).

Here again the Lord contrasts two families. There is an earthly family; there is the heavenly family. An earthly parent transmits life, thus making birth possible. A child is born and begins to grow. Even so there is a Heavenly Father who also transmits life – His own life, eternal life. This He is able to impart to a man's inmost being, so that even though the recipient be already sixty years old, the coming of a new life constitutes an entirely new start. This is his second birth; he is *born again*. This contrast in families was clearly indicated when Christ was told of the presence of Mary and her children. "Then one said unto him, Behold, thy mother and thy brethren stand without, desiring to speak with thee. But he answered and said unto him that told him, Who is my mother? and who are my brethren? And he stretched forth his hand toward his disciples, and said, Behold my mother and my brethren! For whosoever shall do the will of my Father which is in heaven, the same is my brother, and sister, and mother" (Matthew 12:47-50).

Many strange interpretations have been given of the term "born of water." It has been taught that this refers to the act of baptism; that baptism is essential to salvation. Within the confines of the New Testament Church, souls were baptized *after* their conversion, and not while they were being saved. Modern disciples have taught that as in the physical realm conception precedes birth, so in the spiritual realm, faith precedes baptism. It has also been taught that as conception without birth is meaningless and a tragedy, so faith without baptism is null and void. This is not true. There will be thousands of redeemed souls in heaven who never even heard of baptism; there will be thousands more who were utterly sincere in their mistaken belief that baptism was an unessential ordinance. Many devout Salvation Army officers have never been baptized; many ardent Methodists were never immersed; the penitent thief never saw a baptistry, but he has long since found an abiding place in the presence of his Saviour.

Other movements, seeking to atone for the foolishness of their ancestors, teach that baptism for the dead is permissible. A man may be baptized on behalf of his deceased grandmother that she may not be found wanting on the day of judgment. Some earnest people have been immersed so often they believe they are responsible for the salvation of all the heretics who ever disgraced the family tree. This is false; this is not Biblical; this is to be condemned. "For by grace are ye saved, through faith; and that not of yourselves: it is the gift of God; not of works, lest any man should boast" (Ephesians 5:8, 9).

Throughout the New Testament, the term "water" is used to indicate the Word of God, and many and varied are the thoughts which might enrich a sermon. Water cleanses, refreshes, promotes growth, supplies power, supports (in the case of ships), helps to maintain life. All this and very much more is true concerning the Word of God. Thus we read: "Of his own will begat he us with the word of truth" (James 1:18). "Being born again, not of corruptible seed, but of incorruptible, *by the word of God,* which liveth and abideth for ever" (I Peter 1:23).

There exists a most interesting parallel at the beginning of the book of Genesis. We are told that in the beginning God created the heavens and the earth, and that the earth became a waste and void. Tragedy overtook the original creation, and the first chapter of the Bible is the account of God's endeavor to restore a ruined creation. The divine order supplies food for the preacher's thought:

(1) The Spirit moved upon the face of the deep.

(2) God spoke the creative word.

(3) The light shone forth.

The New Testament reveals a similar pattern in the redemption of man.

(1) "And when he (the Spirit) is come, he will reprove the world of sin" (John 16:8).

(2) "Go ye into all the world and preach the Gospel," and ". . . when he, the Spirit of truth, is come, he will guide you into all truth" (Mark 16:15; John 16:13).

(3) "For God who commanded the light to shine out of darkness, hath shined in our hearts, to give the light of the knowledge of the glory of God in the face of Jesus Christ" (II Corinthians 4:6).

Thus was Nicodemus introduced to the doctrine of the regeneration of the soul. God's purpose in Christ was not the improvement of the old life, but the transmission of a new life. The former life may be beautified, educated, taught to say prayers and sing hymns, but when all has been completed, it remains *the old life.* These commendable adjuncts were all exhibited in the life of the sincere ruler. Yet, he was informed that unless he was born from above, his best recommendations would be unable to provide admittance to the kingdom of God. "Ye *must* be born again" suggested urgency. (See the homily dealing with this text.)

> The wind bloweth where it listeth, and thou hearest the sound thereof, but canst not tell whence it cometh, and whither it goeth: so is every one that is born of the Spirit (v. 8).

Can anyone define the wind? Has any person ever seen it? Through the study of the movement of air masses, by determining the direction of the currents, men now predict its coming and diminishing, but the wind remains invisible, almost inscrutable. We see its effect; we sense its presence; we recognize its amazing power, but that is all.

Referring to this verse, the late Reverend A. W. Pink says, "*The wind is irresponsible:* that is to say, it is sovereign in its action. The wind is an element altogether beyond man's control. The wind neither consults man's pleasure nor can be regulated by his devises. So it is with the Spirit. The wind blows where it pleases, when it pleases, as it pleases. So it is with the Spirit.

"*The wind is irresistible.* When the wind blows in the fulness of its power, it sweeps everything before it. Those who have looked upon the effects of a tornado just after it has passed, know something of the mighty force of the wind. It is so with the Spirit. When He comes in the fulness of His power, He breaks down man's prejudices, subdues his rebellious will, overcomes all opposition.

"*The wind is irregular.* Sometimes the wind blows so softly it scarcely rustles a leaf; at other times it blows so loudly, its roar can be heard miles away. With some, the Holy Spirit works so gently, His work is imperceptible to onlookers. With others, His action is so powerful, so radical, revolutionary, His operations are patent to many. Sometimes the wind is only local in its reach; at other times it is widespread in its scope. So it is with the Spirit . . . .

"*The wind is invisible.* It is one of the very few things in nature that is invisible. We can see the rain, the snow, the lightning's flash; but not the wind. The analogy holds good with the Spirit. His Person is unseen.

"*The wind is inscrutable.* There is something about the wind which defies all effort of human explanation. Its origin; its nature; its activities are beyond man's ken. Man cannot tell whence it cometh nor whither it goeth. It is so with the activities of the Holy Spirit. His operations are conducted secretly. His workings are profoundly mysterious.

"*The wind is indispensable.* If a dead calm were to continue indefinitely, all vegetation would die. How quickly we wilt when there is no wind at all. Even more so is it with the Spirit. Without Him there could be no spiritual life at all.

"*Finally, the wind is invigorating.* The life-giving properties of the wind are illustrated every time a physician orders his sick patient to retire to the mountains or to the seaside. It is so with the Spirit. He is the One who strengthens with might in the inner man. He is the One who energizes, revives, empowers. How marvellously full was the figure employed by Christ on this occasion. How much is suggested by this single word *wind . . . .*"

Nicodemus answered and said unto him, How can these things be? Jesus answered and said unto him, Art thou the master (the teacher) of Israel, and knowest not these things? (vv. 9, 10).

This statement suggests that by virtue of his position, THE TEACHER of Israel *should have known* of the need for, and the possibility of, receiving eternal life. We are therefore driven to the conclusion that the Old Testament — the text book for this great Jew — had something to say about the theme. If Nicodemus should have known, it follows *he should have known from his study of the sacred writings.* Where had he failed? What Scripture had remained unnoticed? Which story had continued unintelligible? These are fair questions the answer to which is speedily and easily found.

Almost the first story in the book of Genesis concerned Adam and Eve. We are told that they were placed in the garden of Eden, that they were forbidden to partake of the tree of knowledge of good and evil. Preachers have been too one-sided in their treatment of the text. The importance of a lesser tree has been magnified at the expense of the greater tree — *the Tree of Life.* It should be remembered that God made man — *not a robot.* Man was given a free will, and was expected to use it. We know that because he partook of the fruit of the one tree, the first spot of moral poison fell into his soul. Had he partaken of the Tree of Life, he would have received eternal life. Adam was already a son of God *by creation;* he might have become a son of God *by nature.* When he sinned, man lost his opportunity. "And the Lord God said, Behold, the man is become as one of us, to know good and evil: and now, LEST HE PUT FORTH HIS HAND, AND TAKE ALSO OF THE TREE OF LIFE, AND

EAT, *and live forever* . . . the Lord God sent him forth from the garden of Eden" (Genesis 3:22, 23).

At first there were no restrictions regarding the Tree of Life. Genesis 2:9 reveals that the Tree of Life was in the center of the garden, where man could see it, approach it, partake of it, sit down in its shadow. Had man taken of its fruit, as was evidently God's desire, "he would have eaten, and lived forever." Many theologians stoutly maintain that this is but a fable from a bygone era. It is not my purpose to argue with their findings. As far as Nicodemus was concerned, whether the ancient account was actual historic fact or legendary, it mattered not; at least, *the story was in his Bible.* Therefore he should have been acquainted with its message — the message which revealed three tremendous things.

Provision. God so loved man that a Tree of Life was placed in the midst of the garden. God desired to share His life with the one He had created.

Possibility. Man could approach the tree; there were no restrictions to keep him away. He could take, and eat, and live.

Poverty. Man lost his opportunity, for once he sinned, ". . . God placed at the east of the garden of Eden, cherubims, and a flaming sword, which turned every way, to keep the way of the tree of life" (Genesis 3:24).

It was no new doctrine that God desired to share His life with man. It was true to relate that sin had temporarily blocked the path to the Tree of Life, but through the reconciling work of Christ, God was about to remove the barriers. The royal highway was about to be reopened, and man could return, as it were, to begin again where Adam had failed. The idea that we must suffer because of Adam's transgression is not strictly true. Tragedy has certainly overtaken the human race through man's stupidity, but no man is lost because Adam sinned. Christ restores the possibility of partaking by faith of the Tree of Life. The flaming sword no longer blocks the pathway. Therefore man now has the power to choose, and if he should again be expelled from the garden of grace, it will be through his own folly, and not because of Adam's transgression. All this truth, Nicodemus should have known.

Verily, verily, I say unto you, We speak that we do know, and testify that which we have seen: and ye receive not our witness. If I have told you earthly things, and ye believe not, how shall ye believe if I tell you of heavenly things? And no man hath ascended up to heaven, but he that came down from heaven, even the Son of man which is in heaven (vv. 11-13).

One wonders if the Lord here referred to the general belief of the Jews as a nation, or was He chiding Nicodemus personally for the unbelief within his soul? Three things should be considered.

(1) *His Authority.* "No man hath ascended up to heaven, but he that came down from heaven, even the Son of man which is in heaven." Once again Christ stresses His deity; once again the author of this gospel emphasizes the claims made by his Master. That Christ should be upon the earth and at the same time "still be in heaven" suggests omnipresence. He had been with God, and was even then with God. He who had shared in the eternal plannings of the Father had come to speak of heavenly things.

(2) *His Assurance.* We speak that we do know, and testify that we have seen. It is not without interest that many years later the apostle John used identical words in beginning his first epistle. John had a great memory and had grown to be like his Lord not only in his conduct but in the choice of words by which to impart truth. This could well serve as a standard of efficiency for all preachers of the Gospel. He who had been in the presence of God came forth to say "Thus saith the Lord." He was assured of the truth of His utterances. All ministers should stand in God's presence before they stand in the presence of a congregation.

(3) *His Answer.* Nicodemus had asked, "How can these things be?" and in order to illuminate the mind of the questioner, the Lord once again referred to the rabbi's Scriptures. God's Word is better than any argument. Sometimes, one verse spoken in the power of the divine Spirit may do more good than the most involved and lengthy discussions.

And as Moses lifted up the serpent in the wilderness, even so must the Son of man be lifted up: That whosoever believeth in Him should not perish but have everlasting life (vv. 14, 15).

This is one of the best known and perhaps the easiest to understand of all the Lord's word-pictures, for it is but the work of a moment to turn back the pages of the Bible to find in Numbers 21 the incident to which the Lord referred. "And the people spake against God and against Moses, Wherefore have ye brought us up out of Egypt to die in the wilderness? for there is no bread, neither is there any water; and our soul loatheth this light bread. And the Lord sent fiery serpents among the people, and they bit the people, and much people of Israel died. Therefore, the people came to Moses, and said, We have sinned, for we have spoken against the Lord, and against thee; pray unto the Lord that he take away the serpents from us. And Moses prayed for the people. And the Lord said unto Moses, Make thee a fiery serpent, and set it upon a pole, and it shall come to pass, that every one that is bitten, when he looketh upon it shall live. And Moses made a serpent of brass, and put it upon a pole, and it came to pass, that if a serpent had bitten any man, when he beheld the serpent of brass, he lived" (Numbers 21:5-9). Once again three vital elements stand forth in bold relief to provide every preacher with rich sermon material.

(1) *The Fact of Sin.* Even to this day that part of the world abounds in serpents, and travelers need to walk carefully. It is not too difficult to visualize the heart-rending scenes of a bygone age when through the stupidity of the people disaster overwhelmed the nation. They had despised what God had provided. The "bread of life sent down from heaven" had become despised, and the people's cry, "our soul loatheth this light bread," revealed the animosity which filled their souls. That to which they owed their very existence was now totally rejected, and the resultant displeasure of God was justified. Sin begat danger; and danger led to death. Only when it appeared too late to pray did the people even think of doing so.

(2) *The Fact of a Substitute.* Moses was instructed to make a serpent of brass and to hang it upon a pole. According to the promise of God, this would be the means of deliverance for stricken sinners. Many years later, the Lord cited this incident and suggested the serpent of brass was a type or foreshadowing of His own death. We are justified therefore in expecting to find much food for thought in the narrative.

The serpent has always been the emblem of sin and Satan, and this fact occasioned surprise. How could a serpent be a type of the Saviour? Attention must be given to the details of this verse. Moses might so easily have caught one of the actual serpents in order to nail it to the pole, but that would have been wrong. He was told to MAKE something that *resembled* the serpent. That it was to be made of brass inferred that it had been judged, for in the theological concept of Israel, brass and judgment were practically synonymous terms. When stricken people looked at the brazen serpent, they saw a destroyed destroyer. That which had caused disaster had itself been slain. Romans 8:3 reveals how God sent his own Son *in the likeness of sinful flesh.* He was NOT a sinner, but He associated Himself with sinners; He identified Himself with their guilt that through His death they might be identified with His glory. The apostle Paul wrote, "Christ hath redeemed us from the curse of the law, *being made a curse* for us: for it is written, Cursed is every one that hangeth on a tree: That the blessing of Abraham might come on the Gentiles through Jesus Christ . . ." (Galatians 3:13, 14). It followed then that because He would take our sin to the cross, this would be judged and put away; that which would have destroyed the souls of men would instead be robbed of its power.

(3) *The Fact of Salvation*. The story explains that God did everything to make this salvation possible except one thing. Each sufferer had to look for himself. Men could have been lying within one yard, but had their backs been turned toward the pole, they would have died. It is not sufficient *to know* of the salvation offered; it was not enough even *to believe* this salvation was a reality. *Each man had to look for himself*; otherwise God's provision was useless. As new life began to make its appearance within the camp of gloom, the excitement of the people began to increase, and before long, delivered people were running around looking for others who needed to be saved. If some were too weak to sit up, kindly hands assisted them. Life banished disease; songs dispelled sorrow. When Nicodemus asked how new life could reach a sinner, the Saviour referred to this famous story. How rich would be our preaching if we could discover the art of reading the Gospel on the pages of Old Testament books.

> For God so loved the world, that he gave his only begotten Son, that whosoever believeth in him, should not perish, but have everlasting life. For God sent not his son into the world to condemn the world; but that the world through him might be saved (vv. 16, 17).

This is one of the great treasures of the Bible. Probably it would be true to say that more has been written and said of this verse than of any other in the Scriptures. With their distinctive styles, the commentators have indicated something similar to the following outline:

A *Great Love*   — For God so loved the world,
A *Great Gift*   — that he gave his only begotten Son,
A *Great Opportunity* — that whosoever *believeth* in him
A *Great Deliverance* — should not perish,
A *Great Possession*   — but have everlasting life.

All these divisions may be subdivided, but the purpose of every good commentary is to stimulate thought, and not to do all the thinking for its readers!

> He that believeth on him is not condemned, but he that believeth not is condemned already, because he hath not believed in the name of the only begotten Son of God. And this is the condemnation, that light is come into the world, and men loved darkness rather than light, because their deeds were evil. For every one that doeth evil hateth the light, neither cometh to the light, lest his deeds should be reproved. But he that doeth truth cometh to the light, that his deeds may be made manifest, that they are wrought in God (v. 18-21).

It must be noticed that throughout these verses, faith supercedes action. This was an entirely new concept of theology, for until Christ came, the only salvation offered to man depended entirely upon his observance of Mosaic law. Certain deeds were indispensable in his efforts to merit acceptance with God and the priests. If men deliberately abstained from doing what they were told to do, they stood in danger of damnation. The hierarchy taught that observance of ritual was more important than a man's private prayer. The new doctrine that faith alone was sufficient to gain eternal life was both revolutionary and startling. Naaman was told to wash in Jordan; Israel was told to keep the commandments; prophets and kings were told to fast, and weep, and pray, but now, sinners were told to BELIEVE in the name of the Son of God. This new doctrine was destined to bring deliverance to those who were enslaved to the traditions of men. When Martin Luther rediscovered this same gospel, the fires of the reformation were kindled throughout Europe. Men had been taught that unless they obeyed every dictate of the Roman church, their souls would be damned in the eternal fires of hell. Luther searched the Scriptures diligently until he understood Paul's magnificent statement, "Therefore being justified by faith, we have peace with God through our Lord Jesus Christ" (Romans 5:1).

The faith of the saints is matched by the folly of sinners: ". . . men loved darkness rather than light because their deeds were evil." Compare this verse with chapter 1, verse 5, and evidence is supplied that the hearts of sinful men seem to be unchanging. Prior to the coming of the Saviour, "The light shineth in darkness, and the darkness comprehended it not." After His coming, "the light is come into the world, and men loved darkness . . . ." There are times when even God's greatest provision is unable to arrest the downward tendencies within the human breast. God supplies the light, but He cannot make men love the light. Unfortunately, some men so love the darkness that they will live in it forever. They know of it; probably they might even discuss it; from the distance they might even watch it, but this is not sufficient. *Believing* is the active response of a man's soul. Therefore, ". . . he that *doeth* truth *cometh* to the light, that his deeds may be made manifest that they are wrought in God." Faith without works is dead, and the evidence of the presence of living faith in a man's soul is the transformation of his life. It is not possible for a man to live in the light and at the same time to walk in darkness. By the same standard, it may be claimed it is not possible for a man to live in darkness and at the same time to walk in the light. It was destined that the coming of the Son of God would not only lead to the proclamation of a new message; it would lead to the formation of a new society. This happened when the Gospel begat the Church. The *ecclesia,* or *the called out ones,* found joy in the fellowship of kindred souls. The man who loves the light will never shun the lighthouse; the soul who claims to be the child of the Father will often be found in the Father's house.

HOMILIES

Study No. 12
NICODEMUS . . . WHOSE EDUCATION WAS INCOMPLETE!

There is reason to believe that Nicodemus was one of the outstanding teachers of his day. Even the Lord acknowledged him to be *the* teacher of Israel. The possibility exists that this learned man instructed students and prepared ministers for the pulpits of his time. John 7:50 reveals that Nicodemus held positions of great authority and was entitled thereby to speak in the highest council of the nation. Yet in spite of great learning and academic distinction, this Master of Israel knew nothing of a very important truth. When Christ informed him that he needed to be "born again," the ruler of the Jews was nonplussed, and could only reply, "How can these things be?"

How New

"Ye must *be born again.*" It is hardly possible to appreciate the implications of this message until one fully understands what is sin. The Bible teaches that sin is *a nature* and not merely an act or word. Sinful deeds are the product of a sinful life. Apples do not grow on blackberry bushes! This is taught in the early stories of the Bible. When God created man, Adam was sinless and without blemish. It was quite impossible for temptation to arise from within; Adam was *not* a sinner. Therefore the evil suggestion had to come from without. However, once man yielded, the first spot of moral poison fell into his soul, and he became guilty. Had Adam thereafter observed every law of God, that would not have atoned for his failure. The damage had already been done, and man was no longer without blemish. Ultimately, sons were born to Adam and Eve, but when those boys became adults, Cain rose up and murdered his brother. Yet we do not read that Satan came to tempt him. The idea originated in his own mind and heart. What had been impossible for the father, happened with the boy. The life transmitted from parent to child was, in itself, tainted. It is not foolish to suggest that long before a child knows the difference between good and evil, it is possible, sometimes, to see evil in the child's action. Often in embryonic form the evil temper of a parent is faithfully produced in the small body. David declared, "Behold, I was shapen in iniquity; and in sin did my mother conceive me" (Psalm 57:5).

The Bible teaches that sin is a nature. This is important to every student, for if Christ had been born as we were, *He would have been born a sinner.* It was necessary for God to perform a miracle, for without the virgin birth, there could not have been redemption. "And the angel said unto Mary, Fear not, Mary . . . . thou shalt conceive in thy womb, and bring forth a son, and shalt call his name JESUS. He shall be great, and shall be called the Son of the Highest: and the Lord God shall give unto him the throne of his father David . . . . Then said Mary, How shall this be, seeing I know not a man? And the angel answered and said unto her, *The Holy Spirit shall come upon thee, and the power of the Highest shall overshadow thee; therefore also that holy thing which shall be born of thee, shall be called the Son of God"* (Luke 1:30-35). The people who deny the veracity of the virgin birth may be charming men, but their theology is deplorable. Strictly speaking, the Lord Jesus was neither Jew nor Gentile — He was *the God-Man.* Against this setting, it was possible to appreciate the teaching of the new birth. God's purpose in Christ was not the improvement of an old nature but rather the transformation of a new one. This was something of which the leader of the Jews had never heard.

How Necessary

"Ye *must* be born again." It is easy to imagine how the Lord gently emphasized the urgent necessity for this event. Since entry into the all-important kingdom would be conditioned by whether or not a man had been born the second time, nothing else equalled this in importance. To be denied entrance into God's kingdom would be a tragedy of eternal dimensions. Every Jew acknowledged this fact. However, until this precise moment the only necessary preparation had been conformity to ecclesiastical law, the observance of temple ritual, the commendation of Mosaic teachings. That all this now to be superceded was a staggering statement. Nicodemus was almost speechless as the Lord emphasized the importance of receiving a new life.

Yet to us, the words of Christ are not surprising. The old life may be trained in a college; but it remains *the old life.* It may become cultured, refined, admired, commended by all kinds of people. It may be religiously inclined; might even earn a living doing the work of God, and still be *the old* life. It may appear to be wonderful and yet not be wonderful; may invoke the praises of men, but since the final word rests with God, the commendation of men is insufficient. If God says man's best righteousness is as filthy rags, no argument can change His opinion. Improvement of the old nature may fit one for a place in society; but only the incoming of a new nature entitles one to a place in God's family. "Jesus answered, Verily, verily, I say unto thee, Except a man be born of water and of the Spirit, *he cannot enter into the kingdom of God*" (John 3:5).

How Near

"Ye must be born again." Did the face of the listening minister register surprise as he was reminded of his own need? Was he upset when he was informed that his need equalled that of the people to whom he ministered? "Great Teacher, if the Heavenly Father desires to give me a new life, please tell me how this takes place." The Lord's answer was sublime. "As Moses lifted up the serpent in the wilderness, even so must the Son of man be lifted up: that whosoever believeth in him, should not perish, but have everlasting life." Our world urgently needs a renaissance of spiritual thought. Living as we do in a materialistic age, emphasis has been placed on improving morality and not on the teachings of Christ. I shall never forget the day when I was asked to visit an American school. The headmaster was extremely worried by the delinquency of his students. Thieving, gambling, and sexual intercourse had reached enormous proportions, and he was fearful that grave disasters might overwhelm the life of his institution. He had appealed to the local service clubs for assistance, and his request was repeated when I visited the city. Alas, when I sat in his office, he imposed one restriction which paralyzed me. He begged for my message; he earnestly hoped I would arrest the downward trends among his students — "but would I leave Christ out of my message?" Sorrowfully I had to confess that if I did this, I had no solution for his problems. His students needed "a new heart," which Christ alone could supply. I might succeed in stemming the poison at one point, but if evil were in the blood stream, it would quickly appear elsewhere. The headmaster was a splendid man, but shaking his head, he admitted he could not permit me to speak of the Saviour. I remember his thought-provoking words: "*It makes me sick to think of it. Our forefathers died for their faith, but we are afraid to stand for what we believe. I'm sick.*"

Higher education is excellent, but without the life of God, it may be used to make bigger destructive weapons. Academic distinction is to be desired, but without Christ, it only produces more clever sinners. All men should remember that every day brings eternity a little nearer. There is a kingdom which is not of this world; to be denied entry means indescribable loss. Predominant in importance, superlative in worth, the Saviour's words shine as stars in the sky.

"*Except a man be born again, he cannot see the kingdom of God.*"

Study No. 13
ETERNAL LIFE IN ITS CONTINUING FULLNESS

The Tree of Life in Eden

It should never be forgotten that eternal life is far greater than everlasting life. Eternal life is primarily something of *quality*. Everlasting life is something of *duration* — it never ends. Adam might have succeeded in living forever, as mere man. He was meant to reach higher realms of experience — to share the nature of God; not merely to live endlessly, but to become a son of God by nature. Yet man was not a robot to be impelled by buttons or switches. Adam was given a free will. He was expected to exercise that gift, and thereby to demonstrate his fitness to share in the provision of his Maker. All this has been clearly revealed in the early chapters of Holy Writ. Man had to choose between the Tree of Life and the tree of knowledge of good and evil. The former was situated in the middle of the garden — the place of centrality, where its prominence invited attention; the latter tree was surrounded by prohibitions. When man permitted sin to stain his soul, the way to the Tree of Life was closed — "Lest man should put forth his hand, and take of the tree of life, and live for ever." Adam, therefore, lost his great opportunity, for sin had closed a highway.

The Tree of Life in John 3

I remember a man who complained, "It is not just. Why should I suffer because Adam sinned? It is not *my* fault that Adam went wrong. Why should God punish *me?*" This idea is false. When Christ discussed the topic with Nicodemus, He revealed that what had become an impossibility for Adam was impossible no longer. He said, "Marvel not that I say unto you, Ye must be born again." It was now possible for the Jewish leader to receive a new life — eternal life. This surely signifies that the flaming sword of Adam's day was now to be withdrawn. The question may be asked, "How could this be?" but the answer is unmistakable. The path to the Tree of Life was closed by the existence of sin. If it is now to be reopened, it must be because the hindrance has been overcome. "For God so loved the world, that he gave his only begotten Son, that whosoever believeth in him, should not perish but have everlasting life." If Adam's sin robbed him of the power to choose eternal life, the death of Christ, by removing sin, restored what Adam lost. Once again, man may choose unwisely; but at least *he can choose.* If man now suffers eternal loss, he does so not because Adam went wrong, but because he himself has followed in Adam's footsteps.

The Tree of Life in the New Jerusalem

In describing the New Jerusalem, John says, "In the midst of the street of it . . . was the tree of life . . . and the leaves of the tree were for the healing of the nations." This verse presents a problem. Why should the nations need healing in the eternal kingdom? We have been led to believe that, at that time, all need will have been abolished. This verse harmonizes with the rest of the Scripture. When Christ returns to earth, He will reign for a thousand years, and afterwards, Satan will rally his forces to make a final onslaught on the powers of righteousness. (Revelation 20:7-9). But not all men will follow evil. Many may desire to remain the subjects of the King of Kings. They will be ordinary human beings as we are, so how then can they share in the gift of God which enables men to live as God's children forever? It would seem that the Tree of Life supplies the answer. Whether this be literal or symbolical is not of primary importance. The fact is that God makes it possible for people in all ages TO CHOOSE life, and that always man's destiny is decided by what he does when opportunity knocks at the door. God may offer the Bread of Life, but unless man takes it, he might easily die of starvation. "And the Spirit and the bride say, Come. And let him that heareth say, Come. And let him that is athirst come. And whosoever will, LET HIM TAKE the water of life freely" (Revelation 22:17).

(Reprinted from *Bible Highways*, page 5)

Study No. 14

TWO MEN WHO TRIUMPHED GLORIOUSLY IN THE END

There exists within the New Testament story a friendship which rivals in importance that of David and Jonathan of an earlier age. Nicodemus was a ruler of the Jews; Joseph of Arimathea was an honorable counselor. Both men belonged to the Jewish Parliament, and probably for a while at least, either man feared the other. Nicodemus is mentioned three times in John's gospel, and on each occasion, John referred to him as "the one who came to Jesus by night." In summing up these Scriptures, Dr. Graham Scroggie used the following headings. (1) *His desire for Christ* (John 3:2); (2) *His defense of Christ* (John 7:50, 51); (3) *His devotion to Christ* (John 19:39).

Here ministers are supplied with three vivid scenes, and even a brief time of study might well provide material to make a sermon helpful and attractive. The former homilies may help to depict the coming of Nicodemus during the night hours, the resultant talk with Christ, and the deepening appreciation which finally filled his soul. Secondly, it is not too difficult to describe the Jewish parliament in session, and to hear the sharp exchanges which went across the floor of the house. Had the ruler of the Jews used his knowledge of the book of Daniel and proclaimed what he knew to be true, had he asked for visible evidence that the Messiah be produced or identified, he might have been an evangelist to his people. Alas, he subsided into silence, and a noticeable opportunity was lost for ever. We shall never know how often this great man was haunted by the memory of his failure.

It should be remembered that all the time, just six miles from the city of Jerusalem, was a village called Arimathea. Here Joseph, the honorable counselor resided. We are not told how he first came to believe in Jesus. Perhaps he stood on the outskirts of a meeting; perhaps from a distance he listened to a sermon. We are told that he was ". . . *a disciple of Jesus*, but secretly for fear of the Jews . . ." (John 19:38). There is good reason to believe that he was actually in the house when Nicodemus made a half-hearted attempt to defend Christ. At a later meeting of the Sanhedrin, this same man was opposed to the decision of the majority (Luke 23:50, 51). This timidity might have been a barrier between two very fine men. This was all changed when they united to bury Christ. Joseph supplied the tomb; his colleague brought "a mixture of myrrh and aloes, about a hundred pound weight" (John 19:39). It should be remembered they buried a *dead* Christ. They had no way of knowing the Lord would rise again. As far as they knew they had lost their opportunity of falling at His feet to confess their love. This action was a sure way of throwing caution to the winds. Ashamed of former failures, they now broadcast to the nation that they cared enough to do for Jesus something which even the disciples had not thought of doing. We can only imagine their tumultuous joy when the Saviour rose from the dead. They knew then that He understood; they had triumphed gloriously in the end.

SECTION TWO

Expository Notes on John Baptist's Testimony of Christ

After these things came Jesus and his disciples into the land of Judea; and there he tarried with them, and baptized. And John also was baptizing in Aenon near to Salim, because there was much water there: and they came and were baptized (vv. 22, 23).

The close proximity of the two revival camps begat a situation fraught with peril. (See the notes and homily on chapter 4:1-3.) The site of the meetings had been chosen because *"there was much water there."* This helps us to understand the mode of baptism. In spite of much which has been said to the contrary, New Testament baptism was by immersion. Had the ordinance been that of sprinkling or even pouring, there would hardly have been the necessity for the presence of *much water*. It should be considered again that the Jews did not question the rite of baptism; obviously they knew of this and merely questioned the authority of the preacher to administer the ordinance. Many strange and sometimes weird attempts have been made to read into this and other texts the most amazing interpretations, but the greatest thinkers produced by the Church have agreed that the method and mode of New Testament baptism was that of immersion. Even the Roman Catholic church admits this fact, for the following message has been published officially.

On page 199 of the New Testament, in *The New Catholic Edition of the Holy Bible*, published by the American Catholic Bible Association of 160 Fifth Avenue, New York 10, New York, the following footnote has been added to Romans 6:3, 4.

> St. Paul alludes to the manner in which baptism was ordinarily conferred in the early church — by immersion. The descent into the water is suggestive of the descent of the body into the grave, and the ascent is suggestive of the resurrection to a new life. St. Paul obviously sees more than the mere symbol in the rite of baptism. As a result of it we are incorporated into Christ's mystical body and live a new life.

Bishop J. B. Lightfoot, one of the greatest scholars of the Church of England, said in his 1890 commentary on Colossians 2:12, "Baptism is the grave of the old man, and the birth of the new. As he sinks beneath the baptismal waters, the believer buries there all his corrupt affections and past sins; he emerges thence, and rises regenerate to new hope in the new life."

John Wesley, the founder of the Methodist church, in his *Notes on the New Testament*, at Romans 6:4, says, "We are buried with him. Alluding to the ancient manner of baptizing by immersion."

Perhaps the most striking testimony of all comes from Martin Luther, the founder of the Lutheran church and the progenitor of the Reformation. From the quotation in Theodosia Ernest, Vol. I, page 171, we glean the following:

> The word *baptize* is a Greek word. It may be rendered *immersion* as when we plunge something into water, that it may be entirely covered with water — and though that custom is now abolished among the generality (even children are not entirely immersed but only have a little water poured on them), nevertheless they ought to be completely immersed and immediately drawn out, for the etymology of the word requires it.

Professor Peake, the famous British Methodist, endorsed all this in the *Expositors' Greek Testament*. Referring to Colossians 2:12, he says, "The rite of baptism in which the person baptized was first buried beneath the water, and then raised from it, typified to Paul the burial and resurrection of the believer with Christ."

This then was the mode of baptism practiced in both camps near to Salim. Later, the Church gave to the rite a clearer and more thrilling interpretation, but this Scripture enables us to appreciate the ordinance observed in the meetings of John Baptist. He preached repentance; and when converts responded, he baptized them.

For John was not yet cast into prison (v. 24).

This really should be in parenthesis, and serves as a focusing point in a period of time. Compared with the synoptic record, it enables the incident to forerun the other events described elsewhere.

Then there arose a question between some of John's disciples and the Jews about purifying. And they came unto John and said unto him, Rabbi, he that was with thee beyond Jordan, to whom thou barest witness, behold, the same baptizeth, and all men come to him (vv. 25, 26).

Obviously some animated discussion had taken place, and one thing led to another. The washing of the hands with water, the immersion of the body in baptism — these and other details added fuel to the fires, and finally, Jesus and His disciples were mentioned in the arguments. Spite begat criticism, and the fact that John's audiences were decreasing could not be denied. Had God withdrawn blessing from the Baptist? If so, by what authority did he continue to minister? The increasing crowds in the rival camp suggested that John had outlived his usefulness! These were unpleasant thoughts; the disciples of John might be supporting a losing cause! Unfortunately this was fertile soil in which the seeds of jealousy germinated. One mistake on John's part might have ruined his entire testimony. The Baptist was a true believer; he endorsed his former utterances and stressed he was not the Christ.

He that hath the bride is the bridegroom: but the friend of the bridegroom, which standeth and heareth him, rejoiceth greatly because of the bridegroom's voice: This my joy therefore is fulfilled. He must increase but I must decrease (v. 29, 30).

The text supplies a threefold picture for here we see (1) the bridegroom; (2) the bride; (3) the best man. Certain evangelical expositors see here the foreshadowings of the Marriage Supper of the Lamb, and emphasize details which, to say the least, do not represent the best in exegesis. That Christ is to be the Royal Bridegroom and that one day He will be joined by His Bride is obvious. All this is foretold in prophecy, but John's first thought was the provision of an illustration to quiet the fears of his disturbed disciples. They were upset by the apparent decreasing popularity of their wonderful leader. Somehow they had to learn that the very thing which caused acute disappointment was in itself the greatest commendation of their leader. The increasing greatness of Jesus was precisely what he had predicted. Had it been otherwise, John would have broken his heart! If an excited crowd carried the best man shoulder high from a wedding and left the betrothed couple deserted, forgotten, shamed, the wedding would be a tragedy. John was but the best man who prepared for a great occasion; and when the day of happiness dawned, he himself eagerly anticipated "taking a back seat" that his Friend might be all in all.

> He that cometh from above is above all: he that is of the earth is earthly, and speaketh of the earth: he that cometh from above is above all . . . . For he whom God hath sent speaketh the words of God: for God giveth not the Spirit by measure unto him . . . . He that believeth on the Son hath everlasting life: and he that believeth not the Son shall not see life: but the wrath of God abideth on him (vv. 31-36).

If the closing portions of this narrative were spoken by John Baptist, then evidence is supplied that his spiritual education was still continuing. This type of testimony was something in advance of the sermons preached in the Jordan valley. There, the preacher stressed the need for repentance; here he emphasizes the need for personal faith in Christ. There he spoke of God; but now he testifies of the Father. At first he announced Christ as *the Lamb of God;* now, Jesus is called *the Son of God.* These features suggest that after so many years, the apostle John might have been interpreting John Baptist's message; that he might have been amplifying the preacher's utterance in order to give a better understanding, a clearer picture of what was in the Baptist's mind. Be that as it may, the theme of the passage is chronologically perfect. The chapter began with the question, "How can these things be? — How can a man be born again?" The chapter ends with the answer to that same question: "He that believeth on the Son hath everlasting life . . . ."

HOMILIES

Study No. 15

JOHN BAPTIST . . . . WHO ANSWERED QUESTIONS

In John 3 and Luke 7:16-28 we find the Baptist playing the same role. However, between the two situations exists a world of difference. In the first instance he stood beneath blue skies; he knew the warmth of the sunshine upon his cheek — and the joy of preaching God's word. In the second instance, he had been in a dungeon for 18 months; the thrill of the great meetings was but a memory. John's only contact with the outside world came when his disciples visited the cell to provide a distorted picture of what was happening outside the prison. John was a great man; when he realized he was unable to convince his followers, "he sent them to Jesus." We must not read an expression of doubt into his statement, "Art thou he that should come, or look we for another?" John was not a reed shaken by the wind, believing one day and doubting the next. John sent them to Christ not because he doubted, but because he believed Christ alone could solve their problem.

Ministers and teachers might appreciate the following outline:

The Saintly Man

For every hour that John preached to people, he had known days in the presence of God preparing for his ministry. Dr. Jowett used to say, "A minister's study should be an upper room and not a lounge!" Should any preacher see the faces of a congregation before seeing the face of God?

The Sure Message

When John came forth from obscurity, he knew what he had to say; he knew that for which he had to look. There was no element of uncertainty in him. He had received implicit instructions and these were the rules of his conduct to the end. He spoke of sin, of the Saviour, of salvation, and of everything appertaining thereto. He earned the commendation: "Among those which are born of women, there is not a greater prophet than John the Baptist . . ." (Luke 7:28).

The Superb Manner

In spite of the fiery denunciations of sin which echoed across the Jordan valley, John was a man apart. He never condemned in others what he encouraged in himself, and never tried to steal the limelight for himself. He refused to be jealous; his faith remained unwavering, unswerving; always, he pointed men to his Lord. The effectiveness of his ministry is never seen to better advantage than after his decease — ". . . his disciples came, and took up the body, and buried it, *and went and told Jesus*" (Matthew 14:12).

John had so often pointed them to Christ, he had so often sent them to Him that their problems might be solved, that even from his grave, he seemed to say, "Go to Jesus." "And he being dead, yet speaketh."

Unfortunately our world seems to be suffering an acute shortage of men like John Baptist.

The Fourth Chapter of John

THEME: *Christ Begins to Reach the Samaritans*

OUTLINE:

    I. Jesus hurriedly leaves Judea. Verses 1-3.
    II. Jesus meets a Samaritan woman. Verses 4-30.
    III. Jesus instructs His followers. Verses 31-38.
    IV. Jesus accepts an invitation. Verses 39-42.
    V. Jesus heals the nobleman's son. Verses 43-54.

SECTION ONE

Expository Notes on Christ's Unexpected Departure From Judea

When therefore the Lord knew how the Pharisees had heard that Jesus made and baptized more disciples than John, (though Jesus himself baptized not, but his disciples,) he left Judea, and departed again into Galilee (vv. 1-3).

It has never been customary to abandon anything unusually successful, and the sudden decision to terminate Christ's enthusiastic revival meetings surely surprised His followers. There would have been reason to leave if the meetings were poorly attended, or if fierce opposition threatened their safety, but to depart when everything was going well, appeared inexcusable.

This section, although extremely brief, is potent with meaning. It may be studied under three simple headings. *When* did He decide to leave? *What* had He heard? *Why* did He leave?

(1.) *When did He decide to leave?* The disciples were jubilant! They had only begun their meetings but already great crowds were attending every service. Enthusiasm was increasing constantly and even the disciples of John were aware of the continuing success in the great crusade. They reported to their master, "Rabbi, he that was with thee beyond Jordan, to whom thou barest witness, behold, the same baptizeth, *and all men come to him*" (John 3:26). There was indeed cause for great satisfaction, and it only seemed a matter of time before the entire nation would be swayed by the power of God. The kingdom was indeed at hand! Then suddenly, the Lord seemed to be worried. Momentarily the shadows came to His eyes;

He was burdened. Somehow, the eagerness to preach diminished, and the watching disciples wondered what was taking place. Then, with a sigh, the Lord announced the time had come to depart. The effort would be transferred to another locality. Peter and John and the others were dumbfounded! The most wonderful chance they had ever had in their evangelistic career was being thrown away. We do not know whether or not they endeavored to persuade the Lord to change His decision. If they tried, they failed. The Lord had made up His mind to leave, and the decision was irrevocable.

(2.) *What had He heard?* This answer is easily supplied; there is no need to speculate. He knew the Pharisees had heard He was making more disciples than John. We are not told *how* He knew. Perhaps He had overheard certain conversations; perhaps some unknown person told Him. There exists the possibility that He did not need to be told. The previous studies supplied evidence of His omnipresence; He who could be in heaven and on earth at the same time would have no difficulty in being present — in spirit — at both His own meetings and in the council chambers of His enemies. The apostle John says, "the Lord knew," and with that simple statement, we must be content. The Master considered all the implications of the situation. His eyes, as the eyes of a seer, read the future and recognized the storm clouds on the horizon. Soon the Pharisees might twist the information, and using it to further their evil purposes, would begin to tell people that John and Jesus were in opposition to each other. Spite and jealousy would beget gossip, and once the rumors began to circulate, it would be increasingly hard to refute the allegation.

(3.) *Why did He leave?* He left in order to safeguard His ministry; He left that Satan's insinuations would be stifled at birth. Had He lingered another day; the damage might have been done. John could have all the crowds; His wonderful friend, the Baptist, could enjoy the blessings upon the gatherings. Jesus would start in another place. His timely action, unexpected as it was, revealed a wisdom that is not of this world. He left the district that the blessing might remain. He was a wonderful Saviour.

HOMILIES

Study No. 16

THE ELOQUENT SILENCES OF JESUS

"Never man spake like this man" was one of the most striking things ever uttered concerning Christ; and the helplessness of the officers who were sent to arrest the Lord Jesus ably endorsed their verdict. Words of profound wisdom fell from the Teacher's lips, and it was said that He spoke "as one having authority and not as the scribes." Eloquence and wisdom; simplicity and profundity; clarity of thought, directness of approach, tenderness and fearlessness all combined to place Him in a class of His own. Yet in strange contrast was the astonishing fact that sometimes His silence was more effective than His sermons. Often when circumstances demanded an oration, He calmly considered the matter and then refrained from speaking.

He was silent when we would expect Him to answer prayer (Matthew 15:23).

"And behold, a woman of Canaan came out of the same coasts, and cried unto him, saying, Have mercy on me, O Lord, thou son of David; my daughter is grievously vexed with a devil. *But he answered her not a word.*" This action was apparently inexplicable, but it brought the very best out of the woman's soul. Her faith was tried, and ultimately she went away a better woman. If the Lord immediately and unconditionally answered every prayer, more harm than good would result. Sometimes He accomplishes most by refusing to grant our desires. (See *Bible Cameos*, page 91).

He was silent when we would expect Him to defend a woman (John 8:6).

When the enemies of Christ brought to Him the woman taken in adultery, they said, "Master, this woman was taken in adultery, in the very act. Now Moses in the law commanded us, that such should be stoned: but what sayest thou? This they said, tempting him, that they might have to accuse him. But Jesus stooped down and with his finger wrote on the ground, as though he heard them not . . . ." And we know now that His silence delivered Him from a foul plot. (See homily at chapter 8, Section One.) Words spoken in haste are often repented at leisure, and frequently it is the still tongue that makes a wise head. The Master's silence enabled Him to consider the grave issues at stake; and when at length He answered His critics, His words exhibited great wisdom. His was the most eloquent silence ever known.

He was silent when we would expect Him to continue preaching (John 4:1-3).

"When therefore the Lord knew how the Pharisees had heard that Jesus made and baptized more disciples than John . . . he left Judea and departed again into Galilee." This was one of the most suggestive of all His actions. When the blessing of God was falling in increasing measure, and people were responding to the call of the Gospel, when revival knocked at the door, He quietly withdrew from the scene, and allowed John Baptist to continue the great work. He knew that the enemies were beginning to compare the two camps, and soon their evil tongues would be saying rivalry existed between Christ and His forerunner. Before they had a chance to begin, the Lord graciously went to another district.

He was silent when we would expect Him to defend Himself (Matthew 27:12-14).

"And when he was accused of the chief priests and elders, he answered nothing. Then said Pilate unto him, Hearest thou not how many things they witness against thee? And he answered him to never a word; insomuch that the governor marvelled greatly." (1) Christ was careful not to make others sin. (2) He was patient in bearing reproach. (3) He was willing to endure all things — even a cross — if by so doing He could honor God and help His fellow men. What would we have done in similar circumstances? Pilate marveled — and probably all heaven marveled with him.

He was silent when facing a guilty soul (Luke 23:8, 9).

"And when Herod saw Jesus, he was exceedingly glad: for he was desirous to see him of a long season, because he had heard many things of him, and he hoped to have seen some miracle done by him. Then he questioned him in many words; but he answered him nothing." And thereby hangs a tale — a tale of tragedy and sin. God once declared: "My spirit shall not always strive with man," and Herod provided the infamous example of this fact. He had murdered John Baptist, and thereby sealed his destiny. Even the great Lover of souls had no word of rebuke, of love, or even of advice. He let him die. "He answered him nothing," and that silence preached a sermon which still echoes around the world.

(Reprinted from *Bible Treasures*, page 79.)

SECTION TWO

Expository Notes on Christ's Meeting With the Samaritan Woman

And he must needs go through Samaria (v. 4).

It is not good exegesis to read into a text that which the author never intended to suggest. Therefore cognizance must be made of the fact that there were two highways from Judea to the northern territory of Galilee. One, the shorter of the two routes, went through Samaria; the other crossed the Jordan, skirted the region of the Samaritans, and entered Galilee far to the north. The devout, embittered Jews avoided, whenever possible, contact with the despised

Samaritans and preferred to take the longer route than to journey among people they detested. The *"must"* of this text was not a necessity imposed by geographical restrictions. Had the Lord desired, He could have gone to Galilee by the longer route. Compulsion was begotten by the knowledge that at Sychar's well a sinful woman needed salvation.

Then cometh he to a city of Samaria, which is called Sychar, ear to the parcel of ground that Jacob gave to his son Joseph (v. 5).

An adequate appreciation of this passage is not possible until one gains a clear picture of the historical background of the unpopular Samaritans. The roots of prejudice went deep into history, and the wounds resulting therefrom apparently defied healing. When the land of Canaan was divided among the tribes of Israel, Samaria was given to the tribe of Ephraim and the half tribe of Manasseh. Unfortunately, when insurrection split the nation, these people generally ceased to worship at Jerusalem. Idolatry reared its head, and sin took root in the territory (I Kings 12:25-33.) Later, when the people of the land were carried away captive, the king of Assyria arranged that some of his own people should colonize the land, and thereafter a strange mixture of people were found tilling the soil in Samaria. Of them it has been written, "They feared the Lord, and served their own gods . . ." (II Kings 17:33). When the Judean captives returned to their homeland from Babylon, the Samaritans offered to befriend them, to become partners in an alliance, but when this was refused, they became the most bitter enemies of the returning people. The fourth chapter of Ezra has much to say in regard to this situation.

By direct permission of Alexander the Great, a temple was built on Mount Gerizim, and here, in opposition to the hierachy in Jerusalem, Manasseh and his posterity officiated as high priests. Thus the cleavage between the two people became increasingly acute, and at the time of Christ's sojourn on earth, their bitterness beggared description. Sychar was one of the Samaritan cities and was close to a piece of ground rich in legend and history.

Now Jacob's well was there; Jesus therefore, being wearied with his journey, sat thus on the well: and it was about the sixth hour (v. 6).

At midday, six hours after sunrise, and with very little if any shade, the heat of the sun would have been intense. It was customary for travelers to rest during this period, but a compelling urgency had driven Christ toward His destination. Without food and water, dusty, perspiring, tired, the Lord arrived at the well where He sat to await the coming of the woman. It might be asked how

He knew she would be coming at all? Everyone knew that women of ill fame were obliged to draw water at a well when other, more respected citizens were absent. Yet the possibility existed that she might have had sufficient water at home to last another day, or at least to last a little longer. Obviously *the Lord knew she would be coming.* He also knew the time of her arrival, indeed, He knew everything about her. Jesus was no mere carpenter; His hands had fashioned the planets. The Logos, the Son of God who had helped to make both man and woman, had no difficulty in reading from a distance her every thought. Yet He who had placed the stones in the mountains was glad to rest upon those stones. He who gave birth to the seas, and springs, and rushing torrents knew what it meant to be thirsty. His lips, from which would flow the living water to turn the wilderness into a garden, became parched and dry; He was thirsty. The Master who was timeless, eternal, the I AM, to whom a thousand years were as a day, was so human that He became weary. He needed to sit down, and seeing the well, He paused to rest.

> **There cometh a woman of Samaria to draw water: Jesus saith unto her, Give me to drink. (For his disciples were gone away unto the city to buy meat) (vv. 7, 8).**

Two very simple but potent questions open realms of suggestive thought. Why did not Christ draw water for Himself? Why did the disciples hurry to the city before they quenched their Master's thirst? Undoubtedly, they were hungry, but to wait a few moments longer would hardly have imposed a sacrifice. At midday, the shopkeepers would probably be resting, and therefore the question becomes even more important. They had been on the hot dusty roads for hours; the Master needed water. Alas, the disciples possibly thought of reaching the shade of some tree, some shop, some home. As was always the case, in the hour of the Master's need, they thought only of self. Elsewhere it is said that a cup of cold water given in Christ's name shall not lose its reward. A cup of cold water given to Christ on that memorable day might have found an abiding place on the pages of God's Holy Word.

> **Then saith the woman of Samaria unto him, How is it, that thou being a Jew, asketh drink of me, which am a woman of Samaria? For the Jews have no dealings with the Samaritans (v. 9).**

She was surprised. Either by His garments or by His accent, she recognized Him as a Jew. Possibly she thought Him to be an itinerant Rabbi, and if that were the case, her amazement would have been great, for such men were never permitted to speak to a woman on the street. Why then had He asked her to do what He could have done? Of course, the Lord could have drawn water, but He preferred to wait until His need provided the opportunity to reach a guilty soul. It was written on His heart that eventually a greater sacrifice would be made in order to provide living water for thirsty souls.

> Jesus answered and said unto her, If thou knewest the gift of God, and who it is that saith to thee, Give me to drink, thou wouldest have asked of him, and he would have given thee living water (v. 10).

What a tragedy that the Creator should be in the midst of the people He created and His identity remain unknown. The Baptist said, ". . . there standeth one among you whom ye know not" (John 1:26). The Lord said, ". . . If thou knewest . . . ." Later, as we shall see in chapter 5, the unknown Christ stood at the pool, and for the most part remained unidentified. What blindness! He could be within one yard, yet be missed by a mile! Here is progression of thought.

(1) *Faith begets knowledge.* God is near. He cares enough to help.

(2) *Knowledge begets prayer.* It is possible to ask for living water!

(3) *Prayer begets experience.* He can place a well in a human heart!

The woman had no conception of the greatness of the Stranger; alas, she was not only in the dark, she was also in her sin. To rescue her the Lord made the journey, and the study of the remaining verses reveals an inspired pattern in Christian psychology.

> The woman saith unto him, Sir, thou hast nothing to draw with, and the well is deep: from whence then has thou that living water? Art thou greater than our father Jacob which gave us the well, and drank thereof himself, and his children, and his cattle? (vv. 11, 12).

How amazed she would have been to know that He had actually watched Jacob digging that well! He was greater than the Queen of Sheba, and infinitely greater than Solomon (Matthew 12:42). The woman claimed Jacob as her father because the Samaritans claimed descent from Ephraim and Manasseh (the *Antiquities* of Josephus, ix. 14:3).

> Jesus answered and said unto her, Whosoever drinketh of this water shall thirst again; But whosoever drinketh of the water that I shall give him shall never thirst; but the water that I shall give him shall be in him a well of water springing up into everlasting life (vv. 13, 14).

Godet, in summarizing the varying interpretations of the text, says: "*Living water,* in the literal sense, denoted spring-water, in contrast with water of a cistern, or stagnant water. Genesis 26:19 reads: 'Israel's servants dug in the valley, and found there a well of living water,' that is, a subterranean spring of which they made a well (compare Leviticus 14:5). In the figurative sense, living water is therefore a blessing which has the property of incessantly reproducing itself, like a gushing spring, like life itself, and which consequently is never exhausted. What does Jesus mean by this? According to Justin and Cyprian, baptism; according to Lucke, faith; according to Olshausen, Jesus Himself; according to Calvin, Luthardt, and Keil, the Holy Spirit; according to Grotius, the evangelical doctrine; according to Meyer, truth; according to Westcott, eternal life, consisting in the knowledge of God and His Son, Jesus Christ . . . . It seems to me, that according to Jesus Himself (verses 13, 14) it is, as Westcott thinks, eternal life, salvation, the full satisfaction of all the wants of the heart and the possession of all the holy energies of which the soul is susceptible." (*Godet's Commentary on John*, page 423).

One cannot but contrast the wine of Cana's wedding with the *living* water of this text. That which Christ supplies is infinitely superior to the best of earth's vintages. To drink of worldly refreshment reminds us of ever recurring need — we thirst again. Thus the constant search for satisfaction robs the soul of rest. The quest for inward delight continues unabated day and night through the years until death terminates the endeavor. Yet Christ promised complete satisfaction. The living water would be a springing well; new supplies would automatically arise from the unfathomable depths of God's sufficiency. The living water would be *a gift;* it could neither be purchased nor merited. It would be a *well;* thus the supplies would hardly be meager. It would be *springing* water; therefore it would never run dry. The gift of God would be completely inexhaustible, refreshing, life-giving for ever. It is not too difficult to appreciate the increasing interest of the Samaritan woman as she listened to this absorbing message.

> The woman saith unto him, Sir, give me this water, that I thirst not, neither come hither to draw. Jesus saith unto her, Go call thy husband, and come hither. The woman answered and said, I have no husband. Jesus said unto her, Thou hast well said, I have no husband: For thou hast had five husbands; and he whom thou now hast is not thy husband: in that saidst thou truly. The woman saith unto him, Sir, I perceive that thou art a prophet (vv. 15-19).

When the woman asked for this living water, it became obvious that she thought only of relief from menial tasks. If the benevolent acts of the Stranger could grant assistance, she greatly desired His help. The Lord knew her greatest need was the ability *to see* — to see with the eyes of understanding. His command, "Go call thy husband," was the initial step in revealing her spiritual need. It should be noticed that He did not accuse her of being an outrageous sinner. He knew all the time that she lived in illegitimate intimacy with one whom she had never married, but He made no charge to this effect. And in fairness to this unfortunate woman, we should consider it would have been easy to avoid the confession, "I have no husband." Her statement indicates light was beginning to penetrate where decency had not completely died. Suddenly her sins were revealed, but her amazement counteracted her sense of guilt. The Stranger's eyes had read with ease her closely guarded secret; He knew, but *how* did He know? Suddenly she ceased thinking about possibilities of acquiring supplies of living water; now she was interested in Jesus. However attractive *His gift*, He was more attractive. "Sir," she exclaimed, "I perceive that thou art a prophet." A subsequent homily reminds readers of the progression of her spiritual insight. At first she saw Him as *a Jew*, and asked, "How is it that thou being a Jew asketh drink of me . . . ?" Then with profound respect she said, "*Sir,* give me this water . . . ." Now she recognized the characteristics of *a prophet*, and asked a pertinent question.

> Our fathers worshipped in this mountain; and ye say, that in Jerusalem is the place where men ought to worship. ⟨Jesus said unto her, Woman, believe me, the hour cometh, when ye shall neither in this mountain, nor yet at Jerusalem worship the Father. Ye worship ye know not what: We know what we worship: for salvation is of the Jews. But the hour cometh and now is, when the true worshippers shall worship the Father in spirit and in truth: for the Father seeketh such to worship him. God is a Spirit: and they that worship him must worship him in spirit and in truth (vv. 20-24).

Since Jacob's well was situated at the foot of Mount Gerizim, where the Samaritan temple had once stood (it was destroyed over a hundred years before Christ), the woman undoubtedly pointed and said, "Our fathers worshipped in this mountain." Many expositors read into her words strange motives, but there is reason to believe that having recognized a true prophet, her questions were completely sincere. This prophet was not a religious bigot; He had even asked for a drink of water; He was different! Toward this end the Saviour had been working; why should there be any ulterior motives or questionable thoughts in the woman's mind? Had she called Him a Prophet? then a prophet he would be: Verse 21 pointed onward; verse 22 gently reminded her that the Samaritans were wrong. Verse 23 cuts across the bounds of prejudice and race; He did not speak primarily of good or bad Jews; good or bad Samaritans; He spoke of *true worshippers*, and said, "The Father seeketh such to worship Him."

In this wonderful chapter we begin to detect the outreach of the truth expressed in John 3:16. "For God so loved the world . . . ." Thus was born a fellowship — a fellowship of true believers which could never be confined within the walls of any temple, be it Samaritan or Jewish, or Gentile. The woman called Christ "a prophet"; she was correct. At this time, she had probably forgotten about the living water discussed earlier in the conversation. Now she thought only of Jesus. Gently He revealed her sin. Her morality left much to be desired, but she was not beyond redemption. This prophet was different; His religion had none of the bigotry so evident in others of His rank; He spoke of true believers. God was a Spirit; that is, God was not limited by corporeal form. He could be anywhere; He could be there, then. Sincerity superceded ceremonial; a clean heart was more to be desired than ecclesiastical commendations. Yes, this Prophet was indeed wonderful. Perhaps He even knew when the Messiah would come.

The woman saith unto him, I know that Messias cometh, which is called Christ; when he is come, he will tell us all things (v. 25).

There is something refreshingly wonderful about her testimony, *I know.* She had previously veiled her own feelings and desires in her comments concerning others — *"Our father Jacob . . . our fathers worshipped in this mountain";* thoughts of five husbands and of one not her husband had tended to crowd out that for which Christ patiently waited. Suddenly, as a star shining through the clouds, her testimony came, *"I know that Messias cometh."* She knew also that the word of the Messiah would be authentic.

Jesus saith unto her, I that speak unto thee am he (v. 26).

This was the seventh and final time that He answered the woman, and since seven is the number of completion in Scripture, this represents the final or complete revelation of God to a sinner. His words brought her thirsting soul from the barren wastes of sin's desert to the fountain of sparkling, living water; His wonderful message illuminated her mind until the One, thought to be an itinerant Jew, stood forth as the Messiah, the Son of God. Patience, deep insight into character, unfailing love, and a sound knowledge of Scripture were united in the rescue of her soul. To revert to the language of the synoptic record, He had caught a fish! It is thrilling to remember that this Christ, in calling disciples, promised to make them "fishers of men." Here we have a pattern for all who seek souls. Acquainted as He certainly was with the Law and the Prophets, He was aware of Isaiah's prediction (Isaiah 9:6). Christ's Messianic claim negatives all the teachings which deny His deity. (See the expository notes on chapter 1.)

And upon this came his disciples, and marvelled that he talked with the woman: yet no man said, What seekest thou? or, Why talkest thou with her? (v. 27).

The disciples were surprised when they saw their Master speaking with a woman of ill fame. There existed a rabbinical prejudice which affirmed that a woman was incapable of receiving advanced religious instruction. The writings of the fathers said, "Do not prolong conversation with a woman; let no one converse with a woman in the street, not even with his own wife. Let a man burn the words of the law, rather than teach them to a woman." At that time, the disciples had much to learn.

The woman then left her waterpot, and went her way into the city, and saith to the men, Come see a man, which told me all things that ever I did: is not this the Christ? Then they went out of the city, and came unto him (vv. 28-30).

It will be seen that in the Lord's statement, "I that speak unto thee am *he*," the final word has been printed in italics. This was placed there by the translators to indicate that there was no corresponding word in the Greek Testament. Actually, it was included to make the reading intelligible. Perhaps this was a mistake. The Greek words are very forceful. *Ego eimi* literally means *I am*. Used elsewhere, these words were followed by an amazing manifestation of divine power. (See expository notes on John 18:6.) "I AM" was God's name (Exodus 3:14). Actually, the Lord Jesus said something like the following. "It is I am who speaks with thee." He not only claimed to be the Messiah; He also claimed to be all that Isaiah had predicted of the Messiah — "His name shall be called Wonderful, Counsellor, *The Mighty God, the everlasting Father*, the Prince of Peace." Possibly she had often approached those citizens. Her earlier solicitations were vastly different from the thrilling story which now poured from her lips. The Living Water was already overflowing her soul. Her love for Christ demanded that she try to reach others. In this respect she resembles the disciples who, having met Christ, went out to find their brothers. The citizens, aware of the woman's shortcomings, marveled at her transformation. Her compelling sincerity begat increasing interest, and soon they were hurrying across the fields of Sychar.

HOMILIES

Study No. 17

THE WOMAN WHO RAN AWAY WITH A WELL

It was midday, and an atmosphere of lazy indolence filled the countryside as an outcast woman drew near to Sychar's well to draw water. She was accustomed to come at this hour, for the absence of scornful citizens made the most appropriate time to obtain supplies from the well. As she drew near, she saw the Stranger and heard His request for water: "Then said the woman of Samaria unto him, How is it that thou being a Jew, asketh drink of me, which am a woman of Samaria? for the Jews have no dealings with the Samaritans . . . ." This is a very thrilling story; it suggests certain propositions which students should find challenging.

The Love of God knows no racial barriers

Between the woman and the Saviour were barriers of social, racial, and spiritual differences. These conversationalists were as unlike as it was possible to be; it was not a cause for amazement when she expressed surprise at His request. No other Jew would have acted as He did. Even the disciples had yet to learn that divisions were not permitted in the Kingdom of God. "There is neither Greek nor Jew, circumcision nor uncircumcision, Barbarian, Scythian, bond nor free: but Christ is all and in all" (Colossians 3:11). The love of God sweeps away all barriers dividing His children, for baptized into one family, we own God as our Father and each other as brethren. At least that is the ideal we preach, but it must be confessed with shame that often-times our actions are condemned by our theology. To proclaim this truth, and at the same time deny spiritual freedom and privilege to others whose skin is of a different color, savors of hypocrisy. When the Lord Jesus looked into the face of a sinner, He saw a potential child of the Highest; it was therefore in keeping with the ideals of His ministry that He should make special efforts to reach this outcast.

The Provision of God knows no human limitations

"The woman said unto him, Sir, thou hast nothing to draw with, and the well is deep: from whence then hast thou that living water? . . . . Jesus answered and said unto her, Whosoever shall drink of this water shall thirst again: But whosoever drinketh of the water that I shall give him shall never thirst . . . ." Without well, waterpots, or any other means of obtaining supplies, He calmly announced His ability to implant inexhaustible supplies within human souls. His wells could never run dry; A veritable river of the water of life, clear as crystal, could flow from the throne of God into her heart. Dumbfounded, interested, desirous, she said unto Him, "Sir, give me this water." Christ replied, "Go call thy husband and come hither."

The Vision of God knows no undiscovered secrets

When the woman declared that she had no husband, she opened the way by which the Saviour was able to send the first convicting arrow to her soul. Gradually her perception increased. She had asked for living water, but this could not be granted until she learned more of His identity. Salvation is the product of an intelligent apprehension of His person, a sincere acceptance of His message. With startling accuracy, Christ's words revealed that her secrets were known to Him; yet He did not utter words of condemnation. His attitude was in strange contrast to those of the self-righteous citizens whose dictates made her visit the well at midday. Slowly she was drawing near to the Light of the world and was able to see the stains on her soul. "She said, I know that Messias cometh, which is called Christ: when he is come, he will tell us all things."

The Power of God knows no insurmountable obstacles

"Jesus said unto her, I that speak unto thee am he." Eventually she grasped the meaning of His utterance, and abandoning her waterpots, rushed into the city to electrify the citizens with her thrilling testimony. A well of joy filled her soul as she exclaimed, "Come see a man who told me all things that ever I did. Is not this the Christ?" This woman, untutored, immature, became the first female evangelist of the New Testament. God used her to reach an entire city. Here, evidence is supplied that God is expert at taking the foolish things of this world to confound the wise. Possibly the most polished sermon would have left that city unmoved. A real experience of Christ's power to save, a desire to serve, an infilling of "living water," and with God to assist, even the weakest saint may laugh at impossibilities.

SECTION THREE

Expository Notes on Christ's Talk with His Disciples

The theme of this conversation is service in a harvest field, and since the instruction is sandwiched between the conversion of a sinful woman and the evangelizing of a complete city, these verses occupy a place of outstanding importance. From an unpretentious beginning with a very sinful woman, Christ continued until that same woman became His instrument in reaching a great multitude. There is much food for thought in these verses.

> **In the meanwhile, his disciples prayed him, saying, Master, eat. But he said unto them, I have meat to eat that ye know not of. Therefore said the disciples one to another, Hath any man brought him ought to eat? Jesus saith unto them, My meat is to do the will of him that sent me, and to finish his work. Say not ye, There are yet four months, and then cometh harvest? Behold, I say unto you. Lift up your eyes, and look on the fields: for they are white already unto harvest (vv. 31-35).**

Godet says, "Between Jacob's well, at the foot of Mount Gerizim, and the village of Aschar, at the foot of Ebal, far on into the plain of Mukhna, there stretch out vast fields of wheat. As the disciples beheld the springing verdure on the freshly sown soil, they no doubt said one to another: "We must wait four months until this wheat shall be ripe." The Saviour knew of their conversation and listened as they enquired if someone had brought food during their absence. They did not know that His experience in rescuing a sinner had refreshed both his body and soul. The Lord had proceeded with His individual evangelism, and the success attained justified the haste in which He had made His way to Sychar's well. The woman was the first sheaf of ripened grain, the forerunner of a great harvest. He looked at the wheat fields, and in gentle tones of rebuke indicated a harvest of souls already awaited the reapers. They marveled because He spoke with the woman; they saw the earthly protocol, and knew little of the all-embracing love of the Father. God was no respector of persons; to Him, Samaritan wheat was as beneficial as Judean wheat! Our churches would do well to study these statements. Many are willing to send millions of dollars to far distant places, but shrink from rescuing the unwanted Samaritans who reside a few streets away. Furthermore, there are Christians who would even pay the missionaries to labor in the downtown harvest field, but never go along to help. Some are too dignified to perspire; others, too busy to visit the fields; others, too tired to care; but those who work, and reap, and rejoice in God's wheat fields, find adequate compensation for all their efforts.

> And he that reapeth receiveth wages, and gathereth fruit unto life eternal: that both he that soweth, and he that reapeth may rejoice together. And herein is that saying true, One soweth, and another reapeth. I sent you to reap that whereon ye bestowed no labour: other men laboured, and ye are entered into their labours (vv. 36-38).

A three-fold division of this section might help the reader to a full appreciation of the implications contained therein.

(1) *The laborer's happiness.* God is not a skin-flint! He pays the most excellent wages to all who labor in His wheatfields. Fruit is gathered unto life eternal. Dividends are paid from the Everlasting Bank of Heaven. Earthly wealth might dwindle and disappear; eternal wealth is a prize known only by God's people.

(2) *The laborer's helpers.* One man may sow, another may reap, but always, God gives the increase. God's servant is not expected to become a hermit. Isolation is a word seldom used in heaven's language. To produce a harvest requires the work of many people, and to work harmoniously with them presents one of life's

greatest delights. It was for this purpose the Church was formed; it is within the assembly of saints that people are trained to help with the harvest. The isolationist may enjoy his own company, but his soul becomes lonely.

(3) *The laborer's humility.* When success seemingly crowns the effort, it is necessary to remember that workmen enter into the labors of other men. Other Christians, equally as sincere as the most gifted evangelist, worked long and hard to produce nothing — or so it seemed. But without their preparation even the most gifted preacher might be helpless. Ruth gleaned wheat in the fields, but she did not know until later that kind and loving hands had deliberately dropped the gleanings in her path. It is always wise to remember that, at best, "we are unprofitable servants."

HOMILIES

Study No. 18

REAPING GOLDEN SHEAVES

A Startling Challenge

"Lift up your eyes, and look on the fields; for they are white already unto harvest." As the disciples walked along the streets of Sychar, they passed homes in which the grain was waiting to be reaped. Alas, they had continued their journey! This might also be true of an office, a factory, a place of business, a school, a hospital, a classroom. The fields are white and waiting. Are we too blind to see the challenge? Peter and John were busy buying meat when they might have been talking of their Master.

A Sure Commission

"I sent you . . ." (verse 38). One man may sow a field, but much more help is required to reap the harvest. Christ made the harvest possible, but to reap the human sheaves, He requires the consecrated talents of all His people. He said, "Go ye into all the world, and preach the Gospel." Can a man be justified in making a fortune if his true place is in the harvest field? Can a woman be happy running for high office anywhere, if a village in Africa is waiting for her? Let it be emphasized that God has servants everywhere, but the Christian's task is to discover where the Lord wants *him*, and to get there fast!

A Steady Constraint

". . . other men laboured, and ye are entered into their labours." The Carpenter in Nazareth had many tools in His workshop. There were wooden tools and iron tools; expensive tools and inexpensive ones. Some tools were sharp and others were blunt, but they never quarrelled and never interfered with each other's ministry. Furthermore, the tools were quite useless until the Carpenter lifted them. They never chose their tasks and never complained if they were used on a small job. They existed for one purpose only – to do the Master's will. The plane entered into the work of the saw; the hammer supplemented the work of both, and because all were dependent upon each other, none could boast unless they all boasted together. And as it was, so it is.

A Sublime Contentment

"And he that reapeth receiveth wages . . . ." "And thou shalt be blessed . . . for thou shalt be recompensed at the resurrection of the just" (Luke 14:14). The Master said a cup of cold water given in His Name would gain a reward. If this be the standard by which true service is measured in the harvest fields of the world, then some of God's choicest workers will have an abundant entrance into the everlasting kingdom.

SECTION FOUR

Expository Notes on Christ's Two-day Stay in Samaria

As an introduction let us consider again the words of verses 28-30:

> The woman then left her waterpot, and went her way into the city, and saith to the men, Come, see a man, which told me all things that ever I did: is not this the Christ? Then they went out of the city, and came unto him."

Verse 39 continues the account:

> And many of the Samaritans of that city believed on him for the saying of the woman which testified, He told me all that ever I did. So when the Samaritans were come unto him, they besought him that he would tarry with them: and he abode there two days (vv. 39, 40).

These verses are an adjunct of the passage already considered; they represent the first outreach of Christ's message to a needy world. The instrument used was not a trained disciple but an enthusiastic convert. "We are shown that God is pleased to use feeble messengers to accomplish mighty ends. Frequently He employs weak instruments to make manifest His own mighty power. In this, as in everything else, the Lord's thoughts and ways are different from ours. He employed a shepherd lad to vanquish the mighty Goliath. He endowed a Hebrew slave with more wisdom than all the magicians of Babylon. He made the words of Naaman's servants to have greater effect upon their august master than did those of the renowned Elisha. In making selection for the mother of the Saviour, He chose not a princess but a peasant woman. In appointing the heralds of the Cross, fishermen were the ones called. And so a mighty work was started in Sychar by a converted harlot. 'How unsearchable are his judgments, and his ways past finding out!' . . ." (Arthur W. Pink).

The enthusiasm of the Samaritan people was the more remarkable as there is no evidence that Christ ever performed a miracle among them. They were stirred not by any manifestation of miraculous power, but by the quality of His message. In this connection a contrast in terms is noticeable in the Greek Testament. The people of the city said, "We believed because of his word (*ton logon autou*) and not because of thy saying (*seen lalian*)." That they used the richer words *logos* — the name used by John to describe Christ — suggests they had recognized the depth of His thought and the unmistakable authority with which He spoke. In contrast, the woman's message was but a story, a testimony, a piece of news. This is in keeping with the great principles of evangelism. A preacher's duty is to introduce hearers to Christ. John's statement holds true for all, "He must increase; I must decrease."

And many more believed because of his own word; and said unto the woman, Now we believe, not because of thy saying: for we have heard him ourselves, and know that this is indeed the Christ, the Saviour of the world (vv. 41, 42).

During two never-to-be-forgotten days, the Saviour stayed among His new friends, but we are not told what He did, nor what He said. Where He slept remains a secret of the ages, and what His disciples thought of this delay, we may never know. Obviously, He preached with power, and as a result, many people were drawn closer to God. Some of the early manuscripts do not have "the Christ" in the text. Certain of the Early Church Fathers said these words were added at a later date, for the term "the Christ" was Jewish, and Samaritans would not use anything which identified them with their enemies. To them, the term, "*the Saviour of the World*," would be far more significant; it included them.

There is hardly need for a homiletical section to deal with this very short passage. The following, however, is supplied as a stimulant to thought and a beginning for an evangelistic address.

They heard

"The woman saith to the men, Come see a man who told me all things that ever I did: is not this the Christ?"

They came

"Then they went out of the city and came unto him."

They saw

"They came unto HIM."

They prayed

"They besought him that he would tarry with them."

They believed

"And many more believed because of his own word."

They testified

". . . we have heard him ourselves, and know that this is indeed the Saviour of the World."

SECTION FIVE

Expository Notes on the Healing of the Nobleman's Son

Now after two days, he departed thence, and went into Galilee. For Jesus himself testified that a prophet hath no honour in his own country (vv. 43, 44).

There are numerous expositors who see in this two day stay among the Samaritans a prophetic picture of this age when Christ works specifically among the Gentiles. They affirm that the absence of miracles lends credence to the statement that in this age of grace God's greatest weapon is the Gospel of His grace. When this two-day interval terminates, when two thousand years have expired (for a day is as a thousand years, and a thousand years as a day) Christ will begin a new phase in His ministry and return to the people who in former days rejected Him. See Luke 4:16-30. Whether or not this prophetic message was meant to be in the text, each reader will doubtless decide for himself; this book is not an exposition of prophecy but one of John's gospel. It is hard to avoid the feeling that even John would be surprised if he knew of some things supposedly "discovered" in his gospel!

The Lord returned to His own country knowing that the prospects of a successful campaign were dim. Nevertheless He went. A preacher who avoids the hard tasks can hardly be trusted with the easy ones.

Then when he was come into Galilee, the Galileans received him, having seen all the things which he did at Jerusalem at the feast: for they also went to the feast (v. 45).

It is somewhat difficult to reconcile this verse with its predecessor. One would expect Christ to be snubbed; for if a prophet is without honor in his own country, he could hardly expect a welcome such as was afforded in Galilee at this time. Reference should be made to John 2:23-25, and a comparison made between these verses. The presence of an excited, enthusiastic crowd was not a guarantee that they respected the Saviour. These people had seen certain miracles performed at Jerusalem, and they hoped to be present at

a repeat performance! To them, this was another *Spectacular;* there
was no charge for admittance! There is no suggestion that they
desired to hear His words. They never sat at His feet to worship.
They wished to see miracles, and we can appreciate the Lord's
sadness when He exclaimed, "Except ye see signs and wonders, ye
will not believe."

> So Jesus came again into Cana of Galilee, where he made the
> water wine. And there was a certain nobleman, whose son was
> sick at Capernaum (v. 46).

These verses and those to follow constitute one of the most outstanding parts of John's gospel; here may be found truth of superlative quality. Certain features must be carefully remembered as we
approach this story, for without them it is impossible to grasp the
hidden beauties of this account.

The term *basilikes* here translated "nobleman" implies more than
a man in high standing. *Basileus* means "king," and the word used in
this passage means one probably connected with the royal household, one attached to the king, one enjoying high eminence. The
suggestion has been made that this man might have been Chuza,
Herod's prime minister (Luke 8:3), or even Manaen, Herod's foster-
brother (Acts 13:1).

The town of Cana was situated to the southwest of the sea of
Galilee and not far away from the city of Nazareth. Capernaum
stood on the shores of the Sea of Galilee to the north and was about
17-20 miles away. Consequently it did not take long for the news
to travel from one place to the other.

Tragedy had visited the house of the nobleman in that his child
was seriously ill and near to death. It may be safely assumed that
the best medical attention had already been given — in vain. Death
is no respector of persons; even the wealthy die! The desperate father
anxiously watched the stricken lad, and then came the news from
Cana.

> When he heard that Jesus was come out of Judea into Galilee, he
> went unto him, and besought him that he would come down, and
> heal his son: for he was at the point of death (v. 47).

We are not told *how* he heard; the news might have been brought
by a friend or by a servant. The whole countryside had heard of the
miracle performed earlier at the wedding, and as a result the name
of Jesus was known in every home. Furthermore, verse 45 suggests
that other miracles had thrilled the crowds. Jesus was known everywhere as a great Healer, and His arrival in Cana seemed extremely
opportune. Already criticism of the Lord and His works was being
heard throughout the nation, and the prospect of going on a fool's
errand was not inviting. Yet the father had little choice. It might

cost much if he went to see Jesus; it would cost more if he did not go. If he stayed at home, he would be able to attend his boy's funeral! Desperation took him to Cana in Galilee. The people listening to Christ would recognize instantly that he was a man of eminence and would respectfully make way for his approach to Jesus. They listened and waited for the outcome.

Then said Jesus unto him, Except ye see signs and wonders, ye will not believe. The nobleman saith unto him, Sir, come down ere my child die (vv. 48, 49).

In view of what follows in verse 50, it is hard to believe the Lord's rebuke was directed primarily at the man himself. It is easier to believe, especially after reading verse 45, that the Lord looked at the waiting, watching crowds as He uttered these words. The desperation of the distracted father brushed aside the rebuke, and repeated again the plea of his broken heart.

Jesus saith unto him, Go thy way; thy son liveth. And the man believed the word that Jesus had spoken unto him, and he went his way (v. 50).

This verse is of great worth. The Lord Jesus uttered a promise, which the man accepted without reservation. Let it be noted, however, that *he did not go home immediately.* The statement *"he went his way"* has been misconstrued until it has been taken for granted that the man started for home. This was definitely not so. Either he remained in the service listening to the most wonderful Preacher he had ever heard, or he found a place in which to sleep. And if any man questioned his action, the nobleman replied, "There is no need to go home; my son is fine. I do not need to see him; Jesus promised my child would be well, and that is sufficient for me." There is reason to believe that having watched his boy, day and night for a considerable time, the father now placed his head on a pillow and slept peacefully. The word of healing had been spoken by Christ at the seventh hour, approximately one hour after midday.

At that precise moment, in Capernaum twenty miles away, the members of the nobleman's family were surely gathered around the bedside of the sick child. The lad's restoration proved the father's mission had been accomplished. Their excitement was unsurpassed as they awaited the return of the nobleman. He had approximately twenty miles to travel and could have been home easily in four or five hours. Students are invited to consider this statement. A man of such exalted rank would hardly walk the distance between the two cities. Horses would be available, and it would not be too difficult to hire others for the return journey, if such were needed. Had the man walked home, he could have completed the journey in the time specified, but had he ridden, he would have finished the journey in less time. Whichever interpretation is accepted, the fact remains that he could have been home before six o'clock in the evening. It has been suggested that since a Jewish day ended at sunset, any time after that would have been "the next day." This presents problems, for verse 51 reveals that the servants met their master on the highway. In order to do this prior to six o'clock, they would have needed to start for Capernaum almost as soon as the son was healed. That does not make good sense and can hardly be accepted as sound exegesis. It is far more likely that they waited exuberantly for the return of their master, and when he did not arrive, became anxious. At dawn the next day, their fears increased and they went in search of the nobleman, only to find that, unharmed, he was returning to his home.

> And as he was now going down, his servants met him, and told him saying, Thy son liveth. Then enquired he of them the hour when he began to amend. And they said unto him, YESTERDAY at the seventh hour the fever left him (vv. 51, 52).

This is a picture of *true faith*. Denied, for a while at least, any visible evidence that the miracle had been performed, this man believed the word that Jesus had spoken. "Now faith is the substance of things hoped for, the evidence of things not seen" (Hebrews 11:1).

> So the father knew that it was at the same hour, in the which Jesus said unto him, Thy son liveth: and himself believed, and his whole house. This is again the second miracle that Jesus did, when he was come out of Judea into Galilee (vv. 53, 54).

Possibly the servants inquired of their master the reason for the delay in his homecoming; they had expected him "yesterday." And perhaps the nobleman countered by asking, "Did you ever meet Jesus? He's wonderful. He could not lie. When He told me the boy was healed, I knew all was well." The saving power of Christ spread in ever widening circles and ultimately all within the nobleman's household responded to the charm of the Saviour. "The nobleman believed and his whole house." John might have added that this was not only the second miracle which Jesus did when He was come into Galilee; it was much more. Formerly the Lord changed water; here, He changed lives.

HOMILIES

Study No. 19

THE MAN WHO BELIEVED!

If faith can remove mountains, the question might well be asked, "What is faith?" There is a kind of faith which is hardly faith! The story has often been told of Blondin, the famous tight-rope artist, who once gave a masterly exhibition of his art at the Niagara Falls. As a climax to a brilliant performance, he placed the balancing rod in his mouth in order that he might use his hands to push a specially made wheelbarrow across the rope. A small lad watched breathlessly, and as the great man arrived close to where the boy stood, Blondin saw the youngster cheering. Pausing for a few moments, he said, "Sonny, do you think I could push the wheelbarrow back again?"

"Yes, Sir!"

"And my boy, if you sat in it, do you think I could take you to the other side?"

"Yes, Sir."

"Good! Jump in and I will take you."

"No, Sir!"

The lad possessed faith, but unfortunately he had no trust. Faith without trust is not faith. The nobleman, in contrast, had faith *and* trust, and all that was needed to gain the commendation of the Saviour.

He Needed Christ

His home was a place of tragedy; a boy was dying. Helpless, frustrated, sad, the anxious parent wondered what might be done to avert a tragedy, and then he heard of Jesus. Pride and prejudice were overcome; the urgency of need demanded action. Innumerable people seldom think of Christ until tragedy knocks on the door. Someone has said, "Adversity is the Good Shepherd's *black dog.*" In a general sense it is true of all. As Ephraim of old, who "waxed fat and kicked," we prosper and forget the One whose blessing made prosperity possible. God has to hit hard before we begin to think properly. Sin has placed its hands upon every heart, and since the outcome leads to death, the choice of coming to Christ or not is something none can avoid.

He Sought Christ

Somewhere in distant Cana, the Saviour waited, and eventually the nobleman walked into His presence. Possibly the people were amazed to see this, but throwing caution to the winds, the harassed man begged for assistance. He did not waste time talking with disciples; neither did he ask unnecessary questions. He came straight to the point. His son was in great danger, Christ alone could heal — would He please do so? This man from a bygone age could well become our teacher. Of another further back in time, the Bible says, "In his disease, he sought not to the Lord but to the physicians."

Unfortunately, this man, King Asa, paid for his stupidity with his life (II Chronicles 16:12, 13).

He Believed Christ

The expository notes explained the faith with which the man received the words of the Saviour. Doubts failed to gain a lodging place in his mind. The Teacher had spoken; the miracle had happened. Resting upon this unshakable foundation, the father was content. He knew even before he saw! Later, when Christ was dying, ". . . the chief priests, mocking him, with the scribes and elders, said, He saved others; himself he cannot save. If he be the king of Israel, *let him now come down from the cross,* AND WE WILL BELIEVE HIM" (Matthew 27:41, 42). These men asked for signs as a necessary aid to faith. Another Scripture explains how the Lord reversed that order. "Jesus saith unto Martha, Said I not unto thee, that, *if thou wouldest believe,* THOU SHOULDEST SEE the glory of God?" (John 11:40). The nobleman believed long before he saw the visible evidence of the power of Christ to heal.

He Confessed Christ

A thrilling testimony came from the nobleman's lips. He believed *and his whole house.* We do well to consider the similarity which unites all the initial stories of John's gospel. John Baptist loved Christ and told others. Andrew heard Christ and went in search of his brother Simon. Philip heard the Lord Jesus and afterward could not rest until he had found Nathaniel. Mary, at the wedding, had faith in her son and encouraged the nonplussed servants to do as He commanded. The Samaritan woman talked with the Stranger at the well, and then ran to confess her faith in the nearby city. The one exception to this golden rule was Nicodemus, and yet at a later date, as we shall see, his belated confession revealed that he also had faith in the Saviour of the world. An unashamed confession of the Lord Jesus Christ guarantees that (1) we please God; (2) we grow in grace; (3) we reach others; (4) the kingdom is thereby extended. This is the royal highway to blessing. The ancients walked it constantly; alas, we seem to have lost our way in the dark!

The Fifth Chapter of John

THEME: *Christ . . . Who was equal with God*

OUTLINE:
    I. Christ and His Unequaled Power . . .
        the healing of the impotent man. Verses 1-15.
    II. Christ and His Unprecedented Claims . . .
        making Himself equal with God. Verses 16-30.
    III. Christ and His Unshakeable Evidence . . .
         "for as the Father . . . even so the Son." Verses 31-47.

SECTION ONE

Expository Notes on the Healing of the Impotent Man

After this there was a feast of the Jews; and Jesus went up to Jerusalem (v. 1).

Much has been written in attempts to identify this particular feast, for theologians in many countries propagated their own views and interpretations. Some believe this to be the feast of Pentecost which came fifty days after the Passover (John 2:13); others state it was the Feast of Purim, and still others think it was the Feast of the Tabernacles. From the strictly exegetical and homiletical points of view, I can see no real value in debating at length something of which no person can be absolutely sure. For all practical purposes, it is sufficient to know that a feast was being held in Jerusalem, and in common with every other sincere worshiper, the Lord desired to be present. Furthermore, the presence of a crowd in the city provided an opportunity to preach His message, and if for no other reason, this would have encouraged His going to Jerusalem at this time.

Now there is at Jerusalem by the sheep market a pool, which is called in the Hebrew tongue Bethesda, having five porches (v. 2).

Reference is made to *the sheep gate* in Nehemiah 3:1. "Then Eliashib the high priest rose up with his brethren the priests, and they builded the sheep gate . . . ." In the restoration of the city walls, the temple property, and the religious ceremonies, the sheep gate was considered to be of primary importance. Through the sheep gate came the animals destined for sacrifice, and since worship would be incomplete without the offerings, it was of vital importance that the sheep gate be repaired as soon as possible. *Bovet* says, "The small cattle which entered Jerusalem came there certainly by the east; for it is on this side that the immense pastures of the wilderness of Judea lie." *Riehm's* Dictionary also says, "Even at the present day, it is through this gate that the Bedouins lead their flocks to Jerusalem for sale." Furthermore, another noted commentator has written, "The sheep gate must have been quite near to the temple; for it is from this that, in the ceremony of the inauguration of the walls, the cortege of priests entered immediately into the sacred inclosure. The gate, called at the present day, St. Stephen's, at the north-east angle of the Haram, answers to these data" (Godet's *Commentary on the Gospel of John*).

It has been generally believed that the five porches were but five arches, or entrances in one pentagonal building, at the center of which was the famous pool.

In these lay a great multitude of impotent folk, of blind, halt, withered, waiting for the moving of the water. For an angel went down at a certain season into the pool, and troubled the water: whosoever then first after the troubling of the water stepped in was made whole of whatsoever disease he had (vv. 3, 4).

This Scripture has been attacked by critics continually, and there are many who dismiss the healing of people as fantasy. The idea of sick folk rushing to enter the troubled waters appears to be a little fantastic, and as a result, the account has been rejected by certain famous scholars. Students should beware of accepting anything — positive or negative — without first giving adequate consideration to the subject matter. The story is neither fantastic nor outrageous as some would have us believe.

"There are still known at the present day, in the eastern part of the city of Jerusalem, some springs of mineral water; among others, on the west of the inclosure of the Temple, in the Mohometan quarter, the baths of *Ain-es-Schefa* (*Ritter*, 16th part, page 387). *Tobler* has proved that this spring is fed by the large chamber of water situated under the mosque which has replaced the temple. Another better known spring is found at the foot of the southeastern slope of Moriah; it is called the *Virgin-spring*. We have two principle accounts respecting this pond, those of *Tobler* and *Robinson*. The spring is very intermittent. The basin is sometimes entirely dry; again, the water is seen springing up between the stones. On the 21st of January, 1845, *Tobler* saw the water rise four and a half inches, with a gentle undulation. On the 14th of March, it rose for more than twenty minutes, to a height of six or seven inches, and in two minutes sank again to its previous level. *Robinson* saw the water rise a foot in five minutes. A woman assured him that this movement is repeated at certain times, two or three times a day, but that in summer, it is often observed only once in two or three days. These phenomena present a certain analogy to what is related of the spring of Bethesda. *Eusebius* also speaks of springs existing in the locality, whose water was reddish. This color, which evidently arises from mineral elements, was, according to him, due to the infiltration of the blood of victims . . . .

"The spectacle which this portico surrounding the pool presented, is reproduced in some sort by *Bovet,* describing the baths of Ibrahim, near Tiberias: 'The hall where the spring is found is surrounded by several porticos, in which we see a multitude of people, crowded one upon another, laid upon pallets or rolled in blankets, with lamentable expressions of misery and suffering . . . . The pool is of white marble of circular form and covered by a cupola supported by columns; the basis is surrounded on the interior by a bench on which persons may sit'" (Godet's *Commentary on the Gospel of John,* pp. 455, 456).

Many other references may be quoted in support of the historicity of this narrative; they reveal that the events described by John were neither fantastic nor impossible. On any day of the year at Rotorua in New Zealand, tourists may watch as placid pools are made to erupt by the irresistible powers of thermal activity. At the *Devil's Cauldron,* once every four minutes, the placid pool gurgles and erupts until the whole scene presents a picture of acute agitation. Since these things are so commonplace, why should John's record be questioned?

Indisputably, the erupting waters were rich in mineral content, and it is not impossible that certain individuals received healing by immersion in the water. Doctors in all ages have extolled the benefits of mineral baths, and thousands of patients are sent to thermal areas every year to partake of the facilities offered to the public. Just what we are to infer from the suggestion that healing was confined to the first person to enter the pool is something each student must decide for himself. There are two possibilities. First, it might have been that one man had indeed been helped by his sudden plunge into the water; on the other hand, the person or persons who followed were not helped. From this the superstitions of the people were encouraged to make the statement that only the first man was ever healed. Secondly, as will be seen in a subsequent homily, it is possible that God also had a purpose in this extraordinary event. Almost five hundred years had elapsed since the message of a true prophet stirred Israel, and during all that time, *something* had to preserve faith in a faithless age. The pool was a pulpit; the erupting waters, the preacher. As long as miracles happened in Bethesda, faith could not die. The name Bethesda means "The house of mercy." The pool was aptly named.

> And a certain man was there, which had an infirmity thirty and eight years. When Jesus saw him lie, he knew that he had been now a long time in that case, he saith unto him, Wilt thou be made whole? The impotent man answered him, Sir, I have no man, when the water is troubled, to put me into the pool: but while I am coming, another steppeth down before me. Jesus saith unto him, Rise, take up thy bed, and walk. And immediately the man was made whole, and took up his bed and walked (vv. 5-9).

A comparison is sometimes made between Deuteronomy 2:14 and John 5:5. The impotent man and the impotent nation of Israel suffered in their respective wildernesses for an identical period — thirty-eight years. Both scenes present pictures of tragedy. Verse six supplies three very simple yet interesting phases. (1) *Jesus saw him;* (2) *Jesus knew about him;* (3) *Jesus spoke to him.* It would appear as though the Lord came to the pool specially to meet this man. It is never wise to read strange things into any text, but the fact remains that John spoke of "a *certain* man," and while many people were within reach of the water, it was to one man only that Jesus came. We wonder why this was so, but here we see the predestinating foreknowledge of God. It was in the eternal mind that this man would respond, and in the fullness of time, the opportunity was given for him to do so. In some senses this is the history of every conversion, for all men are surrounded by great multitudes. Yet, however many make profession of faith in great revival meetings, souls are truly saved one at a time. In a very personal and unique sense, the Saviour comes to the side of every man and every woman destined to be healed by His grace. The fact that the man had no friends shows he was helpless; the fact that he had been there for thirty-eight years suggests he was also hopeless. There was nothing he could do toward his salvation except *believe,* but that was sufficient.

The word order of the text is significant: *"Rise, take up thy bed, and walk."*

Faith made him rise. It enabled him to triumph over the thing which held him captive. *His testimony demanded that he take up his bed.* Had he left his couch lying around, another man might have broken his neck! Readers should contrast Luke 5:24 with Acts 9:34. The man with the palsy was told to *take up* his bed; Aeneas was told to *make* his bed. Progress in the future is not possible unless there be restitution in the past. *Growth in grace* demanded that he exercise his legs, that he use the new power given by Christ.

... and on the same day was the sabbath. The Jews therefore said unto him that was cured, It is the sabbath day: it is not lawful for thee to carry thy bed. He answered them, He that made me whole, the same said unto me, Take up thy bed and walk (vv. 9-11).

Here criticism is matched by commonsense. The Jews were already seeking an excuse to undermine the authority and influence of the Saviour. Their teaching that the carrying of any piece of furniture was a violation of Sabbath rest enabled them to pounce upon this man and accuse him of sin. Instinctively he hid behind the Lord. "I only do what He commanded me to do." Let it be constantly remembered that as long as men obey Christ, they never violate any law of the Father.

Then asked they him, What man is that which said unto thee, Take up thy bed and walk? And he that was healed wist not who it was: for Jesus had conveyed himself away, a multitude being in that place (vv. 12, 13).

A. W. Pink says, "He ministered without ostentation. He never sought to be the popular idol of the hour, nor the center of an admiring crowd. Instead of courting popularity, He shunned it. Instead of advertising Himself, He 'received not honor from men.'"

That the Saviour could approach so quietly and leave again so unobtrusively suggests that all men should be careful not to miss an opportunity to be healed. If He comes, only to leave again — He may never return.

Afterward Jesus findeth him in the temple, and said unto him, Behold thou art made whole: sin no more, lest a worse thing come unto thee. The man departed, and told the Jews that it was Jesus, which had made him whole (vv. 14, 15).

Why had the man gone to the temple? Why had he not hastened to his home to share his joy with the members of the family? Why had he not gone to the streets or market place where indisputably he would have been a center of attraction? Did he run to the temple to thank God? The identity of the Healer was still unknown; to whom then could thanks be rendered but to God?

There are three thoughts here to be developed. So many people obtain healing but seldom return to offer thanks. See Luke 17:12-18. "Afterward, Jesus found him in the temple . . . ." Did the Lord seek the man, and was this the Master's way of teaching that even after the initial experience of conversion, much more may follow as we seek to do the Father's will? "Sin no more" supplies evidence to support the conclusion that the man's conduct had not been above reproach, and "lest a worse thing come upon thee" must be a warning of eternal tragedy. It would be difficult to conceive of anything worse than thirty-eight years of suffering. More than half a normal life had already been spent in pain — how then could anything worse happen? His body had indeed been made whole; his soul also could know the healing power of the Lord Jesus. Obviously the man was not ashamed to confess the name of his Benefactor. In answer to the question of why he told the Jews, it would be hard to be dogmatic. (1) Maybe they had commanded that he reveal as soon as possible the identity of the sabbath breaker. (2) It is not impossible that he thought he would gain some privilege by supplying the knowledge they desired. (3) It would be nice if we could be sure this was the inspired, unashamed testimony of a sincere and grateful worshiper.

HOMILIES

Study No. 20

THE POOL OF BETHESDA . . . THE PULPIT WHERE ANGELS PREACHED!

It was the Sabbath day in Jerusalem, and many people had neglected going to church. Bethesda, the sheep market pool, was a scene of lazy indolence, and on the steps surrounding its placid waters, the sick lay in frustrated expectancy. The synagogue service had ended, and some of the worshipers were walking toward the famous place. They passed beneath the arches made by the five porches, and saw before them, "a great multitude of impotent folk, of blind, halt, withered, waiting for the moving of the water. For an angel went down at a certain season into the pool, and troubled the water: whosoever then first after the troubling of the water stepped in was made whole of whatsoever disease he had." Alas, on that Sabbath day the waters were very still!

The Pool that said God still Lived

A great amount of discussion has taken place concerning the accuracy of this story. It has been said that the district was rich in medicinal qualities, and that periodic eruptions in the earth's strata filled the pool with healing propensities. Theologians have said that the incidents always took place during such disturbances, and that every miracle was due to a man's being able to seize his opportunity when subterranean movements liberated elements beneficial to sick people. This however is open to question. Either the account is true or it is not. None of these teachers explained why the healing powers were all exhausted after the first miracle, nor for that matter how, irrespective of the type of disease to be treated, the swirling waters always healed the seeking sufferer. The Bethesda pool was God's pulpit. Malachi had been the last of the prophets, and his ministry had almost been forgotten. The nation possessed a dead formalism, an ornate temple, but no prophet. Yet as long as the pool offered healing to sick souls, it did the work of the temple pulpit. The priestly theologians only spoke of healing; the pool supplied it. Perhaps this was the chief reason why folk were sitting around the still waters when they might have been in church.

The Power that said God still Listened

If the priests had known how to pray as did the people at the pool, there would have been no need for an angel to stir any waters. The need of a world is generally governed by the spirituality of the house of God. Every true sanctuary liberates more healing power than the sheep market pools of the world ever possessed. A dead church sends seekers elsewhere. The hopes and prayers of Israel had been transferred from the temple to the pool. When the waters were suddenly stirred; when wild confusion sent scores of unfortunates tumbling one over the other in a frantic bid to be the first into the water; when someone emerged to cry aloud for joy; everyone realized that once again God had been sufficiently interested in His creatures to ordain another case of healing. Thus God tried to teach His people to be ready to respond whenever He should shew His hand.

The Preacher that said God still Loved

"And a certain man was there which had an infirmity thirty and eight years. When Jesus saw him lie, and knew that he had now been a long time in that case, he saith unto him, Wilt thou be made whole?" There was no fuss, and the conversation was carried on in normal tones. "Sir," replied the sufferer, "I have no man when the water is troubled to put me into the pool: but while I am coming, another steppeth down before me. Jesus saith unto him, Rise, take up thy bed, and walk. And immediately the man was made whole, and took up his bed, and walked: and on the same day was the sabbath." And the proud, pharisaical people immediately misunderstood His motives and accused Him of forgetting the sanctity of God's day. And while they were arguing over the do's and don'ts of the law, the great Healer quietly withdrew. Yet He left behind a sermon without a text. It was the will of God that every man should have a chance of salvation, and since this lonely sufferer had none to help him, the love of God brought healing to his bedside. "Afterward, Jesus findeth him in the temple." It is noteworthy that the man found his way into the sanctuary. God only visited the pool — He lived at the mercy-seat!

SECTION TWO

Expository Notes on the Unprecedented Claims of Jesus

A Necessary Warning

Experience teaches that in the approach to the study of the fourth gospel, the student is apt to avoid certain parts of the book.

In quest of sermon material, the minister naturally leans toward the historical narratives, for the stories told therein are conducive to reproduction. The scenes at the Jordan, the wedding in Cana, the interview with Nicodemus, the account of the Samaritan woman's conversion, and even the healing of the impotent man provide the most wonderful sermon material. We must beware, however, at being drawn irresistibly to stories. The most important parts of John's gospel are found not in the deeds of Jesus but in His sermons. Sections two and three of this chapter are second to none in this regard.

> **And therefore did the Jews persecute Jesus, and sought to slay him, because he had done these things on the sabbath day (v. 16).**

Jesus had now come to the big city! Preaching in the smaller country town was one thing; this was infinitely more important. It was tantamount to having preached in the small villages of England and then entering into Westminster Abbey in London to challenge the doctrines of its clergy. Opposition was to be expected, and it was quickly forthcoming. They would have resisted Him in any case, but the apparent violation of sabbatical rules provided their first excuse for threatening to take His life.

> **And therefore did the Jews persecute Jesus, and sought to slay him, because he had done these things on the sabbath day. But Jesus answered them, My Father worketh hitherto, and I work. Therefore the Jews sought the more to kill him, because he not only had broken the Sabbath, but said also that God was his Father, making himself equal with God (vv. 16-18).**

The charge was now of a far more serious nature. Violating the Sabbath was one thing; blasphemy was another. They claimed He had made Himself equal with God, and it should always be remembered that never on any occasion did He deny the charge. It would have been an easy matter to refute the allegation, but He never did so, for the Jews were speaking the truth — *He did claim to be equal with God.* The fact that He was called *the Son* did not suggest He was inferior to the Father. A son may have more education, more ability, more wealth, more friends than his father ever possessed. A man is called the son of his father to indicate he is of the same essence. Similarly, Jesus was called the Son of God because of this same feature. He was *of God* because He *was* God.

Evangelical commentators have been divided in their interpretation of the following verses. It is vital and necessary to consider *both* viewpoints as we examine the statements of the Saviour. As soon as the Lord had said, "My Father worketh hitherto, and I work," the Jewish leaders charged Him with blasphemy. This calls for serious consideration. Apparently He had violated the rules governing conduct on the Sabbath. He had encouraged a man to carry a bed; and this constituted as grave a charge as though He had Himself carried it. The accusation was stupid and ill-conceived; nevertheless it was a charge. The opening statement of Jesus takes us back through the ages where God had worked in creation. Six days God labored, but on the seventh He had rested. Yet a closer examination indicated that even on the seventh day, all through the centuries, work had continued in creation. The sun did not cease to shine on the sabbath; the corn and the wheat did not cease to grow on the seventh day. The processes of healing were not halted when God's day arrived. There had been a sense in which God had certainly ceased to labor; there was another facet of truth which told that God never ceased to do good, either on the Sabbath or any other day. "My Father worketh hitherto, *and I work.*" On another Sabbath day, He asked, "Is it lawful on the sabbath days to do good or evil? to save life or to destroy it?" (Luke 6:9). This, I feel, is the only logical interpretation of the text; it explains how His enemies were so quick to charge He had made Himself equal with God.

> Then answered Jesus and said unto them, Verily, verily, I say unto you, The Son can do nothing of himself, but what he seeth the Father do: for what things soever he doeth, these also doeth the Son likewise. For the Father loveth the Son, and sheweth him all things that himself doeth: and he will shew him greater works than these, that ye may marvel (vv. 19, 20).

The verse provides an example of the two lines of interpretation forthcoming from the expositors. Some say that because of the affinity existing in the divine Family, it was quite impossible for one member to act independently of the other — that constantly, as the Father indicated, so the Son performed; that as the Son lived and moved and had His being, He did what the Father desired, for He was one in knowledge, ability, desire. Other teachers prefer to remember that Christ did not come to earth to live AS GOD (HE WAS GOD), but He came as the last Adam to show the first Adam how to live. As the God-Man He was absolutely surrendered to do His Father's will, to be led of the Spirit, empowered by the Spirit, and completely filled with the Spirit. Thus, because He — a man — was able to reach this hallowed position in life, His followers similarly may be led, and empowered, and filled. If He acted in all His ways and days as GOD, He could hardly be an example for His followers. Thus although as God He knew the Father's will, as the surrendered Man, He constantly looked for guidance, and lived day to day in utter dependence upon His Father. To say the least, there appears to be a calm prevailing sanity about this interpretation.

> For as the Father raiseth up the dead, and quickeneth them; even so the Son quickeneth whom he will (v. 21).

The *greater works* of the preceding verse seem to point to the power which quickens the dead. The Jewish Scriptures told of such incidents, when God had raised the dead. The son of the Shunammite was raised (II Kings 4:34, 35) and the body of an unidentified man was also quickened by contact with the bones of the prophet (II Kings 13:20, 21). John as yet had made no reference to Christ's power to raise the dead; it would seem as if this were a prediction of what was then still to be revealed. It is not difficult to understand the amazement of the people when they heard Jesus claiming to be able to do what only God had done.

> For the Father judgeth no man, but hath committed all judgment unto the Son: That all men should honour the Son, even as they honour the Father. He that honoureth not the Son, honoureth not the Father which hath sent him (vv. 22, 23).

We must consider these verses against the somber background of Sinai. Towering high above all else in Israel's religious life, the holy mount reminded them of the days when the law of God had been engraved on the tablets of stone. The repetition of "thou shalt not" had formulated their laws and provided the basis upon which the conduct of the tribes should be fashioned. Yet first in position and importance had been, "Thou shalt have no other gods before me." What this meant to the people is seen best from the lawyer's statement in Luke 10:27. When the Lord asked, "What is written in the law? How readest thou?" the man replied, "Thou shalt love the Lord thy God, with all thy heart, and with all thy soul, and with all thy strength, and with all thy mind; and thy neighbor as thyself." The laws of God were not trivial and superficial; any man who trespassed was slain. God had been the judge of Israel; He demanded that all should respect His statutes and honor His Name. How startling then was the announcement of Jesus that He had taken the place of God in all the executive affairs of the divine Family. It is perfectly understandable why the leaders of the synagogues were stunned by His statements.

> Verily, verily, I say unto you, He that heareth my word, and believeth on him that sent me, hath everlasting life, and shall not come into condemnation: but is passed from death unto life (v. 24).

The staggering importance of this verse is found not in the wonderful promise of life everlasting, but that it completely swept away the law, the prophets, and the traditions of the fathers. At one moment, and in one breath, Jesus superceded Moses, and the teachings of Jesus became more important than the ten commandments. Previously they had spent years endeavoring to conform to the requirements of the Mosaic law. Every minute detail of daily life was governed by some remote commandment, and in trying to observe them all, men were daily brought into bondage. They tried so hard, only to fail in their efforts; they hoped so desperately, only to find despair gripping their spirit. Then suddenly Jesus said, "He that heareth my word, and believeth on him that sent me, hath everlasting life." He taught that the elusive prize of the future could now become the glorious experience of the present. The fear of coming judgment could be banished forever by the simple fact that compliance with the teachings of Christ absolved believers from guilt. Many people were incensed with the Jewish leaders because of the opposition they gave to the Saviour; let us read the accounts again and realize that if they had NOT opposed His teachings, that would have been an even greater cause for amazement.

> Verily, verily I say unto you, the hour is coming and now is, when the dead shall hear the voice of the Son of God: and they that hear shall live. For as the Father hath life in himself; so hath he given to the Son to have life in himself; and hath given him authority to execute judgment also, because he is the Son of man (vv. 25-27).

It may seem a little difficult to differentiate between life and eternal life. Christ was about to demonstrate His ability to raise the dead, but *"and now is"* of the text suggests that of greater importance was the fact that all around were people who were beginning to hear the voice of the Son of God, and as a result were already being raised from the deadness of sin. Living faith in the Son of God brought eternal life; acceptance of the promises of the Lord begat assurance — such people would *never* come into condemnation. Jesus was able to make these statements because He had authority to do so. God had not only ordained the giving of life; God had also entrusted to the Son the carrying out of the eternal purposes. As Saviour, He was able to give eternal life; as Judge, He was able to acquit the accused. The Son of God had become the Son of man. He who knew the requirements of the divine also knew the weakness of the human. Acquainted as He was with God and man, He, as no other, could be trusted with the task of assessing the dues of the human race.

> Marvel not at this: for the hour is coming, in the which all that are in the graves shall hear his voice, and shall come forth; they that have done good, unto the resurrection of life; and they that have done evil, unto the resurrection of damnation (vv. 28, 29).

Probably the Lord saw the surprise registering on the faces of His listeners, and this made Him say, "Do not be surprised at this. I will tell you something even more amazing. The time is coming when all the graves shall be opened at the sound of My voice." Those men who heard Him will be condemned, not because they refused to accept His teaching, but because "they loved darkness rather than light." When the miraculous actions of Jesus endorsed all He had uttered, they refused to reconsider their premature decision, and "went about to kill him." Fully understanding what would take place, the Lord predicted the day of final reckoning, and warned that eternal judgment would be meted to those found guilty in the great assize. Obviously Jesus believed there would be a day of judgment. Equally as evident is the fact that He believed some men would be damned. This is truth which needs to be preached from all pulpits. Modern preachers shrink from such pronouncements. Some men, credited with higher education and advanced knowledge, predict that ultimately all men will be saved. To say the very least, it is extremely hard to reconcile their views with the teachings of Jesus. He believed that men could be lost; it might be unfortunate for those preachers who have advised their congregations to the contrary.

> I can of mine own self do nothing: as I hear, I judge: and my judgment is just; because I seek not mine own will, but the will of the Father which sent me (v. 30).

This verse expresses identical truth with that found in verse 19. The Lord could not act independently of His Father. He came to do the Father's will, and consequently, every act and every thought had to be in alignment with divine guidance. This is the guarantee that His sentence will be just. This conclusion not only applies to a future judgment; it also embraced His immediate present. The "I judge" of the text in its present tense suggests that Jesus Christ is the same yesterday, and today, and forever. Had He desired to please Himself, He might have founded an earthly kingdom and become the greatest hero of His time. He preferred to do things the right way at the right time — God's time. His will was to do the will of Him who sent Him to be the Saviour of the world.

In conclusion, and to sum up this remarkable section of John's fifth chapter, let it be emphasized that these claims of Jesus were unprecedented. No prophet, no would-be prophet had ever announced such startling things. There was need for corroboration of His statements. The very reasonableness of the Gospel would, in future, demand that these claims be examined to the finest and most remote detail. Therefore it is not surprising to discover that even within the compass of the same sermon, Jesus proceeded to supply what was needed. Our next section should thrill every student, but first it is necessary to pause and consider the homiletical value of the preceding verses.

HOMILIES

Study No. 21

THE PERFECT REVELATION OF GOD

Within the framework of the Bible, *seven* is the number of completion. God completed the work of creation and rested on the seventh day. This ancient order is repeated continually throughout the Scriptures. Six is a man's number; seven is the perfect number; eight is the resurrection number, and students must ever keep this in mind. It will be seen that the Lord's sermon in the temple was built around such scaffolding. His theme was equality with God, but the supports of that theme were seven strong assertions. Constantly throughout the entire discourse He spoke of "My Father and I"; "the Father and the Son"; "the Son and the Father." If we read these verses quickly, we fall into error. It is best to make haste slowly.

(1) *The Father's Work.* "My Father worketh hitherto, and I work . . . for what things soever he doeth, these also doeth the Son likewise" (verses 17 and 19).

(2) *The Father's Revelation.* "For the Father loveth the Son, and sheweth him all things . . . and he will shew him greater works than these . . ." (verse 20).

(3) *The Father's Power.* "For as the Father raiseth up the dead . . . even so the Son quickeneth whom he will" (verse 21).

(4) *The Father's Judgment.* "For the Father judgeth no man, but hath committed all judgment unto the Son" (verse 22).

(5) *The Father's Honor.* "That all men should honour the Son even as they honour the Father. He that honoureth not the Son honoureth not the Father which hath sent him" (verse 23).

(6) *The Father's Life.* "For as the Father hath life in himself; so hath he given to the Son to have life in himself" (verse 26).

(7) *The Father's Will.* "I seek not mine own will, but the will of the Father which hath sent me" (verse 30).

Intertwined, built around these seven great facts, was the amazing sermon preached by Christ on that memorable day in Jerusalem. The second half of His never-to-be-forgotten oration supplied evidence supporting His claims to deity. If seven is the number of completion, we shall expect to find His evidence resting upon a similar set of facts. It is thrilling to discover that this is indeed the case. However, before we seek further for truth, let us examine carefully the verses as they were written by John.

SECTION THREE

Expository Notes on the Evidence Cited by Jesus

If I bear witness of myself, my witness is not true. There is another that beareth witness of me; and I know that the witness which he witnesseth of me is true (vv. 31, 32).

Certain expositors find difficulties within this text. However, there are two broad lines of interpretation. For example, Pink says, "He speaks hypothetically — IF. '*If I bear witness of myself*' means '*If I bear witness independently of my Father.*' In such case, '*my witness is not true.*' And why? Because such would be insubordination. The Son can no more bear witness of Himself independently of the Father, than He can of Himself work independently of the Father." Pink probably meant by this that as the Father and the Son were *ONE*, it was quite impossible to divorce either from the other. To have spoken or worked independently would have signified discord or disunion within the Divine Family. Consequently such an utterance would have been false or untrue to reality.

There is another interpretation which is a little easier to understand, and perhaps to accept. It was the teaching of the law that evidence should be substantiated by at least two witnesses (Deuteronomy 17:6; Matthew 18:16). Therefore Christ said that His own witness concerning any major teaching would be unacceptable; that is, His hearers would have a right to expect corroborating evidence. Therefore, "If I bear witness of myself; my witness is not considered true." Indisputably there is value in Pink's suggestion, but probably this second suggestion is nearer the truth, for thereupon Christ began to cite *seven* witnesses of His deity. This was, as it were, going the extra mile, and since seven is the number of completion, it would follow that whereas two or three witnesses would have been *enough* and *good* evidence, *seven* witnesses would be irrefutable evidence; it would be unimpeachable, perfect. (See the subsequent homily in regard to the two witnesses.) The "another" of the text is, I believe, the Holy Spirit (John 16:13, 14). Here also is oneness with the Father (See homily at the conclusion of these notes.)

Ye sent unto John, and he bear witness unto the truth. But I receive not testimony from man: but these things I say, that ye might be saved (vv. 33, 34).

This is an obvious reference to John 1:19. The Jewish leaders were *appealing* to John for information. Had John spoken words derogatory to Christ, those leaders would have issued a subpoena requiring the Baptist's presence to denounce an impostor. In contrast to such procedure, Jesus did not appeal to any man for evidence to prove what and who He was. John had indeed borne witness to the truth, but even had he not done so, THE TRUTH would have remained eternal, unassailable. The purpose of Christ's teaching was not to attract the plaudits of men or to gain their popularity. He taught, not to get, but *to give;* not to become the object of their hero-worship, but rather that they might be saved.

He was a burning and a shining light: and ye were willing for a season to rejoice in his light (v. 35).

This surely represents one of the greatest commendations ever given by Christ to man. There is something warm and inviting about the Master's statement. Perhaps we may best understand its implications if we see John Baptist silhouetted against the seven-branched candlestick of the ancient tabernacle in the wilderness. He was a *burning* light; that means he drew fuel from some hidden source of supply. This came from the eternal reservoirs of divine sufficiency. Rubbish will burn and give smoke; he burned and gave light. He was a burning and a *shining* light. His ministry was a light to the people who sat in darkness and the shadow of death. His words actually introduced Christ to the multitudes. A burning and a shining light has never been known to be jealous, to seek its own glory, to endeavor to steal the pre-eminence. The chief and only function' of a light is *to shine,* to dissipate the gloom, to reveal the path, to cheer. John Baptist was all that. His attributes should be welcomed in the experience of every minister of the Gospel. That the people to whom John spoke were only willing to rejoice in his efforts *for a season* suggests that, like their ancestors, they too loved darkness rather than light.

But I have greater witness than that of John: for the works which the Father hath given me to finish, the same works that I do, bear witness of me, that the Father hath sent me (v. 36).

The greatest testimony for Christ was the power which transformed lives. His miracles were outstanding and irrefutable, but unfortunately none were so blind as the people who did not wish to see. The very wonderful and saintly Bishop Ryle emphasized five things relative to the miracles of the Lord Jesus. *"(i) Their number.* They were not a few only, but very many. *(ii) Their greatness.* They were not little, but mighty interferences with the ordinary course of nature. *(iii) Their publicity.* They were not done in a corner, but generally in open day, and before many witnesses, and often before enemies. *(iv) Their character.* They were almost all works of love, mercy, and compassion, helpful and beneficial to man, and not merely barren exhibitions of power. *(v) Their direct appeal to man's senses:* They were visible and would bear any examination. The difference between them and the boasted miracles of Rome on all these points is striking and conclusive. Such amazing manifestations of power were sure indications that Christ did always those things which pleased the Father."

> **And the Father Himself, which hath sent me, hath borne witness of me. Ye have neither heard his voice at any time, nor seen his shape (v. 37).**

There are two possible interpretations of this Scripture. Most of the commentators think it refers to the witness made by God at the Jordan. This could indeed be the case, if we admit the possibility that the people to whom the Saviour addressed His remarks had not been present at John Baptist's meetings. We know that they had not been in sympathy with the Baptist's mission, and had only been sent to ask questions. Thus they might have been absent when God said, "This is my beloved Son in whom I am well pleased," and they had neither "heard God's voice nor seen His shape." On the other hand, if this interpretation is unacceptable, the Lord was citing the fact that "God . . . at sundry times, and in diverse manners spake in time past unto the fathers by the prophets" and in so doing had witnessed concerning the coming Messiah.

> **And ye have not his word abiding in you: for whom he hath sent, him ye believe not (v. 38).**

This was a staggering indictment. The people thus addressed claimed to be the representatives of God; they were exceedingly proud of the fact that they, and they alone, enjoyed the privilege of being His ambassadors on earth. When Christ directly charged that they neither accepted His word nor honored His Son, it was tantamount to saying they were foreigners to the divine purposes and were further away from God than were the despised Samaritans. History subsequently revealed that they never forgave this apparent insult.

> **Search the scriptures; for in them ye think ye have eternal life: and they are which testify of me (v. 39).**

The term *"ereunate tas graphas"* implies more than a casual look at an ancient record. Dr. Henry Thayer speaks of it as being *an examination,* or *a concentrated study of something.* The Amplified New Testament renders the verse, "You search, and investigate, and *pour over the Scriptures diligently,* because you suppose and trust that you have eternal life through them." Such diligence can have but one end — "these writings testify of me. If you do not recognize this fact, then you are totally unacquainted with the message given by God." The prophets spoke of the coming Messiah; and Isaiah clearly stated the Coming One would die for the sins of His people (Isaiah 53). The inference here is very strong. If the Jewish leaders

through lack of enlightenment on the Scriptures did not recognize
Him of whom the prophets spoke, neither did they know life ever-
lasting, the inestimable treasure of which the prophets also testified.
Religion without reality was meaningless.

And ye will not come to me that ye might have life (v. 40).

Perhaps there could be some excuse for a man's inability to understand the written words of the prophets. Scholarship, inherent ability,
competent teaching, and privilege all play an essential part in theological research. A man unfortunately denied these assets might encounter difficulty in his search for enlightenment. Yet a greater condemnation became evident. Christ was available to all; none was
denied access to His school. If men deliberately stayed away, there
could be no excuse for continuing ignorance.

**I receive not honour from men. But I know you, that ye have not
the love of God in you. I am come in my Father's name, and ye
receive me not: if another shall come in his own name, him ye
will receive (vv. 41-43).**

Jesus was not a seeker after vain glory; He never tried to become
the popular hero of His times, but sought only the honor which
comes from above. Such quality of soul, such communion with the
Father provided the insight which enabled Him to read the hearts
and secrets of other men. Their hearts were open as a book. He knew
they did not possess the love of God. Earlier, He said they did not
possess His word in their hearts; now follows the indictment that they
did not possess God's love. They were spiritually bankrupt in spite
of a continuing profession and ritualistic worship. One wonders if
He would lay similar charges at the door of some of the twentieth
century churches! His words have been vindicated throughout the
centuries. Men have come in their own name, have taught the most
outrageous doctrines, but in some remarkable fashion have been
acclaimed brilliant.

**How can ye believe, which receive honour one of another, and seek
not the honour which cometh from God only? (v. 44).**

Within the Greek words *dunasthe umeis* is the thought of ability
or inherent power, such as, "How can ye learn to believe which only
think of acquiring honor from men?" There are certain prerequisites
for graduation in God's school. There is need to unlearn some of the
things which have become preconceived ideas, and to see clearly the
divine standard by which all things are judged. Without these foundation principles, the structure of spiritual knowledge cannot be erected.

**Do not think that I will accuse you to the Father: There is one
that accuseth you, even Moses, in whom ye trust. For had ye**

believed Moses, ye would have believed me: for he wrote of me. But if ye believe not his writings, how shall ye believe my words? (vv. 45-47).

To the Jews, this statement of Christ's would be unpardonable. Moses, the great judge of Israel, would condemn the people into whose hands the sacred writings had been placed. Men who talked of the Scriptures remained ignorant of their true teaching. This gives added force to the earlier statement, "Search the scriptures." These people would be condemned because they believed not the writings of Moses. *God had given His word; God had preserved His word; God was now interpreting His word.* The Lord had done everything possible for their enlightenment and salvation. If through ignorance they remained in the dark, if through sin they rejected the Son, then their blood would be upon their own heads. Moses the great lawgiver would rise in the judgment to condemn them. Indeed, even then, Moses through his writings was already condemning them. No theologian, no preacher, no student should reject the written word, until adequate thought has been given to this solemn statement.

HOMILIES

Study No. 22

THE SEVEN-FOLD WITNESS TO THE CHRIST

(1) "There is another (God the *Holy Spirit)* that beareth witness of me; and I know that the witness which he witnesseth of me is true" (verse 32).

(2) "Ye sent unto *John,* and he bear witness unto the truth" (verse 33).

(3) ". . . the same *works* that I do, bear witness of me" (verse 36).

(4) "The *Father* himself . . . hath borne witness of me" (verse 37).

(5) ". . . the *scriptures* . . . are they which testify of me" (verse 39).

(6) "*Moses* . . . wrote of me" (verse 46).

(7) "If ye believe not his writings, how shall ye believe *my words* when they testify of me?* The final five words are added because they interpret the earlier statement.

Study No. 23

THE TWO WITNESSES WHO FULFILLED GOD'S LAW

The earlier expository notes explained that under the Mosaic law, two witnesses at least were required in any matter of legislation. The testimony of a solitary witness was insufficient to gain a verdict. The following is reprinted from *Bible Pinnacles,* pages 157-158, in order to reveal the completeness of the testimony by which the entire ministry of Christ was safeguarded:

According to Mosaic law, at least two witnesses were required in the conviction of a criminal. "Whoso killeth any person, the murderer shall be put to death by the mouth of two witnesses: but one witness shall not testify against any person to cause him to die" (Numbers 35:30). "One witness shall not rise up against a man for any iniquity, or for any sin, in any sin that he sinneth: at the mouth of two witnesses, or at the mouth of three witnesses, shall a matter be established" (Deuteronomy 19:5). It is most interesting to note that in His relationships with the Lord Jesus Christ, God honored His own laws.

The Two Witnesses of His Royalty (Matthew 3:16, 17)

"And Jesus when he was baptized, went up straightway out of the water: and, lo, the heavens were opened unto him, and he saw the Spirit of God descending like a dove, and lighting upon him: and lo a voice from heaven saying, This is my beloved Son in whom I am well pleased." At the commencement of the public ministry of the Saviour, the remaining two Members of the divine Family witnessed concerning the Third. God the Father audibly announced His approbation; the Holy Spirit endorsed what was said.

The Two Witnesses of His Redemptive Work (Luke 9:28-31)

"And as Jesus prayed, the fashion of his countenance was altered . . . . And behold there talked with him two men, which were Moses and Elias: who appeared in glory, and spake of his decease which he should accomplish at Jerusalem." God's choice of witnesses was most admirable. These two saints of a bygone age represented both the law and the prophets. Moses, whose very name suggested the written word, and Elijah, the foremost of the prophets, appeared to add their testimony to the value of the Son of God. While the synagogue leaders openly proclaimed their allegiance to the ancient patriarchs, Moses and Elijah appeared to speak with Christ concerning the crucifixion. Thus they confessed that Jesus would fulfill all they had believed and promised.

The Two Witnesses of His Resurrection (John 20:11, 12)

"But Mary stood without at the sepulchre weeping: and as she wept, she stooped down, and looked into the sepulchre, and seeth two angels in white sitting, the one at the head, and the other at the feet, where the body of Jesus had lain. And they say unto her, woman, why weepest thou?" The memory of that wonderful morning never left Mary. She heard from the angels the glad tidings of the resurrection, and a little while later, she recognized her Lord. The two angels came to speak of the resurrection, for they had witnessed the thrilling event and were able to comfort the sorrowful woman. Neither the untruths of the Jewish story, nor the false statements of modern teaching, can change the testimony of the two angels who witnessed His triumph.

The Two Witnesses of His Return (Acts 1:9-11)

"While they beheld, Jesus was taken up; and a cloud received him out of their sight. And while they looked steadfastly toward heaven as he went up, behold, two men stood by them in white apparel; which also said, Ye men of Galilee, why stand ye gazing up into heaven? this same Jesus, which is taken up from you into heaven, shall so come in like manner as ye have seen him go into heaven." The return of the Lord Jesus Christ is the greatest hope of the Church, and there are many students who believe the fulfilment of this great promise cannot long be delayed. In the mouth of the two witnesses the testimony has been established. The Gospel story is the most reasonable message in the world, for at each crucial point in the ministry of Jesus, God honored His laws, and through the united testimony of reliable witnesses, endorsed the teaching of the Saviour. "Even so, come, Lord Jesus" (Revelation 22:20).

The Sixth Chapter of John

THEME: *Christ . . . the Bread of Life*

OUTLINE:

      I. Christ feeds the five thousand. Verses 1-15.

     II. Christ walks on the water. Verses 16-21.

   III. Christ speaks in the synagogue. Verses 22-59.

  IV. Christ disturbs the disciples. Verses 60-71.

SECTION ONE

Expository Notes on the Feeding of the Five Thousand

After these things Jesus went over the sea of Galilee, which is the sea of Tiberias (v. 1).

The *Sea of Galilee* was known by several names. First, it was called by this name because its waters came from the east side of Galilee. Sometimes it was called *The Sea of Gennesaret;* this came from the proximity of the fertile plain of Gennesaret which lay at the lake's northwest angle. The plain was said to be about three and a half miles long, and two and a half miles broad (see Luke 5:1). In earlier times the lake was known as *the Sea of Chinnereth.* This was probably so because the city of that name stood on its shores. *The Sea of Tiberias* was one of the later names and probably came from the fact that the city of Tiberias was close to the shore. *Fausset's Bible Encyclopaedia* says, "Nine cities stood on the shores of the lake, of which only two are now inhabited. These are Magdala, consisting of a few mud huts, and Tiberias, sadly changed from its ancient prosperity. Silence now reigns where formerly the din of industry was heard."

And a great multitude followed him, because they saw his miracles which he did on them that were diseased. And Jesus went up into a mountain and there he sat with his disciples (vv. 2, 3).

In studying the verse, two others should be taken in consideration. "But Jesus did not commit himself unto the people, because he knew all men" (John 2:24). "From that time many of his disciples went back, and walked no more with him" (John 6:66). Enormous crowds and surging enthusiasm are not always the evidence of spirituality. The report that another miracle had been performed was sufficient to send people running through the streets; the expectation of a second miracle was sufficient to hold a crowd for long periods of time. The miracles of Christ never wounded anyone; His message did. His supernatural powers amazed them; His indictment of sin angered them. There were, and still are, countless thousands who would welcome His miracles if at the same time His teachings could be avoided. Therefore it must be concluded that a true miracle is not the sudden ability to use a limb, but the complete transformation of character and conduct which are the necessary adjuncts of conversion. Unfortunately, there is little evidence to prove this followed the majority of His miracles. Maybe this sheds a light on a later promise, "Verily, verily, I say unto you, he that believeth on me, the works that I do, shall he do also; and greater works than these shall he do; because I go unto my Father" (John 14:12). More often than not the Lord Jesus was able only to touch a man's body; now through the ministry of the Holy Spirit and His consecrated witnesses, He transforms the lives of innumerable thousands of guilty sinners.

When the Lord retired to the mountain, He was able to sit quietly to consider the dangers and implications of the scene before Him. Oftentimes throughout His memorable ministry, the quiet of the hillside counteracted the tumult of the valley; the communion in the solitudes offset the criticism in the cities. The man who never visits the quiet places can hardly expect to be God's representative to the masses.

> **And the passover, a feast of the Jews, was nigh. When Jesus then lifted up his eyes, and saw a great company come unto him, he saith unto Philip, Whence shall we buy bread, that these may eat? And this he said to prove him: for he himself knew what he would do (vv. 4-6).**

This section seems to be unusually interesting. A dual concern is apparent from the Saviour's utterance. The approach of the passover accounted for the presence of an unusually large crowd; it is not impossible that many of these people were actually on their way to Jerusalem, that they were hungry and faint from travel, and that hearing Jesus was nearby, they sought Him with the curiosity and enthusiasm of any modern tourist. Christ was by no means obligated to feed them, but the presence of need constituted a challenge which could not be permitted to pass unnoticed. However, the feeding of the multitude did not present any major problem. "He knew what he himself would do." A matter of greater concern was the growth in Philip's soul. What did he think? Had he any faith capable of grasping the implications and possibilities of the situation? Was the disciple another curious sightseer, or was he a true disciple approaching graduation in the school of Christ? These were matters of real importance, and the fact that Christ tested His follower reveals the concern with which He regarded the training of the men destined to evangelize the world. The Lord has never had difficulty feeding the hungry people of the world — when He has been able to find believing, consecrated servants ready to do His will. So many people remain hungry because they waste their time counting the problems instead of reaching for the Master's hand.

Philip answered him, Two hundred pennyworth of bread is not sufficient for them that every one of them may take a little (v. 7).

Denarion, unfortunately translated "penny," was the name given to the silver coin in daily use at the time of our Lord's sojourn on earth. In present day value it would be worth 8½ pence (English) or about 10 cents (American). Thus two hundred pence would be the equivalent of approximately seven pounds in English currency or somewhere in the region of twenty dollars. In order to assess its true *purchasing* value, it is necessary to take into consideration that one denarius was enough pay for a full day's work in the vineyard (Matthew 20:2). It should be remembered that in those days, laborers worked at least twelve hours a day. According to present standards of remuneration, a modern workman would expect at least one dollar fifty cents per hour, thus making his daily rate eighteen dollars per day. This does not take into account that men are paid extra for working overtime! Therefore in order to understand the text, we must consider the denarius equal to eighteen dollars. Therefore Philip would have said something tantamount to the following, "$3,600 worth of bread is not sufficient for them, that every one may take a little." By any standard, that would be a lot of bread. Yet if we are to appreciate the magnitude of the miracle performed by the Lord Jesus, it is necessary to see the occurrence through modern eyes.

Earlier expository notes explained that this miracle, in some senses, outshone the others. It was performed before an immense crowd who were able to substantiate the reports soon to circulate throughout the nation. Furthermore, this manifestation of divine power began with the meager supplies brought by a lad. Modern interpretation suggests that the people pooled their luncheon baskets, and there was therefore no need for any miracle. It is hardly necessary to discuss this proposal. Immediately afterward, the Lord used this setting for one of His most profound sermons. He spoke of the Bread of Life sent down from heaven, and it is difficult to find adequate support for His sermon in the suggestion that this was a mammoth picnic made possible by the sharing powers of a good-natured audience.

> One of his disciples, Andrew, Simon Peter's brother, saith unto him, There is a lad here, which hath five barley loaves, and two small fishes: but what are they among so many? (vv. 8, 9).

How did Andrew learn of the lad's lunch? Did the boy overhear the disciples talk, and offer to give his supplies? These are things which every preacher would like to know. (See homily on Andrew, Chapter 1). Thompson's *Land and the Book*, page 449, reveals that the people of Palestine still complain that their enemies leave them nothing to eat but barley! Revelation 6:6 declares that one measure of wheat was worth three measures of barley. Judges 7:13 suggests that Gideon in the estimation of the Midianites was but an insignificant barley cake. The story in John 6 suggests that God has always used the foolish things, the despised things of this world, to confound the mighty! Compare I Corinthians 1:21-25.

> And Jesus said, Make the men sit down. Now there was much grass in the place. So the men sat down, in number about five thousand (v. 10).

Possibly the number present far exceeded the number here announced. If some of these people were on their way to Jerusalem, it is certain that many wives would be traveling with their husbands. We know that at least one boy was present, and unless human nature has greatly altered, the presence of one lad suggests many more were nearby. The crowd surely contained families, and the task of feeding the people was infinitely greater than the mere feeding of five thousand men.

> And Jesus took the loaves; and when he had given thanks, he distributed to the disciples, and the disciples to them that were set down; and likewise of the fishes as much as they would (v. 11).

This is the hallowed standard by which all true ministry must be measured. We take from His hand that which we pass to others. Others may dispense the blessing, but He alone can give it. Alas, many people remain hungry because that which is offered comes from any place other than His Hand. So often when much time has been wasted on unimportant tasks, the preacher seeks desperately for any source of supply that his sermon might be finished in time. Unfortunately, such sermons die on the pulpit steps!

In writing of this text, A. W. Pink has a delightful paragraph in his commentary. On pages 296 and 297, he says, Christ "did not scorn the loaves because they were few in number, nor the fish either because they were 'small.' This tells us that God is pleased to use small and weak things. He used the tear of a babe to move the heart of Pharaoh's daughter. He used the shepherd-rod of Moses to work mighty miracles in Egypt. He used David's sling and stone to overthrow the Philistine giant. He used a 'little maid' to bring the mighty

Naaman to Elisha. He used a widow with a handful of meal to sustain His prophet. He used a 'little child' to teach His disciples a much needed lesson in humility. So here, He uses the five loaves and two small fishes to feed this great multitude . . . . But mark it carefully, it was only as these loaves and fishes were placed in the *hands of Christ* that they were made efficient and sufficient." Contrast Philip's statement, "That every one of them may take a little" with the "as much as they would" of verse 11. In common with the wine of Cana's well, the supplies were equal to every demand made. The people were able to return for a second helping, or even a third, until ". . . they were filled . . . ."

> When they were filled, he said unto his disciples, Gather up the fragments that remain, that nothing be lost. Therefore they gathered them together, and filled twelve baskets with the fragments of the five barley loaves, which remained over and above unto them that had eaten. (vv. 12, 13).

Attention is drawn to the fact that this is the only miracle performed by the Lord which is recorded by all four writers of the gospels. Obviously then, in their concept of things, this miracle occupied pride of place. Consideration must also be given to the fact that this miracle was not the only one of its type. God was very wise when He reminded both Matthew and Mark to record that other occasion when the Lord used seven loaves to feed four thousand men beside women and children (Matthew 15:32-38; Mark 8:1-9). If either Matthew or Mark had forgotten to mention the miracle of the feeding of the *five* thousand, the critics of the Bible would have had a "field day."

Probably the Lord knew His enemies would criticize His actions, and to avoid any charge of unnecessary waste, He commanded that even the fragments be collected. We are not told what happened to the twelve baskets of food, but probably it was carried away by the people who still had many miles to travel before they reached the feast in Jerusalem.

> Then those men, when they had seen the miracle that Jesus did, said, This is of a truth that prophet that should come into the world (v. 14).

Link verses 2 and 14 together and the shallowness of these men is seen clearly. They were not interested in *what He said,* and had no desire to know what He required of them. Sin, repentance, holiness, and the Father's will were never considered. They were getting something for nothing; life had become a joyous new picnic. Work was unnecessary; labor was foolishness. The prophet was all they required to bring heaven to earth! Soon they were to hear His sermons; soon they were to feel the cutting edge of the Word of God; alas, soon they were to cry aloud "Crucify him!"

When Jesus therefore perceived that they would come and take him by force, to make him a king, he departed again into a mountain himself alone (v. 15).

Christ's actions teach us that success begets danger, that a fence on the top of a cliff is better than an ambulance at the bottom! From a purely human point of view it may be admitted that Christ could have yielded to their wishes and allowed them to arrange His coronation service. This however, would have been fraught with peril and without question would have ended in tragedy. Both King Herod and Pontius Pilate would have united to stamp out insurrection. Within days, many of those men would have been left dying on a field of battle, and many more languishing in dungeons. The entire cause of God would be brought into jeopardy, and the initial enthusiasm would give way to deepest despair. Christ recognized the danger and sought refuge in the mountain. And let it be well appreciated — *He went alone.* The presence of disciples might have led to complications. The enthusiastic crowds would follow with ease the tracks of a party, and the disciples might also share the views of the king-makers. Alone, Christ could hide; alone, He could find a quiet place and kneel to pray. Jesus was a very worthy Son of the Highest; the Master was a most wonderful Saviour.

HOMILIES

Study No. 24

CHRIST . . . AND THE BREAKING OF THE BREAD

Many delightful touches in the ministry of Christ were best seen in retrospect. When the Saviour did certain things, His disciples were often too preoccupied to realize the true value of His actions. Yet in after days, when they reviewed the life of their Lord, they were able to compare spiritual things with spiritual, and see things in their true perspective. They remembered certain little characteristics and said, "Only Jesus could have done that — just like that." And perhaps one of the foremost of these was the way in which He took bread and brake it. It is not without significance that the Emmaus travelers who had failed to recognize the Stranger Christ confessed afterward "that he was known of them in the breaking of the bread" (Luke 24:35).

A Gracious Parable

"And when he had taken the five loaves and two fishes, he looked up to heaven, and blessed, and brake the loaves, and gave them to his disciples to set before them; and the two fishes divided he among them all" (Mark 6:41). Many years later, the disciples remembered the exquisite grace with which He handled the meager supplies. All through the heat of the day the great crowd had followed Him. Morning had given place to afternoon, and the setting sun had turned the west to crimson. Shadows were lengthening across the fields when Jesus indicated that He desired to feed the hungry.

(1) *A Great Scarcity.* It seemed ludicrous to place a little boy's lunch before such a crowd, and the disciples may be excused for muttering, "What are five loaves and two fishes among so many?"

(2) *A Great Saviour.* "He took the loaves, and blessed, and break them," and immediately thousands of people partook of it and were fed.

(3) *A Great Satisfaction.* When the meal was finished, no one remained hungry unless he had refused to stretch out his hand. Thus did Christ begin to reveal His eternal purpose to feed hungry souls with the Bread of Life.

A Grim Prediction

"And he took bread, and gave thanks, and break it, and gave unto them, saying, This is my body which is given for you: this do in remembrance of me" (Luke 22:19). The setting sun had lain down to sleep in its bed of shadows, and the glory that had been day had given way to night. The crowds had gone home, and, alone with His disciples, the Lord proceeded to endorse His earlier teaching. He lifted the loaf and as He divided it, said, "This is my body which is broken for you." With His benediction, He gave the bread to them, and commanded them to eat. They remembered how He had said, "The bread of God is he which cometh down from heaven, and giveth life unto the world . . . . I am the Bread of Life: he that cometh to me shall never hunger; and he that believeth on me shall never thirst . . . . I am the living bread which came down from heaven: if any man eat of this bread, he shall live forever" (John 6:33, 35, 51). And very thoughtfully they lifted the broken bread to their lips. At that time, they did not know what His death would mean. It was fantastic to believe their Master was about to die. They hoped and prayed for the kingdom, but in after days they remembered His words and realized how wonderful they had been.

A Glorious Presentation

"And it came to pass, as he sat at meat with them, he took bread and blessed it, and break and gave to them. And their eyes were opened, and they knew him" (Luke 24:30, 31). Perhaps the vanishing Christ smiled as He left them spellbound at the table. He had put the finishing touches on their education; they had graduated at God's university. Did He possess some delightful way in which He handled the bread, or were the nail prints visible to the watching host and hostess? Excitedly they returned to their colleagues in Jerusalem; but whereas they might have cried, "We saw the wound-prints in His hands," they preferred to say, "He was known to us in the breaking of the bread." In retrospect they saw how that He had thrice acted similarly. Viewed together in their proper sequence, the occasions suggested progression. A gracious parable, a grim prediction, a glorious presentation. He had longed to feed the hungry souls of men and women; He had died to make this possible; He had risen again to finish His task. They realized also that in each of these three scenes, one underlying truth had been important. At the great feast, the hungry people had been required to take the bread from the hand of the disciple-server. At the last supper, they had been required to accept the bread from the hand of their Lord; and outside their little village, the Saviour had continued on His way until they invited Him to enter their home. God may provide a sumptuous banquet, but if our arms be paralyzed we may easily starve.

SECTION TWO

Expository Notes on Christ's Walking on the Water

A Notable Omission

This particular incident has been recorded by Matthew, Mark and John, yet only Matthew has added the extra details of Peter walking on the water to go to Christ. The question why this was so seems to be unavoidable. Probably in the final analysis, no one can be dogmatic, but at least some obvious reasons are forthcoming. Mark, as the emanuensis of Simon Peter, would hardly incorporate in his gospel something undesirable to his friend. And it was hardly likely that the apostle would dictate something to glorify his own achievements. Peter would be more likely to include the story of his backsliding to enhance the forgiving grace of his Lord. On the other hand, the theme of John's gospel was the deity of Christ, and nothing could be permitted to steal His preeminence. Furthermore, if John set out to write things omitted from the other gospels, it is understandable why Peter's exploit was rejected. Matthew, however, when he wrote his memoirs saw no reason whatsoever to omit what he considered to be a thrilling account of Christ's saving power. We agree with him.

And when even was now come, his disciples went down unto the sea, and entered into a ship, and went over the sea toward Capernaum (vv. 16, 17).

We are indebted to Matthew for his explanatory notes on this incident. He wrote: "And straightway Jesus constrained his disciples to get into a ship, and to go before him unto the other side, while he sent the multitudes away. And when he had sent the multitudes away, he went up into a mountain apart to pray: and when the evening was come, he was there alone. But the ship was now in the midst of the sea, tossed with waves: for the wind was contrary" (Matthew 14:22-24). In view of the possibility of a conspiracy to make Him king, Jesus considered the dispersing of the crowd the best thing possible. Whether or not the disciples understood and appreciated His motives remains a secret.

And it was now dark, and Jesus was not come to them (v. 14).

Even out of its context, this verse is highly suggestive. The term "darkness" was one of John's favorite expressions; again and again it appeared in his writings. Unregenerate men lived in darkness; rebellious men loved the darkness rather than light because their deeds were evil. "Then spake Jesus . . . I am the light of the world: he that followeth me shall not walk in darkness, but shall have the light of life" (John 8:12). Without Christ, men abide in the shadows, here, and in eternity.

And the sea arose by reason of a great wind that blew (v. 18).

Writing of the sea of Galilee, A. R. Fausset has said, "Sudden and violent storms agitate the waters, sweeping down the ravines and gorges converging to the head of the lake, from the vast naked plateau of the Jaulan and the Hauran and Mount Hermon in the background. It was such a storm that Jesus stilled by a word." There are times when the waters of Galilee are so calm and placid that storms appear to be impossible. And yet, in frighteningly quick time, the air cools in the mountains and winds of hurricane force rush down the hillside to turn the lake into a maelstrom. To be fishing when this takes place is to be in acute and terrible danger. The Lord praying in the hillside may have had evidence to warn Him of an approaching storm, and realizing His followers were in peril, hastened to their rescue. He arrived in time — as He always does.

So when they had rowed about five and twenty or thirty furlongs (three or four miles) they see Jesus walking on the sea, and drawing nigh unto the ship: and they were afraid (v. 19).

It is so easy for us to sit in the calm of a home and pass judgment on these terrified fisherman. They were in danger of death; at any moment their boat could capsize. They were drenched to the skin, and water dashing into their faces almost blinded them. We do not know whether or not they recognized their Master. When they stared in amazement at what seemed to be an apparition, superstition seized their minds and suggested imminent disaster. Their cry of fear was the most natural thing in the world. Mark says, ". . . they were so amazed in themselves beyond measure, and wondered. For they considered not the miracle of the loaves and fishes: for their heart was hardened" (Mark 6:51, 52). It must be remembered that their amazement followed the stilling of the tempest and not while Christ was walking on the waves. Mark adds a significant detail which seems to reflect Peter's reactions on that memorable night. ". . . he cometh unto them walking upon the sea, *and would have passed by them*" (Mark 6:48). Students should compare this with Luke 24:28 ". . . and he made as though he would have gone further." The Master loves to hear the cry of His children; He welcomes an invitation to enter, either a storm tossed boat or a quiet homestead.

> **But he saith unto them, It is I; be not afraid. Then they willingly received him into the ship, and immediately the ship was at the land whither they went (vv. 20, 21).** Mark adds the thrilling detail, ". . . and the wind ceased" (Mark 4:51).

Attention must be given to the fact that once again the Lord used the expression *Ego eimi . . . I AM*, and again a mighty demonstration of supernatural power followed. Compare this verse with John 18:6: "As soon therefore as he had said unto them, I AM, they went backward and fell to the ground." See also Exodus 3:14 and study expository notes on John 4:26. If Christ had been a mere man, none of these utterances would have been intelligible. I AM is God's name, and each time it was used by the Lord, amazing power was liberated to accomplish the impossible. Even the waves were hushed before Him, and ". . . immediately the ship was at the land whither they went."

HOMILIES

Study No. 25

The Stilling of the Storm

Experience teaches that sometimes there are far greater storms within human hearts than ever blew on Galilee. Nevertheless, two truths shine as stars against the darkness of the night. (1) *Foreknowledge.* As the great I AM, the Master knew of the approach of the hurricane. It was no secret that soon the lake would be lashed to fury. Nevertheless in spite of this, "He constrained His disciples to get into a ship and to depart to the other side." (2) *Foreplanning.* If He knew of the approach of the storm, He also knew what He intended to do when its force threatened the safety of those He loved. Christ was never too late, never too early; He always arrived at the right time to effect a rescue. Wisdom appropriates this great truth for itself. Happy indeed is the mariner who sees not the storm but the Saviour.

A Great Storm

The Bible speaks of many storms — of one kind and another. The widow at Nain was almost swamped by the waves of grief, yet Christ arrived in time to rescue her (Luke 7:11-18). Saul of Tarsus was overwhelmed by conviction, yet outside the walls of Damascus, Christ stilled the waves and brought peace to his troubled heart (Acts 9:1-6). The nobleman of Capernaum was frantic with worry, but Christ solved his problems (John 4:46-54). The thief was almost drowned amid waves of indescribable guilt, but Christ was there to lift him (Luke 23:42, 43).

A Great Saviour

(1) *How wonderful.* He walked on the waters; He could not sink. He was Master of every situation.

(2) *How wise.* It appeared as though He would have passed by. The request, "Lord, teach us how to pray," was being answered in a most unusual way. Sometimes He permits us to enter the storm because only there can He teach life's greatest lessons.

(3) *How willing.* Immediately when they asked Him to enter the ship, He did so, and the perilous waves began to subside. The disciples had rowed hard and long to do what He accomplished in a moment. Strong arms are good; powerful oars are fine; a knowledge of seamanship is invaluable, but the presence and power of Christ are worth all put together.

A Great Stillness

"And the wind ceased." Probably the water was still running from their clothing; their hair was saturated; the boat almost water-logged, but the wind was no longer howling; the waves were flattening out; the stars were shining, and the shoreline was just ahead. In describing another scene, the Evangelist said, "And there was a great calm." Matthew 8:26. This kind of miracle has been repeated many times in the experience of Christians. The Lord is never far from those who trust Him.

SECTION THREE

Expository Notes on Christ's Sermon in the Synagogue

> The day following, when the people who stood on the other side of the sea saw that there was none other boat there, save that one whereinto his disciples were entered, and that Jesus went not with his disciples into the boat, but that his disciples were gone away alone . . . . when they had found him on the other side of the sea, they said unto him, Rabbi, when camest thou hither? (vv. 22-25).

Obviously the people had not entirely abandoned their plans to crown Christ king; perhaps too they were beginning to be hungry again. They therefore sought for Jesus, and knowing the only boat had departed without Him, they were curious to know what had happened. After seeking in vain, they decided to go to Capernaum, knowing that ultimately Jesus would rejoin His followers. When they heard that He was already there, they wanted to know how this had been possible. The presence of a small armada of vessels considerably increased the crowds, but it appears they were quite certain none of these vessels accounted for Christ's quick transit across the lake. Every sincere student finds here evidence to corroborate John's account. Had there been any possible way of explaining the presence of Christ in Capernaum at this time, the Lord's enemies would have been quick to reveal it. Indeed they would have called Him an imposter for permitting His followers to propagate falsehood.

> Jesus answered them and said, Verily, verily, I say unto you, Ye seek me, not because ye saw the miracles, but because ye did eat of the loaves, and were filled. Labour not for the meat which perisheth, but for that meat which endureth unto everlasting life, which the Son of man shall give unto you: for him hath God the Father sealed (vv. 26, 27).

The Amplified New Testament has translated this passage: "Stop toiling, and doing, and producing for the food that perishes and decomposes in the using, but strive and work and produce rather for the lasting food which endures continually unto life eternal. The Son of man will give or furnish to you that, for God the Father has authorized and certified Him and put His seal of endorsement upon Him." Christ was recommending a readjustment in their sense of values; He was urging a shifting of emphasis. It cannot be that He was advising them to cease working for daily food; that would have been folly. He was telling them to concentrate less on the search for material things, and instead to seek other avenues where the rewards would be eternal. This would bring them to His feet, for His ministry bore the imprint of the Father's hand; He had been authorized, empowered to grant life everlasting. The seal of the divine was bestowed by the Holy Spirit at His baptism. Compare Ephesians 1:13.

> Then said they unto him, What shall we do that we might work the works of God? Jesus answered and said unto them, This is the work of God that ye believe on him whom he hath sent (vv. 28, 29).

It is frequently difficult to ascertain the motives which prompted certain questions. What did these people mean by "the works of God"? Were they seeking the power that could multiply loaves and fishes? Were they anxious to discover the secret which would gain for them increasing popularity with the people? Were they aspiring to greatness where work would be unnecessary? Were they truly sincere, pricked in their hearts, and asking how they could do works which would indeed be pleasing to God? It would seem from the text they were only thinking of material gain, for with the next breath they asked for signs. The fact that signs had already been given meant nothing. Here, as in other places of the Bible, man's effort was contrasted with God's grace. Man always seeks *to do* something, as if salvation depended upon human merit. God's will is that men *might believe*. Eternal life is a gift; by faith sinners accept it. If any work comes into the pattern, it comes afterward, when those already in possession of everlasting life serve Christ to reveal gratitude. Men do not work to get this life; they work because they already have it.

> They said therefore unto him, What sign shewest thou then, that we may see, and believe thee? What dost thou work? Our fathers did eat manna in the desert; as it is written, He gave them bread from heaven to eat. Then Jesus said unto them, . . . Moses gave you not that bread from heaven; but my Father giveth you the true bread from heaven. For the bread of God is he which cometh down from heaven, and giveth life unto the world (vv. 30-33).

What hypocrisy was this! He had just performed the miracle of the loaves and fishes, and the accuracy of the account could be established by the testimonies of thousands of people. They excused their action by suggesting that Moses had given a sign; however, they forgot to add that in spite of all that Moses did, their forefathers murmured against him. Furthermore their statements were inaccurate. Moses did not give bread from heaven. Moses merely prayed and *God gave manna from heaven*. The text supplies a tremendous contrast! ". . . *that bread*" and ". . . *the true bread*." Any student, after a short period of concentrated study, may find here food for thought, food to make sermon preparation a delight.

> Then said they unto him, Lord, evermore give us this bread (v. 34).

At first sight it seems that a great impression had been made upon their minds; however, subsequent verses reveal that unbelief continued to reign in their hearts. Unless they uttered their request with a faint touch of mockery in their tone, the Lord's rebuke would hardly be justified.

> And Jesus said unto them, I am the bread of life: he that cometh to me shall never hunger; and he that believeth on me shall never thirst. But I said unto you, That ye also have seen me, and believe not. All that the Father giveth me shall come to me; and him that cometh to me I will in no wise cast out (vv. 35-37).

The underlying truths of this Scripture are so obvious that ministers are invited to consider them under the following headings.

(1) *God Attracting.* "All that the Father giveth me shall come

to me." "No man can come to me, except the Father which hath sent me draw him: and I will raise him up at the last day" (verse 44). We detect here the great doctrine of predestination. The Church was promised to Christ before the world began, and since we are part of the gift, our Heavenly Father must do His utmost to honor His promise.

(2) *Man Assenting.* ". . . he that *cometh* to me shall never hunger; and he that *believeth* on me shall never thirst." The Greek word translated "believeth" is a very potent word. Dr. J. H. Thayer renders it thus: *"The conviction and trust to which a man is impelled by a certain inner and higher prerogative and law in his soul."* The call of God begets an urge which man must obey. The convicting power of the Holy Spirit reveals need; but to meet the need, man himself is required to act intelligently to take what God offers.

(3) *Christ Accepting.* ". . . and him that cometh to me I will in no wise cast out." The translation as given in the Amplified New Testament is very thrilling: ". . . him that comes to me, I will most certainly not cast out — I will never, no never reject one of them who comes to me." An intensified search through the gospel narrative fails to reveal any instance when Jesus failed to welcome a penitent soul. "Whosoever will may come, and him that cometh, I will in no wise cast out."

> For I came down from heaven, not to do mine own will, but the will of him that sent me. And this is the Father's will which hath sent me, that of all which he hath given me I should lose nothing, but should raise it up again at the last day. And this is the will of him that sent me, that every one which seeth the Son, and believeth on him, may have everlasting life: and I will raise him up at the last day (vv. 38-40).

It is hardly possible to study these weighty utterances without detecting again the strong underlying truths of predestination. Nevertheless, it is necessary to exercise care, for it is so easy to read into the text that which was never meant to be there. We shall better understand this passage if we consider it under three headings.

(1) *God Planning.* Three times in quick succession, the Lord speaks of *the Father's will.* The Lord's coming to earth was the result of plans conceived in the mind of God before the world was. "For I came down from heaven not to do mine own will but the will of him that sent me." God's will was immediately explained under two subheads. (a) ". . . of all which he hath given me I should lose nothing" and (b) ". . . that every one which seeth the Son and believeth on him, may have everlasting life . . . ." We are therefore reminded that God had prearranged plans and the Son's mission to men was the carrying out of that which had been decided in heaven. God's plan is clearly revealed as being *conceived in heaven, carried*

out on earth, and *brought to full fruition at the end of time.* Now all this concerns a specified company of people. It was the will of the Father and the desire of the Son that "many . . . be brought to glory." Paul sheds light on the subject, for Romans 8:29 says, "For whom he did foreknow, he also did predestinate to be conformed to the image of his Son . . . ." Because God is infinite, He is able to see the end from the beginning. *He knew* those who would respond to His call, and was able to plan intelligently that such converts be conformed to the image of His Son. An earthly parent may look ahead and see that on a certain date a son will graduate from college. Knowing this, the father begins to make preparation that when that day arrives his boy can either proceed to the university or enter a business house. Foreknowing, a man can plan intelligently. So with God. He knew that certain people at a certain time would be brought, as it were, to graduation point; that faith would elevate their souls from the lower ranks of unbelief. Therefore, He devised a plan by which they could climb higher, and be conformed to the image of the eternal Son. The idea that some souls are predestined to be damned is incompatible with Scripture and foreign to the nature of God.

(2) *Christ Preserving.* Once again this truth is clearly defined under three subheads. (a) First, Christ had to find these people. That they would be drawn to Him, the Lord had no doubt, nevertheless, He constantly looked for those whom the Father had promised. (b) Having found them, Christ had to keep them, and furthermore, (c) He had to keep them until the end of time when they would be raised with an incorruptible body. At a much later date, John said, "Beloved, now are we the sons of God, and it doth not yet appear what we shall be: but we know that, when he shall appear, we shall be like him; for we shall see him as he is" (I John 3:2). This work was destined to be accomplished through the indwelling power of the Holy Spirit. See expository and homiletical notes on John 7:37-39.

(3) *Man Perceiving.* ". . . every one which *seeth* the Son, and *believeth* on him, may have everlasting life . . . ." It is very essential that note be made of the word order of this text. *Seeing precedes believing.* In other words, God reveals the Son before man can effectively believe on Him. Paul declared, ". . . *it pleased God . . . to reveal his Son in me*" (Galatians 1:15, 16). Salvation begins not with man's brilliance but with God's grace. Some men look at Christ and see but little; others look to see the Word made flesh, the Son of God who loved us and gave Himself for us. It follows that what a man sees governs his actions. Nevertheless the old adage is still true, "None are so blind as the people who do not wish to see." When Christ claimed that He would raise the dead at the last day, this, to the

Jews, was another claim to deity. Those who believed in a resurrection affirmed that only God could raise the dead.

> The Jews then murmured at him, because he said, I am the bread which came down from heaven. And they said, Is not this Jesus, the son of Joseph, whose father and mother we know? how is it then that he saith, I came down from heaven? (vv. 41, 42).

If evidence be needed to support the interpretation of the preceding verses, here it is. In spite of Christ's amazing miracles, the leaders still asked for a sign; in spite of His wonderful teaching, they saw Him only as the son of a tradesman. Whatever modern sects may teach, the people who lived and moved in the presence of Christ clearly understood His claim to pre-existence. He claimed that He had come down from heaven. Continually they charged him with this, and NEVER DID HE DENY THE CHARGE. It was perfectly true. HE CLAIMED EXACTLY WHAT THEY SAID. For this He did not apologize. Students will understand that these are the things which help to make John's memoirs unique. *This is the Gospel of God the Son.*

> Jesus therefore answered and said unto them, Murmur not among yourselves. No man can come to me, except the Father which hath sent me draw him: and I will raise him up at the last day. It is written in the prophets, And they shall be all taught of God. Every man therefore that hath heard, and hath learned of the Father, cometh unto me (vv. 43-45).

Emphasis should be placed not upon the drawing power of the Father, but upon man's inability to come on his own initiative. Man is lost. Isaiah 53:6 likens him to a wandering sheep, and it has well been said that the natural tendency of a lost sheep is to *"get more lost."* Cows, pigs, horses, pigeons have the ability to find their way home, but sheep continue to go further away. Therefore, since men are as sheep, left to themselves they go further into the wilderness of sin. If and when they come home, they do so because the voice of the Shepherd has called them. It is this fact that gives strength to the Saviour's challenge, "No man can come except . . . the Father draw him." The fact that Christ refers to Isaiah 54:13 endorses this interpretation. "And all thy children shall be taught of the Lord." Once again by a neat circumlocution we are back where we began. There is in the text a message (1) to be preached, (2) to be heard, (3) to be accepted, and (4) to be consummated.

> Not than any man hath seen the Father, save he which is of God, he hath seen the Father. Verily, verily, I say unto you, He that believeth on me hath everlasting life. I am the bread of life (vv. 46-48).

This is but a repetition of that which has gone before. With great deliberation, the Lord repeats continually His amazing statements.

He had been with God; He had seen God; He had heard God; He was of God; His word was the word of God; He could give eternal life which was God's life. See homily at the end of this study.

> Your fathers did eat manna in the wilderness, and are dead. This is the bread which cometh down from heaven, that a man may eat thereof, and not die. I am the living bread which came down from heaven: if any man eat of this bread, he shall live forever; and the bread that I will give is my flesh, which I will give for the life of the world (vv. 49-51).

It is obvious from these memorable words that Christ had now taken the place occupied by the Tree of Life in the Garden of Eden. (See Genesis 3:22-24, and the homily and expository notes in John 3). The power of choosing life or death had been restored to man, but the fruit of the new Tree of Life was to be the flesh and blood of the Saviour. Broad horizons of immense possibilities were now opening before sinful man. As with Adam, so with his descendants. To choose wisely would mean the joyful experience of everlasting life ; to choose unwisely would mean a wandering in sin's wilderness through time and even into eternity.

> The Jews therefore strove among themselves (angrily contended with one another) saying, How can this man give us his flesh to eat? (v. 52).

Indisputably there is progression of thought in these words. Prior to this point, Christ had affirmed He was the Bread of Life, but now He speaks of His flesh and blood. Later, in John 13:24, He was to say, ". . . Except a corn of wheat fall into the ground and die, it abideth alone: but if it die, it bringeth forth much fruit." Bread is produced by crushed wheat; the Bread of Life was to be produced from a body broken. Already Christ is foretelling His death; the shadow of Calvary has fallen across His soul. It is easy to appreciate the difficulty of His hearers. To them it seemed fantastic that He should speak in this fashion. Had we been placed in their position, we too would have been deeply disturbed. Their condemnation came, not because they failed to grasp the true meaning of His utterances, but because they failed to investigate His claims, to discover what He meant. Prior to this, the Lord had performed great miracles and it was not possible to find misdemeanors in His conduct. The nobility of His character, the supernatural power exhibited in His miracles, the profundity of His thought demanded a careful examination of His claims. This was not forthcoming; the leaders flew into a rage and began to accuse Him of blasphemy. Their actions were inexcusable.

> Then Jesus said unto them, Verily, verily, I say unto you, Except ye eat the flesh of the Son of man, and drink His blood, ye have

no life in you. **Whoso eateth my flesh, and drinketh my blood, hath eternal life; and I will raise him up at the last day. For my flesh is meat indeed, and my blood is drink indeed (vv. 53-55).**

Throughout the centuries these verses have been the focal point in the most animated discussions. The Roman doctrines of transubstantiation have implied that to become a true Christian, one must become a cannibal. It should be remembered that at the time these things were uttered by Christ, the Last Supper had not even been mentioned. The fact that someday the Church would break bread and partake of the communion service was completely unknown. It could not have been possible that Christ was referring to the sacraments when He enunciated these doctrines.

Matthew Henry in commenting on John's gospel states the position admirably: "What is meant by eating this flesh and drinking this blood? It is certain that it means neither more nor less than believing in Christ. *Believing in Christ* includes these four things, which *eating and drinking* do. *First,* it implies an appetite to Christ. This spiritual eating and drinking, begins with *hungering* and *thirsting,* (Matt. 5:6). 'Give me Christ or else I die.' *Secondly,* an *application* of Christ to ourselves. Meat *looked upon* will not nourish us, but meat *fed upon.* We must so accept of Christ as to appropriate Him to ourselves. *Thirdly,* a *delight* in Christ and His salvation. The doctrine of Christ crucified must be meat and drink to us; most pleasant and delightful. *Fourthly,* a *derivation of nourishment* from Him, and a dependence upon Him for the support and comfort of our spiritual life, and the strength, growth, and vigour of the new man. It is *to live upon Him* as we do upon our meat. When afterward He would institute some sensible signs, by which to represent our *communicating* of the benefits of His death, He chose those of *eating* and *drinking,* and made them *sacramental* actions" (*Matthew Henry's Commentary on the Whole Bible* in one volume; Grand Rapids: Zondervan Publishing House, p. 338). As we take food, so also by faith we take of Christ, that what He accomplished at the cross may become part of our spiritual being, making us strong to do His will.

He that eateth my flesh, and drinketh my blood, dwelleth in me, and I in him. As the living Father hath sent me, and I live by the Father: so he that eateth me, even he shall live by me (v. 56).

Attention is drawn to the thought-provoking fact that John has changed the tense of his verb. In verse 53, he uses the aorist tense of the verb denoting something completed in the past. Now the apostle uses the perfect tense to denote something which is continuous. In the past, by one single appropriating action of faith, a man partook of Christ to receive life. "Except ye *eat* . . . ye have no life." Then the soul continues to eat — that is, every day — he comes for new supplies, and thereby grows in grace. "He that eateth . . . dwelleth in me, and I in him." This is a perfect expression of New Testament doctrine, for while being born into the family of God is certainly a marvelous experience, to grow into the likeness of the Saviour is even more wonderful. We obtain life by coming to Him; we thereafter *"live by Him"* in daily communion.

> **This is that bread which came down from heaven: not as your fathers did eat manna, and are dead: he that eateth of this bread shall live for ever. These things said he in the synagogue, as he taught in Capernaum (vv. 58, 59).**

This was probably the greatest sermon ever heard in that ancient sanctuary. Continually Christ repeated His salient points, for unlike the science of modern homiletics where repetition is considered a fault, He was determined His hearers would have no doubt as to the things He wished to say. Students may like to count the number of times the Lord mentioned each of the following:

> I am the Bread of Life.
> I came down from heaven.
> I will raise him up at the last day.
> He that believeth on Me.
> Hath everlasting life.
> The Father that sent Me.

HOMILIES

Study No. 26

THE EXPANDING FULLNESS OF CHRIST

Within the scope of John's great gospel we discover Christ's claim to be equal with God. The *ego eimi*, the I AM, the name of God, continually makes an appearance, but it is worthy of note that on seven different occasions the Lord expanded this inspired title. If the Christian life be a pilgrimage through time toward eternity, these seven verses reveal certain requirements for the journey.

(1) *"I am the Bread"* (John 6:41).

This is the strength every pilgrim needs as he walks the road. The food for his soul comes only from the Lord Jesus.

(2) *"I am the Light of the world"* (John 8:12).

There is no guarantee the Christian will always live in unbroken sunshine. "Days of darkness still come o'er me; sorrow's paths I sometimes tread." Yet light from the Lord Jesus will shine on the road, for He walks at our side.

(3) *"I am the Door"* (John 10:9).

This is the access or means of entrance to the Royal Highway. It is not possible to begin unless one enters at the appointed place.

(4) *"I am the Good Shepherd"* (John 10:11).

Sometimes the journey leads through enemy territory. It will be necessary to wrestle against principalities and powers. Sometimes the dangers may be too great for Christ's sheep. The staff and rod of the Shepherd guarantee safety.

(5) *"I am the Resurrection and the Life"* (John 11:35).

This supplies the needed power for the journey. Sometimes men grow weary, but "they that wait upon the Lord shall renew their strength." Resurrection life may be known throughout the entire pilgrimage.

(6) *"I am the Way, the Truth, and the Life"* (John 14:6).

We shall never get lost if we stay close to Him, for He is the way; we shall never be confused if we listen to His advice, for He is the Guide.

(7) *"I am the True Vine"* (John 15:1).

We shall neither starve nor waste time on the journey. The bread will feed us; the Vine will fill us with divine life; constantly pilgrims will bear fruit to His glory. The walk to the celestial city will not be burdensome exacting affair, but a joyous experience of living union with Christ.

SECTION FOUR

Expository Notes on the Division Among the Disciples

Many therefore of his disciples, when they had heard this, said, This is an hard saying; who can hear it? (v. 60).

It may be necessary to remember that the Greek word translated "disciples" is *matheetees*, which really means a pupil. The followers of Christ were not called "Christians" until a later date (Acts 11:26). The ancient philosophers delivered their lectures while they walked around a garden or some suitable enclosure. Their students followed, listened, and learned. Similarly, the pupils of Christ — His adherents — followed Him, some to partake of loaves and fishes, others to listen to His words. These people were not Christians as we now understand the term, they were not all devoted to Christ and His cause. That some of them were soon to leave must be attributed to the idea that His teachings were now making demands they were not prepared to grant.

When Jesus knew in himself that his disciples murmured at it, he said unto them, Doth this offend you? What and if ye shall see the Son of man ascend up where he was before? It is the spirit that quickeneth; the flesh profiteth nothing: the words that I speak unto you, they are spirit, and they are life (vv. 61-63).

Attention is again drawn to the fact that the teachings of Christ were more important than His miracles. His supernatural acts were but endorsements of the amazing things He said. Already in this remarkable chapter He has spoken of *His divine origin;* He was the Bread which came down from heaven. Already He has predicted that His body would be broken and His blood shed, that believing men might eat His flesh and drink His blood. Now the Lord plainly foretells that death can never hold Him captive. The day must come when He who came down from heaven must ascend "where He was before." He had come to earth to conform to a divinely made schedule; when the time arrived, every detail of God's plan would be fulfilled. Yet all this would be meaningless unless the Holy Spirit breathed life and understanding into their minds. "But as it is written, Eye hath not seen, nor ear heard, neither have entered into the heart of man, the things which God hath prepared for them that love him. *But God hath revealed them unto us by his Spirit: for the Spirit searcheth all things, yea, the deep things of God"* (I Corinthians 2:9, 10).

> But there are some of you that believe not. For Jesus knew from the beginning who they were that believed not, and who should betray him. And he said, Therefore said I unto you, that no man can come unto me, except it were given him of my Father (vv. 64, 65).

It was quite impossible to deceive the Lord. He knew the motives of all who stood in His presence; and the observance of religious ordinances was no substitute for true devotion. The Lord repeats His earlier statements that the response of faith was dependent upon the call of the Father. The doctrine that some persons are born to be damned finds no support here. All travelers in the Middle East know the shepherds permit their flocks to mingle at the watering holes. When the time comes for each shepherd to leave, the man calls, and his sheep respond. The only sheep that will not respond *are those that are sick.* God calls everyone, but unfortunately the sickness of sin interferes with the response of some people; they prefer to lie down in the mud rather than follow the Shepherd to the green pastures.

> From that time, many of his disciples went back, and walked no more with him (v. 66).

This was no fault of the Saviour. These disciples left Him *because they did not like what He said.* The voice and the message of the Saviour had reached them all, but while some lingered to hear more, others preferred to go away. This is precisely what the Lord had predicted. And if additional evidence is required to support this conclusion, one has only to examine the modern world.

It is not difficult for any speaker to gain a following, but once the message begins to impose hardship, his disciples decrease immediately. The call of Christ is not to attend a picnic, but to take up a cross and carry it!

> Then said Jesus unto the twelve, Will ye also go away? Then Simon Peter answered him, Lord, to whom shall we go? thou hast the words of eternal life. And we believe and are sure that thou art that Christ, the Son of the living God (vv. 67-69).

Matthew Henry says, "Christ will detain none against their will; His soldiers are volunteers, not conscripted men." The answer supplied by Simon Peter reveals that he was more attracted to the teaching of Christ than to His miracles. He did not say, "Thou art the greatest Healer Israel has ever known." Peter said, "Thou hast the words of eternal life." This proves his ears had been more active than his eyes. He had seen much; he had heard more. "Faith cometh by hearing, and hearing *by the word of God.*"

> Jesus answered them, Have not I chosen you twelve, and one of you is a devil? He spake of Judas Iscariot the son of Simon: for he it was that should betray him, being one of the twelve (vv. 70, 71).

Throughout the centuries, theologians and others have sought the reason for the inclusion of Judas in the disciple band, and some have even wondered if Christ should have called the man. They suggested that it would have been better if he had been denied discipleship in order to keep him from temptation. This is but one side of a very sad picture. Possibly the Lord Jesus HAD to accept Judas; maybe there was no alternative. Unfortunately this is a theme seldom considered within the theological circles. Many eminent scholars have stated that Judas was Satan's imitation of the Son of God. Of no other except the Antichrist has the term been used, *"the son of perdition."* Then again, of Judas alone was it recorded, ". . . from which Judas by transgression fell, *that he might go to his own place"* (Acts 1:25). Here are great mysteries, but one thing is clear. Judas had staked his all. He was a reckless gambler. He lost because he had not the ability to see God's way was better than his own. Possibly, Judas was the direct challenge of Satan to Christ. Was it possible for the Son of God to remain sweet with a snake in His bosom? If the evil one directly challenged the Saviour, Christ had no alternative. Judas became a follower, not primarily because Christ called him, but because Satan provided him. (See homily on John 14:21-30.)

HOMILIES

Study No. 27

THE PARTING OF THE WAYS

Three types of people are seen here, and in some strange way they remind us of people whom we meet every day.

The Men Who Backslid

"From that time many of his disciples went back, and walked no more with him." Some of these people had been with Him for quite a time; they had partaken of the loaves and fishes, and probably, for a while, had been most enthusiastic concerning the great Leader. It is not difficult to hear their excited chatter as they talked of His exploits. Yet there is reason to believe that real faith was not in their hearts. They followed Him as long as He pleased them; they questioned Him when they did not agree with His teaching; they forsook Him when real discipleship loomed on their horizons. When Jesus was asked for signs of His return, He predicted that in the last days because iniquity should abound, the love of many would wax cold. The Bible supplies many examples of the people who endeavor to excuse their inexcusable actions (Luke 14:18-20.)

The Men Who Believed

"And we believe and are sure that thou art that Christ, the Son of the living God." Simon Peter was the spokesman for the rest of his brethren. These men had heard the call and had followed. They made innumerable mistakes, and Peter particularly was to know the bitterness of remorse which would send tears rolling down his cheeks. Nevertheless, these men truly loved their Master, and for His sake went out to turn the world upside down.

The Man Who Betrayed

It is truly solemnizing to consider how near a man may come to Christ and yet be lost. It is almost frightening to consider how often one might hear the words of Christ and yet remain uninstructed. Even though Judas were the offspring of Satan (compare Genesis 6:1-3), the fact remains that for three years the Saviour showered love upon him. The Bible teaches that a man is not lost because of Satan's action; a man is lost because of *his own decision*. Some men have asked what would have happened if Judas had truly repented and asked Christ for pardon. To such questions we are not able to supply adequate answers, for *Judas never asked for pardon*. What he did, he did deliberately, and for that he alone can be held responsible. (For further details, see the homily on John 14:13.)

The Seventh Chapter of John

THEME: *Christ at the Feast of Tabernacles*

OUTLINE:

      I. Christ cannot be intimidated. Verses 1-13

     II. Christ cannot be silenced. Verses 13-44

    III. Christ cannot be arrested. Verses 45-53.

SECTION ONE

Expository Notes on Christ's Secret Journey to Jerusalem

After these things Jesus walked in Galilee: for he would not walk in Jewry, because the Jews sought to kill him (v. 1).

We have now reached a new phase in the gospel story. Christ has spoken in the large city; His message has stirred the religious heart of the nation. The repercussions to His statements and deeds were serious indeed, for now there is no pretense about the actions of the Jewish leaders. Their decision that Jesus must be removed at any cost predicted trouble. This was to be fully expected, for the statements made by the Saviour were diametrically opposed to everything they had ever believed. The commandment, "Thou shalt not kill," had been conveniently forgotten; Jesus must die. From here on evidence of the deity of Christ is supplied not only in His words, but in the things which His enemies could not do. It seems incredible that one apparently defenseless man could survive, but Jesus appeared to have a charmed life. His enemies planned and schemed, but their efforts were in vain. Jesus could not be intimidated nor frightened.

Now the Jews' feast of tabernacles was at hand (v. 2).

It now becomes evident that John's sixth chapter spans a period of six months. John 6:4 reads, "And the passover, a feast of the Jews, was nigh." John 7:2 speaks of the Feast of Tabernacles. Leviticus 23:5-34 reveals that whereas Passover was held on the fourteenth day of the first month, the Feast of Tabernacles was held on the fifteenth day of the seventh month. All this adds importance to John's statement, "And there are also many other things which Jesus did, the which, if they should be written every one, I suppose that even the world itself could not contain the books that should be written" John 21:25).

His brethren therefore said unto him, Depart hence, and go into
Judea, that thy disciples also may see the works that thou doest.
For there is no man that doeth anything in secret, and he himself
seeketh to be known openly. If thou do these things, shew thyself
to the world. For neither did his brethren believe in him (vv. 3-5).

His brethren were His brothers, the sons of Mary and Joseph,
and their statement reveals how utterly ignorant they remained of
His purpose and mission. For them, spiritual insight did not exist.
The "if" which prefaced their request suggests that an element of
doubt, perhaps scorn, maybe a desire for self importance, were all
seeking an outlet. It was as though they said, "If what is said of
you be true, why waste precious time in these insignificant villages?
Go to the city where thousands can watch your miracles. Then if
the rumors be really true, they can make you a king, and we can
find a better job in the administration of your kingdom. If all they
say of you be untrue, then the sooner the falsehood is exposed, the
better for all concerned." It seems unbelievable that these men had
lived with Christ for thirty years and yet knew nothing about him.
Their familiarity had bred contempt.

Then Jesus said unto them, My time is not yet come: but your
time is alway ready. The world cannot hate you; but me it hateth,
because I testify of it, that the works thereof are evil (vv. 6, 7).

The Lord's days were all planned in heaven; He did nothing
without thoughtful preparation. The time and opportunity to go to
the feast were not ripe, but since they did always the things they
desired, their time was always ready. They were men without
conviction, discernment, courage. They never criticized the world,
and never denounced evil. They "minded their own business" and
never made enemies. Therefore the world had no cause to hate them.
They waited to see which party would get into power, and then supported it! Moral issues and spiritual values had no appeal. God
could look after His affairs; they would look after their affairs. Jesus
was different. He came to do the will of God; He denounced evil.
He was spiritual; they were carnal. He was from above; they were
earthy.

Go ye up into this feast: I go not up yet unto this feast; for my
time is not yet full come. When he had said these words unto
them, he abode still in Galilee. But when his brethren were gone
up, then went he also up unto the feast, not openly, but as it were
in secret (vv. 8-10).

It was required of every male in Israel to present himself before
the Lord at least three times every year. At other times attendance
at religious ceremonies was optional, but at the feasts of Passover,
Pentecost, and Tabernacles attendance was compulsory. "Three times
in a year shall all thy males appear before the Lord thy God in a

place which he shall choose; in the feast of unleavened bread; and in the feast of weeks, and in the feast of tabernacles: and they shall not appear before the Lord empty" (Deuteronomy 16:16). Therefore in advising His brethren to go to the feast, the Lord, as He was always careful to do, complied with the requirements of the Mosaic law. Any other advice would have invited and merited criticism from the Jewish leaders. He did not say that He would not attend the feast; He merely said, "I go not up *yet* . . . ." People generally traveled to Jerusalem in groups or caravans. Each new arrival was met by crowds and afforded a joyous welcome, for this was the feast of joy. Christ desired to arrive secretly — quietly, unostentatiously — for His Father's purpose could be better served that way. The pilgrims traveled the highway; He probably traveled along the byways. Sometimes the longest way round is the shortest way home!

Then the Jews sought him at the feast, and said, Where is he? And there was much murmuring among the people concerning him: for some said, He is a good man: others said, Nay; but he deceiveth the people. Howbeit no man spake openly for him for fear of the Jews (vv. 11-13).

Ugly rumors were circulating in the city; sinister whispers were being heard in the market place. Premonitions of trouble filled many hearts. The Jewish leaders were hostile; the joyful festival of harvest was likely to be marred by civil strife. Eyes became furtive; people became suspicious, and in such soil, the seeds of untruth germinated rapidly. Had Christ appeared at this time, disaster would have ruined His visit; His enemies could have prosecuted Him for several reasons. (See the following homily.)

HOMILIES

Study No. 28

THE AMAZING CHRIST

It was during this feast, that officers of the law were sent to arrest the Saviour. Their failure to do so and their resultant report make good reading. They said, "Never man spake like this man." Their testimony could easily be enlarged, for we are now able to declare, "Never man lived, thought, acted, yielded, overcame, preached, rescued, died, or rose again, as did Jesus of Nazareth. He was the altogether lovely One, the incomparable Christ." This brief first section of John 7 provides three glowing examples of the fact.

How Constrained

This was two-fold, for the pull came from different directions. His brethren urged Him to go to the city, to demonstrate His powers, to become increasingly popular, and having captured the affections of the masses, to do what had to be done. From the heart and throne of God came the sure guidance that a better way could be found to do all these things in a different way. The Lord had great vision and probably recognized here a new edition of an old temptation. A strange similarity of motive may be detected in Luke 4:5-8. "And the devil, taking him up into a high mountain, shewed unto him all the kingdoms of the world in a moment of time. And the devil said unto him, All this power will I give thee, and the glory of them: for that is delivered unto me; and to whomsoever I will give it. IF THOU THEREFORE WILT WORSHIP ME, ALL SHALL BE THINE. And Jesus answered and said unto him, Get thee behind me, Satan: for it is written, Thou shalt worship the Lord thy God, and him only shalt thou serve." It should be noted carefully that the Lord never denied the devil's power to give these rewards; neither did He challenge the statement that all these things belonged to the evil one. Christ knew this was true. During two thousand years, missionaries have labored and died to evangelize the heathen. It appears that all this could have been done in a moment. Satan offered to surrender his territory immediately. The anguish of the cross could have been avoided, and a very difficult road made easy — at a price. Hollow victories are defeats in disguise. All that glitters is not gold, and the Lord was an expert connoisseur of true values.

How Careful

Within the first thirteen verses of this chapter, jewels of truth lie hidden just beneath the surface. Christ was careful (1) to seek His guidance from God and not from men, and (2) to avoid unnecessary trouble. *Foolish* bravery is not a part of the Christian's armor. Had the Lord reached the city when everything was in a turmoil, His arrival would have caused a riot. (3) The Feast of Tabernacles was a time of thanksgiving when people came to worship God and return thanks for the bounties of harvest. The streets would be filled with booths, tents, or temporary homes made of branches. Civil disturbances could have caused many injuries. His absence at the crucial moments prevented disaster. (4) Had he stolen the limelight, His enemies could have accused Him of interfering with the main purpose of the feast — of usurping the glory due to God. It must be remembered that while Jesus claimed to be equal with God, never on any occasion did He try to push His Father from the center of the picture. Being equal with God did not mean that He superseded God. The men had been commanded to attend the feast and give thanks to Jehovah. The fact that Christ did not make an appearance for at least three days enabled them to do this without hindrance. (5) He was careful to attend the feast, for otherwise the leaders could have charged Him with violation of the Mosaic law. *All* males were expected to be present. We are told that Christ was tempted in all points as we are, but just how often and in what ways this took place, we shall never know. The fact that He foresaw every attack of Satan, and victoriously offset it proves that He was indeed a very wonderful Saviour.

How Courageous

Never at any time did Jesus shirk His duty; never on any occasion did thought of personal discomfort turn Him from the appointed path. Prudence, not fear, made Him journey to the city secretly. Tact, not timidity, made Him delay His appearance in the temple for three days. He waited until God unmistakably opened the way for advance, and then went up into the temple to teach. These same attributes were exhibited throughout His life and were evident even in His decease. ". . . who for the joy that was set before him, endured the cross, despising the shame, and is set down at the right hand of the throne of God" (Hebrews 12:2).

SECTION TWO

Expository Notes on Christ's Sermon in the Temple

Now about the midst of the feast Jesus went up into the temple and taught (v. 14).

"The fifteenth day of this seventh month shall be the feast of tabernacles for seven days unto the Lord" (Leviticus 23:34). The Lord either delayed His arrival, or secreted Himself somewhere in the city for about three days, and then with great deliberation made His way to the temple. As the preceding homily suggested, His timing was perfect.

And the Jews marvelled saying, How knoweth this man letters, having never learned? (v. 15).

This was probably one of the most stupid things they ever uttered. Obviously there were depth of thought and beauty of expression in the Lord's sermon, and this aroused their curiosity. It would have made for easier understanding and greater clarification had they asked, "How can he do these things since He never studied *in our college!?*" That he had been with God in the eternal university; that His wisdom designed the planets, the flowers, the mountains; and that His creative instincts had even given music to the birds, were things beyond the powers of their comprehension. Man is apt to manufacture a mold, and while this may be very fine and useful, man should never be surprised if sometimes God makes His own mold! These words have been used as a sounding board for all kinds of silly statements. The fact that God brought John Baptist from the undiscovered school in the wilderness did not automatically infer that every known school was accursed. God is the God of the unexpected; there is variety in all His acts. If the world's only flower were a daisy, if the world's only bird were a crow, if the world's only animal were a donkey, what a queer world it would be! God called Elijah from a mountain village; Luke from a medical school; Saul of Tarsus from a theological seminary; Amos from the fields, and many others from universities, steel works, coal mines, fishing boats, and a hundred other places. Education is excellent; academic distinction to be desired; but primarily, the thing for which all should look is the imprint of the hand of God upon a man's ministry. Sometimes an insignificant grain of wheat in God's good earth will yield more than a ton of grain stored in the barns of an elaborate agricultural college!

> Jesus answered them and said, My doctrine is not mine, but his that sent me. If any man will do his will, he shall know of the doctrine, whether it be of God, or whether I speak of myself. He that speaketh of himself seeketh his own glory: but he that seeketh his glory that sent him, the same is true, and no unrighteousness is in him (vv. 16-18).

The literal rendering of the Greek text is, "If anyone desire His will to practice, he shall know . . . ." The word translated *"desire"* is *thelo* and this is unusually strong. It means much more than a fleeting wish or a superficial longing. Dr. J. H. Thayer translates it, *"to seize with the mind,"* or *"to be resolved."* This means a deeply rooted desire to know and be in the will of God. This suggests that everything else is brought into captivity to this guiding principle. To know the will of God necessitates a nearness, a oneness with God, and such proximity demands purity of motive, cleanness of soul, and open lines of communicative thought between God's throne and the human mind. To compare this with the indictment, "These people draw near to me with their lips, but their hearts are far from me," is to understand why the Jews failed to appreciate the greatness of the One preaching in the temple precincts. Continually, the Lord referred to His Father, His Father's will, His Father's word; and but for the desire that in all things God should have the pre-eminence, such repetition would seem needless. The Lord was not soliciting support for His earthly kingdom; He sought hearts in which His Father could be enthroned. Consequently, no unrighteousness could be associated with His words or His motives.

> Did not Moses give you the law, and yet none of you keepeth the law? Why go ye about to kill me? The people answered and said, Thou hast a devil: who goeth about to kill thee? (vv. 19, 20).

Here their statements boomerang upon their own heads. They had earlier accused Christ of being untrained, unlettered; now He accuses them of being possessors of the law and yet being untrue to its teachings. The law of God said, "Thou shalt not kill," and while they accepted the commandment in their minds, their hearts were already preparing to do what God expressly forbade. Consequently they were hypocrites. This was a very serious charge, and however true, it was nevertheless not destined to ease the tension of those moments. Probably some of the listeners were people who had come up to worship at the feast, and unaware of the true facts, could hardly believe that their revered leaders were guilty of such inexcusable conduct. They therefore accused Christ of being demon-possessed, or insane.

> Jesus answered and said unto them, I have done one work and ye all marvel. Moses therefore gave unto you circumcision; (not because it is of Moses but of the fathers) and ye on the sabbath day circumcise a man. If a man on the sabbath day receive circumcision, that the law of Moses should not be broken; are ye angry at me, because I have made a man every whit whole on the sabbath day? Judge not according to the appearance, but judge righteous judgment (vv. 21-24).

A. W. Pink has correctly said, "It is to be observed that Christ here refers to circumcision as belonging to 'the law of Moses.' For a right understanding of the teaching of Scripture concerning the law, it is of first importance that we distinguish sharply between 'the law of God' and 'the law of Moses.' The law of God is found in the ten commandments which Jehovah Himself wrote on the two tables of stone, thereby intimating that they were of lasting duration. This is what has been rightly termed *the moral law*, inasmuch as the Decalogue (the ten commandments) enunciates a rule of conduct. The moral law has no dispensational limitations, but is lastingly binding on every member of the human race. It was given not as a means of salvation, but as expressing the obligations of every human creature to the great Creator. The '*law of Moses*' consists of the moral, social, and ceremonial laws which God gave to Moses *after* the ten commandments. The law of Moses *included* the ten commandments as we learn from Deuteronomy 5. In one sense, the law of Moses is wider than 'the law of God,' inasmuch as it contains far more than the Ten Commandments. In another sense it is narrower, inasmuch as 'the law of Moses' is binding only upon Israelites and Gentile proselytes, whereas 'the law of God' is binding on Jews and Gentiles alike. Christ clearly observes this distinction by referring to circumcision as belonging not to 'the law of God' but as being an essential part of 'the law of Moses,' which related only to Israel" (A. W. Pink's *Commentary on John*, Vol. I, page 389).

In all ages, the letter of the word has been apt to kill; it has been the Spirit that has given life. When God commanded that no work should be done on the sabbath day, he did not follow it with another command that all men should stay in bed on the seventh day. Some things had to be done on the day of rest. Cows had to be milked and animals fed. The sick had to be attended and every essential task necessary for the maintenance of life performed. If the letter of the law were to be strictly enforced, then no priest should be expected to work on the Sabbath. In proof that they did work, the Lord cited the acts of circumcision which, although considered to be essential, indisputably meant that someone had to work on the Sabbath. And however meritorious circumcision might appear to be, it could not compare with the healing of the impotent man. The people were biased in their judgment, and this was unfair. Therefore Jesus said, "Judge righteous judgment."

> Then said some of them of Jerusalem, Is not this he, whom they seek to kill? But, lo, he speaketh boldly, and they say nothing unto him. Do the rulers know indeed that this is the very Christ? Howbeit, we know this man whence he is: but when Christ cometh, no man knoweth whence he is (vv. 25-27).

Obviously not all the listeners were unaware of the avowed purpose to kill Jesus. They marveled, first, at the courage and message of the Saviour, and then at the absence and apparent impotence of their own leaders. "Have they now decided that this is the Christ? Is that the reason why they are permitting Him to continue His preaching unmolested? No, that cannot be, for we know where this man belongs; we also know the place from which he came. Whatever the rulers have decided, this man cannot be the Christ, for when He comes, we shall not know *whence He is.*" It is not wise to read into the text something which may not be there, but to say the least, this final statement is most attractive. It cannot mean that they were unaware of the Messiah's origin or birthplace. They all knew that Messiah would be born ". . . in Bethlehem of Judea: for thus is it written by the prophet. And thou Bethlehem, in the land of Juda, art not the least among the princes of Juda; for out of thee shall come a Governor, that shall rule my people Israel, whose goings forth have been from of old, from everlasting" (Micah 5:2). What then is inferred from this statement, "When Christ cometh, no *man* knoweth WHENCE he is"? There are eminent Bible teachers who believe this is a reference to the fact that Jews believed the Messiah would be supernaturally born of a virgin. This would be in fulfilment of yet another prophecy. "Therefore the Lord himself shall give you a sign; *Behold a virgin shall conceive,* and bear a son, and shall call his name Immanuel" (Isaiah 7:14).

> Then cried Jesus in the temple as he taught, saying, Ye both know me, and ye know whence I am: and I am not come of myself, but he that sent me is true whom ye know not. But I know him for I am from him, and he hath sent me (vv. 28, 29).

There seems to be a clear indictment in this utterance of Christ. He affirmed that they *did* know, and that their sin was not committed in the darkness of ignorance but in the full light of realization. They were sinning against the light. Their own Scriptures revealed what they needed to know, but even if their neglect had prevented acquaintance with the revealed word of God, He Himself had spoken to them. Thus, what the written Word had been unable to do for them, the living and spoken Word had already done. HE HAD TOLD THEM WHENCE HE CAME, and if they refused to believe, they alone could and should shoulder the responsibility of rejection.

> Then they sought to take him: but no man laid hands on him, because his hour was not yet come (v. 30).

Jesus was quite invincible until the moment when of His own free will, He surrendered Himself to the mob. (See the homily at the end of this section.)

> And many of the people believed on him, and said, When Christ cometh, will he do more miracles than these which this man hath done? The Pharisees heard that the people murmured such things concerning him; and the Pharisees and the chief priests sent officers to take him (vv. 31, 32).

The faith of the believers was crippled by fear. The word translated "murmured" is *gogguzo*, which means to speak in a low tone, to whisper, to speak secretly. It was this spreading of rumors, this whispering in the streets which stirred the rulers to positive action. Officers were sent to apprehend the Preacher. This nonsense should be stopped immediately! Alas, the officers of the law only made one mistake. (See homily at the end of Section Three.)

> Then said Jesus unto them, Yet a little while am I with you, and then I go unto him that sent me. Ye shall seek me and shall not find me: and where I am, thither ye cannot come (vv. 33, 34).

Three things were obvious to Christ; they should also be clear to us. (1) Christ knew that His ministry would not be indefinite; it would end in death. (2) Christ knew that the grave would never hold Him; it was destined that He should return to heaven. (3) Christ knew that because of their sin, some souls would never share His eternal glory. He did not say that they *should* not go where He would be; he used a stronger term "thither ye *cannot* come." Then, He was with them; they had to learn that to lose an opportunity was to lose it forever.

Then said the Jews among themselves, Whither will he go, that we shall not find him? will he go unto the dispersed among the Gentiles? What manner of saying is this that he said, Ye shall seek me and shall not find me: and where I am, thither ye cannot come? (vv. 35, 36).

Unfortunately these people were blind and foolish. They had no conception of the magnitude of Christ's statement; they saw no danger to themselves. They were the children of Abraham, and their conformity to law and tradition would surely guarantee a place in God's kingdom. They lulled themselves into a false sense of security and paid for it with their souls. "The dispersed among the Gentiles" meant the Jews who lived outside of Palestine. The people considered the possibility of His instructing the accursed Gentiles if and when He were excommunicated by their rulers.

In the last day, that great day of the feast, Jesus stood and cried, If any man thirst let him come unto me and drink. He that believeth on me, as the scripture hath said, out of his belly shall flow rivers of living water (vv. 34, 38).

Three and a half days had elapsed since He first made His appearance in the temple. The feast had reached its great climax, and the city's supplies of water were getting low. Every pilgrim was thirsty! The Lord had just been reminded of the "dispersed among the Gentiles," and of the Gentiles themselves. A great new world opened before His vision, and His startling cry concerning living water amazed the multitudes. Long afterward, when John wrote his memoirs, he was careful to explain the meaning of Christ's message.

But this spake he of the Spirit, which they that believe on him should receive: for the Holy Spirit was not yet given; because that Jesus was not yet glorified (v. 39).
(See the homily at the end of this section.)
Many of the people, therefore, when they heard this saying, said, Of a truth, this is the Prophet. Others said, This is the Christ. But some said, Shall Christ come out of Galilee? Hath not the scripture said, That Christ cometh of the seed of David, and out of the town of Bethlehem, where David was? (vv. 40-42).

See expository notes on John 1:21 for reference to "that Prophet." These people were filled with prejudice, for to them even the loveliest lily would be stained if it grew in foreign soil! They were adept at quoting Scripture, but were inexperienced at seeking their true meaning. Even Satan can quote scripture, but texts out of their context can be made to mean anything. This verse gives credence to the remarks made earlier concerning the people's belief that the Messiah would be born of a virgin.

So there was a division among the people because of him. And some of them would have taken him; but no man laid hands on him (v. 43).

Compare this verse with Matthew 10:34-37, and see again the homily at the end of this section.

HOMILIES

Study No. 29

THE LION THAT LOOKED LIKE A LAMB!

It must have been exceedingly difficult for the disciples to understand and appreciate the contrasting phases of their Master's life. Almighty strength seemed wedded to weariness; invincibility to perpetual frustration. The Lord who stilled the raging tempest slept through most of the storm. The Christ whose words paralyzed the multitudes permitted two of their number to bind Him with cords. He who claimed to be equal with God allowed Himself to be crucified on one of the trees He had made. He appeared to be utterly invincible, but when they thought their Master could never be captured, He submitted and was led away. This was all so confusing. Throughout His ministry, and particularly in that part of it remembered and recorded by John, the words "His hour was not yet come" and "the hour is come" played a most important part. God had appointed a time and a place when His Son should die, and until that moment arrived Christ was beyond the reach of His foes. This may be appreciated best when seen against another of John's pictures.

Christ before the throne

"And I wept much, because no man was found worthy to open and to read the book, neither to look thereon. And one of the elders saith unto me, Weep not: behold, the Lion of the tribe of Juda, the Root of David, hath prevailed to open the book . . . . And I beheld, and lo, in the midst of the throne . . . stood a Lamb as it had been slain" (Revelation 5:4-6). It is truly significant that when the elder looked at the Eternal Son, he saw the Lion of the Tribe of Juda. Yet when a redeemed sinner looked at the same Son, he saw not the Lion but *the Lamb*. And in that one thrilling Scripture we see the dual nature of the Lord Jesus. It was not possible for any man or army to overwhelm the Lion. Yet on the other hand it would have been wrong for the Lamb to fight! "He was oppressed, and he was afflicted, yet he opened not his mouth: he is brought as a lamb to the slaughter, and as a sheep before her shearers is dumb, so he opened not his mouth" (Isaiah 53:7). This is the truth which enables us to appreciate some of the seemingly bewildering passages found in the Gospel.

Christ on the brow of the hill

"And all they in the synagogue, when they had heard the things spoken by Jesus, were filled with wrath, and rose up, and thrust him out of the city, and led him unto the brow of the hill whereon their city was built, that they might cast him down headlong. But he passing through the midst of them went his way" (Luke 4:28-30). It seems incredible to us that the mob would suddenly lose its power, that their apparently helpless Captive could suddenly turn and, without having a hand placed upon Him, calmly walk through the midst of the infuriated crowd. "His hour was not yet come."

Christ in the garden

"And, behold, one of them which were with Jesus stretched out his hand, and drew his sword, and struck a servant of the high priest's, and smote off his ear. Then said Jesus unto him, Put up again thy sword into his place . . . . Thinkest thou that I cannot now pray to my Father, and he shall presently give me more than twelve legions of angels?" This tremendous statement is worthy of consideration. "A legion was the largest division of the Roman army, of which it was, in order and armament, the miniature; 6000 foot soldiers in addition to a body of horse" (A. R. Fausset). Therefore twelve legions would be at least 72,000 angels. It is the potential of this company that is amazing, for in II Kings 19:35 we are told that one angel went into the camp of the Assyrians and smote 185,000 men. On this simple basis it is possible to say that twelve legions of angels could have slain 13 billion, 320 million people (13,320,-000,000) which indisputably represented far more people than were to be found in the entire Roman Empire. Yet the same Christ who controlled unlimited power allowed Himself to be nailed to a tree. Compared with this dynamite, even the hydrogen bombs are but firecrackers! How impossible then to take Christ before the appointed time.

Christ before Pilate

"Then saith Pilate unto Jesus, Speakest thou not unto me? knowest thou not that I have power to crucify thee, and have power to release thee? Jesus answered, Thou couldest have no power at all against me, except it were given thee from above . . ." (John 19:10, 11). Within reach of the governor's voice were many soldiers waiting to obey his command; behind the man Pilate lay the authority of the Caesars. Yet all this could do nothing without the permission of the Almighty. These are the details which endorse the text, "His hour was not yet come." See Matthew 26: 18, 45; John 7:30; 12:23; 13:1, 17:1.

Study No. 30

THE OVERFLOWING LIFE

The gospel of John is the book of the Holy Trinity, for here as in no other place the Father, the Son, and the Holy Spirit are mentioned continuously. John 7:39: "In the last day, that great day of the feast, Jesus stood and cried, saying, If any man thirst, let him come unto me, and drink. He that believeth on me, as the scripture hath said, out of his belly shall flow rivers of living water. (but this spake he of the Spirit . . .)" It could be that the Scripture the Lord had in mind was Isaiah 58:11. "And the Lord shall guide thee continually, and satisfy thy soul in drought, and make fat thy bones: and thou shalt be like a watered garden, and like a spring of water, whose waters fail not." Happy indeed is that man of whom such words may be truly spoken. The early chapters of the fourth gospel provide a thrilling progression of thought.

The Beginning of the Spring

"Except a man be born . . . of the Spirit" (John 3:5). Regeneration is the direct work of the Holy Spirit in conviction, conversion, and initiation into the family of God. Furthermore when a man is truly converted to Christ, he becomes a temple in which the Holy Spirit resides. "The Spirit itself beareth witness with our spirit that we are the children of God" (Romans 8:16). "Now if any man have not the Spirit of Christ, he is none of his" (Romans 8:9). "Know ye not that ye are the temple of God, and that the Spirit of God dwelleth in you . . . the temple of God is holy, *which temple ye are*" (I Corinthians 3:16, 17).

The Full Well

". . . but the water that I shall give him, shall be in him a well of water springing up into everlasting life" (John 4:14). Springing, or *bubbling up* waters can lead only to one thing — *a full well*. This presupposes certain things. It is possible for a spring to be choked. Compare Genesis 26:18, 19: "And Isaac digged again the wells of water, which they had digged in the days of Abraham his father; for the Philistines had stopped them . . . . And Isaac's servants digged in the valley, and found there a well of springing water." It is possible for a man to be a Christian, for the Holy Spirit to reside in his heart, and yet for all the channels of communication to be blocked by sin. To surrender one's soul is but a beginning. Conversion precedes holiness and the full surrender of one's faculties. "I beseech you therefore, brethren, by the mercies of God, that ye present your bodies a living sacrifice . . ." (Romans 12:1). When the Christian's heart is fully yielded, the indwelling Spirit fills his life — the well is full.

The Overflowing River

". . . out of his inner man shall flow rivers of living water" (John 7:38). A continual inflow leads inevitably to a constant outflow, and this river turns a desert into a watered garden. This makes Christian service a joy; this alone brings glory to Christ and success to service. However, care should be taken to consider that a prerequisite is the enthronement of Christ. "The Holy Spirit was not yet given; *because that Jesus was not yet glorified.*" This is still true in the daily experience of some Christians. A private coronation of Christ must precede a personal Pentecost.

SECTION THREE

Expository Notes on the Officers' Inability to Arrest Jesus

> Then came the officers to the chief priests and Pharisees; and they said unto them, Why have ye not brought him? The officers answered, Never man spake like this man (vv. 45, 46).

This verse should be linked with verse 32: ". . . the Pharisees and the chief priests sent officers to take him." The words translated officers is *hupeeretes* and is used in Matthew 5:25. It refers to a magistrate's officer or representative — possibly the equivalent of the modern policeman. That these men had the legal authority to arrest Jesus none can deny. Possibly they too were interested in the exploits of the Preacher and waited until the end of His sermon before interfering. That was a mistake from the legalistic point of view, for they almost became converts. It is significant that they did not say, "Never man performed miracles as this man does." They had been captivated by His message.

> Then answered them the Pharisees, Are ye also deceived? Have any of the rulers or of the Pharisees believed on him? But this people who knoweth not the law are cursed (vv. 47-49).

This appears to have been the angry and ironic reaction of proud men whose aims had been defeated. When they accused the people of being unacquainted with the demands and teaching of the law, they indicted themselves, for they were the teachers of the law. Either they had failed in the task, or had expressed themselves in terms which the common people could not understand. In any case, this too would have been failure — failure of another kind. So many people accuse others when blame lies nearer home.

> Nicodemus saith unto them, (he that came to Jesus by night, being one of them,) Doth our law judge any man, before it hear him, and know what he doeth? (vv. 50, 51).

It is to the eternal credit of Nicodemus that he tried to defend Christ; it would have been easy to remain silent. Obviously the interview recorded in John 3 had not been in vain. With his immense knowledge of the law, Nicodemus might have offered a more spirited defense, but at least he did say something. (See the homily at the end of Section One in John 3.)

They answered and said unto him, Art thou also of Galilee? Search, and look: for out of Galilee ariseth no prophet (v. 52).

Unfortunately, Nicodemus lost a golden opportunity to refute their statement, for one of their foremost prophets had arisen from Galilee. II Kings 14:25 declares, "He restored the coast of Israel . . . which he spake by the hand of *his servant Jonah, the son of* Amittai the prophet, *which was of Gathhepher.*" At the end of any Bible is a map showing the ancient kingdoms of Judah and Israel. It can be seen there that Gathhepher was in Galilee across from the southern tip of the Sea of Galilee on the western side. Poor Nicodemus, he was so overwhelmed by the bitterness of his colleagues, timidity paralyzed his brain.

And every man went unto his own house (v. 53).
The feast was now over; the crowds began to disperse.

HOMILIES

Study No. 31

THE INCOMPARABLE CHRIST

Isaiah wrote, "For unto us a child is born, unto us a son is given: and the government shall be upon his shoulders: and his name shall be called, Wonderful, Counsellor, The mighty God, The everlasting Father, The Prince of Peace" (Isaiah 9:6). This illuminating prophecy provides the finest Old Testament introduction to the Lord Jesus. No other person could have names such as these, and no other could belong to the same category as He. The Saviour stands alone in splendid magnificence; alone, because by virtue of His person and power, He is unequalled.

Unique in His Preaching — "Never man spake like this man" (John 7:46).

The leaders of the Jewish nation were very annoyed. They had had enough of this meddlesome Carpenter. They considered His teachings to be obnoxious; His fearlessness was unpardonable arrogance, and the time had come to silence the upstart. ". . . and the Pharisees and the chief priests sent officers to take him" (John 7:32). Poor fellows! They only made one mistake, and we cannot blame them. The people were saying, "When Christ cometh, will he do more miracles than these which this man hath done?" The officers of the law may be excused for the interest which made them linger on the outskirts of the crowd. Probably they planned to arrest Him when the service terminated, when the people had dispersed, and when there was less likelihood of a disturbance among the disciples. As they listened to His message, their hearts were charmed by the power of the Preacher. They heard the Lord say, "If any man thirst, let him come unto me and drink," and as they saw needy people responding to the invitation, they knew this was no ordinary speaker. He was forceful, sincere, fearless. No man spake of God, of eternity, of pardon, as He did. The meeting ended; the officers looked at each other and, helplessly shaking their heads, returned to their masters. When they were asked to explain their conduct, they replied, "Never man spake like this man."

Unique in His Power — ". . . a colt . . . whereon yet never man sat" (Luke 19:30).

"And it came to pass when he was come nigh to Bethphage and Bethany, at the mount called the mount of Olives, he sent two of his disciples, saying, Go ye into the village over against you; in the which at your entering ye shall find a colt tied, *whereon yet never man sat*: Loose him, and bring him hither." And all who are acquainted with the fury of unbroken animals regard this feat with amazement. It is not easy to break the resistance of a young colt. Until man has mastered it, its resentment can be volcanic. Yet in the presence of Christ, this unbroken colt was perfectly docile. And when the Lord calmly sat on its back, the little beast probably lifted a proud head and rejoiced in the privilege of carrying the Lord of Creation. No other man could have acted similarly. Many accomplished riders would have succeeded in staying in the saddle, but no other man could have instantly subdued the natural rebellion of the young animal. Could it be that the Last Adam was demonstrating the power which God had given to the First Adam? (Genesis 1:26). And did the unbroken colt condemn arrogant people? "Christ came unto his own, and his own received him not." The beast of the field was wiser than the people who watched it. (See Zechariah 9:9).

Unique in His Passion — "A new sepulchre, wherein was never man yet laid" (John 19:41, 42).

"Now in the place where he was crucified there was a garden; and in the garden a new sepulchre, *wherein was never man yet laid.* There laid they Jesus therefore because of the Jews' preparation day; for the sepulchre was nigh at hand." Thus was Isaiah's prophecy fulfilled. Seven centuries before the coming of Christ, he had foretold, "And he made his grave with the wicked, *and with the rich in his death*" (Isaiah 53:9). Nicodemus and Joseph gently laid to rest the body of their Master, and quietly went home. No other had ever lain there; no other had died as He died. Christ was unique in all His preaching; He was unique in all His actions; He was unique in death. He came to give to us *His message, His power; His love.* He was, and is, the Incomparable Christ. "The chiefest among ten thousand . . . he is altogether lovely" (Song of Solomon 5:10, 16).

(Reprinted from *Bible Treasures,* page 113).

The Eighth Chapter of John

THEME: *Christ, the Light of the World*

OUTLINE:

    I. The Light Radiating . . .
      to a sinful woman. Verses 1-11.
    II. The Light Revealing . . .
      the guilt of the people. Verses 12-30.
    III. The Light Receding . . .
      to leave them in darkness. Verses 31-59.

SECTION ONE

Some Necessary Introductory Remarks

Unquestionably, this story presents one of the outstanding features of John's gospel. Nevertheless, the account is not found in several of the earliest manuscripts. It has been affirmed that the early fathers of the Church deliberately cut this story from the text lest its message should encourage adultery. They apparently feared that the Saviour's words to the adulterous woman, "Neither do I condemn thee," read out of their context, might condone one of the greatest evils of that day. If the report is accurate, if the early church leaders did in fact do this, they were wrong, for John's gospel could never be quite as wonderful as it is without this tremendous story. Readers are warned that particular attention must be given to every detail for much truth has been enshrined in the first 11 verses of this eighth chapter of John.

Expository Notes on the Woman Taken in Adultery

Jesus went unto the mount of Olives (v. 1).
The feast was over; the people were already on their way home.

Within the hearts of the Jewish rulers, bitter opposition was increasing. The future seemed ominous. Tomorrow and all the tomorrows of the near future would bring increasing problems. Under these pressing circumstances what could Jesus do?

> There is a place of full release,
> Near to the heart of God;
> A place where all is rest and peace,
> Near to the heart of God.

The Saviour climbed into the solitudes, and found strength to offset the difficulties. Throughout the night He communed with His Father, and when dawn broke over a sleepy world, He was ready to meet the challenge of the new day.

> And early in the morning he came again into the temple, and all the people came unto him; and he sat down and taught them. And the scribes and Pharisees brought unto him a woman taken in adultery; and when they had set her in the midst, They say unto him, Master this woman was taken in adultery, in the very act. Now Moses in the law commanded us, that such should be stoned: but what sayest thou? This they said, tempting him, that they might have to accuse him (vv. 2-6).

Probably many of the Pharisees had been awake all night; but alas, whereas the Lord had communed with heaven, they had plumbed the depths of evil. To decide to arrest Christ was easy; to do it was altogether different. Then some crafty lawyer conceived a fool-proof plan. His associates listened to his schemes, concurred, and during the night hours, a sinful woman was arrested. When the news came that Jesus was already speaking to an early morning congregation in the temple, the Jewish leaders went forth to put into operation one of the most sinister plots ever made against the Son of God. The adulteress was thrust into Christ's presence and publicly denounced. The proud upholders of the law were quite sure of her guilt, for "*she was taken in the act.*" They were also sure that the law of Moses had already condemned her; she should be stoned. However they wanted to know what Jesus had to say about the entire affair. They asked their evil question and then waited expectantly for the Saviour to make his first mistake. If he had answered, "Stone her," the people would have shuddered and left Him, for the murderous stones would have been out of harmony with the tenderness of His touch. On the other hand, if He had forbidden the stoning, they could arrest Him for breaking the law. Apparently, it mattered not what answer He gave, they could defeat Him either way. John expressed truth when he wrote, "This they said tempting him, that they might accuse him."

> But Jesus stooped down, and with his finger wrote on the ground, as though he heard them not (v. 6).

The words "as though he heard them not" are not in the old manuscripts and were placed in our translations to make good reading. The important section of the text is that which concerns the writing of the Saviour. This is the only place in the gospel story where the Lord is said to have written something. Since the inception of the Church, teachers have asked what he wrote. There are three possibilities.

(1) The accusers of the woman had just stated, "Moses in the law commanded us that such should be stoned." This was only a half truth. What the law actually said was, "If a man be found lying with a woman married to an husband, *then they shall both of them die, both the man* that lay with the woman, *and the woman*: so shalt thou put away evil from Israel" (Deuteronomy 22:22). The charge against the woman stated "she was caught *in the act.*" Why then had they permitted the man to escape? If these men were so anxious to obey the law, if they were so incensed against the outrageous conduct of the woman, they should have apprehended *both* the culprits. This was part of an evil scheme to trap Christ. In actual fact, they could have captured this woman on any night. Over a long period of time they had known of the existence of her kind, but had given no attention to her. Probably they had even engaged a man for this act, and had paid for his assistance. If Christ actually wrote the law as it was given by Moses, the words BOTH stood out in bold relief accusing the leaders of hypocrisy.

(2) Maybe the Lord wrote some of the secrets of their own lives, and if this were the case, it might explain why "convicted by their own conscience, they went out one by one, *beginning at the eldest,* even unto the last . . . ." Probably the eldest went first for he had most to hide — he had lived longest! The Lord was able to read the hidden secrets of men's hearts; nothing was hidden from Him. If therefore an old rabbi pressed forward to read the words written by Christ, the fact that he read something intimately connected with himself would be frightening. When Christ answered, "He that is without sin among you, let him first cast a stone at her," the men would be afraid to take the initiative lest Christ reveal what the rabbi preferred to remain unmentioned. The threat of open denunciation would be terrifying, and no Jewish leader was prepared to take this risk.

(3) Finally, there remains the possibility that Christ wrote the glorious old Testament predictions that God is full of compassion and overflowing in mercy. "But thou, O Lord, art a God full of compassion, and gracious, longsuffering, and plenteous in mercy and truth" (Psalm 86:15). See also Psalm 111:4 and Psalm 112:4. The fact must not be overlooked that since the Lord continued to write on the ground, before He finished, all three might have been written.

So when they continued asking him, he lifted up himself, and said unto them, He that is without sin among you, let him first cast a stone at her. And again he stooped down and wrote on the ground. And they which heard it, being convicted by their own conscience, went out one by one, beginning at the eldest, even unto the last: and Jesus was left alone, and the woman standing in the midst (vv. 7-9).

See the homily on John 4:3 regarding "The Silences of Jesus." Here the divine Family, in unbroken unity, rescued a sinful soul. The law of God spoke from the ground; the Son of God was almost on His knees alongside; the Spirit of God moved among the people. Patiently the Saviour waited until the Holy Spirit drove away the accusers, then suddenly directed His first words to the woman.

> **When Jesus had lifted up himself, and saw none but the woman, he said unto her, Woman, where are those thine accusers? hath no man condemned thee? She said, No man, Lord. And Jesus said unto her, Neither do I condemn thee: go, and sin no more (vv. 10, 11).**

Much has been written about this paragraph, and the strangest interpretations have been given from pulpits. The preliminary words to this study explained that the Early Church Fathers omitted the account from the records fearing Christ's words might encourage adultery. More recently, other commentators explained the words of Jesus provided an insight into the character of God — that the Almighty cannot be other than kind and forgiving, that finally all men must be saved. The woman was one of the most sinful people of her day and fully deserved death. Christ hastened to her rescue to teach mankind ultimate punishment will never fall upon anyone.

Neither of these interpretations expound accurately the text itself. The question must be asked, *when* did Jesus refuse to condemn her? He never denied her guilt; she was an adulteress, and certainly merited stoning. Unless hidden truth be discovered within the text, the entire paragraph must be out of harmony with the other parts of the narrative. Preceding the Lord's announcement was the woman's confession. She had replied, "No man, LORD." Readers will remember another verse: "Wherefore I give you to understand, that no man speaking by the Spirit of God calleth Jesus accursed: and that no man can say that Jesus is the Lord, but by the Holy Ghost" (I Corinthians 12:3). While the convicting power of God drove the accusers away, the woman came closer. Her thrilling answer, "No man, LORD," suggests faith had reached her heart. She might have called Him by several other names; instead she called Him *Lord.* The Bible teaches that faith is capable of saving a soul. Continually throughout the fourth gospel, the apostle John emphasized this truth. "This is the work of God that ye believe on him whom he hath sent" (6:29). ". . . he that believeth on me shall never thirst" (6:35). ". . . he that believeth on him may have everlasting life . . ." (6:40). Having enunciated this fact, the Lord Jesus now supplied living evidence that *it worked!* One of the most despicable citizens had just believed on him; living faith had flooded her soul. This led to three things.

(1) *Her sins could be forgotten.* He did not chide her; He never even mentioned her unfortunate past — ". . . for I will forgive their iniquity, and I will remember their sin no more" (Jeremiah 31:34).

(2) *She need not fear the judgment day.* The Lord did not condemn her. God does not exact punishment or payment for that which has been forgiven.

(3) *She was required to face the future, determined "to sin no more."* In this way she could repay the Lord for His kindness and demonstrate to others the reality of the work in her life.

HOMILIES

Study No. 32

THE BIRTH OF A SOUL

The life story of this unfortunate woman might be written under six headings. Together, they present a composite picture of redeeming grace.

Her Fall

Somewhere in her unrevealed past, she began losing her grip upon everything decent. We are not told how this happened; we must not condemn her. Perhaps she was born in a slum where an unkind combination of circumstances united to ruin her virtue. She became a woman of the streets, and each night went into the darkness to break the heart of God.

Her Fear

The adulteress was very surprised when officers arrested her. The sudden urge to restore morality to the city was so unexpected. The leaders were aware of her existence and had they been anxious to reform the city's underworld, they could have taken her much earlier. As far as she knew there had been no revival of true goodness and this high-handed action nonplussed her. Throughout the night she was kept under guard, and when her accusers talked of the penalty of stoning, she trembled.

Her Friend

When the woman was thrust into the presence of another Man, her eyes reflected the bitterness of her heart. People who had helped damn her soul now demanded her execution. All men were the same — liars, hypocrites, accursed! She probably expected the new Judge to endorse their verdict; at any moment she would be sentenced to death. But Jesus stooped down and with His finger wrote on the ground, and in the ensuing silence, she waited hopelessly. When He appeared to be defending her, the accused wondered if she were dreaming. It could not be true!

Her Faith

We have no way of knowing the length of time she gazed at the Lord. We only know that the longer she looked, the more she saw. Slowly the light burst upon her soul, and she knew Christ was not an ordinary man. This Person was good, and kind, and merciful; this Jesus was like God. When He spoke to her, fear vanished. When he asked a question, her tremulous lips answered, "LORD." A new woman was already beginning to emerge from the darkness of the past. Her soul, clean as a lily, arose from the depressing filth of former indiscretions.

Her Forgiveness

Though no actual word of pardon was ever spoken, His wonderful eyes probably expressed all that needed to be said. Growing and glowing faith filled her with strange ecstasy; she felt clean, and free, and happy. Perhaps for a while, it seemed too good to be true, but His reassuring smile banished doubt. Her regrettable past had gone; she hoped it had gone forever.

Her Future

When he said, "Neither do I condemn thee" relief filled her soul; when He added, "go and sin no more," a rugged determination inspired her to face the future. We do not know the remaining part of her life story. Maybe there came days when the pressure of economic worries and the pull of the old life united to drag her down. It is nice to think that in such moments the memory of His words and the vision of His face helped to hold her fast.

This was a new conception of morality; this was a new vision of God. The law given by Moses had been concerned with the stamping out of evil; the Gospel of God's grace was concerned with the emancipation of sin's slaves. Moses spoke of stones; Christ spoke of mercy. The Saviour's portrait of God was entirely different from anything that had ever been revealed. A new light of exceptional brilliance was beginning to shine in the darkness. It revealed the hatefulness of sin; the exceeding kindness of God; the charm and desirability of the Lord Jesus Christ. It is problematical whether any other New Testament story would have been adequate to endorse the Lord's claim.

"I am the Light of the World."

SECTION TWO

Expository Notes on the First Half of Christ's Sermon in the Treasury

Then spake Jesus again unto them, saying, I am the light of the world: he that followeth me shall not walk in darkness, but shall have the light of life (v. 12).

Succeeding as it did the account of the woman taken in adultery, this text occupied pride of place. The Lord's grace had shone into the darkened depths of a sinful soul; Christ was indeed the Light of the World. Mention has already been made of the sevenfold reference to the I AM statements of Jesus as found in this gospel. This *I AM* is the second of the seven. We are indebted to the apostle John for a threefold reference to God. *God is Spirit* (John 4:24); *God is Light* (I John 1:5); *God is Love* (I John 4:8).

The term "light" is significant as it expresses itself in well defined ways.

Light reveals. A man in total darkness may have no idea whatsoever as to the nature of his surroundings. He can feel the page of a book, and be unaware of what is written thereon. A light shining upon a path makes all the difference between wandering and getting to a destination. "The whole world is lost in the darkness of sin," but Jesus came to be the Light, to reveal the mind of God, and to shine clearly upon the path to heaven.

Light guides. A mariner may have spent years taking his ship across the oceans. He might be conversant with maps and charts, but if he be lost in a fog, if he be a prisoner in a world of impenetrable darkness, his vessel and crew may be in terrible danger. Yet if a beam of light suddenly reaches the vessel, despair gives place to hope. The friendly light from the shore indicates the way to a safe harbor. There are many human vessels adrift on life's ocean; innumerable souls are in danger of perishing, but Christ came to be a guiding Light. The clear, shining, radiant teaching reveals the way to safety.

Light cheers. When a man is hopelessly lost in strange country, the light in the window of a homestead means hope, cheer, joy. It promises the presence of other humans; and suggests a home, help, friends. This has been the bulwark of every evangelist, for often the nature of his work takes him to strange territory where loneliness can be acute. When a Christian family comes into view, fellowship within the radiant circle of light performs a miracle.

Light heals. The entire world has become aware of the value of infra-red lamps, of the advantages of permitting certain rays of light to fall upon damaged limbs. Many homes now possess their own specially equipped rooms where families enjoy the luxury once only known in clinics. Light is one of the God-appointed channels of healing, and this too harmonizes perfectly with the Gospel of Christ. "He heals the broken-hearted and supplies strength for the weary."

Light warns. Reference has already been made to the lighthouse. Sometimes the light is placed on a jagged coral reef to warn people of danger and urge mariners to set a safer course. This chapter in John's gospel supports the conclusion that Christ was God's greatest Lighthouse. He warned men of eternal danger and urged them to change their ways.

Light blinds. This is most solemn and thought-provoking. Unwary animals stare impotently at the lights of an oncoming vehicle. The lamps which warned them were unheeded until it was too late to move. Thus it is with the Gospel. John said, "And I saw the dead, small and great, stand before God . . . and they were judged every man according to his works" (Revelation 20:12, 13). Indisputably the Light will still be shining; but souls will be judged and found wanting. Jesus said, "I am the Light of the World"; wise people consider His statement. How dark is that darkness where His light is not permitted to shine. "He that followeth Christ shall not walk in darkness, but shall have the light of life."

> The Pharisees therefore said unto him, Thou bearest record of thyself; thy record is not true. Jesus answered and said unto them, Though I bear record of myself, my record is true: for I know whence I came, and whither I go; but ye cannot tell whence I come, and whither I go (vv. 13, 14).

The Pharisees taught that God was the Light of the World; to them this new utterance was another claim to deity. This was unacceptable and they accused Him of lying. There is no need to look for remote meanings in the text. The Lord merely affirmed that He told the truth, that their inability to comprehend was not His fault. They were in the dark; they loved to be in the dark. If they preferred to live and walk in this fashion, it would be impossible to appreciate the joys of walking in the sunshine.

> Ye judge after the flesh; I judge no man. And yet if I judge, my judgment is true: for I am not alone, but I and the Father that sent me (vv. 15, 16).

The Lord stressed that their judgment was based upon what they saw and heard, and that often their decisions were influenced by preconceived notions. They argued, "He is but the son of a tradesman, how then can He be the Light of the world? This man that knoweth not letters, how can He teach us?" Their decision was formulated even before they examined the true evidence — they judged after the flesh. The Lord added, "I do not judge that way — that is, according to your standards, after the manner of the flesh." When judgment was necessary, the Lord judged righteously. His verdict was just; the Father endorsed the sentence.

> It is also written in your law, that the testimony of two men is true, (that is, reliable and valid in a court of law — Deuteronomy 19:5). I am one that bear witness of myself, and the Father that sent me beareth witness of me (vv. 17, 18).

This was another claim to deity. The Father and the Son spoke identical words. They both testified to the same message; to reject the teaching of Jesus was to reject entirely the message of the Father. (See earlier homily on "The Two Witnesses.")

> Then said they unto him, Where is thy Father? Jesus answered, Ye neither know me, nor my Father: if ye had known me, ye should have known my Father also (v. 19).

With undisguised scorn, they looked around to see if they could identify the second witness. Possibly their lips curled as they asked, "Where is thy Father?" The Lord's answer was a cutting indictment for He seemed to say, "If He were actually standing here, you would be unable to recognize Him. You have no idea of His likeness; no appreciation of His virtue; no appetite for His message. I belong to His family, but you do not recognize Me; how then could you know My Father? You are in the darkness of sin, and are unable to see anything."

> These words spake Jesus in the treasury, as he taught in the temple: and no man laid hands on him; for his hour was not yet come (v. 20).

This text supports the historicity of the foregoing account. The treasury was situated in that part of the sacred house known as "The Forecourt of the Women." The sinful woman could not have been brought to any other part of the temple as her presence would have defiled the sanctuary. In this section of the building were placed the chests into which the people placed their money. This utterance identifies the place in which Christ preached His memorable sermon. (See earlier notes for exposition of "His Hour Was Not Yet Come.")

> Then said Jesus again unto them, I go my way, and ye shall seek me, and shall die in your sins; whither I go ye cannot come. Then said the Jews, Will he kill himself, because he saith, Whither I go ye cannot come (v. 21).

Three vital things seem to be suggested in the text:

(1) *Opportunities do not last indefinitely.* At that time, the Lord was actually with them. His words were instructing them;

His power waited to meet their every need. Soon, this would end, for the time of His departure was approaching.

(2) *Opportunities, lost, seldom return.* "Ye shall seek me, and shall die in your sins." How solemn that the day should ever dawn when men would seek in vain. Possibly the Lord foresaw the dread days of the year 70 A.D. when rivers of blood were to flow from the stricken city. Possibly He heard the prayers of people who desperately cried for help, only to discover they had prayed too late.

(3) *Opportunities denied mean eternal tragedy.* ". . .whither I go ye cannot come." It should be carefully noted that He did not say, "Ye shall not come," for that would imply a decision, which under more favorable circumstances might be revoked. He said, "Ye *cannot* come — ye are unable to come." To die in sin means to be lost forever; to forget to preach this solemn truth is to be unfaithful to God and to men. Unfortunately the people failed to understand His teaching. They were extremely religious, they could not be in danger!

> And he said unto them, Ye are from beneath; I am from above: ye are of this world; I am not of this world. I said therefore unto you, that ye shall die in your sins, for if ye believe not that I AM, ye shall die in your sins (vv. 23, 24).

Jesus did not avoid repetition; John did not apologize for repeating what he had written several times. The theme of this gospel was the deity of Christ, and here the author emphasized something of unusual significance. To deny the deity of Christ was to damn one's soul. *"If ye believe not that I AM, ye shall die in your sins."* This explains why John's message was so unyielding, so emphatic when at a later date he denounced the apostate teachers who challenged the Gospel of Jesus (I John 4:1-3). There are teachers today who deny both the deity of Christ and the fact of eternal condemnation. The question must be asked, If a man is not WITH Christ in eternity, *where will he be?*

> Then said they unto him, Who art thou? And Jesus saith unto them, Why do I even speak to you? I am exactly what I have been telling you from the first (v. 25 *The Amplified New Testament*)

The Pharisees repeated their earlier questions. They knew precisely what He claimed, and ultimately crucified Him for saying such things. In spite of the sustained attempt to destroy His testimony, the Lord maintained to the end. He was the Light of the World. He revealed *the sinfulness of sin, the shallowness and insufficiency of traditional religion, the holiness of the Father, the dangers of eternal damnation, and the only way by which sinners could escape.* "I am exactly that which I have told you from the beginning."

I have many things to say and to judge of you: but he that sent
me is true; and I speak to the world those things which I have
heard of him. They understood not that he spake to them of the
Father (vv. 26, 27).

Consider three things: (1) *His prediction:* "I have many things
to say and to judge of you." An earlier text declared that all judgment had been given into the keeping of the Son. There is reason
to know that when the Book of God is open, the words of the
Saviour Himself will condemn those from whose hearts He was
excluded. (2) *His patience:* Had He so desired, He could have punished them then; instead, He sighed and sought consolation in the
company of His Father. (3) *His preaching:* His mission to earth
was not finished; He had a message to deliver. Beyond the boundaries
of that small country, a world of far reaching horizons awaited His
message. He was the Light of the *world;* through the ministry of
trusted servants, the Gospel should be preached to every nation.

Then said Jesus unto them, When ye have lifted up the Son of
man, then shall ye know that I AM, and that I do nothing of
myself; but as my Father hath taught me, I speak these things.
And he that sent me is with me: the Father hath not left me
alone; for I do always those things that please him. As he spake
these words, many believed on him (vv. 28-30).

Linked with verse 18, ". . . the Father that sent me beareth
witness of me . . . ," this passage represents one of the most profound
parts of the fourth gospel. (Examine carefully the following homily.)
This concluded the first half of the Lord's discourse. If it were followed by a break in delivery, then it was during the interim that
certain listeners expressed their enthusiasm and professed to accept
His teaching. The *"if"* of the following verse suggests their faith was
not yet accepted by Christ as permanent. There are times when
actions speak louder than words!

HOMILIES

Study No. 33

THE DIVINE PREACHER AND HIS GREATEST SERMON!
(John 8:18; John 8:18, 19)

The Lord Jesus Christ was a man of supreme confidence. He
was never surprised into rash action; He walked calmly along the
path of His Father's will. When the crowd endeavored to push Him
over the brow of a hill, He passed through their midst unharmed.
When Peter would have attacked the enemies in the Garden of
Gethsemane, the Lord told him to put away his sword, for had it
been necessary twelve legions of angels could have been summoned
to His assistance. Yet of all such instances of overflowing confidence

found in the New Testament, one of the greatest is one of the lesser known. One day, when critics refused to accept His authority, Jesus said, "When ye have lifted up the Son of man, then shall ye know that I am . . . . He that sent me is with me: the Father hath not left me alone . . . . The Father that sent me beareth witness of me." The Lord Jesus fully realized that when His own voice would be unable to testify, the Father would bear witness of Him. The way in which this prediction was fulfilled revealed the greatest truth. At the appointed time, God preached His sermon — WITHOUT WORDS.

God witnessed to the purpose of the cross

It was nearly midday at Calvary when the watching crowds first became aware of the changes in the heavens. They had been gazing intently at the sufferers, and many had taunted Christ with their sneers and jeers. Then someone noticed the changing sky and expressed amazement, for it seemed that the sun was dying. "Now from the sixth hour there was darkness over all the land until the ninth hour." And God had commenced His sermon! He could not have done a greater thing to witness to the purpose of the cross. Such an event had never taken place before; it has never been repeated. The king of the celestial realm was blotted out by an accumulation of dark clouds brought together from all parts of the heavens. As fearful eyes watched the phenomenon, men wondered if the sun would ever be visible again. Then after three hours the welcome radiance filtered through the gloom, and it appeared as though a resurrection had taken place in the sky. God blotted out the sun in order to testify to the other miracle taking place on the cross. There, the eternal Son was dying amid the darkness of a world's sin; yet the catastrophe was not to be forever, for after three days, He rose again, nevermore to die.

God witnessed to the path of the cross

"And behold, the veil of the temple was rent in twain from the top to the bottom." Horrified priests stood appalled as the rending sound destroyed the silence of the sacred house. Unseen hands rudely tore the great veil to reveal the mercy seat. Only the high priest had seen that sacred emblem, for on the day of atonement, he alone was permitted to enter within the holiest place. Now everything had changed. Christ had died to open a new and a living way to the throne of grace, and the rending of the veil demonstrated the fact that what had been a private footpath walked by one privileged leader had now become an open highway. Anyone could approach the Father. It was not without significance that the break came "from the top to the bottom." Had it commenced on earth, priests might have seized the veil and brought it together again. The rending came from heaven and continued to the floor, so that even the smallest could have access to the place of communion.

God witnessed to the power of the cross

"And the graves were opened; and many bodies of the saints which slept arose, and came out of the graves after his resurrection, and went into the holy city, and appeared unto many." Probably there were many sorrowful hearts in Jerusalem, where loved ones were sadly missed. Bereavement had removed the joy from homes, and families had been left to mourn. Then this miracle took place. The risen ones seemed to say, "Why do you weep? Dry your eyes for we are not dead. The Lord has died for us, and through His triumph, we live — absent from the body and at home with the Lord." In this extraordinary manner God completed His preaching. His wordless message provided the greatest sermon ever delivered in this world, and justified the confidence expressed in the prediction of the Saviour. It was heaven's testimony to the value of the death of Christ.

(Reprinted from *Bible Pinnacles*, page 95.)

The Jewish leaders anticipated that the cross would destroy Christ's hopes of a kingdom; they firmly believed that once His voice had been hushed in death, His message would never again be heard. They were wrong in their deduction. "When ye have lifted up the Son of Man, then shall ye know that I AM." "He that sent me is with me." ". . . . he beareth witness of me . . . ." God was a marvelous Preacher; He never wasted words!

SECTION THREE

Expository Notes on the Second Half of the Sermon in the Treasury

Then said Jesus to those Jews which believed on him, If ye continue in my word, ye are my disciples indeed; and ye shall know the truth, and the truth shall make you free (vv. 31, 32).

Faith without works is dead. Faith opens the door; but works is the evidence that Someone has entered to transform character. There is a faith which is hardly faith. (See expository notes on "The Nobleman's Son," chapter 4:46-54). Good works are not the condition for receiving everlasting life; but they are the evidence that the faith exercised is *genuine* faith. At conversion, the light shines into the temple; in continuing consecration the light shines into *every part* of the temple. Faith brings the light to one's soul; continuing faith supplies exercise for the tongue to speak, the heart to love, the hands to serve, the feet to walk in ways pleasing to Christ. Such devotion to Christ breaks the power of indwelling sin and sets free the one hitherto enslaved. Let it be well considered that the only key to unlock the chains of slavery is *the Truth*. The Lord said, "I am the way, the truth, and the life . . ." (John 14:6).

> **They answered him, We be Abraham's seed, and were never in bondage to any man: how sayest thou, Ye shall be made free? (v. 33).**

This was an outrageous statement, and supported the later conclusion that they were liars. Abraham's children had been in bondage on at least two occasions. They were slaves in Egypt and in Babylon. More potent still was the simple fact that even as the leaders spoke, their land was occupied by the Roman legions. In a deeper and more tragic sense, they were bondmen to sin.

> **Jesus answered them, Verily, verily, I say unto you, Whosoever committeth sin is the servant of sin. And the servant abideth not in the house forever: but the Son abideth ever. If the Son therefore shall make you free, ye shall be free indeed (vv. 34-36).**

The New Testament uses three vital words to describe the condition of an unregenerate person. (1) *Amartolos* means "a sinner." This infers that one has broken the moral law, that one has become guilty of moral imperfections. (2) *Doulos* means "a slave." This reveals a sad deterioration within the soul. The evil which made the man a sinner has now overwhelmed him; he is not the master in his own house. (3) *Exthros* has been translated "an enemy." Dr. Thayer states that it is properly translated "hostile; hating; opposing; one who bitterly opposes the divine government" (Luke 10:19). (See also I Timothy 1:15 for "sinners"; John 8:34 for "slaves"; Romans 5:10 for "enemies.") This apparent strengthening of the power of evil was tragic. The entrance of evil made man a sinner; the increasing strength of that same evil made man a slave; the continuing increase of that evil made man an enemy of God, for now he is not only a slave, he loves his sin and fights for it. "The house" as mentioned in the text probably refers to "the house of Abraham" to which the Jews claimed to belong. Christ said they were as servants; as slaves, and therefore they had no abiding place in the household. Their position as contrasting with a true son was but a temporary arrangement. They could be dismissed at any moment; they did not possess any abiding union with the true family — they were of another household and were sadly in need of the emancipating power of the Lord Jesus.

> **I know that ye are Abraham's seed; but ye seek to kill me, because my word hath no place in you. I speak that which I have seen with my Father: and ye do that which ye have seen with your father (vv. 37, 38).**

Three "fathers" are in the text. (1) Abraham, the father of the faithful; (2) God, the Father of the Lord Jesus; and (3) Satan, the father of evil doers. The fact that humans could belong to the family of Abraham and at the same time be a child of the devil was a serious statement. It will be recognized instantly that never at any time did the Lord try to become a popular preacher, never did He "play to the gallery." He was the *TRUTH*, and sometimes the cutting edge of the truth was very sharp.

> **They answered and said unto him, Abraham is our father. Jesus saith unto them, If ye were Abraham's children, ye would do the works of Abraham. But now ye seek to kill me, a man that hath told you the truth, which I have heard of God: this did not Abraham. Ye do the deeds of your father. Then said they to him, We be not born of fornication; we have one Father, God (vv. 39-41).**

The setting for this paragraph undoubtedly is found in the fact that Abraham had taken to him the servant girl Hagar, and that she had borne Ishmael. He was indisputably the seed of Abraham, but he was not the son of promise. This distinction is emphasized in Romans 9:6-8: ". . . For they are not all Israel, which are of Israel. Neither, because they are the seed of Abraham, are they all children: but, in Isaac shall thy seed be called. That is, They which are the children of the flesh, these are not the children of God: but the children of the promise are counted for thy seed." Abraham was *"the father of all them that believe"* (Romans 4:11). These were irrefutable facts from the Jewish Scriptures, and even as Christ expounded the truth, the listeners realized the implications of His statements. They suspected that He was about to infer that they were as tainted as the Samaritans or the Arabs and this so enraged them that they began to contradict themselves. The opening and closing remarks of the last paragraph are in conflict.

> **Jesus said unto them, If God were your Father, ye would love me: for I proceeded forth, and came from God; neither came I of myself, but he sent me. Why do ye not understand my speech? because ye cannot hear my word. Ye are of your father the devil, and the lusts of your father ye will do. He was a murderer from the beginning, and abode not in the truth, because there is no truth in him. When he speaketh a lie, he speaketh of his own: for he is a liar and the father of it. And because I tell you the truth, ye believe me not (vv. 42-45).**

The picture has become darker! In the preceding verses, the Jews were seen as slaves; now they are revealed as enemies serving under God's greatest opponent, Satan. The words *"lust," "murder,"* and *"lies"* do not make good reading. Satan had not *abode in the truth.* Positionally, Lucifer, the son of the morning, had been in the sphere of privilege. By creation, he had descended from God, but he rebelled against the Most High and fell from his high estate. Thus he forfeited what might have been a great inheritance and became

an enemy, the accursed one. See Ezekiel 28:11-15 and remember that
in a literal sense, the king of Tyre could hardly fit the description.
Consider also the following passage from Isaiah 14:12-15. "How art
thou fallen from heaven, O Lucifer, son of the morning! how art thou
cut down to the ground, which didst weaken the nations! For thou
hast said in thine heart, I will ascend into heaven, I will exalt my
throne above the stars of God: I will sit also upon the mount of the
congregation, in the sides of the north: I will ascend above the
heights of the clouds; I will be like the most high. Yet thou shalt be
brought down to hell, to the sides of the pit . . . ." Christ's illustration
and teaching concerning this point were apt but tragic. He inferred
that like their father these people had been in the position of privilege,
but this was being forfeited. They were falling, and were now in
danger of being cast down to hell. This teaching was unprecedented
and destined to arouse the most bitter resentment. Soon His listeners
would stone him.

> Which of you convinceth me of sin? And if I tell you the truth,
> why do ye not believe me? He that is of God heareth God's words:
> ye therefore hear them not because ye are not of God. Then
> answered the Jews and said unto him, Say we not well that thou
> art a Samaritan and hast a devil? (vv. 46-48).

The Lord invited them to indicate any weakness in His theological utterances; He invited them to reveal any imperfection in His
character. He had explained the truth of their own Scriptures; His
conduct was above reproach. If these things were untrue, the opportunity was provided to say so publicly. The fact that they resorted
to the use of unpleasant names indicated "never man spake like this
man." They charged Him with being a Samaritan or an enemy of
the nation; they accused Him of being devil-possessed. They accused
Him of something of which they themselves were guilty.

> Jesus answered, I have not a devil; but I honour my Father, and
> ye do dishonour me. And I seek not mine own glory: there is one
> that seeketh and judgeth. Verily, verily, I say unto you, If a man
> keep my saying, he shall never see death (vv. 49-51).

In view of the fact that these words are but the introduction to
another stupendous utterance of Christ, it is sufficient at this juncture
to remind readers that the ministry of Christ was (1) *sanctified* —
"I honor my Father"; (2) *selfless* — "I seek not mine own glory"; (3)
startling — "If a man keep my saying, he shall never see death."

> Then said the Jews unto him, Now we know that thou hast a devil.
> Abraham is dead, and the prophets; and thou sayest, If a man
> keep my saying, he shall never taste of death (v. 52).

Actually the words used are different. The Lord spoke about
seeing, or becoming a spectator of death, whereas they charged him

concerning the tasting of death. However, they may be excused for this. They knew what He meant, for in Matthew 16:28, the Lord said, ". . . There be some standing here, which shall not TASTE of death, till they see the Son of man coming in his kingdom." Obviously then, the statement, "tasting death," was not new to His sermons. His hearers understood what He was trying to say. It seemed to be fantastic and unreal because the best of earth's men had succumbed either to disease or old age. Without spiritual understanding and insight, the Jews were unable to grasp the inner meaning of His message and concluded He was controlled by an evil spirit. (See the very important homily at the end of this section).

Art thou greater than our father Abraham, which is dead? and the prophets are dead: whom makest thou thyself? (v. 53).

But for the tragic circumstances in which the question was asked, the Master might have smiled. Students might find in the following the most excellent sermon material.

Greater than Abraham — "Before Abraham was, I AM" (John 8:58).

Greater than Jacob (John 4:12).

Greater than Solomon — "Behold, a greater than Solomon is here" (Matthew 12:4).

Greater than Jonah (Matthew 12:39, 40).

Greater than John the Baptist — "He . . . is preferred before me" (John 1:27).

Greater than the temple — ". . . in this place is one greater than the temple" (Matthew 12:6).

Greater than angels — Being . . . much better than the angels" (Hebrews 1:3).

Greater than Aaron or the priests (Hebrews 10:11, 12).

Jesus answered, If I honor myself, my honor is nothing: it is my Father that honoreth me; of whom ye say, that he is your God. Yet ye have not known him; but I know him: and if I should say I know him not. I shall be a liar like unto you: but I know him, and keep his sayings. Your father Abraham rejoiced to see my day: and he saw it, and was glad (vv. 54-56).

Never were the creeds of two worlds seen in such bold relief and such sharp contrast. There is a fame which is self sought, self engineered, self enjoyed. And there is an honor which God alone can bestow. The one is transient; the other eternal. "By faith, Moses . . . chose rather to suffer afflictions with the people of God, than to enjoy the pleasures of sin for a season; esteeming the reproach of Christ greater riches than the treasures in Egypt: for he had respect unto the recompense of the reward" (Hebrews 11:24-26). To share in such honor, to enjoy the commendation of the Father was of paramount concern to the Son. Anything in opposition to this was a lie. The realization of this project was the greatest star in Christ's sky, and even from afar, Abraham's keen vision saw it. One cannot help but ask if this were a reference to the incident on Mount Moriah. "And Isaac spake unto Abraham his father and said, . . . where is the lamb . . . ? And Abraham said, My son, *God will provide* HIMSELF a lamb for a burnt offering . . ." (Genesis 22: 7, 8).

> Then said the Jews unto him, Thou art not yet fifty years old, and hast thou seen Abraham? Jesus said unto them, Verily, verily, I say unto you, Before Abraham was, I AM (vv. 57, 58).

This was the supreme claim of the Christ, and it left no room for conjecture. Either He was, or He was not, what He claimed to be. If He were not God, the eternal I AM, then He was either mentally unbalanced or guilty of being the world's greatest liar. It would appear that many of today's sects need to find another book to endorse their teachings. The Jesus of John's gospel was God.

> Then took they up stones to cast at him: but Jesus hid himself, and went out of the temple, going through the midst of them, and so passed by (v. 59).

The Light of the World was now receding; the expected climax had been reached; they desired to kill him. They were indeed the children of the evil one; they were truly described by the Greek word *exthros* . . . "they were bitterly opposing the government of heaven." Nothing more could be done for them; they loved darkness rather than light, therefore the light quietly withdrew. The people had yet to learn this was one of the saddest days in Jewish history.

HOMILIES

Study No. 34

THE NASTIEST TASTE IN THE WORLD

The term "death" has a threefold interpretation in the Scriptures. (1) Death is the termination of life's earthly journey. It is the experience which, through sickness, accident, or age, eventually overcomes man, and removes him from conscious association with fellow beings. (2) Death is used to express the state of unregenerate men. They are said to be dead in trespasses and sins; and by that term is inferred the fact that they are unresponsive to the promptings of the Spirit of God. (3) Death is the ultimate tragedy which overwhelms the guilty. When a sinful world appears before the throne of God, each man will be judged according to the facts written in God's records. "And they were judged every man according to their works. And death and hell were cast into the lake of fire. This is the second death" (Revelation 20:13, 14). There are certain texts of holy Scripture which can only be understood when they are examined in the light of these facts.

Death and the Critics

And the Lord Jesus said, "Verily, I say unto you, There be some standing here, which shall not taste of death, till they see the Son of man coming in his kingdom" (Matthew 16:28). This was an outstanding utterance, and can only mean one thing. It will be immediately recognized that neither of the first two interpretations can possibly explain the text. The people to whom Christ referred were hypocrites, and were said to be "whited sepulchres", bigoted zealots who were expert at finding fault in all hearts but their own. They were already *dead in sin*. We do not know how long they survived, but it is perfectly safe to say they were buried long ago, while the promise of Christ's coming still awaits fulfilment. It follows that the only possible interpretation of the text is the one which takes our thoughts to the future. Christ recognized the undying hatred of His enemies and boldly predicted that before final doom overtook His critics, they would witness His triumph. And in that one statement He reaffirmed His faith in the survival of the soul. He recognized that physical death was not annihilation but an introduction to a new world. He also declared His belief in the final judgment. "They shall not taste of death *till* they see the Son of man coming in his kingdom."

Death and the Christ

"But we see Jesus, who was made a little lower than the angels for the suffering of death, crowned with glory and honor; that he by the grace of God *should taste death for every man*" (Hebrews 2:9). The Lord Jesus was never dead in sin, for "he was in all points tempted like as we are, yet without sin" (Hebrews 4:15). It is also extremely difficult to understand how His succumbing to physical weakness could materially affect every man. Unless there be spiritual truth connected with His sacrifice, then a death two thousand years ago could hardly affect modern people. The *second death* means separation from God, a state of inexpressible remorse, the outcome of lost opportunities, the inevitable reward of sin. "Christ tasted death for every man." He took our sins and went into the darkness. When the three hours of impenetrable blackness gave place to the new dawn, Christ uttered a cry of glad relief. He said, "My God, my God, why didst thou forsake me?" The aorist tense of the verb is used in this connection, revealing something completely accomplished in the past. The work was finished, the struggle had ended. Christ had been in the dark so that we could remain in the light for ever.

Death and the Christian

"Then said the Jews unto him, Now we know that thou hast a devil. Abraham is dead, and the prophets; and thou sayest, If a man keep my saying, he shall never taste of death" (John 8:52). It is not difficult to appreciate the problems of those Jewish listeners. It seemed fantastic that this Carpenter should speak such apparent absurdities. Yet as Paul afterward declared, "These things are spiritually discerned." Jesus said unto Martha, "I am the resurrection, and the life: he that believeth in me, though he were dead, yet shall he live: And whosoever liveth and believeth in me, shall never die" (John 11:25, 26). Once again two interpretations are instantly ruled out. Since we were born in sin and shapen in iniquity, and since countless thousands of saints have passed through the valley of the shadow of death, the text can only mean one thing. The Christian will never know the anguish of eternal condemnation, because in Christ he has been pardoned. The Lord Jesus said, "They shall not come into condemnation" (John 5:24). We shall never taste the bitterness of eternal death, because He tasted it for us.

The Ninth Chapter of John

THEME: *The Spiritual Growth of the Blind Beggar*

OUTLINE:

    I. The blind beggar receives his sight. Verses 1-7.

    II. The blind beggar repeats his story. Verses 8-34.

    III. The blind beggar recognizes his Saviour. Verses 35-41.

SECTIONS ONE TO THREE

The ninth chapter of John tells the remarkable story of the beggar blind from birth, and is the outworking of the theme, "The Light of the World." This account is a practical demonstration of the truth taught in the previous chapter. *There* Christ *said* He was the Light of those who sat in darkness; *here* He *proves* it. Throughout the former chapters, John reveals how the Jews resisted the Light and preferred to remain in darkness; here, the apostle sets forth the thrilling account of a man who earnestly desired the light and who, step by step, left the darkness behind. This is not merely a story of the opening of blind eyes, it is the unfolding of a greater drama wherein the eyes of his understanding were enlightened. It is better that we examine the entire chapter before we consider homiletical suggestions.

> **And as Jesus passed by, he saw a man which was blind from his birth. And his disciples asked him, saying, Master, who did sin, this man or his parents, that he was born blind? (vv. 1, 2).**

It is hardly possible to appreciate the implications of this text without first understanding its theosophical background. Among the people of Palestine were those who believed in the doctrine of reincarnation. Today the same kind of people teach that a man must know six hundred emanations — that is, he must live six hundred times, and advance in every one, to reach perfection. If a man progresses well in one life on earth, the next time he is born he begins on a higher level of opportunity. On the other hand, if a man fails in this life, the next time he returns to earth the present failure is punished in that he will be handicapped in some measure. When the disciples suggested this man might have sinned before he was born, they were re-echoing the teaching of their times. They wondered if this man were being punished by God for something done during a former sojourn on earth. The only alternative to this conclusion seemed to be that the beggar's parents had sinned secretly in their pre-marital relations. Some citizens probably remembered Exodus 20:5. "Thou shalt not bow down thyself to any graven image, nor serve them: for I the Lord thy God am a jealous God, *visiting the iniquity of the fathers upon the children unto the third and fourth generation* of them that hate me." It was considered possible that the beggar's affliction was occasioned by the sin of his grandparents.

Jesus answered, Neither hath this man sinned, nor his parents: but that the works of God should be made manifest in him (v. 3).

Care should be taken not to remove this text from its context. That the parents of this beggar were sinners, Christ did not deny. He merely stated that their sin was not the direct cause of their son's affliction. It was better and wiser to remember that in the overruling providence of God all things could be made to work together for good to the people who loved the Lord. God had permitted this ailment in order that a sinner could be brought to Christ, that God should be glorified. God, who is able to see the end from the beginning, planned this episode for a dual reason. The beggar was fully compensated for his part in the proceedings, for he was not only given physical sight; he was brought to know Him whom to know is life eternal. Had he never been blind, he might not have known spiritual enlightenment. God always goes the extra mile in paying His accounts!

I must work the works of him that sent me, while it is day: the night cometh when no man can work. As long as I am in the world, I am the light of the world (vv. 4, 5).

This statement was ominous! "The night cometh" and "As long as I am in the world" suggest that already He was seeing clearly the end of His stay among the disciples. Soon it would not be possible to hear Him, to touch Him, to come to Him. Soon the day of opportunity would give place to the darkness of inability. It was necessary therefore to grasp every opportunity of rendering honor to God and service to men. A light is only of value when it shines.

When he had thus spoken, he spat on the ground, and made clay of the spittle, and he anointed the eyes of the blind man with the clay, and said unto him, Go, wash in the pool of Siloam, (which is by interpretation, Sent.) He went his way therefore, and washed, and came seeing (vv. 6, 7).

Writing of the Pool of Siloam, A. R. Fausset says, "It is *Shelach* in Nehemiah 3:15, A. V. 'Siloah,' 'Shiloah' (Isaiah 8:16), 'Siloam' (John

9:7 and 11). Every other pool has lost its Bible designation. Siloam, a small suburban tank, alone retains it. It is a regularly built pool or tank . . . near the fountain gate . . . . It is partly hewn out of the rock, partly built with masonry, measuring 53 feet long, 18 feet wide, and 19 feet deep. A flight of steps descends to the bottom . . . . To it Christ sent the blind man to wash the clay from his eyes . . ." (*Fausset's Bible Encyclopedia and Dictionary,* page 652).

It is significant that Christ did not promise sight to this blind beggar. The miraculous powers of God are activated by faith in a man's soul. The beggar was unable to see what was taking place before him; the first thing he knew was that two lumps of wet clay were placed upon his eyes. Within seconds those patches of clay could have been removed; instead, the beggar preferred to let them remain. He presented a strange sight as he hurried to the pool, for when people suggested he might remove the clay immediately, he shook his head and replied, "Jesus told me *to wash* it away. Nothing else will do." Christ had made no promise; but already the man's soul was expectant. When he reached the famous pool, he counted the steps as he descended; then he scooped up the water and washed away the clay and the darkness. Such faith could not go unrewarded. This set the pattern for New Testament evangelism. First, men must hear the word of Jesus; secondly, they must believe and obey it; thirdly, they must "wash"; and finally, the light will come. This was but the beginning of another miracle; this was a bridgehead in the man's life; the starting point of infinitely greater triumph in the conquest of his soul.

> The neighbours therefore, and they which before had seen him that he was blind, said, Is not this he that sat and begged? Some said, This is he: others said, He is like him: but he said, I am he (vv. 8, 9).

The man had now become the center of attraction; soon the entire city talked of him, and soon, an immense crowd of people increased the embarrassment of the beggar. The decisiveness of his testimony was to be commended. There were many things he had yet to learn, but he made no attempt to be other than he was. His indisputable testimony regarding his identity silenced the speculation of bystanders and prepared the way for steady growth within his soul.

> Therefore said they unto him, How were thine eyes opened? He answered and said, A man that is called Jesus made clay, and anointed mine eyes, and said unto me, Go to the pool of Siloam and wash: and I went and washed and I received sight (vv. 10, 11).

This description was marvelously accurate. The man did not mention the fact that Christ had stooped down to spit upon the ground and make clay with His fingers. This he did not know, for he had been unable to see what the Lord was doing. He only became aware of the Lord's intentions when two lumps of clay were spread over his eyes. Of necessity, his testimony had to begin there. He did not exaggerate; he made no attempt to make mountains out of molehills; he did not use the incident as an excuse to advertise his own oratorical prowess. He merely stated what he knew to be the truth and this was his unwavering practice to the end of the long interrogation which followed. He knew nothing of the Lord's claims; he had never heard the matchless sermons already delivered by Jesus. He knew that *a man* called Jesus had made clay and sent him to the pool. Let it not be forgotten that as yet he was only a babe in Christ. Very soon an evident deepening will be visible in his appreciation and understanding of his Benefactor. There are people who affirm that Christ was only a man. They admit He was a very good man — some even suggest that He was the best of all men — yet He was not God. The fact remains that if Christ were NOT God, He was not even *a good man*. To claim to be equal with God when one is not, is either the evidence of mental illness or moral imperfection. If Christ were only a man, He should have been confined to an institution or castigated as the world's greatest liar.

Then said they unto him, Where is he? He said, I know not (v. 12).

The transparent honesty of the man's testimony makes refreshing reading. What he knew, *he knew;* what he did not know, he readily admitted. He was not a genius; he made no claims to fame. He was a beggar who had been fortunate in meeting Jesus. He might never become a member of the Sanhedrin; he had little hope of becoming a ruler of the synagogue, but he had met Jesus, and of that he was certain. Where Jesus had gone, he did not know, but he did know where Jesus *had been,* for he also had been there. Such reasoning is difficult to overcome.

They brought to the Pharisees him that aforetime was blind. And it was the sabbath day when Jesus made the clay, and opened his eyes. Then again the Pharisees also asked him how he had received his sight. He said unto them, He put clay upon mine eyes, and I washed and do see. Therefore said some of the Pharisees, This man is not of God, because he keepeth not the sabbath day. Others said, How can a man that is a sinner do such miracles? And there was a division among them (vv. 13-16).

This was a real test of the beggar's courage. It was one thing to testify before the neighbors in the street; it was another to stand before the leaders of the people, before the eminent rulers whose power could either make or break a man. The Pharisees made no secret of their opposition to any who challenged their authority and teaching. Already they had taken up stones to kill Jesus. The beggar recognized the dangers before him. It should be considered that he did not even know whether or not he would ever meet Jesus again. Weaker men might have succumbed to the temptation of diluting the testimony in order to make friends in high places. A little cooperation at the right time would have gained the commendation of the leaders. The man might have asked, "What have I to lose. I must live; I need friends. Where is Jesus? God helps those who help themselves; I must walk circumspectly; I must play it safe!" This man was delightfully guileless. He played it safe by telling the truth. He might never see Jesus again, but at least, he intended to be true to His memory.

Someone within the Pharisaic circle was not ashamed to raise an objection to the consensus of opinion. It was not possible for Christ to be a sinner! Was the objectionist Nicodemus? It was unfortunate that the leaders thought more of the preservation of the Sabbath than of the emancipation of souls. They had forgotten that "the sabbath was made for man, and not man for the sabbath," "The letter of the word killeth; it is the Spirit that giveth life." It is tragically possible to be an ardent student of the written word and at the same time to be a stranger to its truth. It is possible to quote texts and not to possess charm and grace, the true characteristics of a saint. A sound heart is better than an academic mind; yet happy indeed is the man who is able to lay both at the feet of Christ.

They say unto the blind man again, What sayest thou of him, that he hath opened thine eyes? He said, He is a prophet (v. 17).

The danger became more acute. Hitherto they had only asked about the way in which sight had come; now they sought the man's opinion of Jesus. Prior to this point, the beggar had only been expected to reiterate a story; now he must confess allegiance. The former could only result in an argument; this could invite persecution. While the argument proceeded in the street, the beggar considered the implications of the miracle. A Man had opened his eyes; yet surely He was more than a man, for all the other men he had met had never been able to do what this One had done. He was a good Man; He was God's Man, for only God's power flowing through Him could accomplish the impossible. Throughout the ages, God had been able to find men to anoint as prophets. Moses, Elijah, Elisha, Jonah, Isaiah, and many others had been God's good men, but they had never opened the eyes of one born blind. Jesus had done this; therefore He was the equal of all the prophets.

Perhaps He was God's latest and best Prophet. "What do I think of Jesus? He is a prophet."

> But the Jews did not believe concerning him, that he had been blind, and received his sight, until they had called the parents of him that had received his sight (v. 18).

Religious life within the country followed two well-defined patterns. Mention has already been made of the fact that there were both Pharisees and Sadducees in the nation. The Jews — a term repeatedly used by John — probably represented Sadducee leaders who were bitterly opposed to Christ for two reasons. He challenged their authority and proclaimed a life beyond the grave. On the other hand, the Pharisees gladly accepted His message concerning the resurrection, and some at least were kindly disposed toward him. It was significant that the most virulent opposition always came from the *Jews.* Hoping to discredit the testimony of the beggar, they demanded the presence of the man's parents. They were seeking desperately for a loophole through which to offset the challenge of this annoying testimony. They could not afford to be wrong again!

> And they asked them saying, Is this your son, who ye say was born blind? how then doth he now see? His parents answered them and said, We know that this is our son, and that he was born blind: But by what means he now seeth, we know not; or who hath opened his eyes, we know not: he is of age; ask him: he shall speak for himself. These words spake his parents, because they feared the Jews: for the Jews had agreed already, that if any man did confess that he was Christ, he should be put out of the synagogue. Therefore said his parents, He is of age; ask him (vv. 19-21).

"The fear of man bringeth a snare, but whoso putteth his trust in the Lord shall be safe." These intimidated parents were conscious of the first half of the ancient verse; they were so terrified they forgot the sublimity of the closing statement. To be excommunicated and expelled from the synagogue would have far reaching repercussions. This would not only mean a loss of privilege in that worship within the sanctuary would be denied; it could mean starvation, for no employer would invite the attention and opposition of the rulers by assisting one whom they had publicly disgraced. To be excommunicated was tantamount to becoming outcasts; they would be moral lepers deprived of every vestige of social respectability. They forgot the commandment, "Thou shalt not bear false witness against thy neighbor" (Exodus 20:16).

One wonders what might have taken place had they boldly confessed their gratitude to Christ. If (1) a mother's love, (2) a son's testimony, and (3) the power of God had united to defend the action of the Saviour, the forces of evil would have been routed. Unfortunately, the fear of a woman's heart paralyzed her tongue, and her courageous boy was cast out. This mother was destined to live with her conscience. She never forgot her unpardonable failure, and she lost the greatest opportunity of a lifetime. Probably she retained her synagogue membership but lost the respect of the citizens, for they recognized her guilt and probably criticized her conduct. Her husband shared in her decision and in her condemnation. The Bible says, "That if thou shalt confess with thy mouth the Lord Jesus, and shalt believe in thine heart that God hath raised him from the dead, thou shalt be saved" (Romans 10:9). Faith without confession *is a man lame from his birth!*

> Then again called they the man that was born blind, and said unto him, Give God the praise: we know that this man is a sinner (v. 24).

Thus they admitted defeat. They had tried desperately to discredit the testimony of a young convert; they had tried in vain to break the story; now they changed their tactics. Their methods were clever but transparent. Yes, Jesus had done this thing; but since God was almighty, He could overrule the actions of sinners that His Name should be magnified. It had been written, "Surely the wrath of man shall praise thee: the remainder of wrath shall thou restrain" (Psalm 76:10). Here then was a living example of the old utterance. God was gracious; He had seen the unfortunate beggar, and for reasons best known to Himself had used a sinner to accomplish His purpose. There was nothing strange nor new about this; He had done it often. "Now therefore, behold, the Lord hath put a lying spirit in the mouth of all these thy prophets . . ." (II Kings 22:23). This was an ingenious attempt to turn the beggar away from Christ. It sounded and appeared meritorious to give praise to God; Jesus must be at fault in that He tried to obtain that which rightly belonged to God. It was indeed clever, but the interrogators had not reckoned on the growth of the convert's soul.

> He answered and said, Whether he be a sinner, I know not; one thing I know, that, whereas I was blind, now I see. Then said they to him again, What did he to thee? how opened he thine eyes? (vv. 25, 26).

The third degree methods of interrogation and the brain-washing of modern times seem to have descended from antiquity. It was hoped that under the incessant strain of repeated questioning, some flaw would appear in the testimony. One slip would have been sufficient to challenge the entire account. The beggar would not be intimidated; he refused to be hurried. The intricacies of theology were completely unknown, but he had been blind. There were innumerable facets of truth which he was unable to recognize, but he could see the sun, the sky, the streets, the people. This was indisputable. He was prepared to continue the discussion as long as this fact retained its place of centrality.

> He answered them, I have told you already, and ye did not hear: wherefore would ye hear again? will ye also be his disciples? (v. 27).

Here is unmistakable growth. The little word *also* is most illuminating. It implies that the beggar had already become a disciple. The prophets of old had disciples; Elijah called a young man Elisha, and the two of them traveled together until Elijah was taken into heaven. Elisha afterward had a school of the prophets, and the young men gave allegiance to him (II Kings 6:1-4). The philosophers of more recent date had also followed the same pattern in that their disciples or students accompanied them on their travels and gleaned words of wisdom from the conversations of the revered leaders. Jesus also had disciples who followed Him everywhere. If it were permissible, the beggar would seek admission to this noble band. His decision was made; he would be a disciple of Jesus. Perhaps he smiled as he asked, "Is it possible that you seek information because you also are contemplating discipleship?"

> Then they reviled him and said, Thou art his disciple; but we are Moses' disciples. We know that God spake unto Moses: as for this fellow, we know not from whence he is (vv. 28, 29).

They were quick to understand the implication of his former statement. "Thou art his disciple." Happy is that convert who can make his allegiance so clear that within seconds his hearers have no illusions about his testimony. Of this passage, A. W. Pink (Vol. II, page 91) has written, "We know that God spake unto Moses — Such knowledge was purely intellectual, something which they venerated as a religious tradition handed down by their forebears; but it neither moved their hearts nor affected their lives. And *that* is the real test of a man's orthodoxy. An orthodox creed, intellectually apprehended, counts for nothing if it fails to mold the life of the one professing it. I may claim to regard the Bible as the inspired and infallible Word of God, yea, and be ready to defend this fundamental article of the faith; I may refuse to heed the infidelistic utterances of the higher critics, and pride myself on my doctrinal soundness — as did these Pharisees. But of what worth is this if I know not what it means to *tremble* at the Word, and if my walk is not regulated by its precepts? None at all! Rather will such intellectual light serve only to increase my condemnation."

Compare the statement, " . . . as for this fellow, we know not from whence he is" with the earlier confession, ". . . but when Christ cometh, no man knoweth whence he is" (John 7:27), and evidence is supplied that these people were not only inconsistent, they were liars.

> The man answered and said unto them, Why herein is a marvellous thing, that ye know not from whence he is, and yet he hath opened my eyes. Now we know that God heareth not sinners: but if any man be a worshipper of God, and doeth his will, him he heareth. Since the world began was it not heard that any man opened the eyes of one that was born blind. If this man were not of God, he could do nothing (vv. 30-33).

Out of context, the beggar's statement would be untrue. God does hear the cry of sinners, and the sacred writings supply many examples of the kindness of God in responding to the appeals of the most unworthy people. The Jews had just pronounced that Jesus was a sinner; they believed Him to be a sinner of the worst type. His acts and deeds were said to be anti-God; how then could God help such a sinner to fight against true goodness? God heareth not sinners! This they themselves taught, for never in the entire record of Jewish history had any man succeeded in opening the eyes of one born blind. Sensational answers to prayer had been limited to those who worshiped the Father in spirit and truth. The conclusion was inescapable; if their teachings were accurate, Jesus would have been unable to do what He had done. Either their sermons in the synagogue had been misleading, or their opinion of Christ was utterly wrong. In any case, they were making a mistake and should apologize either to misled congregations or a maligned Prophet. If they were blind, by whose authority were they empowered to instruct others?

> They answered and said unto him, Thou wast altogether born in sins, and dost thou teach us? And they cast him out (v. 34).

What blessed loneliness! The calamity feared by his parents had now fallen upon him. Excommunicated, he could no longer expect help from the citizens; seeing, he could no longer beg; homeless, he could no longer return to his people without causing acute embarrassment. Alone, but not discouraged, he went into isolation. The man's testimony had made enemies; the leaders were very annoyed. When men lose their temper, they betray the fact that they are smaller than the thing which upsets them. This probably was their greatest indictment.

> Jesus heard that they had cast him out; and when he had found him, he said unto him, Dost thou believe on the Son of God? He answered and said, Who is he, Lord, that I might believe on him? And Jesus said unto him, "You have seen him; in fact, He is talking to you right now" (*Amplified New Testament*). And he said, Lord, I believe. And he worshipped him (vv. 35-38).

Possibly one of the disciples told the Lord what had befallen the convert, and instantly the Master went in search of the outcast. There is something warm and inviting about the phrase, "*and when he had found him."* It presents a picture of the Saviour hurrying along the streets eagerly seeking the man He had befriended. It should be remembered that the beggar had never seen the face of the Lord. Earlier that day he had heard His voice, but since the miracle at Siloam, the Saviour and the beggar had not met. Probably there was a gentleness about the Master's voice which awakened memory, but full realization burst upon the convert's mind, when he exclaimed joyfully, "Lord, I believe." When Christ permitted the beggar to worship Him, He affirmed once more that He was indeed God. It was an unchallenged law that men should worship the Lord their God and Him only were they allowed to serve. When John fell to worship the heavenly messenger, he was rebuked. "And I fell at his feet to worship him. And he said unto me, See thou do it not: I am thy fellow servant, and of thy brethren that have the testimony of Jesus: worship God . . ." (Revelation 19:10). This represented the thrilling climax to the growth of the beggar's soul. (See the following homily.)

> And Jesus said, For judgment I am come into this world, that they which see not might see; and that they which see, might be made blind (v. 39).

This utterance was solemn but true. He came to save sinners, but the very fact that He had come increased the responsibility of all who were aware of His coming. *To know* was to be responsible; *to reject* was to be condemned. The light of the world resembled the sun in the firmament. Its clear shining light provided the guidance and help so necessary on life's journey. Yet if one continued to gaze arrogantly into the sun's face, the same light would cause blindness. The same sun which melted fat, hardened clay. The abiding effects of the sun's rays were decided not by the sun, but by that commodity upon which it fell. The gospel message was either the savor of life unto life, or death unto death. The Sun of Righteousness was always constant; alas, men's hearts were different, and therein lay the secret of this text.

> And some of the Pharisees which were with him heard these words, and said unto him, Are we blind also? Jesus said unto them, If ye were blind, ye should have no sin: but now ye say, We see; therefore your sin remaineth (vv. 40, 41).

The interpretation of this statement could be very far reaching. If you were blind, if the light had not reached you, if you were still in the dark, ignorant and uninformed, you could not be held responsible for your deeds. Responsibility is measured by understanding. Does this infer that the unevangelized heathen who never heard the Gospel might have a better chance in the day of judgment than many of the great teachers of religion? People cannot be expected to answer for something of which they never heard. The proud Pharisees of Jesus' day claimed to be the servants of God, they were the interpreters of the Mosaic law. Upon them the light shone. They were NOT uninformed; they knew, therefore they would be required to answer for their deeds. Their sin remained before God; their outlook remained bleak and uninviting.

This concludes that section of John's gospel wherein the Saviour taught that He was the Light of the World. His sermon relating to the theme had been followed by a practical demonstration of its truth. In a dual sense, a man had been brought from darkness to light. He had been given physical sight enabling him to appreciate God's great world; he had been given spiritual sight enabling him to recognize God's wonderful Son. At the beginning of the account (verse 3), Christ had said, ". . . Neither hath this man sinned, nor his parents: but that the works of God should be made manifest in him." Thus it follows that God deliberately planned that this man should suffer infirmity. Probably this caused much unhappiness and some doubt. Possibly the man even questioned the wisdom and kindness of God. Yet, ultimately the divine action was fully justified, and the man compensated beyond his wildest dreams. His remuneration was eternal.

HOMILIES

Study No. 35

THE GROWTH OF A SOUL

In the ninth chapter of John's gospel we have the remarkable record of the growth of a soul. A blind beggar who daily sat in the gateway of his city suddenly felt clay placed upon his eyes and heard the strange command, "Go, wash in the pool of Siloam . . . ." He went his way therefore, and washed, and came seeing." Soon afterward he became the center of a great crowd of people arguing about his identity. The Pharisees complained that the Sabbath had been violated; the crowd argued about the man himself. Then someone approached the beggar to ask how the healing had taken place. The reply given enables us to appreciate the man's first conception of the Saviour.

A Man that is called Jesus (v. 11)

Let us try to understand things from the beggar's point of view. He was not a theological student and seems to have been a poor man. A voice of indescribable sweetness suggested the journey to the pool, and in responding, the man received sight. At first, his entire conception of the Stranger was that he had been a man who had paused on the roadside to speak to him. This, of course, was perfectly correct, but no sincere convert can ever remain long at such low levels of comprehension. If Christ be only a man, we are obliged to admit He was a very strange man. He claimed to be the Messiah, and the Scriptures had already declared of the coming Messiah, "His name shall be called . . . The Mighty God, The everlasting Father . . ." (Isaiah 9:6). When a mere man claims to be equal with God, he exhibits evidence of insanity.

He is a Prophet (v. 17)

The heated arguments continued until the crowd divided. Feelings were somewhat strained when some of the people again asked the beggar, "What sayest thou of him that he hath opened thine eyes? He said, He is a prophet." A little reflection had enabled the man to realize his Benefactor was more than an ordinary man. He ranked with the great men of Jewish history. He was a prophet who spoke with the authority of the Most High. The crowd then visited the home of the beggar, and soon a new storm of angry discussion burst over his head. He had no time to enjoy his new experience for he became the center of animated debate.

He is my Master (v. 27)

"Then said they to him again, What did he to thee? how opened he thine eyes? He answered them, I have told you already, and ye did not hear: wherefore would ye hear it again? will ye also be his disciples?" We should consider the word *also*. It represents the man's confession that he had decided to follow Jesus. If the ancient prophets had disciples, this Prophet would also have them; as far as the beggar was concerned, he intended to be among the number. The Jews were quick to understand the meaning of his words, for they replied, "Thou art his disciple; but we are Moses' disciples." Then the convert commenced to preach, and his reasoning was so astute, his critics could only reply, "Thou wast altogether born in sins, and dost thou teach us? And they cast him out."

Jesus the Son of God (v. 38)

"Jesus heard that they had cast him out; *and when he had found him,* he said unto him, Dost thou believe on the Son of God?" The Lord Jesus was most gracious in seeking the outcast, but it should be remembered that the man had never seen the face of Jesus, and could hardly be expected to recognize a Stranger. He probably wrestled with his thoughts before he replied, "Who is he, Lord, that I might believe on him? And Jesus said, . . . It is he that talketh with thee. And he said, Lord, I believe. And he worshipped him . . . ." Thus the growth in the man's soul was brought to full fruition. It would be thrilling if we could discover what happened to the man in the months and years which followed. He could not beg for he was no longer blind. Employment would be denied, for the rulers had publicly excommunicated him. What then could he do? Did he become one of the additional disciples when the original twelve increased to seventy? Did he seek other blind men and lead them to Christ? He refused to be brow-beaten by bombastic leaders, and such courage surely found a place among those who later turned the world upside down.

The Tenth Chapter of John

THEME: *Christ, God's Good Shepherd*

OUTLINE:

      I. The Shepherd Describes. Verses 1-21.
     II. The Shepherd Discerns. Verses 22-38.
   III. The Shepherd Departs. Verses 39-42.

SECTION ONE

A Necessary Introduction to Christ's Parable of the Sheepfold

The tenth chapter of John's gospel supplies one of the best loved portions of the New Testament. The parable of the Good Shepherd has thrilled people in every age, but there is reason to believe its true application remains undiscovered by the vast majority of Christians. Unless this section is considered as a whole, unless its verses are viewed in their true context, there is danger they might teach something not true. Various interpretations have been given of the sheepfold; for example, some teachers have made it to mean heaven, the true fold of all God's sheep. This cannot be true, for how can any thief or robber climb up by another way to heaven? In a vain effort to understand verse 2, other preachers have hardly known how to proceed, for if Christ be the Door (verse 9), how then can He enter by Himself into Himself? Indisputably, this is a most wonderful passage of Scripture, but it needs to be studied carefully; otherwise students may fall into error.

This parable speaks of *two folds* and *three doors*. There is a fold and the door into which and through which the shepherd enters (verse 2). It should be noted very carefully that the Shepherd's ministry *begins inside the fold*. The idea of going out into the wilderness in search of a lost sheep is definitely *not* here. The sheep are already within the fold, and the purpose of the Shepherd is to enter and lead them *out*. (verse 3). Verse 7 speaks of the "door of the sheep" — that is, the means of exit by which the true sheep leave their fold. Then finally, in verse 9 we read of another door, the door by which God's sheep enter into the second fold. Unless these things are understood from the beginning, the parable will certainly become distorted. Furthermore it should be remembered that this parable follows the excommunication of the man who was born blind. He was one of Israel's sheep who resided within the fold of Judaism. Then a door to deliverance was opened, and Christ led him out of the bondage of ecclesiastical restrictions into the glorious freedom of the children of light. The parable of the Good Shepherd is really a corollary of the account given in the previous chapter. Chapter 9 describes how the Good Shepherd found one of God's sheep in bondage and led him forth into green pastures. Chapter 10 explains why this took place.

Finally, before the study of the verses begins, it might be well to understand what is meant by a sheepfold. The people of Palestine were, for the most part, nomads. They led their flocks over the hills and valleys as their forefathers had done throughout the ages. The shepherd always went first; the sheep, knowing his voice, followed. At night, the animals were always brought to a strong enclosure. Walls over ten feet high surrounded the area, and entrance was gained through one door. Throughout the hours of darkness the sheep might be attacked by wild animals or stolen by Bedouins who often raided the sheep fold. Therefore, the protecting walls were always high and strong and a guard remained in the doorway. When several shepherds used the same sheepfold, they took turns at guarding the sheep; one man stayed on duty while the others went home to rest. At other times, a special man was employed to act as the guardian of the sheep. He knew every shepherd and refused to allow unauthorized persons to enter the fold. At dawn, the shepherds called their animals and led them to the feeding grounds. Western shepherds need dogs, but in Palestine, sheep respond to the shepherd's voice. Against this background we should understand the chapter.

Expository Notes on Christ's Parable of the Sheepfold

Verily, verily, I say unto you, He that entereth not by the door into the sheepfold, but climbeth up some other way, the same is a thief and a robber. But he that entereth in by the door, is the shepherd of the sheep (vv. 1, 2).

Two important details must be kept in mind. (1) The shepherd was NOT the door, and (2) this parable was spoken to religious leaders who claimed to be shepherds of God's flock. These men had demonstrated they were not true shepherds, for they sought to destroy Christ and had excommunicated one of God's true children. *They were the thieves and the robbers* who had not entered by God's appointed way into God's appointed work. In contrast to their questionable entry, every detail of the Lord's coming had been accurately foretold; nothing had been left to chance. The prophets revealed the manner and place of His birth, and their predictions had been fulfilled. He was indeed the true Shepherd; He had nothing to hide.

> To him the porter openeth; and the sheep hear his voice: and he calleth his own sheep by name and leadeth them out. And when he putteth forth his own sheep, he goeth before them, and the sheep follow him: for they know his voice (vv. 3, 4).

Many teachers of the church have been at variance in regard to the identity of "the porter." The duty of this man was that of guarding the sheep until the shepherd arrived, and then of introducing the leader to the flock. The porter was often in the direct employ of the true owner of the sheepfold. He knew the owner; he also knew the shepherds, and could be trusted to refuse admittance to all but authorized people. There appear to be two schools of interpretation in regard to the identity of God's "porter." When Christ came to the Hebrew sheepfold, the one who welcomed and admitted him was John Baptist. The wilderness preacher was in the direct employ of the divine Owner, and recognized the true Shepherd. Other Christian teachers affirm that the Keeper of the Gate was the Holy Spirit, that He had watched over the flock of God's elect from the beginning. Actually there appears to be little if any difference between these two. If the porter were John Baptist, he gained his inspiration from the Holy Spirit. On the other hand, if the porter be the Divine Spirit, He undoubtedly used the wilderness preacher. The main thing is that in the fullness of time, God's Good Shepherd came to the fold and called all those who belonged to God's true flock. They heard His voice, and followed whithersoever He led them. Actually this was a scathing indictment of the Pharisees. They had heard the Shepherd's voice, but refused to follow Him. This was all the evidence required to prove they did not belong to God's flock. On the other hand, the beggar had heard the voice of the Son of God, and recognized the true Shepherd.

> And a stranger will they not follow, but will flee from him: for they know not the voice of strangers. This parable spake Jesus unto them: but they understood not what things they were which he spake unto them (vv. 5, 6).

There are none so deaf as those who do not wish to hear; there are none so blind as the people who have no desire to see. All men should be aware of the fact that there are false shepherds. Against these the apostle John uttered his sternest warnings. They would call the sheep and endeavor to lead them astray. Yet every true child of God possesses, to a measure at least, the spirit of discernment. "The Holy Spirit witnesseth with our spirit." The genuine message of God awakens within the soul an instant response; that which is not conceived in the mind and heart of God only awakens a growing suspicion. Elsewhere in the Testament, God draws a line of demarcation between the sheep and the goats; here, that line is seen in bold relief. God's Good Shepherd had been calling for several months, and the nation had been divided. Old and young, fishermen, publicans, sinners were responding; yet others — rulers, rabbis, Pharisees — were critical, antagonistic, murderous. Blinded and deafened by preconceived ideas, *"they understood not . . . ."*

> Then said Jesus unto them again, Verily, verily, I say unto you. I am the door of the sheep. All that ever came before me are thieves and robbers: but the sheep did not hear them (vv. 7, 8).

This was the door of exit. This was not the way in, but the way out — of Judaism and bondage. Christ did not teach that all prophets who preceded His appearance were thieves and untrustworthy. Throughout the ages God had ordained and used saintly men, but these had never divided the flock of God. Furthermore, none of them had ever claimed to be the true Shepherd of Israel. God's prophets predicted that in the fulness of time God would send the Messiah. Unfortunately, others not sent by God had claimed glory for themselves and had led men astray. They had indeed been thieves and robbers. (See Acts 5:35-39). The time had now come when God intended to do a new thing in the earth, and toward that end, the Good Shepherd was already calling out a people sanctified to His Name. The same idea was carried over into the Christian Church, for the word *ecclesia,* translated "church," means *the called out ones.* The people who responded to the Gospel of Christ were separated from sin and baptized into the fellowship of a new body — the Church. Old things had indeed passed away, behold, all things were now new.

> I am the door; by me if any man enter in, he shall be saved, and shall go in and out, and find pasture (v. 9).

This is the door of entry, and is in direct contrast to the door of exit mentioned earlier. God was calling people into a new fold. The invisible walls would be high, offering protection; the pasture would be rich, offering nourishment; the door would be open, offering a welcome. Here and in verse 11 are two additional phases in the ever expanding ministry of the Logos. (See the earlier homily on the seven I AM titles of John's gospel, Ch. 6, Sec. 3.) "I am the door" *indicates how we may enter* into God's true sheepfold. "I am the good shepherd" reveals what we must do *after we have entered.* As good sheep we follow Him through whose saving grace we were introduced to the fellowship of saints.

(1) *A door is a means of entrance.* A building without a door is a vault sealed in death. A divine plan without a door would be meaningless, unreachable, useless. Christ came to be the means whereby those who were afar off might be made nigh. There was but one door in Noah's ark; there was only one door in the Tabernacle in the wilderness. "Neither is there salvation in any other: for there is none other name under heaven given among men; whereby we must be saved" (Acts 4:12). *There is but ONE Door.*

(2) *A door is a means of separation.* To be on the one side of a closed door means to be separated or cut off from those on the other side. Seldom is a door used as an ornament! Doors are made to be used, and when this is done, a person passes from one place to another. There is a vast difference between being inside and outside; when the door is closed, it is not possible to be on both sides at once. It is thus with Christians. To respond to the claims of Christ means forsaking the company of those without, to turn one's back upon that which is evil, and with calm deliberation to identify oneself with the people of God.

(3) *A door is a means of protection.* When the icy blasts of a mid-winter storm beat upon a home, a closed door becomes a shelter. Behind its solid strength is warmth, comfort, protection. When wild beasts or evil men would enter a home, a strong door becomes a bulwark. When Christ announced that He was the Door, He not only invited sinners to seek refuge in His kingdom, but also promised in every time of stress and storm to be near to help. "I will never leave thee" seems to be the talk of a truly Good Shepherd.

(4) *A door is a means of exclusion.* An open door issues an invitation; a strong door promises protection; but a locked door is something to be feared. Matthew 25:10-12 suggests that all men should strive to enter the kingdom of God while the door is open. The time must come when the door will close. "Afterward came also the other virgins, saying, Lord, Lord, open to us. But he answered and said, Verily I say unto you, I know you not."

Whether God's sheep *go in to worship,* or *out to serve,* their nearness to the Shepherd is the guarantee their souls will be fed with the bread of life (see John 6). God prefers gardens to deserts, and to follow His guidance means to reach green pastures and be beside still waters (Psalm 23).

> The thief cometh not but for to steal, and to kill, and to destroy: I am come that they might have life, and that they might have it more abundantly. I am the good shepherd: the good shepherd giveth his life for the sheep (vv. 10, 11).

The thief, the arch-enemy, could mean anybody at war with the purposes of the True Shepherd. The Bedouins often raided the sheepfold in search of food. They slaughtered the sheep and caused havoc among the flock. They had no real affection for the animals and thought only of the satisfaction of selfish motives. This was certainly true of the Jewish leaders who listened to Christ. Jesus, God's good Shepherd, was different. He loved the children of God and demonstrated this by laying down His life for them. (For notes on *the abundant life,* see the homily at the end of this section.)

> But he that is an hireling, and not the shepherd, whose own the sheep are not, seeth the wolf coming, and leaveth the sheep, and fleeth; and the wolf catcheth them, and scattereth the sheep. The hireling fleeth because he is an hireling, and careth not for the sheep. I am the good shepherd and know my sheep, and am known of mine (vv. 12-14).

The *Amplified New Testament* translates verse 13 as follows: "Now the hireling flees because he merely serves for wages, and is not himself concerned about the sheep — cares nothing for them." His task is a job and not a calling. If he could find more remunerative employment, he would gladly accept it even if the wolf killed all the sheep. The picture is devastating. The true cause of God is not even remotely associated with the hireling's heart. He is employed to do something, and even though he hates the task, he does it for what he can get out of it. Yet even wages cannot hold him to his position when his own person is threatened with danger. This was not only an indictment of the under-shepherds of Christ's day, it applies to other religious leaders who exist today. Only fools would deny that the flock of God is still plagued by the presence of such men. It is a cause of grief that the Christian ministry is considered by many to be one of the easiest ways of earning a living!

> As the Father knoweth me, even so know I the Father: and I lay down my life for the sheep. And other sheep I have which are not of this fold: them also I must bring, and they shall hear my voice; and there shall be one fold, and one shepherd (vv. 15, 16).

Between the Father and Son existed perfect affinity. Either One knew what the Other desired, and the fact that Christ spoke of His coming decease suggested this important event had been planned from before the foundation of the world. The cross would not be an accident, the unfortunate end of a mob's stupidity. Jesus was meant to die; He wanted to die, for this would become the agency by which other sheep would be attracted to the one great fold of God.

Many and varied have been the opinions expressed about the

"other sheep" and the "other fold," but interpretation of this verse is not difficult. Christ was speaking to Jews and had already indicated that He had entered Israel's fold to lead God's sheep out of bondage. He had come to proclaim His Gospel to the entire world. Jews and Gentiles were to be welded into one glorious unity, and that unity would reach culmination in the fellowship of the Church. Christ realized there were many true believers outside the fold of Judaism, and He intended to seek them as soon as possible. He knew of souls to be rescued in Africa, India, China, America, Europe, the islands of the sea, the jungle villages, and a thousand other places. Not all are evil who never heard; not all are good who have heard. Yet in this great outer world of the Gentiles were many destined to be God's sheep. These He intended to bring that there should be one flock under one Shepherd. This work is still going on, and it is stimulating and thrilling to know that someday divisions among Christians will be completely unknown.

> Therefore doth my Father love me, because I lay down my life, that I might take it again. No man taketh it from me, but I lay it down of myself. I have power to lay it down, and I have power to take it again. This commandment have I received of my Father (vv. 17, 18).

Within this great passage, the cross and the Resurrection stand forth in all their splendor. Christ was utterly invincible. His enemies might just as well try to pluck the stars from the sky as to try and take His life. Unless by His own volition He laid it down, He would never die. Yet even when He decided to die, He still retained the power to raise Himself from the dead. He was the Lord of life; He was God, the eternal One. That He would die, nevertheless, was clear, for He came to do the Father's will. It was appointed that He should die, that through His cross other sheep in distant flocks might be brought to the one true fold of God. Let it be emphasized with great force that if these words were spoken *by a mere man,* they provided evidence to support the conclusion that the speaker was insane. This Speaker was God, and it was this simple yet tremendous claim which infuriated His enemies.

> There was a division therefore again among the Jews for these sayings. And many of them said, He hath a devil, and is mad; why hear ye him? Others said, These are not the words of him that hath a devil. Can a devil open the eyes of the blind? (vv. 19, 20).

The question, "Why hear ye him?" might be contrasted with the divine command in Matthew 17:5: "This is my beloved Son . . . *hear ye him.*" The Lord said, "Think not that I am come to send peace on earth: I came not to send peace but a sword" (Matthew 10:34). It was inevitable that the message of Christ would lead to division.

Either He *was* what He taught, or He was *not*. It was not possible to assume a position of neutrality in regard to the amazing things He claimed. When some of His enemies accused Him of being mentally unbalanced, they indicated a depravity of heart of which no man could be proud. That others were charmed by His words suggests there were nobler souls in Israel. It would be nice to believe that among the dissenting Pharisees were Nicodemus and Joseph of Arimathea.

HOMILIES

Study No. 36

Jesus, the Shepherd of the Sheep

Throughout the Sacred Writings, prophets, seers, disciples gave to the Messiah many names. Approximately 85 titles were given to Christ, but the name "the *Shepherd*" seems to be one of the best loved. From time immemorial the saints thought of God as being the Shepherd of Israel, and Psalm 23 became engraved on the hearts of countless believers. The New Testament uses the term in a three-fold way.

The Good Shepherd . . . Redeeming

"I am the good shepherd: the good shepherd giveth his life for the sheep" (verse 11). There were all kinds of shepherds; unfortunately, some were a disgrace to their calling. There were false shepherds who deserted their flocks in time of danger, and inexperienced shepherds unable to find good pasture. A good shepherd was one who loved his animals. He cared for their health; he planned wisely how to find and retain adequate pasture, and never deserted them in time of peril. He sought shade from the fierce heat of the wilderness; he found shelter in time of storm, and provided safety when enemies threatened. A good shepherd loved his sheep so much that he lived among them most of his time. They were like his children, and responded to his voice. When Jesus said, "I am the Good Shepherd," He expressed all that is best in Christian teaching.

The Good Shepherd . . . Rising

"Now the God of peace, that brought again from the dead our Lord Jesus, *that great shepherd of the sheep,* through the blood of the everlasting covenant, Make you perfect in every good work to do his will . . ." (Hebrews 13:20, 21). A *good* shepherd is not necessarily a *great* shepherd. A good shepherd refers to reliability; a great shepherd exhibits the characteristics of a genius. When the former hardly knows what to do, the great shepherd will be solving his problems. A good shepherd may be a wonderful man in times of plenty, and yet be frustrated and defeated when drought, famine, and disease begin to destroy the flock. It is then that the great shepherd takes over. He never admits defeat; his medicines save life; his patience, ability, bravery, and knowledge of many things are invaluable in the struggle against enormous odds. A man might be a very good shepherd and yet never become a great shepherd. Similarly, a man may be a very good preacher without necessarily being a great one. Within the confines of a small parish, a man may be considered a first class politician, yet when surrounded by the nation's best and most prominent parliamentarians, the villager might appear insignificant and mediocre. To be good is not necessarily to be great, but happy indeed is the shepherd of whom both terms are true. In every emergency of life, Jesus is both the good and the great Shepherd. He heals, guides, safeguards, cares. He is indeed God's wonderful Son, who rose again from the dead to become the leader of God's sheep.

The Chief Shepherd . . . Returning

Writing to early Christians, Peter said, "And when the chief shepherd shall appear, ye shall receive a crown of glory that fadeth not away" (I Peter 5:4). The previous verse indicates that a necessary condition for such a reward was being "ensamples to the flock." Peter recognized that the pastors of the churches were serving under the supervision of the Chief Shepherd. Their thoughtful, faithful service would not pass unnoticed nor stay unrewarded. When Christ ascended to heaven He left instructions that His followers should go into all the world to make disciples — to reach those other sheep which were not of the original fold. From His vantage point at God's right hand, the Lord was able to watch their labors and appreciate their earnest efforts. Ultimately He would return to reward His faithful servants. This has been the hope of the church in all generations. When Christ returns to establish His kingdom, then shall there be one flock and one Shepherd, even as He predicted.

These three phases of the life and ministry of God's Good Shepherd may be seen clearly in the successive Psalms, 22, 23, and 24.

The Good Shepherd . . . Redeeming

"My God, my God, why hast thou forsaken me? . . . All they that see me, laugh me to scorn; they shoot out the lip, they shake the head saying, He trusted on the Lord that he would deliver him: let him deliver him seeing he delighted in him . . . . I am poured out like water, and all my bones are out of joint . . . . my tongue cleaveth to my jaws; and thou hast brought me into the dust of death . . . . They parted my garments among them and cast lots upon my vesture" (Psalm 22).

The Good Shepherd . . . Guiding

"The Lord is my shepherd; I shall not want. He maketh me . . . . he leadeth me . . . . He restoreth my soul. I will fear no evil: for thou art with me . . . . thou preparest a table before me . . . . thou anointest my head with oil. Surely goodness and mercy shall follow me all the days of my life, and I will dwell in the house of the Lord for ever" (Psalm 23).

The Good Shepherd . . . Reigning

"Lift up your heads, O ye gates; and be ye lift up, ye everlasting doors; and the King of glory shall come in. Who is this King of glory? The Lord strong and mighty, the Lord mighty in battle . . . . Who is this King of glory? The Lord of hosts, he is the King of glory" (Psalm 24).

Study No. 37

JESUS . . . AND THE LIFE MORE ABUNDANT

Regeneration, wonderful as the experience might be, is but the introduction to God's great world of truth. As birth must be followed by growth, so conversion must be followed and superceded by holiness. "That we henceforth *be no more children* . . . But speaking the truth in love, *may grow up* into him in all things" (Ephesians 4:14, 15). The systematic teaching of the New Testament has much to reveal concerning this important theme.

An Abundant Life

The Lord Jesus said, " . . . I am come that they might have life, and that they might have it more abundantly" (John 10:10). Eternal life is the priceless gift which reaches the sinner through personal faith in the Lord Jesus Christ. Language cannot express the inestimable worth of this superlative treasure, but we do well to remember that *life abundant* is to *life* what a reservoir is to a pool. A drink of cool, refreshing water may revive a thirsty traveler, but it cannot satisfy all the requirements of his future. Eternal life brings to a man a taste of the reviving springs of God's unfailing supplies, but the Lord Jesus never promised that this experience alone would meet the Christian's every need. He planned to make it possible for heaven's limitless supplies to flood human souls, that daily needs should be supplied by the inflow of divine sufficiency.

An Abundant Grace

The apostle Paul wrote, ". . . they which receive abundance of grace . . . shall reign in life by one, Jesus Christ" (Romans 5:17). It will be recognized immediately that this statement introduces a theme of great import. Conversion – the receiving of eternal life –

introduces the believer to a spiritual kingdom. This new experience takes him to *a place of power within the kingdom.* "They shall REIGN in life." As the late Dr. Campbell Morgan said, "They shall trample under foot the very powers by which they were overcome." Inbred sin would be defeated by this spiritual conqueror who received abundance of grace from God. It is helpful to link another text with this verse. "Let us therefore come boldly unto the throne of grace, that we may obtain mercy, and find grace to help in every time of need" (Hebrews 4:16). Grace is obtained when we draw near to God; abundant grace is obtained when we continue to draw near to God. Conversion is marvelous; continuous communion is better.

An Abundant Joy

". . . the grace of God bestowed on the churches of Macedonia; how that in a great trial of affliction the abundance of their joy and their deep poverty abounded unto the riches of their liberality" (II Corinthians 8:1, 2). This presents a delightful study in extremes. Affliction and joy, poverty and liberality, are brought together as though they belonged to each other. Indeed, this is the case, for when a man has advanced into the realm of abundant blessing, he proves in daily experience that all things are made to work together for his good. He joyfully exclaims, "I have learned in whatsoever state I am, therein to be content." Affliction is but the somber setting against which the scintillating jewel of joy is displayed. Deep poverty encourages faith to be active, and man reaches forth unto the inexhaustible riches of Christ. If we may be permitted to change the simile, it may be said that abundant life is the fertile soil; abundant grace is the healthy plant; abundant joy is the radiant bloom which sends forth its fragrance to attract and enchant all who come within its domain.

An Abundant Entrance

The apostle Peter supplied the glorious climax to this stimulating study. He wrote in his second epistle, ". . . brethren, give diligence to make your calling and election sure: for if ye do these things, ye shall never fall: For so an entrance shall be ministered unto you abundantly into the everlasting kingdom of our Lord Jesus Christ" (II Peter 1:10, 11). *An abundant entrance.* Let us compare an ordinary citizen returning to his home after a brief holiday, with a national hero returning from the distant fields of battle. The one man returns unnoticed; the other is awaited by excited, cheering crowds. The one man is forgotten; the other is given the freedom of the city. Both men obtain an entrance, but only one is given *an abundant entrance.* It would appear as if something like this happens in heaven. All Christians obtain an entrance, for their citizenship is registered in God's city. Yet the King will be waiting to say to some of His subjects, "Well done, thou good and faithful servant." Perhaps the angels will line the streets of gold, the redeemed will sing the songs of the Homeland. Perhaps our loved ones already there will accompany us to the palace of the King. Surely, these are the characteristics of an abundant entrance into the everlasting kingdom. It can be ours if we gain distinction in the battles of life.

(From *Bible Treasures,* pages 115, 116)

SECTION TWO

Expository Notes on Christ's Continued Teaching in Solomon's Porch

And it was at Jerusalem the feast of dedication, and it was winter. And Jesus walked in the temple in Solomon's porch (vv. 22, 23).

This feast began on the 25th of Chisleu (December) and commemorated the purging of the temple and the rebuilding of the altar after Judas Maccabaeus had driven out the Syrians in the year 164 B.C. It also coincided with the anniversary of the evil day when Antiochus Epiphanes desecrated the temple in 167 B.C. The feast continued for eight days and was celebrated, as was the feast of tabernacles, with much singing and joy. The Hallel was sung in the temple daily. The feast was often called the Feast of Lights, for this was a special occasion when the Jews illuminated and decorated their homes. The temple for the most part would be continually crowded, and this might explain why Jesus walked on the outside, that is, in Solomon's porch, a part of the temple which, according to Josephus, remained from the reign of Solomon. It rose from a great depth and was said to be supported by a wall "400 cubits high, formed of immense stones, some twenty cubits long" (A. R. Fausset).

This tenth chapter brings to conclusion that part of Christ's ministry in which He directly preached to and reasoned with the Jews. It is therefore significant that He is now found on the outer side of the sanctuary. He had been rejected; His message had been criticized. His learned listeners had accused Him of blasphemy and were now rejected themselves. Their house was being left unto them desolate for "they knew not the time of their visitation."

Then came the Jews round about Him, and said unto him, How long dost thou make us to doubt? If thou be the Christ, tell us plainly. Jesus answered them, I told you, and ye believed not: the works that I do in my Father's name, they bear witness of me (vv. 24, 25).

Compare this with the methods used by the Jews in interrogating the blind beggar in John 9. Again and again they asked him to repeat his story. They had already heard his testimony but hoped a discrepancy might appear in the continued repetition of the account. They were not seeking truth; they were looking for something to criticize. The identical technique was used here. The Pharisees transferred blame from themselves to Christ. They inferred He was responsible for their unbelief as He had not spoken intelligently of His theme. They insinuated that He was a poor teacher; that as students, they had little if any chance to learn. In view of the persistent evil of these leaders, one wonders why Christ continued to preach to them. Only the sustained grace of God could withstand such insults. The Lord then indicated a change of method. If their ears were blocked, He would appeal to their eyes. ". . . . the works that I do . . . they bear witness of me." How great is the grace of God. If one method fails to reach a sinful heart, He tries another. He never ceases to strive with sinners until every avenue of redemption has been fully explored. If finally the Lord abandons man, He does so because nothing more can be done.

But ye believe not, because ye are not of my sheep, as I said unto you. My sheep hear my voice, and I know them and they follow me. And I give unto them eternal life; and they shall never perish, neither shall anyone pluck them out of my hand (vv. 26-28).

Two families are seen again in bold relief. The Lord said plainly that His listeners were not of His sheep — they belonged to an alien flock; they followed another shepherd. Probably they remembered how He had said unto them, "Ye are of your father the devil." This was not a studied insult but a plain statement of fact. They did not belong to God, and were not among the chosen sheep; they were lost. Yet it must never be forgotten: they were lost because *they refused to be found.* One truly conscious of being lost does not argue with a guide who offers to reveal the way home. Jesus said, "My sheep hear my voice . . . and *they follow me.*" The true sheep thus indicate they are indeed God's sheep, and to them is given eternal life. The terms used in the New Testament are most interesting. *Everlasting,* as such, refers to duration in time, *eternal* refers to quality in essence. God's true sheep are not only assured of deathless existence; they are lifted to lofty realms to share the life of God — they become partakers of the divine nature. They are not merely God's children by adoption, nor by creation, but are linked with the Eternal Father by *nature.* God's life is transmitted to repentant men; they are born again into the family of the Highest, and through grace are able to say, "Abba Father."

As sheep can never become goats; as horses can never become cows; as cats can never become dogs, the children of God can never become the children of Satan. Christians may backslide, but they can never perish. Christians may lose their joy, their usefulness, their fellowship, their eternal rewards, but they cannot lose their eternal life *for it is eternal*. Prodigals, they might wander to a far country, and finally live with the swine. They might soil their garments, ruin their reputation, and destroy every vestige of decency, but nothing can change the life which flows in their veins. God does not accept a man one week, only to banish him the next. A *man's happiness* depends on his holding to Christ; *his safety* depends upon Christ's holding him. The Christian's joy is sometimes impaired through backsliding, nevertheless his destiny is never in doubt. In spite of much that has been said to the contrary, the eternal security of the believer is taught within the Scriptures. When a man is saved by the grace of God, he is saved *forever*. See homily at the end of this section.

> My Father which gave them me is greater than all; and no man is able to pluck them out of my Father's hand. I and my Father are one (v. 29).

Again we encounter the great truths of predestination running through John's gospel. The saints, the sheep, were foreseen from before the foundation of the world. God who sees the end from the beginning knew that certain people would respond to the call of the good Shepherd. He therefore gave them, in promise, to the Shepherd. If from eternity God could see that men would respond, surely He could see a little farther, to know whether these people would endure to the end. He knew those who would TRULY respond, and *these* He gave to His Son. A great amount of heresy has been taught in Christendom because preachers looked at people and not at the promises of God. Indisputably, thousands of people have professed faith in Christ only to dishonor their profession in times of adversity. It can never be stressed too much that *professing* Christ does not necessarily mean *possessing* Him. Many thousands of children of very tender age have been urged to make a decision which they were not able to comprehend. Evangelists who count their converts in hundreds after a meeting of very young children exhibit their own stupidity and do irreparable harm to the cause of Christ. Eternal life is the gift of God to a sinner who intelligently apprehends Christ. This miracle of grace is endorsed by the transformed life which follows. The man who says he has accepted the new life but prefers to live the old life resembles the American communists who say Russia is the best country in the world, but who prefer to "rough it" in the United States! To repeat what has already been said — when a man is saved, he is saved forever. He may be a disappointing Christian; he might even grieve his Heavenly Father, but once a son, always a son. Such was the teaching of Christ, and His claim to divine equality provided the guarantee that His Father endorsed the teaching.

> Then the Jews took up stones again to stone him. Jesus answered them, Many good works have I shewed you from my Father; for which of those works do ye stone me. The Jews answered him, saying, For a good work we stone thee not; but for blasphemy; and because that thou, being a man, makest thyself God (vv. 31-33).

One cannot help but wonder how often the Lord had been persecuted and threatened with death. Psalm 88:14, 15 suggests that attacks had been made on His life even during the silent years prior to His appearance in the Jordan Valley. "Lord, why castest thou off my soul? Why hidest thou thy face from me? I am afflicted and ready to die *from my youth up*: while I suffer thy terrors, I am distracted." Light always challenges darkness; good always rebukes evil. We are not given details of "the silent years," but the text suggests that even among the young people of Nazareth were those whom Satan used to persecute the Son of God. The people liked His works; they rejected His message, and since in the economy of God these belong to each other, the Jews were finally deprived of both. Yet of one thing there can never be any doubt. *They understood that He made Himself equal with God.* They accused Him of blasphemy because He did this, and it must be emphasized that never on any occasion did Jesus deny the charge. He *did* make the claim; He made it again and again, and He did so because He WAS God. This is the theme of the fourth gospel; it was to make this clear that John wrote this book. If the deity of Christ be denied, this gospel should be removed from the Bible.

> Jesus answered them, Is it not written in your law, I said, Ye are gods? If he called them gods, unto whom the word of God came, and the scripture cannot be broken; say ye of him, whom the Father hath sanctified, and sent into the world, Thou blasphemest; because I said, I am the Son of God? (vv. 34-36).

This verse has created difficulties for some readers, and excuses for others who do not accept the deity of Christ. The Lord referred to the words of Asaph as recorded in Psalm 82. The ancient writer had lamented over the corruption of Israel's judges. They had been appointed by God to execute justice, to pass sentence according to the written law. As such, they acted for God, for when they lived up to their high calling, when they judged in accordance with God's command, they were acting as God, for they did His work. The ancient writer said, "Ye are gods; and all of you are children of the most High. But ye shall die like men, and fall like one of the princes." Asaph therefore had called the judges *gods*. This account was written and preserved in books *which the Jews held to be sacred*. The Lord was using their own doctrines to refute their allegations. In so many words, He was asking, "Why do ye not accuse your ancient leader of blasphemy? Why do you revere his words if they were wrong? And if he were right, why do you accuse me of blasphemy when I appear to say the same thing?" The ancient judges had become corrupt and had forfeited the moral right to hold high office. In contrast, the works of Christ continued to glorify the Father; the blind had been made to see; the outcast had been drawn into the Father's embrace. This added force to the following statements.

> If I do not the works of my Father, believe me not. But if I do, though ye believe not me, believe the works: that ye may know, and believe, that the Father is in me, and I in him (vv. 37, 38).

Constantly the Lord repeated what He had already said many times. His message was endorsed by His works; His claims were substantiated by His Father who permitted those works. If Christ's deeds had been at variance with the divine will, God could have prevented them. God had blessed the Son; He had anointed Him and not denied what the Son continued to claim. If the Son were guilty, then God shared His guilt. Therefore, said Jesus, ". . . though ye believe not me, believe the works, that ye may know, and believe." He could do no more; the die was cast.

HOMILIES

Study No. 38

THE HAND . . . THAT HOLDS SHEEP AND THE HONOR OF GOD!

The shepherds and their flocks had come to the river, and while the men discussed their problems, their fleecy charges jostled each other around the sparkling water. Eventually the calls of the shepherds echoed across the countryside, and immediately each flock followed its master. Westerners find it hard to believe that a shepherd's voice can attract sheep from a surging collection of animals at a river bank, but such is the way of the East. The disciples probably smiled when Jesus said, "I am the good shepherd . . . My sheep hear my voice, and I know them, and they follow me: And I give unto them eternal life; and they shall never perish, neither shall any man pluck them out of my hand. My Father, which gave them me, is greater than all; and no man is able to pluck them out of my Father's hand." Indisputably this was one of the Lord's most wonderful sermons.

God's Great Grace

It is almost incomprehensible that sinners should be able to obtain a place among the followers of Christ. It has been said that a sheep is the only animal incapable of finding its way home. There may be exceptions to this rule, but it is undeniable that the innate characteristic of a sheep is to wander. Perhaps Isaiah had this in mind when he said, "All we like sheep have gone astray; we have turned every one to his own way . . ." (Isaiah 53:6). Yet the entire scene is changed when affection born of knowledge links the sheep with a shepherd. Instead of straying, the sheep are drawn irresistibly after the one who cares for them. Such is the power of grace. Straying sinners are united to the Good Shepherd by the bonds of love, and His voice is sufficient to attract them from places of danger. He said, "My sheep hear my voice . . . and they follow me."

God's Great Grip

"And I give unto them eternal life, and they shall *never* perish, neither shall any man pluck them out of my hand." We do well to remember that eternal life is *eternal life.* When a man becomes a child of God, he becomes one *forever.* If the priceless treasure disappears after one month, it can hardly be eternal. A son may decide to change his name, but nothing can alter the fact that he remains the child of his parent. The father may be very grieved by the conduct of his boy, but nothing can change the affinity of nature. The son may be a poor son; an uneducated son, a disappointing son, but if he has ever been a son, he stays a son. Thus it follows that God's transmission of life to the soul is something accomplished eternally. We may lose our grip on God but He cannot lose His grip on us. "No man can pluck them out of my Father's hand." And if any further evidence were needed to support this statement, I Corinthians 5:1-5 would be sufficient. There Paul speaks of the worst backslider known to the church. His sin was inexcusable and unprecedented. His evil influence had been so spread abroad that the apostle could not even pray for his restoration. "Let him die, then men will forget what has happened." ". . . deliver such an one unto Satan, for the destruction of the flesh, *that the spirit may be saved* in the day of the Lord Jesus." This poor prodigal was as much his Father's son when he was filthy in the far country as when he was clean at home. Alas, he had lost everything except his soul. A Christian's security depends completely upon the strength of God's hand. It is truly wonderful to hold on to God, but it is infinitely more wonderful to remember that He is holding us.

God's Great Glory

God has never broken a covenant promise. His honor is at stake in the strict observance of every undertaking. Charles Haddon Spurgeon, the famous English Baptist minister, is reputed to have said, "If there were one soul in hell upon whom were the marks of the precious blood of Christ, all heaven would be away to the rescue." If God permitted one of His children to perish, He would be a liar. His honor is at stake in the promise made by Christ, and perhaps this is the reason why the Saviour spoke of the *double-grip*. He said, ". . . neither shall any man pluck them out of *my hand* . . . . and no man is able to pluck them out of *my Father's hand*." The objection has been made that a man might jump out of God's hand! However, since God holds the world in the hollow of His hand, the backslider would need to be a superlative athlete to jump *that far*. The doctrines of eternal security do not provide license for sin. The reality of individual salvation is expressed in loyalty to Christ. If a man loves the Lord, he will endeavor to keep His commandments. The new birth entails more than mere conformity to church law; it is far more than identification with any particular body of worshipers. It is union with Christ. No man can be truly united with Christ and not wish to follow Him fully. "My sheep hear my voice, *and they follow me*." Such people are safe in the keeping of Christ and can never be lost.

> My name from the palms of His hands
> Eternity will not erase:
> Impressed on His heart it remains,
> In marks of indelible grace.
> And I to the end shall endure,
> As sure as the earnest is given;
> More happy, but not more secure,
> When glorified with Him in heaven.

SECTION THREE

Expository Notes on Christ's Departure From Jerusalem

Therefore they sought again to take him: but he escaped out of their hand (v. 39).

The end had never for a moment been in doubt. They had continued the interrogation, not in a genuine attempt to gain information but in the vain hope that a slip of the tongue would embarrass Jesus. His transparent honesty, His flawless evidence, His direct challenge to their own imperfection aroused their deepest animosity, and when they could no longer engage Him in debate, their anger provided a veneer for their impotence. Yet they might just as well have tried to empty the ocean. It was not possible to capture the impregnable One until He was willing to permit their deed. However, there were other details now to be considered. Maddened and infuriated by their own helplessness, these bigoted leaders might vent their spleen on other people — the other sheep of the flock. Knowing all this, Jesus quietly withdrew. It is wise to remember His example. There are times to speak; there are other occasions when it is better to be silent. Spiritual warfare demands the study of advance and retreat. Sometimes, the longest way round is the shortest way home.

And went away again beyond Jordan into the place where John at first baptized; and there abode (v. 40).

Among the old familiar landmarks, Jesus found rest; amid the freshness and purity of God's good handiwork, He relaxed. Even greater storm clouds were beginning to gather on His horizon; He needed new strength to offset the challenge of the future, and to obtain this, Christ withdrew from the noisy city. Most tired ministers seek relaxation on a golf course, or in a fishing boat, or on a river bank. Jesus went into the solitude where none but God could intrude. Probably we should be better fitted for our tasks if we emulated His example.

> There is a place of quiet rest,
>   Near to the heart of God.
> A place where sin cannot molest,
>   Near to the heart of God.
> There is a place of comfort sweet,
>   Near to the heart of God.
> A place where we our Saviour meet,
>   Near to the heart of God.
> There is a place of full release,
>   Near to the heart of God.
> A place where all is joy and peace,
>   Near to the heart of God.
> O Jesus, blest Redeemer,
>   Sent from the heart of God,
> Hold us, who wait before Thee,
>   Near to the heart of God.

And many resorted unto him, and said, John did no miracle: but all things that John spake of this man were true. And many believed on him there (vv. 41, 42).

This was one of the greatest compliments ever paid to the Baptist. The testimony of the onlookers was accurate. John never performed any miracle; he never *tried* to perform one. He knew the task to which he had been appointed, and to the very end of his ministry was true to his commission. Of him it was well said, ". . . Among those that are born of women, there is not a greater prophet than John the Baptist." He was a prince among preachers, a saint among men, yet ". . . he that is least in the kingdom of God is greater than he" (Luke 7:28). This does not mean to infer that the most disappointing Christian was greater than John Baptist. John for a forerunner of the Lord who in turn came to establish a spiritual kingdom. To be the least *inside* that kingdom is to be greater than the greatest *outside* that kingdom. John Baptist was truly a great man outside the kingdom — that is, before Christ came; nevertheless, once John entered into the kingdom of God, he became an even greater man than he ever was before. Thus did Christ teach the superlative value of spiritual realities; thus did He urge men to seek those things which are above.

HOMILIES

Study No. 39

THE HALLMARKS OF A TRUE PROPHET

A prophet is one who fears God and no one else. A true prophet of God looks so often into the face of his Lord that other faces cease to be important. John Baptist was said by Christ to be the greatest prophet, and a study of the New Testament suggests why this was so.

He was selfless

"And the same John had his raiment of camel's hair, and a leathern girdle about his loins; and his meat was locusts and wild honey" (Matthew 3:4). The power of John was such that without much difficulty he could have had friends in high places. A word spoken in the right place, a suggestion made to the right people, and the preacher could have been domiciled in the most luxurious accommodation possible. He preferred to remain where he was.

He was courageous

"But when he saw many of the Pharisees and Sadducees come to his baptism, he said unto them, O generation of vipers, who hath warned you to flee from the wrath to come?" (Matthew 3:7). Possibly some of the modern professors would brand this as poor psychology, a lack of tact, an inexcusable error. If the effect of the critics' ministry was even comparable with that of John Baptist, the moderns would be entitled to a hearing. John Baptist lived so close to God, he forgot to be afraid of anyone. He had no idea how to become a soothsayer!

He was powerful

He had no radio nor television programs; he never had a sponsoring committee, and had no organized team going ahead to prepare the way. He never spent a cent on advertising, and had no church, mission hall, choir, young people, or any other to guarantee assistance, yet ". . . there went out unto him, all the land of Judea, and they of Jerusalem, and were all baptized of him in the river of Jordan, confessing their sins" (Mark 1:5).

He was humble

Such astonishing success would have "gone to the head" of most evangelists, but this preacher remembered to say, ". . . There cometh one mightier than I after me, whose shoes I am not worthy to stoop down and unloose."

He was holy

Even ungodly men recognized the quality of his life. "For Herod feared John, knowing that he was a just man and an holy . . . ." This was the king's only complaint. John was so close to God that he hated sin; he was so sure of God's message, he could not be silenced (Mark 6:20).

He was commended by Christ

". . . Jesus began to speak unto the people concerning John, What went ye out into the wilderness for to see? A reed shaken by the wind? A man clothed in soft raiment? Behold they which are gorgeously apparelled, and live delicately, are in kings' courts. But what went ye out for to see? A prophet? Yea, I say unto you, and much more than a prophet . . ." (Luke 7:24-28).

John Baptist was a man whom God could use. There are still vacancies for all men of his type.

The Eleventh Chapter of John

THEME: *The Raising of Lazarus From the Dead*

OUTLINE:

    I. The Delayed Miracle. Verses 1-46.
    II. The Decisive Meeting. Verses 47-53.
    III. The Discreet Master. Verses 54-57.

SECTION ONE

Expository Notes on the Raising of Lazarus

It is generally agreed in theological circles that the eleventh chapter of John presents one of the most vital episodes in the life and ministry of the Saviour. Nevertheless, John alone records the raising of Lazarus and this fact suggests questions. Matthew Henry prefaces his expository notes on the incident with these words: "The raising of Lazarus to life . . . is recorded only by this evangelist; for the other three confined themselves to what Christ did in Galilee, and scarcely ever carried their history in Jerusalem until the passion-week; whereas John's memoirs relate chiefly to what passed in Jerusalem. It is more largely recorded than any other of Christ's miracles because it was an earnest of that which was to be the crowning proof of all — Christ's own resurrection."

Before we begin the detailed study of the chapter, it might be well to remind ourselves that while all Scripture is given by inspiration of God, interpretations sometimes differ. Since the inception of the Church, preachers have praised the devotion of Mary of Bethany, and many still regard her as second only to Mary the mother of the Lord. Throughout the gospel story her charm and grace appear, and even the Lord commended her rare insight into spiritual necessities. Probably these details account for the fact that commentators praised the virtues of this remarkable disciple, and few if any dared to suggest that occasionally she too could make mistakes.

Mention is now made of this fact because within the compass of the study of this chapter, students must examine the record in the light of two possibilities. Mary of Bethany has always been regarded as a shining example of Christian resignation; her patience in suffering, her unfailing trust in Christ even in times of adversity, her love and adoration have been the theme of innumerable sermons. This old and very popular interpretation may well be justified but, to say the least, there is another side to the picture which, though it may not flatter this wonderful woman, will at least remind us that she was human. Mary's trust may not have been flawless; perhaps like millions of her sisters, in the face of acute disappointment she became hurt, doubtful, reproachful. If this were indeed the case, it in no manner detracts from her loveliness; rather, it endears her to all the family of God. As we consider the chapter itself, John's record will explain why mention has been made of the two-fold interpretation of this thrilling miracle.

> Now a certain man was sick, named Lazarus, of Bethany, the town of Mary and her sister Martha. (It was that Mary which anointed the Lord with ointment, and wiped His feet with her hair, whose brother Lazarus was sick.) Therefore his sisters sent unto Him, saying, Lord, behold, he whom thou lovest is sick (vv. 1-3).

Here we are introduced to the most famous home of the first century. John alone, in the eleventh and twelfth chapters of his gospel, makes mention of Lazarus, who seems to have been a younger brother, a man of quiet disposition and great affection. Some commentators have even suggested that he was the wealthy young ruler who came to Christ to ask how he could inherit eternal life. Many and varied have been the theories and suggestions made throughout the Christian era, but it is wiser and safer to stay close to the text. There is no conclusive evidence that such was the case.

However, one detail deserves mention for, to say the least, its possibilities are certainly interesting. Ganneau discovered close to Jerusalem an ancient tomb, probably dating back to the first century, in which were found the names of Simon, Martha, and Lazarus. Concerning this and other relevant matter, Fausset says, "The subordinate position of Lazarus at their feast in Christ's honor (John 12:2) makes it likely he was the youngest. Moreover, the house is called that of Simon the leper, (Matthew 26:6; Mark 14:3) who was probably their father." (See notes on the following chapter.) "Their friends from Jerusalem (John 19:19) according to John's use of 'The Jews' were of the ruling elders and Pharisees. The feast, the costly ointment, the family funeral cave, all bespeak good social position." The Lord had been welcomed to this home, and was greatly attracted to the young brother. It was perfectly natural and true for the sisters to say, "Lord, behold, he whom thou lovest is sick." Looking back over a half century, John seems mindful of the fact that there had been others Marys, and other women who had similarly worshiped the Lord, and was careful to identify the woman about whom he was to write.

We have no means of knowing whether the statement contained in verse 3 represents the entire message sent to Jesus. If this were all, then it is worthy of note that these sisters did not make any request. Had they said, "Lord, behold, he whom thou lovest is sick; please come quickly to help him and us," the reading would have been logical and understandable. Possibly they had so much confidence in their Master that it was unnecessary to ask anything. To know the existence of need would be sufficient to bring Christ immediately. Faith saw no difficulties and anticipated no problems. It only remained to tell Christ, *and before they could call He would answer.* This, unquestionably, was most wonderful, but there are times when, as the heavens are high above the earth, God's ways are higher than ours. Sometimes we see human needs so clearly that we forget that God sees them too. There can be no doubt that the faith within the two sisters strengthened the belief that Christ would respond eagerly to their unspoken petition. This He did not do, and the resulting situation was surely filled with great drama.

When Jesus heard that, he said, This sickness is not unto death, but the glory of God, that the Son of God might be glorified thereby (v. 4).

Death, as we know it, is a termination of life upon this earth; it is a permanent farewell to loved ones and home. In this intimate and sad sense, the death of Lazarus was not death. There can be no doubt that he had truly died, but in view of the plans of Christ to restore Lazarus to his family, this incident was not truly "unto death." Three things deserve consideration, for they relate intimately to human suffering.

(1) *God Perceived.* The Lord was not surprised when He heard of the catastrophe overwhelming the home in Bethany. Whether or not He actually planned the unwelcome occurrence we do not know. There are many who declare that all sickness is out of the will of God; that anything which causes suffering should never be accepted; that such things should be offset and overcome by triumphant faith. Be that as it may, that God foresaw the coming of this illness is beyond doubt, for subsequent events provided a living example of the text, "And we know that ALL THINGS work together for good to them that love God, to them who are the called according to His purpose" (Romans 8:28).

(2) *God Permitted.* Had God desired, He could have preserved the health of Lazarus and prevented the sickness which led to a premature death. That He did not do this provides food for thought.

If a God of love permits suffering, then all sickness cannot be classified as needless. If we believe that God sees the end from the beginning, if we believe that God earnestly cares for those who trust Him, then we should learn to look beyond our overcast skies. Faith sees not the darkness of the heavens but the sun which turns clouds to rain.

(3) *God Planned.* "... *that the Son of God might be glorified thereby.*" Afterward, Mary and Martha were able to look back to see in every detail of those trying events the fulfilment of the will of God. Nevertheless, experience belongs to the past; faith belongs to the future, for "... faith is the substance of things hoped for, the evidence of things not seen" (Hebrews 11:1). Happy indeed is that soul who is able to sing:

> God holds the key to all unknown,
> And I am glad.
> If other hands should hold the key
> Or if He trusted it to me,
> I might be sad.

Now Jesus loved Martha, and her sister, and Lazarus. When He had heard therefore that he was sick, he abode two days still in the place where he was (vv. 5, 6).

By any standard this must remain a strange verse. The word "therefore" appears to be the key to unlock its hidden treasures. Human reasoning suggests Christ's great love for this family would send Him hurrying to Bethany, but that was not to be. *The delays* of the Lord were always begotten by unerring wisdom. God not only does the right things; He does them at the right time.

> God moves in a mysterious way,
> His wonders to perform;
> He plants His footsteps in the sea
> And rides upon the storm.
> Deep in unfathomable mines
> Of never failing skill;
> He treasures up His bright designs
> And works His sovereign will.

Sometimes God is more able to respond to the prayers of His children by doing nothing.

Then after that saith he to his disciples, Let us go into Judea again. His disciples say unto him, Master, the Jews of late sought to stone thee; and goeth thou thither again? Jesus answered, Are there not twelve hours in the day? If any man walk in the day, he stumbleth not, because he seeth the light of this world. But if any man walk in the night, he stumbleth because there is no light in him (vv. 7-10).

With great deliberation, the Lord allowed His friends to enter into their period of distress, and only when it was quite obvious that

Lazarus had died did He leave His meetings. The objection made by the disciples was quite logical, but the Lord's answer suggested there comes a time when necessity demands action. Fear of reprisals and the threat of persecution should never hinder our walking with God. It is wrong to proceed when God says, "Halt"; it is equally foolish to linger when God says, "Walk."

> These things said he; and after that he saith unto them, Our friend Lazarus sleepeth; but I go that I may awake him out of sleep. Then said his disciples, Lord, if he sleep, he shall do well. Howbeit, Jesus spake of his death, but they thought he had spoken of taking rest in sleep (vv. 11-13).

Apart from this incident, there was nothing spectacular about the man Lazarus; in every other story relating to the Bethany home Mary and Martha occupied pride of place. There is no record that he ever preached, or sang, or testified of Christ. It is not said that he ever brought anyone to Jesus, but the Master's words, "our friend," suggests this silent man had endeared himself to the Lord and His followers. His life had been eloquent, his charm inescapable, his influence captivating. He had won an abiding place in the affections of the most intimate followers of Christ, and this remarkable victory had been achieved without ostentation and fuss. Perhaps we should consider this fact. Some men need to advertise their virtues in order to make people aware they are alive. Happy is that man whose silence is always golden.

That Christ should refer to death as "sleep" seems to be in keeping with Scripture. It has been well said that no man ever died in the presence of Christ. Had such happened it would have been an irrefutable challenge to the Lord of life. When Luke wrote of the homecall of Stephen, he declared, "And when he had said this, *he fell asleep*" (Acts 7:60). Following the same pattern of expression, Paul said, "For if we believe that Jesus died and rose again, even so them also *which sleep in Jesus will God bring with him*" (I Thessalonians 4:14). As far as the saints are concerned, the resurrection of Christ meant the death of death. The analogy of sleep suggests two vital things.

(1) *Sleep soothes.* Without rest in sleep, life would become unbearable. Excessive toil leads to weariness and, for this, sleep alone is the cure. Sleep is the link between the past and the future; under its amazing influence tired minds are refreshed; human weaknesses overcome.

(2) *Sleep strengthens.* A man may go to his bed unspeakably weary; he rises strengthened to meet the demands of the new day. Along the highways of life, sleep is not a terminus but a junction. There we change trains, so that with replenished supplies we can

make better progress after a new start. The soothing power of sleep looks back; the strengthening power of sleep looks ahead. In both these respects the term aptly describes a believer's death. We do not know what duties, what opportunities for further service await us in the new world. We know only that to fall asleep in Christ is to know the soothing and healing power of His grace. We gain from the experience a new energy to fit us for true citizenship in the eternal city.

> Then said Jesus unto them plainly, Lazarus is dead. And I am glad for your sakes that I was not there, to the intent ye may believe; nevertheless let us go unto him. Then said Thomas, which is called Didymus, unto his fellow disciples, Let us also go, that we may die with him (vv. 14-16).

A most interesting and rewarding Bible study for all students is the tracing of the things which caused gladness for Christ. *Thomas* in Hebrew and *Didymus* in Greek mean "a twin." It is therefore most likely that this disciple was one of twins, and reference was always made to him in the light of this fact, possibly to differentiate between him and others who bore the same name. It is worthy of consideration that the disciple famous for his lack of faith should exhibit such great devotion. Probably this man puts us to shame. He preferred to accompany Jesus to death rather than to remain and live alone. Thomas believed that life without Christ would have been worse than death. All backsliders should give earnest consideration to this remarkable confession.

> Then when Jesus came, he found that he had lain in the grave four days already (v. 17).

A comparison of John 10:40 with verses 3 and 17 of chapter 11 indicates Christ could not have been more than a day's journey from Bethany. If this were indeed the case, we must allow a day for the servant to carry the message to Christ; another two days to include the delay of the Saviour, and a further day for Christ to come to Bethany. Thus, the possibility must be considered that Lazarus may have died even before Jesus received the information of the illness of his friend. Climatic conditions necessitated the early funeral of the deceased, and thus allowing for all the delays, the arrival of Christ could not have been until the body had already been interred four days. These are but suggestions but if they be correct, it endorses the wisdom of Christ. Premature haste was totally unnecessary, for Lazarus was already dead. A miracle performed immediately after death would have been challenged, for the Jews would have been ready to deny that death had taken place. Some would have affirmed Lazarus was only in a very deep sleep or coma, and that no miracle had been performed. The deterioration in the state of the body after four days would have been indisputable, and it was for this supporting evidence that Christ waited. Martha was quite correct when she said, ". . . Lord, by this time he stinketh" (verse 39).

> Now Bethany was nigh unto Jerusalem, about fifteen furlongs off: And many of the Jews came to Martha and Mary, to comfort them concerning their brother. Then Martha, as soon as she heard that Jesus was coming, went and met him; but Mary sat still in the house (vv. 18-20).

The fact that Bethany was only two miles from the city enables us to understand why "many" of the Jews were able to visit the stricken home. The fact that so many desired to do this supports the earlier conclusion that this family was both wealthy and influential. (See notes on opening verses.) When the unexpected messenger announced the approach of Jesus, the news produced different reactions in the sorrowing sisters. Martha hurried to greet Him, but Mary sat still in the house. It is at this point that the interpretation of the text begins to present problems. Why did not Mary accompany her sister and go forth to welcome the Saviour? Throughout the centuries, commentators have stated that this was the rest of faith; that the saint who sat at His feet to hear His word, who had not even asked that the Lord come to heal her brother, was content to wait calmly for His coming. She believed firmly that whatsoever He did would be correct. This might well be, and it is not the wish of this author to lay any charge falsely against a noble woman of a bygone age. Yet a careful examination of the text suggests there is room for another interpretation. It would hardly be possible to read the account without feeling bitter disappointment when Christ failed to respond instantly to the urgent need of those who loved Him. When the tragedy had happened, when the funeral was over, it was difficult to decide which was the greater blow: the death of Lazarus or the disappointing actions of the Master — He had failed them in the hour of their greatest need! It is essential in good exegesis to consider the possibility that Mary had been hurt. Why then should she hurry to Jesus when He had been so slow in coming to her? If this were the reason for her staying at home, let us reflect on the unpleasant truth that, had we belonged to that family, we might have acted similarly. (See homily at the end of this section.)

> Then said Martha unto Jesus, Lord, if thou hadst been here, my brother had not died. But I know, that even now, whatsoever thou wilt ask of God, God will give it thee (vv. 21, 22).

It is difficult to decide which was the more important: (1) The raising of Lazarus, or (2) the spiritual education of a devoted family. The Lord had already been the Guest in the household and His message had therefore often been told to these people. Yet it would seem that their outlook was rather limited. To them Jesus appeared as a marvelous Teacher, a true Friend, a possible Messiah. As yet they had not confessed His deity; it is possible that they had never realized this possibility. Sometimes God has to use new and drastic methods to shake us from the grip of self-satisfied complacency. At first sight, Martha's confession appears to be a thrilling, triumphant testimony, but a closer examination reveals flaws in her spiritual conception. "If thou hadst been here, my brother had not died" suggests victorious faith, but why say, "If thou hadst been here"? Was a miracle dependent upon Christ's nearness? The Lord had already healed from a distance (see John 4:50). "But I know, that even now, whatsoever thou wilt ask of God, God will give it thee," suggests that even the raising of Lazarus was considered a probability — IF JESUS PRAYED. The power to raise the dead was something which even Jesus needed to obtain. It was as though she said, "Ask, dear Lord, ask the Father, and perhaps He will help you do this thing." Her faith was a giant — in chains. Contrast this with the stirring testimony of the centurion who said, ". . . speak the word only, and my servant shall be healed" (Matthew 8:8). The bringing of Lazarus from the tomb was the work of a moment; the spiritual education of Martha necessitated years of patient instruction.

> Jesus saith unto her, Thy brother shall rise again. Martha saith unto him, I know that he shall rise again in the resurrection at the last day. Jesus said unto her, I am the resurrection and the life; he that believeth in me, though he were dead, yet shall he live: and whosoever liveth and believeth in me shall never die. Believest thou this? (vv. 23-26).

Here we reach another stage in the expanding fullness of Christ. This is another of the great "I AM's" of Jesus. Sharing the faith of the Pharisees that death was not the termination of existence, Martha was sure that, in the fullness of time, her brother would join the saints who would be called from their graves. In that day the invincible power of God would make it a time to be remembered, for death would be swallowed up in victory. Her confession of faith inspired the remark that in Christ the day had already dawned. He whose power would open the graves was even then standing in her presence. His word at that moment was identical with the word to be spoken in the last days and, therefore, He had no need to ask anyone — not even God, for He was God.

> She saith unto him, Yea, Lord: I believe that thou art the Christ, the Son of God, which should come into the world — for whom the world has been waiting (v. 27 *The Amplified New Testament*).

Suddenly she seemed to understand what Christ was saying, and the thrilling confession of her soul surpassed anything she had ever uttered. There was no need for further conversation; the lesson in soul culture had terminated. The following verse suggests, however, that it was at this moment Jesus inquired concerning the whereabouts of Mary.

> **And when she had so said, she went her way, and called Mary her sister secretly saying, The Master is come, and calleth for thee. As soon as she heard that, she arose quickly, and came unto him. Now Jesus was not yet come into the town, but was in that place where Martha met Him (vv. 28-30).**

We do not know all that Martha said, nor how she said it. Perhaps she spoke only for a few seconds; perhaps she spoke for five or ten minutes but, at the conclusion of her message, Mary was on her feet ready to come to Christ. A simple study of the various verses reveals five suggestive steps: (1) *She heard;* (2) *she came;* (3) *she saw;* (4) *she fell at His feet;* (5) *her problem was solved.* We must not conclude our investigation without asking, Why did not the Lord go with Martha? If Mary were hurt, would He not have been more able to administer the Balm of Gilead? Why did He remain where He was, waiting until Martha's important mission had been successfully concluded? It is well to remember that to have sat at His feet in the past is no guarantee that we sit at His feet always. Our lack of faith limits the power of Christ; sometimes our stupidity needs to be corrected in the strangest of ways. Matthew Henry's commentary supplies more food for thought in this connection:

"When Martha went to meet Jesus, *Mary sat still in the house.* Some think she did *not* hear the tidings, while Martha, who was busy in the household affairs, had early notice of it. Others think she *did* hear that Christ was come, but was so overwhelmed with sorrow that she did not care to stir. Comparing this story with that in Luke 10:38 we may observe the different tempers of these two sisters. Martha's natural temper was active and busy; she loved to be here and there, and at the end of everything. This had been a snare to her when by it she was not only careful and cumbered about many things, but hindered from the exercises of devotion: but now in a day of affliction this active temper did her a kindness, kept the grief from her heart, and made her forward to meet Christ, and so she received comfort from Him the sooner. On the other hand, Mary's natural temper was contemplative and reserved. This had been formerly an advantage to her, when it placed her at Christ's feet to hear His word, and enabled her, there, to attend upon Him without those distractions with which Martha was cumbered. Yet now in the day of affliction, that same temper proved a snare to her, made her less able to grapple with her grief, and disposed her to melancholy" (Matthew Henry).

> The Jews then which were with her in the house, and comforted
> her, when they saw Mary, that she rose up hastily, and went out,
> followed her, saying, She goeth unto the grave to weep there
> (v. 31).

There is something very precious about this verse. Martha's
message had been delivered secretly, and therefore those who might
have heard, and retold it with many additions had she been less
discreet, thought Mary's sudden departure the forerunner of a new
outburst of grief. There are those who specialize in revealing the
faults of others; Martha's love was of that rare type which covers
a multitude of sins.

> Then when Mary was come where Jesus was, and saw Him, she
> fell down at His feet, saying unto him, Lord, if thou hadst been
> here my brother had not died (v. 32).

Mary used the same words used by her sister. She had the same
faith, but the chains limiting it seemed a little stronger. "If thou
hadst been here . . . ." Nevertheless, she had come to the Master's
feet and this was her proper place. The New Testament writers
were careful to indicate that each time Mary of Bethany was in
the presence of Christ, "she was at His feet." (1) ". . . a sister called
Mary, which also sat at Jesus' feet and heard His word" (Luke 10:40).
(2) "Then when Mary was come . . . she fell down at His feet"
(John 11:32). (3) "Then took Mary a pound of ointment . . . and
anointed the feet of Jesus . . ." (John 12:3). (See homily at the end
of Section One of Chapter 12.)

> When Jesus therefore saw her weeping, and the Jews also weeping
> which came with her, he groaned in the spirit, and was troubled.
> and said, Where have ye laid him? They said unto him, Lord,
> come and see. Jesus wept (vv. 33-35).

Everything within the range of this simple passage of Scripture
is subservient to the dynamic statement, "*Jesus wept.*" We never
read that Jesus laughed, but on at least three occasions we know
that He wept. Matthew Henry declares: "Christ gave this proof of
His humanity, in both senses of the word; that, as a man, He *could*
weep, and that as a merciful man, He *would* weep." Nevertheless,
nothing can hide the amazing wonder that He who had been responsible for the creation of the universe, He who was so divine, so strong,
so omnipotent, was also so human that His cheeks became wet with
tears. It is almost incomprehensible that the eyes which could see
the end from the beginning should be blurred by tears; that the
Creator responsible for the songs of the birds should be choked by
grief; that the King of angels in whose presence the sons of God
had sung together for joy should suddenly lose His own song and
become "a Man of sorrows and acquainted with grief." (See the
homily at the end of this section.)

Then said the Jews, Behold how he loved him. And some of them said, Could not this man, which opened the eyes of the blind, have caused that even this man should not have died? (vv. 36, 37).

Varied emotions found expression in this verse. Some of the onlookers saw compassion in the tears of Jesus; others misread the signs and almost accused the Lord of indifference. They were probably thinking, "This man could have helped Lazarus, and the fact that He did not proves His love was not genuine. Had He truly loved this family He would have been here earlier." It behooves us to give earnest consideration to this text, for in some measure we are all guilty. It matters not how many miracles Christ performs on our behalf, the fact remains that unless He continues to do precisely as we desire, we permit doubts to dim our vision.

Jesus therefore again groaning in himself cometh to the grave. It was a cave, and a stone lay upon it. Jesus said, Take ye away the stone. Martha, the sister of him that was dead, saith unto Him, Lord, by this time he stinketh: for he had been dead four days. Jesus saith unto her, Said I not unto thee, that, if thou wouldest believe, thou shouldest see the glory of God? (vv. 38-40).

The scene here represented was one at which even the angels might have been astonished. The tomb, silent, somber, saddening, issued its challenge. The crowd, hushed except for an occasional sob; Martha and Mary, just a little frightened and apprehensive; Martha particularly fearful of the unpleasant repercussions sure to follow if the entrance to the tomb were opened; Jesus, supreme, confident, divine. He knew exactly what He intended to do and no power on earth or in hell could stop Him. (1) *Deep distress.* He groaned in His spirit. The sorrows of a world were beginning to break His heart. (2) *Disturbing doubt.* Mindful that her brother's body would now be decomposing, that the unpleasant after effects of death would be inescapable, Martha was nervous and ill at ease. (3) *Divine declaration.* Believe — believe, and thou shalt see. True faith knows no defeat, but faith without works is dead. Faith cannot reach the corpse unless willing hands roll away the stone. It is well to remember this. Some people expect God to do everything, but this He will not do. *Faith* believes that Christ can raise the dead; *obedient faith* rolls away the stone; *expectant faith* looks into the darkness; *rejoicing faith* takes off the graveclothes. It will be remembered that at the cross the onlookers said, "Let Christ the king of Israel descend from the cross, *that we may see and believe*" (Mark 15:32). Man has always sought a sign. Unless some supernatural manifestation be forthcoming, man excuses his inability to believe. The divine law reveals that without faith it is impossible to please God. Man must believe first, and then all things become possible.

Thus the Lord reminded Martha of an unchanging principle, "Believe
. . . and thou shalt see."

> Then they took away the stone where the dead was laid. And
> Jesus lifted up His eyes and said, Father, I thank thee that thou
> hast heard me, And I knew that thou hearest me always: But
> because of the people which stand by I said it, that they may
> believe that thou hast sent me (vv. 41, 42).

Martha's statement reminded the Lord of the apparent hope-
lessness of the case; the putrefaction of the dead body suggested
nothing could now be done. The best thing to do with an impossibility is to bring it to God. This, the Lord had already done. The
text suggests that secret, silent prayer can be as effective as an
audible petition. Indeed, it would be extremely beneficial for all
ministers if their audible prayers were first poured secretly into the
ears of a Heavenly Father. Audible petitions *can be* ostentatious;
silent prayers expressed in the secret place bear the hallmark of
reality. The Lord never prayed any prayer but what it was answered,
and this constitutes a challenge to all His followers. The phrase
that they may believe is repeated continually throughout this gospel.
Everything the Lord said and did was consecrated to the supreme
task of bringing men to saving faith. This must ever be our example,
for nothing else can be as important as the task of leading souls to
Christ.

> And when he thus had spoken, he cried with a loud voice, Lazarus,
> come forth. And he that was dead came forth, bound hand and foot
> with graveclothes: and his face was bound about with a napkin.
> Jesus saith unto them, Loose him, and let him go (vv. 43, 44).

Perhaps it was providential that Christ called Lazarus by name,
for so great was the manifestation of divine power, others too might
have responded had the name been omitted. The day will come when
every grave and every tomb will give up its dead, but on that
particular day in Bethany, Lazarus alone responded; he alone had
been summoned. Where had he been for four days? Did he remember anything of the unrevealed experiences? Did he ever speak
of them? Some day we may have the chance to ask him, but
probably he awakened as from a sleep, and the glory of his new day
made the night insignificant. We might ask why the power of the
Lord did not release the body from the graveclothes even as it had
released the spirit from the grip of death. To do such a thing would
have been a mistake. In fulfiling the command of Jesus, men went
forward to handle this body; they came into close contact with Lazarus and had first-hand knowledge that this was no fake. The power
of their sustained testimony became irrefutable and this adds emphasis to the Lord's statement that He desired men to believe. Possibly

the people merely loosened the graveclothes enabling Lazarus to walk to his home, where within the privacy of his own room, he changed into more serviceable attire. The graveclothes belonged to a life being left behind. Raised from the dead, he intended to walk in newness of life, and this should be the standard by which Christians live. (See the homily at the end of this section.)

> Then many of the Jews which came to Mary, and had seen the things which Jesus did, believed on him. But some of them went their ways to the Pharisees, and told them what things Jesus had done (vv. 45, 46).

It matters not what Jesus did, or does; there will always be those who object to His teachings. The Gospel is either the savor of life unto life, or death unto death. Ministers can never perform such a sensational miracle as that performed by Christ in Bethany; they should never be discouraged unduly then if their efforts be criticized by those whose hearts are evil. Yet since one soul is of more value than the world, and since there are always those "who believe on Him," no service is vain; His word cannot return void. How great was the joy of those who worshiped Christ; how tragic the plight of those who looked and saw nothing. It is possible to be within sight of heaven and yet to remain evil.

HOMILIES

Study No. 40

MARY OF BETHANY AND THE ECLIPSE IN HER SOUL

This is one of the most human stories of the Bible; its counterparts may be found in every city of the world. Tragedy has lain bare the noble soul of Mary of Bethany, for two crushing blows have fallen upon her. Her brother has died; and *Jesus of Nazareth has failed her.* "Now a certain man named Lazarus was sick . . . . Therefore his sisters sent unto Jesus, saying, Lord, behold he whom thou lovest is sick." And with that statement went the hopes and prayers of two sincere hearts.

The Strange Delay

"When Jesus had heard therefore that Lazarus was sick, he abode two days still in the same place where he was." The messenger was permitted to return alone, and the apparent indifference of the Saviour surely dealt a most painful blow to those who anxiously awaited His coming. When Lazarus died, the grief of his sisters was greatly intensified — Jesus had failed them. To them, His action seemed both heartless and inexcusable. Each time Mary considered the problem, the tendency to become bitter increased in her soul.

Perhaps only the people who have similarly suffered will appreciate her anguish. The problems of sickness and suffering are ever before us; but when eager, anxious prayers remain unanswered, even the strongest faith can be shaken. The Lord Jesus deliberately stayed away, and in her acute disappointment Mary forgot to consider that His action might have been dictated by wisdom.

The Suggestive Delay

"Then after that saith he to his disciples, Let us go into Judea again . . . . Then Martha, as soon as she heard that Jesus was coming, went and met him; *but Mary sat still in the house.*" Why did she linger at home? Her sister went to meet the Lord, and the entire world knows of the confession that soon fell from her lips. But when asked about Mary, Martha had to explain the cause of her sister's absence. And is it not significant how Jesus abruptly discontinued His walk toward the beloved home! When Mary eventually came to Him, "Jesus was not yet come into the town, *but was in that place where Martha met him*" (verse 30). Why did He not accompany Martha and so save time? The Lord Jesus was very wise. The raising of Lazarus would not be as difficult as the healing of a wounded soul. Was Mary a little bitter? Was she still hurt because Christ had failed to respond in the hour of her greatest need? The new delay, the delay in Christ's entry into the town, is most suggestive. When Mary heard that Jesus was calling for her, her great love swept aside all hindrances and she arose and came quickly.

The Sublime Delay

And when Jesus came to the tomb, "He lifted up his eyes, and said, Father, I thank thee that thou hast heard me." The prayer of the Saviour was all-embracing. The vision of man might have been limited to the tomb and the possibility of a miracle; He looked beyond, to the transformation taking place in the hearts of His followers. Until that day, He had been to the Bethany family a Friend and a possible Messiah; but Martha had now exclaimed, "Yea, Lord, I believe that thou art the Christ, the Son of God which should come into the world." Some day, Lazarus would die again; but if Jesus be the Son of God, new meaning might be found in His message, "Let not your heart be troubled . . . . I go to prepare a place for you . . . that where I am there ye may be also." The victory won in their souls that day far exceeded the triumph obtained at the tomb. It was for this reason that Christ delayed His response to the prayer of the two sisters. Had He immediately responded, they would have lost their greatest blessing. The eclipse was but a shadow; it passed away, and Mary's path to the sunshine was clearly revealed. This pathway has never become overgrown. It remains open for all weary travelers.

(Reprinted from Bible Cameos, page 141.)

Study No. 41

GOD IN TEARS!

The shortest verse in the Bible is probably one of the greatest. Every student of Scripture appreciates the wonder of the miracles, yet it is problematical whether any supernatural display of healing power could ever present a greater sight than that of tears on the Lord's cheeks. It surpasses understanding that the King of angels should weep, and it is almost incomprehensible that He who had known eternal splendor should become acquainted with the heartbreaks of sinful men. There are three instances of such weeping recorded in the Word of God and a study of these texts reveals progression of thought.

He Wept Because Sin Had Hurt the World

The death of Lazarus brought great grief to his sorrowing sisters and it is easy for us to appreciate the poignancy of the scene described in John 11:33, "When Jesus saw Mary weeping, and the Jews also weeping which came with her, he groaned in the spirit and was troubled." And within a few moments the watching crowd saw that "Jesus wept." Some of the greatest thinkers of the Church have advanced reasons for this expression of grief. (1) *He wept in sympathy for His friends.* Yet this reason can hardly be acceptable, for why should Christ weep in sympathy when He knew that Lazarus would soon be restored to his sisters? (2) *He wept because He was about to bring Lazarus back into a world of sin.* It is difficult to accept this explanation, for the Saviour had already said that this event would bring glory to His Father. (3) *He wept because of the irreparable suffering which had been brought to God's fair world.* Many graves would be in the vicinity of the tomb of Lazarus, and Christ knew that behind each burial place was a tale of woe. Disease and death had appeared to mar man's joy, and the scene around Christ was anything but what God had intended. Sin had hurt the world, and the contemplation of the tragedy hurt the Saviour. He wept.

He Wept Because Sin Was About to Hurt His People

"And when he was come near, he beheld the city, and wept over it, saying, If thou hadst known, even thou, at least in this thy day, the things which belong unto thy peace! but now they are hid from thine eyes. For the days shall come upon thee, that thine enemies shall cast a trench about thee, and compass thee round . . .

and shall lay thee even with the ground . . . because thou knewest not the time of thy visitation" (Luke 19:44). When the Lord Jesus wept over the city of Jerusalem, the crowds ceased their shouting, "Hosannah to the Son of David," and as they slowly went away into the streets, the disappointed disciples realized they had lost their greatest opportunity of establishing the Kingdom. The tears of their Master had banished thoughts of glory. He wept because Israel's rejection of their Messiah would bring inescapable destruction to the city of David. The Lord knew all that would shortly take place, and the fact that their fate seemed to be thoroughly deserved could never take the pain from His heart. Had He been able to save the people, He would have done so; but, alas, there were certain things which even Christ could not do.

He Wept Because Sin Was Beginning to Hurt Him

"Christ . . . who in the days of his flesh, when he had offered up prayers and supplications with strong crying and tears unto him who was able to save him from death, and was heard in that he feared" (Hebrews 5:7). In describing the scene in the Garden of Gethsemane, Luke declared, "His sweat was as it were great drops of blood falling down to the ground." The writer to the Hebrews added the significant detail that tears mingled with the blood. Already the Lord Jesus was feeling the weight of a world's iniquity; already, He was beginning to taste the bitterness of His cup of sorrow. The garden conflict was the introductory stage of the triumph of the cross. The greatness of His desire to save the lost carried Him through that night of agony; but we shall never know how much our sins hurt the Son of God. It is significant that the epistle to the Hebrews mentions "strong crying and tears." His anguish was not expressed in silent weeping but in agonized sobs.

How greatly Jesus must have loved us!

(Reprinted from *Bible Pinnacles*, page 125.)

Study No. 42

THE CHARACTERISTICS OF THE NEW LIFE IN CHRIST

This is the account of the three resurrections made possible by the ministry of the Lord Jesus. The apostle Paul said, "If ye then be risen with Christ, seek those things which are above, where Christ sitteth on the right hand of God. Set your affections on things above, not on things on the earth" (Colossians 3:1, 2). This was the best advice ever given to converts, for it was to be expected that when they renounced the old life, the characteristics of the new would be seen daily in their actions. The requirements of the new life are clearly illustrated in the miracles of the Saviour. The gospel records contain three accounts of His raising the dead; and when these Scriptures are compared, an interesting sequence of thought is discovered.

Confession: Converts should learn to talk for Christ

The city street was strangely hushed; it was a place of mourning. The people watched the sad procession making its way toward the cemetery; and all grieved for they knew this was the second time death had devastated the same home. First, the husband had been taken; and now the sorrowing widow had lost her only son. She was haggard; she moved as one in a daze, as she followed the bier. The bystanders waited until the funeral had passed, then they too continued their journey. "Now when Jesus was come nigh to the gate of the city, behold, there was a dead man carried out, the only son of his mother, and she was a widow: and much people of the city was with her. And when the Lord saw her, he had compassion on her." Slowly, He moved across to her side, and gently resting His hand upon her shoulder whispered, "Mother, do not cry." "And he came and touched the bier: and they that bare the young man stood still. And he said, Young man, I say unto thee, Arise. And he that was dead, sat up, and *began to speak*" (Luke 7:11-16). Resurrection joys would have been marred if the young man had remained dumb forever. He had a story to tell; and furthermore, it was his duty to tell it.

Communion: Converts should feed on the Bread of Life

The scene in the bedroom was heartbreaking; the little girl was dead. The mother's anguish was pitiable; sobs shook her body. Those who stood near furtively wiped their eyes. This was a tragedy; the little girl was only twelve years of age. And then the door opened to admit Jairus, the father of the deceased. He had brought Jesus and three disciples. Momentarily the ruler of the synagogue was overcome; his daughter had been the joy of his life. The three disciples silently watched as their Master went across to the bedside to say, "Little girl, wake up." They were thrilled when the color began to return into the ashen cheeks. They saw the eyelids flicker, and then quite suddenly, the child was smiling. "And her spirit came again, and she arose straightway: *and he commanded to give her meat*" (Luke 8:51-55). "Mother," He said, "give her something to eat. She is hungry and needs food." In like manner, all who have risen with Christ need spiritual nourishment that their new life might be maintained. (1) They must feed on the Word of God. (2) They must enjoy fellowship with the people of God. (3) They must know intimate communion with the Son of God.

Consecration: Converts should walk in newness of life

Lazarus had been in his grave four days, and the hearts of his sisters were very sore as they stood before the sepulcher. They had brought Jesus to see the grave. Suddenly the Lord raised His voice and said, "Lazarus, come forth. And he that was dead came forth, bound hand and foot with graveclothes: and his face was bound about with a napkin. Jesus saith unto them, *Loose him, and let him go*" (John 11:44). Had Lazarus remained in his graveclothes, the liberty of the new life would have been seriously curtailed. How could he walk when his feet were tied? How could he work when his hands were bound? How could he speak distinctly when a cloth held his jaws in a vice? The Lord said, "Loose him and let him go." It was a similar thought which prompted Paul to send his message to the Colossians. Worldliness hinders the freedom of the Spirit. It is the duty of the saint to "lay aside every weight, and the sin which doth so easily beset us, and to run with patience the race that is set before us" (Hebrews 12:1). In this way the Christian consummates his confession and communion. When he shakes off the garments of the old life, he is capable of surrendering his feet, hands, and lips to do the will of God. "If ye then be risen with Christ, seek those things which are above, where Christ sitteth on the right hand of God" (Colossians 3:1). There should never be any three-legged race in the Christian experience.

(Reprinted from *Bible Treasures*, page 97)

Sections Two and Three

Expository Notes on the Emergency Session of the Jewish Council

Then gathered the chief priests and the Pharisees a council, and said, What do we? for this man doeth many miracles. If we let him thus alone, all will believe on him: and the Romans shall come and take away both our place and nation (vv. 47, 48).

It would almost seem as though someone had pushed the panic-button. The influence of Christ was spreading in ever widening circles; the fame of His mighty exploits was known in all parts of the land. Even His enemies were now forced to admit the validity of His miracles. If the present trend continued, the entire population would soon be among His disciples. Something should be done and done quickly. Increasing public acclaim could lead to but one thing — His coronation, and if this became a fact, the wrath of the Emperor would be turned in their direction. This conclusion was exceedingly hypocritical, for it was the dearest hope of every Jew that someday, the power of a new kingdom would guarantee the departure of the hated Romans. The excuse was shallow and sinful.

> And one of them, Caiaphas, being the high priest that same year, said unto them, Ye know nothing at all, nor consider that it is expedient for us, that one man should die for the people, and that the whole nation perish not (vv. 49, 50).

Caiaphas displayed his ego-centricity when he announced the ignorance of his colleagues. He was a self-made deity worshiping at his own shrine. He had no qualms about the expediency of the death of Jesus. If a choice had to be made between the wholesale destruction of the nation by the Romans, and the death of this infuriating preacher, the problem was easy to solve. Even the Accused, if He were honest, would be obliged to admit that the counsel of the high priest was logical and sound!

> And this spake he not of himself: but being high priest that year, he prophesied that Jesus should die for that nation; and not for that nation only, but that also he should gather together in one the children of God that were scattered abroad (vv. 51, 52).

When John wrote his gospel a half century later, this utterance had assumed new importance. The apostle believed an unseen Power had suggested the words to the mind of the prelate, that the voice of the Eternal Spirit had found expression in the words of Israel's leader. John saw in the prediction of the priest the glorious fact that through the death of Christ the other sheep of other folds would be brought together into the unity of the one supreme fold where one Shepherd would lead His flock. The statement, *"And not for that nation only"* is in perfect harmony with John 3:16 and I John 2:2.

> Then from that day forth they took counsel together for to put him to death. Jesus therefore walked no more openly among the Jews; but went thence unto a country near to the wilderness, into a city called Ephraim, and there continued with His disciples (vv. 53, 54).

Christ did not leave because He was afraid; He left because it was the only correct thing to do. His hour had not yet come. When the appointed hour of crucifixion arrived, He would utter no protest. His departure was in itself an indictment against His enemies. They had not known the time of their visitation; He therefore withdrew and went toward the wilderness, sure evidence that in the broader outlines of God's activities, even if the people of Palestine rejected His Message, there would be other places in which He would be received. Little is known of Ephraim; we should learn to look for Christ where He may least be expected. Amid the quietness of the unknown, the Lord rested and prepared for the great trial soon to come.

And the Jew's passover was nigh at hand: and many went out of the country up to Jerusalem before the passover to purify themselves (v. 55).

Mosaic law required that all worshipers at the feast should be clean; that any defilement be removed before the worshipers drew near to the altar. The fact that many were mindful of this edict suggests there were people in Israel "who had not bowed the knee to Baal." Their early arrival in the city provided the opportunity to obey the Mosaic injunction, and at the same time to seek and hear the famous Teacher. Happy indeed are those moderns who have learned to combine these features.

Then sought they for Jesus, and spake among themselves, as they stood in the temple, What think ye, that he will come to the feast? (v. 56).

An empty temple is always a sad sight. People thronged the aisles and stood in the adjacent courtyards, but in the most important sense the sanctuary was empty; Christ was missing. He had been there; His voice had thrilled hearers; His amazing power had been manifest, but all this belonged to history. The religious leaders had rejected him; their house was left desolate. And lest any misinformed person should reach a wrong conclusion, John wrote another verse:

Now both the chief priests and the Pharisees had given a commandment, that, if any man knew where He were, he should shew it, that they might take (arrest) Him (v. 57).

The leaders of the nation who professed to be mindful of the commandments of God now issued their own commandment. God had said, "Thou shalt not kill"; the priests conveniently forgot that edict and "went about to kill Jesus." The city of God was now filled with suspicion and whispering. Paid informers walked the streets; rumors were increasing; fear stalked the pavements. What preparation for meeting God at the passover!

HOMILIES

Study No. 43

THE NECESSITY FOR MAKING A DECISION

The priests and Pharisees had gathered from all parts of Jerusalem; special messengers had summoned them to the emergency session of the nation's senate. The red lights of warning were shining throughout the land; the irresistible, inescapable Carpenter threatened the security of the country. Something had to be done quickly or the government would fall. Increasing crowds were following the new leader; the watchful eyes of the Romans were reading the signs; the mighty Sanhedrin must act immediately.

A Necessary Decision: "What Shall We Do?"

"Then gathered the chief priests and the Pharisees a council, and said, What do we? for this man doeth many miracles. If we let Him alone, all will believe on Him: and the Romans shall come and take away both our place and nation" (John 11:47, 48). Something had to be done; a decision had to be made. To remain neutral in face of the mounting tension was impossible. Inactivity on their part would leave every road clear for the advance of the Carpenter. To do nothing would be an open invitation for Him to do everything. They were aware of three things:

(1) *His power could not be denied.* They said, ". . . this man doeth many miracles." They were not ignorant of the claims being made by the Preacher, and they had heard many of His sermons. They were convinced miracles were performed in His meetings although some of their number declared this had been made possible by an alliance with Beelzebub. To know these things increased their responsibility. Inactivity, indifference now would be unpardonable!

(2) *His preaching could not be forgotten.* He would not be silenced. The threat of physical danger; the opposition of the nation's most influential leaders meant nothing to Him. Officers of the law failed to arrest Him; violence did not frighten Him; their best laid plans had not silenced His voice. Continually, His message reached their ears, and they were becoming tired of the ceaseless worry now beginning to play havoc with their peace of mind. Something had to be done.

(3) *His presence could no longer be tolerated.* "If we let him thus alone, all will believe on him, and the Romans shall come . . . ." To be neutral was to invite disaster. They forgot that the Romans had already come and that they were more likely to know oppression without Christ than they ever would be if He were their Leader. It would be better to face the Gentile oppressors *with* Christ, than to face God *without* Him. These things are most pertinent to the people of all ages.

A Notable Discernment: "Be Careful What You Do!"

The scene had changed, but the issue remained the same. Months had elapsed, and the decision made by the earlier session had been carried through to a successful conclusion. The infuriating Nazarene had been crucified, but unfortunately their hopes of a respite had not been realized. It was now proclaimed that Jesus had risen from the dead to give added impetus to the Gospel. Upstart, unlearned fishermen were turning the world upside down, and the people were bewitched. Something had to be done quickly; there could be no turning back. The chief offenders had been brought before the House, but things were getting out of control. "Now when they saw the boldness of Peter and John, and perceived that they were unlearned and ignorant men, they marveled; and they took knowledge of them, that they had been with Jesus. And beholding the man which was healed standing with them they could say nothing against it."

Then someone expressed the thought of every leader, "What shall we do to these men . . . that it spread no further among the people, let us severely threaten them . . . ." History had repeated itself. Knowledge was being sacrificed upon the altar of expediency. At a later session of the Senate, the problem was again discussed, but this time ". . . stood there up one in the council, a Pharisee, named Gamaliel, a doctor of the law, had in reputation among all the people, and commanded to put the apostles forth a little space. And said unto them, Ye men of Israel, *take heed to yourselves what ye intend to do as touching these men . . .*" (see Acts 5:34-42). The policy outlined by this great man seemed to be a contrast to that of the councillors who discussed the claims of Christ. At the earlier meeting, the High Priest declared, "We cannot afford to be inactive"; here, Gamaliel said, "We cannot to afford to do anything." Three thoughts demand examination.

(1) *We cannot afford to do anything hurriedly.* Subsequent events might prove that they who act hastily repent eternally. He who goes to war without first sitting down to count the cost might reach the bankruptcy court or the grave. The matter must be considered carefully, for in former days would-be messiahs faded into insignificance.

(2) *We cannot afford to do anything haphazardly.* What is done must be done with all our power. We must never start something we are unable to finish. There remains the possibility that in opposing this movement, we might be fighting against God. Let us therefore wait until we have further light on the matter; it could be that the problem will resolve itself; it could be that God may do what must be done.

(3) *We cannot afford to do anything hopelessly.* Unless our hearts be dedicated to the downfall of this movement, unless our consciences be free from every vestige of doubt, how can we carry our efforts to a successful conclusion? ". . . if this counsel or this work be of men, it will come to nought. But if it be of God, ye cannot overthrow it; lest haply ye be found to fight against God." "Gentlemen, let us wait and see what will happen; when we have more evidence, we shall be able to decide our policy." Splendid, Gamaliel,

but how long do you intend to wait, and who will decide when you know enough?

A Noble Determination: "... but one thing I do."

To know about Christ means to make a decision concerning Him; there can be no position of neutrality. At first glance the advice given by Gamaliel seemed to be begotten by wisdom, but within a few weeks, Saul of Tarsus, one of his best students was transformed by the power of the risen Christ. Soon the fiery persecutor was preaching the faith which once he destroyed. Obviously, the famous teacher heard of the conversion of his student; naturally, he followed with interest the exploits of the man whom once he taught; constantly he became increasingly aware of the growth of the Church, but alas, continuing silence betrayed the fact that once again knowledge was being sacrificed upon the altar of expediency. As the professor retreated further into his world of watchful silence, the former student carried the banner of Christ throughout Asia and challenged the power of pagan dynasties. Paul's life and ministry may be classified under three headings:

(1) *His Decisive Surrender.* That he also had known moments of mental confusion; harassing doubts, and a troubled conscience is indisputable. Yet in contrast to the attitude of his professor, the student reached the place where knowledge dictated action. He exclaimed, "Lord, what wilt thou have me to do?" (Acts 9:6).

(2) *His Dedicated Service.* "But what things were gain to me, those I counted loss for Christ. Yea, doubtless, and I count all things but loss for the excellency of the knowledge of Christ Jesus my Lord: for whom I have suffered the loss of all things, and do count them dung, that I may win Christ" (Philippians 3:7, 8). The ministry of Paul as told in the Acts of the Apostles is one of the epic stories of all times. He blazed the pioneer trail for Christianity throughout the known world.

(3) *His Distinguished Success.* At the close of his earthly pilgrimage he was able to write, "For I am now ready to be offered, and the time of my departure is at hand. I have fought a good fight, I have finished my course, I have kept the faith. Henceforth there is laid up for me a crown of righteousness, which the Lord, the righteous judge, shall give me at that day ..." (II Timothy 4:7, 8). It should be remembered that Paul wrote of the JUDGE — and not of the Saviour. Paul was apparently conscious of the fact that to the best of his ability, he had served the Lord faithfully. Constantly throughout the continuing difficulties of life, he had answered the question "What shall I do?" by saying, "This one thing I do, forgetting those things which

are behind, and reaching forth unto those things which are before, I press toward the mark for the prize of the high calling of God in Christ Jesus.

Let us therefore, as many as be perfect, be thus minded" (Philippians 3:13-15).

The Twelfth Chapter of John

THEME: *The Final Journey to Jerusalem*

OUTLINE:

    I. The Supper in Bethany. Verses 1-11.
    II. The Entry Into Jesusalem. Verses 12-19.
    III. The Events Within the City. Verses 20-50.

"Let us see what honours were heaped upon the head of the Lord Jesus even in the depths of His humiliation. (1) Mary did Him honour, by anointing His feet at the supper in Bethany (verses 1-11). (2) The common people did Him honour, with their acclamations of joy, when He rode in triumph into the city of Jerusalem (verses 12-19). (3) The Greeks did Him honour, by enquiring after Him with a longing desire to see Him (verses 20-26). (4) God the Father did Him honour, by a voice from heaven (verses 27-36). (5) He had honour done Him by the Old Testament prophets (verses 37-41). (6) He had honour done Him by some of the chief rulers, though they had not the courage to own it (verses 42-43). (7) He claimed honour for Himself, by asserting His divine mission (verses 44-50)" (Matthew Henry).

SECTION ONE

Expository Notes on the Anointing of Christ by Mary

> Then Jesus six days before the passover came to Bethany, where Lazarus was which had been dead, whom he raised from the dead. There they made him a supper; and Martha served: but Lazarus was one of them that sat at the table with him.

The hour had come; the Lord saw clearly that the storm was about to break over His head. This would be the final visit to Jerusalem; this would be His last chance to stay a little while in Bethany. There, amid the warmth of the affection of His friends, He would be cheered and strengthened to face the ominous future. Perhaps He planned to arrive some days before the Passover that this respite might be beneficial to Himself and to those He loved. John remembered that the Master arrived almost a week before the feast on the eighth day of Nisan (Leviticus 23:5), but does not indicate whether or not the supper was arranged to welcome Him. Matthew (26:1-13) and Mark (4:1-11) suggest that the supper might have been held within two days of passover. There is nothing conclusive about the various Scripture references. Possibly, in view of the Lord's imminent departure from Jerusalem, the friends in Bethany arranged a farewell feast, and if this were indeed the case, it would add meaning and virtue to Mary's love-gift. Matthew and Mark agree that this feast was held in Bethany. That a similar feast with similar results was also held in the house of Simon the Pharisee has given occasion for very much debating within theological circles. Some interpreters suggest that Simon the Pharisee and Simon the Leper were the same person; that the sinful woman of Luke 7:36-50 was Mary of Bethany. This is totally unacceptable for obvious reasons. Simon the Pharisee was openly critical of the Lord; Simon the Leper was undoubtedly grateful, for he owed his life to Jesus. The sinful woman mentioned by Luke broke her box of ointment as a confession that sin was being renounced; Mary broke her box indicating her love was being outpoured. (See homily at the end of this section.)

Dr. E. W. Rice says, "There are nine Simons named in Scripture: (i) Simon Peter; (ii) Simon Zelotes, the Canaanite (Matthew 10:4); (iii) Simon, the brother of our Lord (Matthew 13:55); (iv) Simon, the Leper, (Matthew 26:6); (v) Simon the Cyrenian, who bore the cross (Matthew 27:32); (vi) Simon the Pharisee, (Luke 7:40); (vii) Simon the sorcerer of Samaria (Acts 8:9); (viii) Simon the Tanner (Acts 9:43); (ix) Simon the father of Judas (John 6:71). Whether all of these were different persons, or some were the same persons having different titles or names, is uncertain."

Readers are again reminded of the notes on the preceding chapter which suggested Simon the Leper might have been the head of this family in Bethany. There exists the possibility that the father of Mary, Martha, and Lazarus might have been a leper, that Christ had found and cleansed him, thus making possible a family reunion. On the other hand, Simon might have been a neighbour of Martha and Mary, and a common love for Jesus had united their households. If this were the case, the home of the former leper might have been impoverished, and the aid offered by Martha in preparing a supper would have been gladly welcomed by the man who greatly desired to express his appreciation to the Master. Four very simple but thought-provoking features seem to be closely associated with this man:

(1) *He had been fearful.* Leprosy was a dreaded disease necessitating separation from family and friends. Unless a miracle were performed, the sufferer knew he would remain an outcast until death released him from agony. Through every day and night of existence, the leper would hardly be free of the mental anguish which constantly affirmed his case was hopeless.

(2) *He had been found.* There had been a day when the im-

possible happened; somewhere, somehow, he had come in contact with Christ. Divine grace had been manifest and eternal love overflowed to reach a man in his misery. The impossible had taken place; the leper had found new life.

(3) *He was fervent.* Unlike others mentioned by Luke (17:12-19), this man constantly remembered the grace which rescued him. Gratitude filled his heart, and when the opportunity came to do something for his Saviour, he did what was possible.

(4) *He desired fellowship.* There had been a time when he came because he wanted *to receive* something; now he is present because he desires *to give* something. Formerly he desired salvation; now he yearns to sit with the Master, to listen to His voice, to rejoice in His presence, to learn at His feet. Simon the Leper set an example which all men should follow.

"And Martha served." Formerly she had been rebuked because her service had begotten criticism of Mary. She exhibited true greatness by returning to her task. Others, going to extremes, would have joined Mary at the Lord's feet, but had Martha done this, she would have been wrong. Some are called to serve in kitchens; others are commissioned to preach; both deserve equal commendation when the service is cheerfully done for the glory of Christ. Martha never complained the second time, and let it be candidly admitted, there is evidence to prove the Lord and His disciples had good reason to be grateful to the untiring lady who knew how to cook a meal. Lazarus sat at the table with Jesus. This was perfectly natural, for where else should any one raised from the dead be when the Lord was presiding at a feast! Let it be considered that Jesus sat at the table in Bethany; He sat at the table at the last supper (Luke 22:14); He sat at the table in Emmaus. Happy are all those who know the privilege of sitting with Him.

> Then took Mary a pound of ointment of spikenard, very costly, and anointed the feet of Jesus, and wiped his feet with her hair: and the house was filled with the odour of the ointment (v. 3).

The Greek text *murou nardou pistikes polutimou* reads: "ointment of nard, pure, and of great price." Matthew 26:7 has the word "barutimou" which means "of weighty value — of very great worth." Dr. Rice says, "This costly perfume was made from the stem of a plant of the valerian family, probably *Nardostachys Jatamansi,* found in India. The finished product was very precious indeed and the assessment of its worth by Judas further indicates its value in the markets of that day. The covetous disciple estimated its value to have been three hundred pence, but in view of the fact that one penny represented a full day's wage for a worker in the vineyard (Matthew

20:2), this box or flask of costly perfume equalled the wages of a workman for almost one year. Comparisons are odious but some conception of its value might be gained from the fact that in comparative contemporary values, its worth in America today would be in the region of two or three thousand dollars. That Mary possessed such a rare treasure suggests, as earlier indicated, that this home in Bethany was one of the better homes to grace the district. The broken box, or empty flask, revealed the overflowing love of this woman's heart; the escaping odor not only filled the house, it entered the street, filled the town, and in ever widening circles of blessedness proceeded to fill the world.

> Then saith one of his disciples, Judas Iscariot, Simon's son, which should betray him, Why was not this ointment sold for three hundred pence? This he said, not that he cared for the poor; but because he was a thief, and had the bag, and bare what was put therein (vv. 4-6).

It is not to be supposed that Judas stole all that was placed into the common fund, for indeed if this were the case, both Jesus and His disciples must have seemed stupid and slow to recognize what was taking place. The probability is that Judas "pilfered the collections" (*Amplified New Testament*). and that in retrospect, John after fifty years was expressing the inward character of Judas rather than his previously established conduct.

> Then said Jesus, Let her alone: against the day of my burying hath she kept this. For the poor always ye have with you; but me ye have not always (vv. 7, 8).

Professor A. T. Robertson says of the word *entaphiasmos:* ". . . it is a rare substantive from the late verb *entaphiazo* — to prepare for burial. Matthew 26:12; John 19:40 . . . . 'Preparation for my burial' is the idea here. The idea of Jesus is that Mary had saved this money to use in preparing His body for burial. She is giving Him the flowers before the funeral . . . . This is Mary's glory that she had some glimmering comprehension of Christ's death which none of the disciples possessed." (*World Pictures in the New Testament,* Volume V; pages 217, 218).

The impending departure and death of the Son of God were obvious, but only Mary discerned what was about to take place. That she seized the opportunity to give to Him the best she had suggests she was a woman of true spirituality; she had not sat at His feet in vain. (See homily at the end of this section.)

> Much people of the Jews therefore knew that he was there; and they came not for Jesus' sake only, but that they might see Lazarus also, whom he had raised from the dead (v. 9).

The quiet peacefulness of Bethany had been rudely disturbed.

News of the resurrection of Lazarus had startled and thrilled the surrounding countryside, and when the arrival of Jesus was publicized, the crowds rushed excitedly to see whatever could be seen. The prospect of seeing Christ and Lazarus together was most inviting. Alas, the ruling Jews did not share the joyful expectation of the increasing crowds. They had committed themselves to a policy and with every passing day became more and more enslaved to pre-arranged plans. They had tied a noose in the rope of public affairs and their decision to murder Christ was slowly tightening around their own necks.

> But the chief priest consulted that they might put Lazarus also to death; because that by reason of him many of the Jews went away, and believed on Jesus (vv. 10, 11).

The commandments of God had now been forgotten; nothing mattered except the overthrow of the influence of the Nazarene. Every vestige of support for the Carpenter must be ruthlessly destroyed and since the radiant personality of Lazarus now drew people to Christ, he too must die! The cause of Judaism was being menaced; this could not be permitted. The apparent danger to His friend probably accounted for the fact that within hours the Lord had left Bethany for the last time.

HOMILIES

Study No. 44

MARY OF BETHANY WHO DID NOT WAIT FOR THE FUNERAL

If I were a woman, I should be very proud to own Mary of Bethany as my sister. She has been mentioned three times in the New Testament and these Scriptures, when placed together, supply a most interesting progression of thought. It would seem that only Mary anticipated the death of her Master. While the other disciples dreamed of and hoped for the coming Kingdom, she looked into the Lord's eyes and read aright their grim purpose. Then, fearful lest she might lose her opportunity, she gathered up her choicest treasure and gave it to Christ. She placed her flowers in His hand, rather than on his grave.

Mary Listening

The kitchen in the Bethany home was a busy place. Jesus and His disciples were coming to lunch. Both Mary and Martha were thrilled at the prospect, in spite of the fact that much additional preparation would be necessary. When the party arrived, the sisters cordially welcomed them, and then Martha excused herself and hurried away to serve the meal. Alone, with many jobs to do, she became increasingly flustered and when she sought her sister's help, discovered that Mary had followed Jesus into the parlor. Undoubtedly, Martha tried hard, but eventually she opened the door and said, "Lord, dost thou not care that my sister hath left me to serve alone? bid her therefore that she come and help me" (Luke 10:40). Poor Martha! It was necessary to serve lunch for about twenty that day, and only one pair of hands was available for the task. Then Jesus smiled and gently replied, "Martha, Martha, thou art careful and troubled about many things: But one thing is needful, and Mary hath chosen that good part that shall not be taken away from her." Martha was perfectly satisfied and never complained again. The Lord Jesus loved a good listener, and Mary loved to listen. We shall never know all that she heard as she sat at the Master's feet; we shall never know fully the impact made upon her soul. She mastered her lessons and graduated in a hallowed school.

Mary Learning

The scene had changed: the home at Bethany had become a place filled with sorrow. The cruel hand of death had taken away the beloved brother; Lazarus was dead. Then Mary heard of the approach of the Lord, and the events which followed His coming were rich in drama. The sorrowful sisters directed Christ to the tomb, and there witnessed His greatest manifestation of miraculous power. The Lord calmly looked at the place of shadows and said, "Lazarus, come forth," and, to the surprise of all the crowd, "Lazarus came forth, bound hand and foot with graveclothes." Probably the sisters hardly remembered reaching their home that day. Wonder, excitement, joy thrilled their entire beings; but later as they listened again to His gracious words, they became conscious of the gathering of even deeper shadows. The enraged Jews were bitter because the new miracle had thrilled the crowds. Against the somber background of their new plottings the words of Jesus were easily remembered: "The Son of Man must be delivered into the hands of sinful men and be crucified." Mary listened intently, and ultimately understood the meaning of His words.

Mary Loving

"Then Jesus, six days before the passover, came to Bethany" and at request of Simon the Leper went with His friends to visit the convert's home. Probably Simon owed the greatest of all debts to Jesus. Somewhere out in the country the Lord had touched and transformed him and, although the old name still clung to him, Simon was no longer a leper. In that simple home, Mary listened and learned again; and, realizing that this was her final opportunity, she "took a pound of ointment of spikenard, very costly, and anointed the feet of Jesus, and wiped his feet with her hair; and the house was filled with the odour of the ointment" (John 12:3). The disciples were indignant at the apparent waste, but Jesus said, "Why trouble ye the woman? . . . in that she hath poured this ointment on my body, *she did it for my burial.*" It thus became obvious that Mary's training, rich in spiritual contact with her Lord, was bearing fruit. She read aright the meaning of the shadows in His eyes; she foresaw correctly the events soon to take place and, before it was too late, she poured her richest treasures at His feet. Perhaps if we listened more we also might learn more. If this happened, we would not wait so long to bring our treasures to the Master.

(Students are invited to compare this homily with its predecessor).

Study No. 45

Two Women . . . Who Did the Same Thing

How can a man obtain the forgiveness of sin? There have been numerous answers to this important question. It has been suggested that man must endeavor, by his own merit, to increase his credit account in the bank of heaven. It has also been taught that the granting of forgiveness is the prerogative of certain ecclesiastical leaders, that one must conform to particular church laws in order to obtain the coveted treasure. Other people prefer to seek their answer within the Bible.

A Woman's Conviction

Somewhere within the shadowy hovels of an eastern city, a poor woman prepared for her nightly escapade. She was a great sinner and regularly went out to break the heart of God. We do not know what ugly combination of circumstances had brought her to such low levels of morality, nor do we know whether or not she cared. She took from its resting place her box of perfume and, appreciating its powers of attraction, used it to adorn her person. Then, extinguishing the lamp, she slipped into the darkness and her night had begun. Somewhere she probably saw a crowd and, hearing the voice of a Stranger, drew near to come face to face with Jesus. We can only guess as to the nature of His message, but we are sure His words reached her soul. Soon she forgot the purpose of her coming into the city and retraced her steps homeward. She had met Jesus and His words could never be forgotten. She felt unclean; she hardly knew what to do; she loathed herself. Thus she took the first step along the pathway to pardon. Before we proceed, it might be well to recall that in the small town of Bethany was another woman, a women destined to do precisely what the sinner would soon do. Mary first heard the voice of the Saviour when her sister Martha invited the Teacher into her house. What she heard, what she saw, we do not know. She also realized her sinfulness, but the pathways of these women to reach the same conclusion were somewhat different.

A Woman's Contrition

Mechanically the sinner lifted her precious box of ointment but, as her fingers closed around the treasure, she prepared to make her greatest decision. If she accepted and followed the Teacher's way of life, she would never again need this questionable adornment; the purpose for which it was meant would be non-existent in her life. Should she take it to Him? How would she earn her living? How would she obtain bread? It was sufficient to remember she needed cleansing, that never again would she grieve God. She made inquiries at the meeting place and ascertaining that Jesus had gone to dine with Simon the Pharisee, followed to the well-known home. "And behold, a woman of the city, which was a sinner, when she knew that Jesus sat at meat in the Pharisee's house, brought an alabaster box of ointment, and stood at his feet, behind him, weeping, and began to wash his feet with tears, and did wipe them with the hairs of her head." Her conviction had deepened to contrition. We must not confuse these two steps. Conviction reveals man's sinfulness; contrition reveals man's sorrow for sin. Many people have known conviction of soul, yet have persistently pursued their path of evil. Contrition is much nearer to God's heart than conviction. Compare this with the scene in the home of Simon the Leper, and consider that Mary's action was not a confession of sin but the outpouring of her affection. The one woman anointed the Lord because she was about to abandon a life of sin; the second woman anointed the Lord because He was about to die for sinners.

A Woman's Confession

"She anointed His feet with the ointment." Bowing before the mounting storm of criticism, she listened to the words of the Lord and found peace. He alone understood the confession behind the broken box. He knew she was trying to say, "Lord, I shall never need this again, for the old life is now dead." "And he said unto her, Thy sins are forgiven . . . thy faith hath saved thee; go in peace." And while the onlookers saw just a broken box, He saw a broken heart and tenderly healed it. The perfume of the ointment slowly filled the room and then escaped to fill the world; it is still with us. We imagine the woman's home-going; and if sleep seemed elusive that night, maybe she still thought of His words, "Thy sins are forgiven . . . go in peace." She was not commanded to reach new heights of morality in order to atone for former failure; nor was she instructed to bow before the priest in the synagogue. The only confessional box she ever knew was the small one broken in His presence. How can a man obtain the forgiveness of sins? He must realize his need; he should be ashamed of his guilt; he should seek the Saviour. Two women — two broken boxes — two confessions. The former takes us in thought to the depths of human depravity; the latter lifts us to the heights of true devotion. The first woman brought her guilty soul and regrettable past to Jesus; Mary of Bethany brought her warm, true, wonderful affection. As long as she lived she would love her Lord; she would never forget Him. Between these extremes stands the Son of God; the picture suggests He is able to save *from the uttermost to the uttermost, them that believe on Him.*

SECTION TWO

Expository Notes on the Triumphant Entry Into Jerusalem

On the next day much people that were come to the feast, when they heard that Jesus was coming to Jerusalem, took branches of palm trees, and went forth to meet him, and cried, Hosanna: Blessed is the King of Israel that cometh in the name of the Lord (vv. 12, 13).

The other evangelists describe how two disciples were sent in search of the colt, how this unbroken animal was brought to Jesus; and there exists the possibility that somewhere along the road, the news had been told that Jesus was about to enter the city. Very quickly these tidings spread through the streets, and consequently the welcoming crowds increased rapidly. They were not conscious of the fact that the overruling providence of God was fulfilling prophecy even in their excitable actions. Centuries earlier Zechariah had predicted, "Rejoice greatly, O daughter of Zion; shout, O daughter of Jerusalem: behold thy king cometh unto thee: He is just and having salvation; lowly, and riding upon an ass, and upon a colt the foal of an ass" (Zechariah 9:9). Sometimes the hand of God is doing most when we are least conscious of the fact. Sometimes He works hardest when we think He is doing nothing. That the Lord was able to ride an unbroken colt supplies food for thought. Any other rider would have encountered trouble, and the less skillful would have been thrown to the ground. The young colt probably recognized the Lord of Creation, and having more sense than humans, considered it life's greatest privilege to serve the Son of God. Thus John wrote:

And Jesus, when He had found a young ass, sat thereon; as it is written, Fear not, daughter of Zion: behold, thy king cometh sitting on an ass's colt (vv. 14, 15).

It might be beneficial to compare this entry into Jerusalem with another yet to take place. John wrote, "I saw heaven opened, and behold a white horse; and he that sat upon him was called Faithful and True, and in righteousness he doth judge and make war. His eyes were as a flame of fire, and on his head were many crowns . . ." (Revelation 19:11, 12). The first entry led to His rejection; the last one ends in His coronation. The former left Him pitiably alone, for even His friends deserted Him; the last great entry will be a time of supreme rejoicing when, finally, "every knee shall bow, and every tongue shall confess that He is Lord to the glory of God the Father." The citizens of old presented the Saviour with a crown of thorns; the people of the future will accept Him as their Messiah, and "in that day there shall be a fountain opened to the house of David and to the inhabitants of Jerusalem for sin and for uncleanness" (Zechariah 13:1). "Yea, every pot in Jerusalem and in Judah shall be holiness unto the Lord of Hosts: and all they that sacrifice shall come and take of them, and seethe therein: and in that day there shall be no more the Canaanite in the house of the Lord of Hosts" (Zechariah 14:21).

> These things understood not his disciples at the first; but when Jesus was glorified, then remembered they that these things were written of him and that they had done these things unto him (v. 16).

Some things are seen more clearly and better understood when viewed in retrospect. This fact should remind us that even when we fail to comprehend to the full that which is taking place, we should remember there is a Hand that shapes our destiny. What God has decreed will come to pass and, although occasional battles may appear to have been won by the forces of evil, the final victory rests with God.

> The people therefore that was with him when he called Lazarus out of his grave, and raised him from the dead, bare record. For this cause the people also met him, for that they heard that he had done this miracle. The Pharisees therefore said among themselves, Perceive ye how ye prevail nothing? Behold, the world is gone after him (vv. 17-19).

The text reveals the influence of Jesus was spreading in ever widening circles. The people present at the miracle in Bethany had borne witness to what they had seen and the crowd of pilgrims from every part of the nation listened to the exciting story, and joined the people expectantly awaiting the Healer. Soon Jerusalem was filled with an electrifying excitement, and the enemies of the Lord, frustrated, powerless, bitter, faced the prospect of defeat. Their confession, ". . . the world is gone after him" seems strangely related to another confession made much later of the Lord's disciples: "These that have turned the world upside down, are come hither also" (Acts 17:6). The two verses are startlingly suggestive. First, the Lord attracts to Himself and then, through the ministry of His consecrated servants, proceeds to set the world the right side up!

It will be noticed that John omits many of the details connected with the Lord's entry into Jerusalem. It will also be remembered from the introduction to this commentary that John set out to write those things which, for some reason or other, the earlier writers had omitted from their accounts. The omissions of the fourth gospel support that conclusion.

HOMILIES

THE INCOMPARABLE CHRIST

See homily at the end of Section Three, Chapter 7

GOD IN TEARS

See homily at the end of Section One, Chapter 11

SECTION THREE

Expository Notes on the Events Which Followed the Coming of the Greeks to Christ

And there were certain Greeks among them which came up to worship at the feast: The same came therefore to Philip, which was of Bethsaida of Galilee, and desired him, saying, Sir, we would see Jesus. Philip cometh and telleth Andrew; and again Andrew and Philip tell Jesus (vv. 20-22).

We are not told whether the request of the visitors was granted but it is difficult to believe that Jesus would permit such a desire to pass unnoticed. Archeologists have unearthed an inscription which makes it clear that Greeks were not permitted to enter certain parts of the temple. All aliens were forbidden to pass beyond the temple courtyards, and it would therefore appear that at the time of the request, Jesus might have been within the prohibited areas. The Greeks did the only thing possible; they approached one of the disciples in the hope that their request would be relayed to the Lord. The probability is that these Gentiles were converts to Judaism and had come to worship at the feast. Hearing of the presence of the great Teacher, they who had learned so much desired to learn more. That Philip hesitated to act in the matter until he had first consulted Andrew suggests that between these two disciples existed the strongest bonds of understanding and fellowship. Philip probably believed that "two heads were wiser than one," and the result of that conclusion was evident in that both the disciples took the request to Christ. (See the

homily at the end of Section Three Chapter 1: "Andrew . . . the
Patron Saint of Personal Workers.)

> **And Jesus answered them saying, The hour is come, that the Son
> of Man should be glorified. Verily, verily, I say unto you, Except
> a corn of wheat fall into the ground and die, it abideth alone: but
> if it die, it bringeth forth much fruit (vv. 23, 24).**

The request brought to the Saviour stirred the depths of His
soul. Mention had already been made of the other sheep in other
folds; John had already stressed the fact that God loved the entire
world. Throughout the fourth gospel, the phrase is used, "His hour was
not yet come." Now, however, everything seems to change. The coming
hour has already arrived; a ministry hitherto limited to the narrow
confines of Palestine is about to cross borders and boundaries in a
limitless outreach to a lost world. The hopeless will be cheered, and
the people who for long had sat in darkness would see a great light.
Yet this work would never be crowned by complete success until the
power of the Cross became effective in the transformation of sinful
man.

Redeeming love would flow through a cross; God's lighthouse
would be erected on a green hill outside a city wall. Using language
easy to understand, Christ referred to a grain of wheat. Healthy, attractive, desirable, if it remained on a shelf, on a table, in a dish, it
remained alone. If it died, its death could produce a harvest. Had
Christ remained in heaven, even had He stayed alive on earth, He
would have been alone. The implications of this text are tremendous.
No teacher in history ever imparted such profound truth, yet Christ
declared His instruction would be sufficient to produce a harvest of
souls. The amazing power of His miracles astonished the world and
made impossibilities a thing of the past. There were people who
probably said He could do anything, but this was not the case. He
could open blind eyes, cleanse lepers, enable the lame to walk, but
while His touch healed bodies, His death alone removed sin.

> **He that loveth his life shall lose it; and he that hateth his life in
> this world shall keep it unto life eternal. If any man serve me, let
> him follow me; and where I am, there shall also my servant be:
> if any man serve me, him will my Father honour (vv. 25, 26).**

Enunciating the great principles of His kingdom, Jesus set the
example for all Christians. *To live* in the fullest possible way is *to die*,
and to die is gain. To be crucified with Christ is to know the power of
an endless life; to reach the cross is to find a key to heaven's richest
treasures. Four features are revealed in the text: (1) *Salvation.* Dr.
Rice says: "Man is subject to a law which reigns in the natural world.
The wheat that would save itself from falling into the ground, after a
time, would lose its life and power to grow. He who is willing to

sacrifice his life in this world will, through a new creation, similar to the growth of the wheat germ, come into life eternal." (2) *Service.* The Cross through which life flows to our souls becomes the symbol of our creed. Knowing what it has done for us, we proceed to tell others about it. In doing this we obey our Lord, for this was precisely what He commanded. (3) *Security.* If we do His will we can never be far from Him; and this maxim applies both in time and in eternity. (4) *Success.* The ultimate end is never in doubt, for God has promised, "I will honor those who honor me." It is the overflowing, outflowing power of the Holy Spirit which turns service to joy and effort into an enduring success. This reward attends those who walk with Christ in the fulfillment of the divine will.

> Now is my soul troubled; and what shall I say? Father, save me from this hour; but for this cause came I unto this hour. Father, glorify thy name. Then came there a voice from heaven, saying, I have both glorified it, and will glorify it again (vv. 27, 28).

At first glance the Lord's statement seems surprising, for it was expressed amid congenial circumstances. We could be excused for expecting the Lord to say, "Now is my soul thrilled — had not the Greeks expressed a desire to see Him? Sometimes life's joys and sorrows are closely associated; often one is dependent upon the other. Consider: (1) *The Lord disturbed* — "Now is my soul troubled." (2) *The Lord deliberating* — "What shall I say?" (3) *The Lord determined* — "For this cause came I unto this hour." (4) *The Lord's decision* — "Father, glorify thy name." Mention has already been made that the Lord's prayers were always answered. He never prayed with any selfish motive; He never asked for a thing that was out of the will of God. This was the third time that God had honored Him with testimony from the clouds. It is tragically thought-provoking that while the custodians of the temple were opposing Christ and planning to murder Him, the Lord of the temple endorsed His teaching and honored His mission. (See the homily at the end of this section.)

> The people therefore, that stood by, and heard it, said that it thundered; other said, An angel spake to Him. Jesus answered and said, This voice came not because of me, but for your sakes (vv. 29, 30).

It is not surprising that the bystanders failed to understand what God said. They had failed to recognize the voice of the Son; how could they expect to recognize the voice of the Father? They spoke with the same accent, and enunciated the same truth. To know the One is to appreciate the Other; to believe the One is to recognize the One who sent Him. Nevertheless, even though omniscience foresaw the ultimate unbelief of the people, righteousness demanded that no stone be left unturned in the attempt to win the lost. Therefore, said Jesus, "This voice came not because of me but for your sakes."

> Now is the judgment of this world: now shall the prince of this world be cast out. And I, if I be lifted up from the earth, will draw all unto me. This He said, signifying what death He should die (vv. 31-33).

Obviously these remarkable words were meant to follow and expound the Father's statement, "I will glorify it (my name) again." This would be done in fourfold way: (1) *Through the exaltation of righteousness.* The crisis, the judgment of this world is at hand. Sin may appear to triumph; evil may apparently conquer, but the righteousness of God must be vindicated. (2) *Through the defeat of Satan.* The arch enemy is about to be routed; the forces of evil are to be overthrown; the kingdom of darkness will be made to yield. (3) *Through the honoring of the eternal Son.* Christ, so soon to be lifted up on a cross, would be lifted further until in the presence of high heaven He would be crowned with glory and honor. Ultimately even His enemies would be made His footstool. (4) *Through the conquest of a lost world.* At the temptation in the wilderness Satan had offered to Christ the kingdoms of the world. That the Lord never disputed Satan's ability to do as he promised suggests the entire world was indeed in Satan's Grip. Sometimes the longest way around is the shortest way home — what Satan offered is now to be taken from him by other means. Souls would be liberated from the thralldom of sin and brought to the feet of the Redeemer. Thus would God honor His promise and glorify His Name.

> The people answered Him, We have heard out of the law that Christ abideth forever: and how sayest thou, The Son of Man must be lifted up? who is this Son of Man? (v. 34).

There seems to be something shallow and hypocritical about this outburst. They were mindful of those Scriptures which appeared to support their own point of view; they forgot, perhaps conveniently so, the other Scriptures which endorsed the teaching of Jesus. Probably they were thinking of Psalm 110:4; Isaiah 9:7; Daniel 2:44; Micah 4:7, Nevertheless, the whole of Isaiah 53 was also an integral part of their Scriptures, and in this utterance, the prophet predicted the death of the Lord's Anointed. All students must learn rightly to divide the word of God, for a text out of its context can be made to mean anything. This inquiry of the Jews did not carry the hallmark of sincerity.

> Then Jesus said unto them, Yet a little while is the light with you. Walk while ye have the light, lest darkness come upon you: for he that walketh in darkness knoweth not whither he goeth. While ye have the light believe in the light, that ye may be children of light. These things spake Jesus, and departed, and did hide himself from them (vv. 35, 36).

This is one of the greatest passages of John's gospel, for much truth is enshrined within a few words. The Lord obviously referred to His earlier announcement when He declared Himself to be the Light of the World. Now in quick succession He outlines five very vital steps:

(1) *A Great Announcement:* ". . . the light is with you." "There is no need to stumble in the darkness for the embodiment of Truth now stands in your midst. He who knows the mind of the Father is here to instruct you, to guide you, to help you."

(2) *A Growing Awareness:* "The light is with you 'yet a little while'." "Take advantage of the fact and walk while ye have it." The Lord knew the day was fast approaching when the light would no longer be shining. He was urging His listeners to "seek the Lord while he may be found."

(3) *A Grim Assertion:* ". . . that ye may become the children of light." This was tantamount to an insult, for the people to whom He spoke were proud that they were children of Abraham. To them had been given the responsibility and privilege of preserving and proclaiming the Mosiac Law. They firmly believed that if they were not God's children, then God had no children! The Lord was repeating in a new way what He had already said to Nicodemus — "Ye must be born again."

(4) *A Glorious Alternative:* Even though they were not the children of light, there was no need to despair; the highway to the sunshine was open. "While ye have the light . . . walk." "While ye have the light . . . believe." Thus could all men become children of light.

(5) *A Grievous Absence:* As though to endorse what He had just taught, the Lord withdrew and hid Himself. Thus did He indicate the darkness would prevail when He was not present. He was the Sun of Righteousness who had arisen with healing in His wings; His nearness presented opportunity; His departure meant tragedy. Thus did he announce His message but, unfortunately, the people had cataracts upon their eyes.

But though He had done so many miracles before them — right before their eyes — yet they still did not trust in Him and failed to believe on Him. So that what Isaiah the prophet said was fulfilled, Lord, who has believed our report and our message? And to whom has the arm (the power) of the Lord been shown — unveiled, revealed? Therefore, they could not believe — they were unable to believe. For Isaiah has also said, He has blinded their eyes, and hardened and benumbed their (callous, degenerated) heart: — He has made their minds dull — to keep them from seeing with their eyes and understanding with their heart and mind, and repenting and turning to Me to heal them. Isaiah said this because he saw His glory and spoke of Him. *The Amplified New Testament* (vv. 37-41).

To many readers, this passage may present problems, but a
better understanding is made possible in the light of two facts. The
early chapters of the book of the Exodus teach that when Pharaoh
continued to harden his heart against the commands of the Lord, the
patience of the Almighty became exhausted, and finally God hardened
the heart of the monarch — the Holy Spirit ceased to strive with him.
This truth had been enunciated and vindicated in earlier times when
Noah's indifferent audiences suddenly discovered that God, who had
offered mercy, ultimately denied it. This is a basic truth throughout
Scripture, and sinful men have always been urged to seek the Lord
in the day of opportunity. The earlier chapters of John's gospel reveal
how the Light of the World had shone in the midst of the nation; the
claims of the Eternal had been enunciated; miracles had been performed again and again, but the people who might have learned to
love Christ, "took up stones to stone him." The Lord, therefore, pronounced judgment, ". . . your house is left unto you desolate because
thou knowest not the time of thy visitation." John saw in the tragic
indifference of these evil people the fulfillment of a prediction made
by the prophet; the evidence that even His long suffering is controlled
by righteousness.

> Nevertheless among the chief rulers also many believed on him;
> but because of the Pharisees, they did not confess him, lest they
> should be put out of the synagogue; for they loved the praises of
> men more than the praise of God (vv. 42, 43).

Possibly both Nicodemus and Joseph of Arimathea belonged to
this fearful group. They realized that continuance in synagogue
service would be virtually impossible if the wrath of the high priest
broke over their heads. Gamaliel, the President of the Theological
College, would hardly be permitted to instruct Israel's youth if the
Senate did not endorse his teachings. (See the homily at the end of
Section One of Chapter 3.)

> Jesus cried and said, He that believeth on me, believeth not on me,
> but on him that sent me. And he that seeth me seeth him that
> sent me. I am come a light into the world, that whosoever be-
> lieveth on me should not abide in darkness (vv. 44-46).

Attention is drawn to the fact that John is now concluding his
account of the public ministry of the Lord. Hereafter, the apostle
deals with the instruction, guidance, encouragement of the disciples
as they prepared for the evangelization of a lost world. It is worthy
of note, therefore, that John's key words and phrases appear again
in this passage. Christ came to challenge the power of darkness, to
make a way of escape possible for all who sat in the shadow of death.

> And if any man hear my words; and believe not, I judge him not:
> for I came not to judge the world, but to save the world. He that

rejecteth me, and receiveth not my words, hath one that judgeth him: the word that I have spoken, the same shall judge him in the last day (vv. 47, 48).

If Christ came to save the world — then the world needed saving. We might well ask — FROM WHAT? If Christ continually spoke of a judgment at the last day — then there must be a day of judgment; otherwise, He was misleading His listeners. If Christ affirms that words spoken long ago will be used as evidence at the great assize, then records, detailed and correct records, are being kept in heaven. If all these things are true, it could be to the eternal credit of men to consider the implications of these facts.

> For I have not spoken of myself; but the Father which sent me, he gave me a commandment, what I should say, and what I should speak. And I know that his commandment is life everlasting: whatsoever I speak therefore, even as the Father said unto me, so I speak (vv. 49, 50).

The ministry of Jesus was not a haphazard occurrence, not the product of quick thinking, the evidence of spontaneous brilliance. It was carefully planned in eternal council meetings. What had been decided in eternity was being proclaimed in time; what the Divine Family had unanimously affirmed was being preached by the appointed Messenger. Rejection of the message would be suicidal — to reject Christ was to reject God. These were the things claimed by Jesus. Either He spoke truth or He did not. If the former be the correct interpretation, then there is no other word comparable in importance to be found anywhere on earth. If He were false in His claims, someone should begin to explain the secret of His amazing power, the increasing effectiveness of His saving grace, the transformed homes through all generations, and the undeniable fact that His message alone seems to be competent in the solving of a world's problems.

HOMILIES

Study No. 46

SERMONS FROM THE SKY

All true preaching begins in heaven. From thence comes the living word, the power of the Holy Spirit, and the blessing of the Almighty. Without these the most eloquent men in the world are but tinkling cymbals. All who would testify of the Saviour should take as their example the three occasions when God preached from His cloudy pulpit. At the beginning, in the middle, and again at the conclusion of Christ's earthly ministry, God bore witness concerning His Son. These Scriptures form a comprehensive commentary on the Person of Christ.

God witnessed concerning the Purity of His Son (Matthew 3:16, 17)

When John Baptist first appeared in the Jordan valley, few people could have visualized the things soon to take place. The peaceful countryside filled with eager listeners, and the baptismal services eloquently told of the power of John's ministry. One day Jesus came to be baptized and, as the crowd watched, "The Spirit of God descended like a dove . . . upon him: and lo a voice from heaven, saying, This is my beloved Son, in whom I am well pleased." In order to appreciate the magnitude of this statement, we must remember that sin is a nature. Most people think of sin as being an act of evil; for example, a man may commit murder, adultery, steal, or blaspheme. These are but expressions of evil, fruit on a tree, the inevitable outcome of something infinitely deeper. Why does a man do these things? Surely it is because the life within him produces such deeds. This is clearly indicated in one of the oldest of Bible stories. Before Adam could sin it was necessary for Satan to tempt him. It was not possible for sin to arise from Adam's soul — there was no sin there to arise. Yet later, when Cain murdered his brother, the wicked thought originated in his own being. What happened with the son could not have happened to the father — that is, before his initial transgression. Sin tainted the nature of the first man, and this was transmitted to man's offspring. Thus, whereas Adam had been created without blemish, his sons were born sinners. Thus did David say, "Behold, I was shapen in iniquity; and in sin did my mother conceive me" (Psalm 51:5). Attention is specially drawn to the following statement: *Without the miraculous conception, Jesus of Nazareth would have been borne a sinner.* Within the most intimate intimacy of the loveliest lady of that time, the Holy Spirit performed the miracle — "A virgin conceived and brought forth a son." Thus the last Adam commenced His journey as pure as did the first Adam. However, in the case of Christ, every temptation was overcome, and at the beginning of His public ministry God was able to say, "This is my beloved Son, in whom I am well pleased."

God witnessed concerning the Preaching of His Son (Matthew 17:5)

"And behold a voice out of the cloud, which said, *This is my beloved Son, in whom I am well pleased;* HEAR YE HIM." By the addition of a single sentence God increased the scope of His testimony concerning the Lord Jesus. After His baptism in Jordan, Christ was tempted, and then began His public ministry. Soon the people were aware that His message was different from anything they had ever heard. He spoke of the necessity of being born again. He maintained that conformity to ecclesiastical law and traditions of the fathers were insufficient to merit the commendation of God. He warned of eternal tragedies, and even foretold that some of the exponents of Mosaic Law would be found wanting in the day of judgment. Such teaching was diametrically opposed to the prevailing theological concepts acceptable to the Jewish leaders. Consequently, they opposed the new Teacher by all means within their power. Thus it became necessary for God to endorse the teaching of His Son. At the Mount of Transfiguration, the disciples heard the voice from the cloud stressing the simple statement, *"Hear ye him."* As the Living Word, Jesus was the expression of the highest authority; no earthly wisdom could supercede His knowledge of the counsels and purposes of God, and therefore it behooved all men to consider the words of the Lord Jesus. That Christ was termed the Son of God did not signify He was less than the Father. Christ was called the Son of God to indicate He was of the same essence; He was one with the Father, in knowledge, in purpose, in power.

God witnessed concerning the Passion of His Son (John 12:28)

As the shadow of the cross began to darken the horizon of Jesus, His soul became troubled, and He said, "What shall I say? Father, save me from this hour: but for this cause came I unto this hour. Father, glorify thy name. Then there came a voice from heaven, I have both glorified it, and will glorify it again . . . . Jesus answered (the people) and said, This voice came not because of me, but for your sakes . . . I, if I be lifted up from the earth, will draw all men unto me" (verses 27-32). Thus did God speak beforehand of the death of His Son. The tragedy of the cross was destined to become the greatest triumph of all time, the medium whereby the Father would be glorified and the Son exalted as the supreme head of His redeemed people. Calvary was to become a lighthouse to guide life's travelers to an everlasting harbor of refuge. No one can dispute the fulfilment of the Saviour's word, for the power of redeeming love represents the greatest force on earth. The Lord Jesus Christ occupied the supreme place in the affections of God; and if He be relegated to any other position in our hearts, then our folly will rival the love of God in dimensions.

The Thirteenth Chapter of John

THEME: *Christ Begins the Intimate Instruction of His Disciples*

OUTLINE:
 I. The New Parable. Verses 1-17.
 II. The New Problem. Verses 18-35.
 III. The New Prediction. Verses 36-38.

A *Necessary Introduction to the Study of Section One*

This chapter represents an important place in the ministry of the Saviour. Earlier, His words were spoken primarily to the Jewish nation and more particularly to its leaders. His message was rejected and, as a result, "the Jewish house was left desolate." The Lord now begins to prepare for a fresh onslaught upon the powers of evil. Beyond the boundaries of Palestine lay the undiscovered continents where millions of "other sheep" waited to be gathered into the one true fold of the Great Shepherd. The disciple band would shoulder the responsibilities of taking the message of redemption to those who sat in darkness. In order to do this efficiently, they needed special training, and it was to this end the Lord now devoted His attention.

It must be remembered that throughout the entire life and ministry of the Saviour, the disciples thought only of the possibility of establishing an earthly kingdom; the suggestion that their Messiah might be crucified was abhorrent. These preconceived notions had to be destroyed, and their eyes opened to recognize eternal truth. Constantly the Master had warned of the impending death at Jerusalem, but His words failed to impress His followers. It became necessary therefore, for the Lord to change His methods; instead of preaching another sermon, He proceeded to give an object lesson.

SECTION ONE

Expository Notes on the Washing of the Disciples' Feet

Now before the feast of the passover, when Jesus knew that his hour was come that he should depart out of this world unto the Father, having loved his own which were in the world, he loved them unto the end (v. 1).

It will be recognized that attention is now focussed upon the disciples. The forthcoming Passover feast was destined to be decisive; storm clouds filled the sky. Soon the Lord would return whence He came, and this small band of followers would be left as lambs among wolves — "and having loved his own, he loved them unto the end." The disciples were filled with imperfections; their service would be exceedingly faulty, Simon Peter would deny Him, and the others forsake Him in the hour of sorrow; yet nothing could diminish the overflowing love of the Master's heart. ". . . *he loved them to the end.*" Compared with this great affection, our best efforts appear puny and pitiable.

> After supper being ended, the devil having now put into the heart of Judas Iscariot, Simon's son, to betray him . . . (v. 2).

A great amount of discussion has taken place regarding the identity of this particular supper. Some commentators maintain that this could not have been the final "Lord's Supper" as the events recorded here took place after the supper had ended. Other teachers agree with Matthew Henry who says: "It has generally been taken for granted by commentators that Christ's washing His disciples' feet, and the discourse that followed it, were the same night in which He was betrayed, and at the same sitting wherein He ate the passover and instituted the Lord's supper. This evangelist, making it his business to gather up those passages which the others had omitted, industriously omits those which the others had recorded. This occasions some difficulty in putting them all together." Certain things might be argued for both viewpoints; the important thing is that these events really happened.

> Jesus knowing that the Father had given all things into his hands, and that he was come from God, and went to God; he riseth from supper, and laid aside his garments; and took a towel, and girded himself. After that he poureth water into a basin, and began to wash the disciples' feet, and to wipe them with the towel wherewith he was girded (vv. 3-5).

The late Dr. F. B. Meyer saw in this paragraph a cameo of the plan of salvation, and paraphrased it: "He rose from His kingly throne, and laid aside His garments of royalty; and took the towel of humanity and wrapped it around Himself. After that He poured out His precious blood, and made possible the cleansing of His disciples. And because He was truly human and divine, He was able to complete that which He commenced — to perfect them with the humanity wherewith He was girded." Emphasis is placed upon the fact that the Lord used new methods to impart truth. Hitherto the spoken word had failed to enlighten their souls; now Christ *showed* them the meaning of His utterances. He awakened their understanding to the somber fact He was more concerned with the removal of sin than in the establishing of a kingdom. A kingdom without people would hardly be a kingdom; and unless sinners could be transferred from that other kingdom of darkness, Christ's domain would remain empty.

> **Then cometh he to Simon Peter: and Peter saith unto him, Lord dost thou wash my feet? (v. 6).**

We have no way of knowing if Peter were the first disciple to have his feet washed. Some think he had resentfully watched the operation as it took place with his colleagues, that finally his outburst indicated what had been smouldering within his breast. Others think the Lord deliberately went to Peter first, that what then transpired overcame the objections of the other disciples and permitted the operation to proceed unchallenged. Obviously Peter was upset, but the correct interpretation of his words is far from easy.

> **Jesus answered and said unto him, What I do thou knowest not now; but thou shalt know hereafter. Peter saith unto him, Thou shalt never wash my feet. Jesus answered him, If I wash thee not, thou hast no part with me (vv. 7, 8).**

In His own inimitable style, the Lord said, "Peter, I know this action puzzles you; you cannot appreciate what I am doing. Do not worry, even if you do not comprehend at this moment, you will eventually. When the Holy Spirit comes, He will testify of Me, and guide you into the truth. Therefore, even though you may not like My action, at least, obey My commandment. Simon Peter, your foot, please!" Unfortunately Peter had already decided what he intended to do. His reply brought tension to the hearts of all who listened.

It is somewhat difficult to decide whether he was proud or humble. Perhaps his entire attitude was colored by resentful pride; for example: "Lord, my feet do not need to be washed. I washed them myself a few minutes ago, and they are spotless. Thank you very much, but I am not willing that you should do this to me." On the other hand, necessity demands the consideration of the alternative. Peter might have been exceedingly humble as he whispered, "Lord, I am not worthy that you should wash my feet. I am but a servant; You are the Son of God. Lord, I should be washing Your feet, and not You, mine." However, in the final analysis, it matters not whether he was to be commended for humility or denounced for arrogant pride, the fact remains that both were wrong when Christ waited for Peter's surrender. The Lord was teaching that cleansing is not possible without the cooperation of the sinner. God may provide it; but man must accept it. (See the important homily at the end of this section.)

The Lord's reply, "If I wash thee not, thou hast no part with me," shattered Peter's ego, and subdued his rebellious spirit. This was another version of the Lord's earlier message to Nicodemus, "Ye must be born again." Without the new birth, even the great teacher of Israel would be unable to see the kingdom. Similarly, unless Peter were washed by Christ, his claims to discipleship would be null and void. The Lord expressed vital truth when, in so many words, He declared, "The people who are My disciples are washed by Me. Those who are not cleansed by Me do not belong to Me. Therefore, Simon Peter, whether you like it or not, you are obliged to make a decision. Either you are Mine, or you are not Mine; it depends upon whether or not you are willing to be cleansed." The far-reaching implications of this text are tremendous, for to have no part or fellowship with Christ here inevitably means a similar fate in the world to come. Thus in one moment, the entire scope of redemption was made clear to the men who were destined to preach the Gospel to a needy world.

> Simon Peter saith unto him, Lord, not my feet only, but also my hands and my head. Jesus saith to him, He that is washed needeth not save to wash his feet, but is clean every whit: and ye are clean, but not all. For he knew who should betray him; therefore said he, Ye are not all clean (vv. 9-11).

Probably the Lord bowed His head quickly to proceed with the feet washing, and thus Peter missed the sparkle which turned the Master's eyes to stars. He knew that at last He had succeeded in dropping eternal seeds into the fertile soil of Simon's heart. Later, impulsive Peter rushed from one indiscretion into another. Graciously the Saviour reminded him that once a man had been cleansed by divine grace, it only remained to maintain the cleanliness of his daily walk. Saints should realize that the initial cleansing in the precious blood of Jesus is forever; the medium by which the daily cleansing operates is the continual application of the water — the Word of truth. The teaching which infers that the application of baptismal waters is the medium of soul cleansing is false. If the literal washing had cleansed away sin, then Judas would have been saved.

> So after he had washed their feet, and had taken his garments, and was set down again, he said unto them, Know ye what I have done to you? Ye call me Master and Lord: and ye say well; for so I am. If I then, your Lord and Master, have washed your feet; ye ought also to wash one another's feet. For I have given you an example, that ye should do as I have done to you (vv. 12-15).

A. W. Pink draws attention to the fact that the disciples never addressed their Lord as "Jesus." This statement is correct and reminds of the trenchant attacks made against this practice by Sir Robert Anderson. If a citizen of London, England, addressed the ruling monarch by his Christian name, it would be deemed unpardonable ignorance, a total lack of respect, and a complete breach of etiquette. The disciples followed One who was indeed the reigning Monarch of an everlasting kingdom; consequently their deep respect and true adoration always ascribed to their Leader the titles to which He was due. They called Him "Lord" and "Master," but never Jesus. Sinful men and even devils used the term, but no Christian should emulate their example. Our approach to God and the brethren should be characterized by deep humility, and this was the burden of the words which came from the Master's lips. If He, the Lord of Glory, could stoop to wash the disciples' feet, no task should be considered too menial for those who profess to be His followers. He supplied the example for all Christian conduct.

> Verily, verily, I say unto you, The servant is not greater than his Lord; neither he that is sent greater than he that sent him. If ye know these things, happy are ye if ye do them (vv. 16, 17).

Within the Christian Church is a very fine body of people who affirm that literal footwashing was commanded by the Lord Jesus. Consequently a highlight of their church is the ceremony at which, often with many tears, they wash each other's feet. This, to them, is a time of deep heart-searching, confession of sin, and rededication to do the will of God. Other sections of the church do not agree that this was the specific command of Christ, and occasionally between these equally devout people, dissension has arisen. Either one condemns the other — the one for refusing to obey, the other for misinterpreting the Word of Truth. Sometimes in saying the right thing in the wrong way, even a saint may fall into error. Anything which draws a soul closer to Christ is to be commended; any carnal criticism of a brother is to be condemned. Quality of doctrine is most excellent, but quality of living — holiness, Christlikeness — is even better. While both are desirable, the fact must be faced that it is possible to have a very enlightened mind and yet at the same time possess a cold critical heart. If a Christian loves to wash his brother's feet, let him proceed as long as he does not use boiling water! If his critical words denounce others who do not follow his example, he exhibits the fact that his soul needs more cleansing than his feet.

A. W. Pink correctly analyzed the incident when he declared: "That that which the Lord Jesus here did to His disciples looked beyond the literal act to its deep symbolic significance is clear from these facts: First, *the Lord's* word to Peter, 'What I do, thou knowest not now' (13:7). Certainly Peter knew that his feet had been literally washed. Secondly, *the further* words of Christ to Peter. 'If I wash thee not, thou hast no part with me.' There are multitudes of believers that HAVE A PART WITH CHRIST *who have never practiced foot washing as a religious ordinance.* Thirdly, *His words:* 'Ye are clean, but not all.' Judas could never have been thus excepted if only literal foot-washing were here in view. Fourthly, *His question:* 'Know ye what I have done to you?' clearly indicates that the Lord's act in washing the feet of the disciples had a profound *spiritual meaning* . . . 'For I have given you an example, that ye should do as I have done to you.' We take it that the force of these words of Christ is this: "I have just shown you how spiritual love operates; it ever seeks the good of its objects, and esteems no service too lowly to secure that good."

HOMILIES

Study No. 47

PETER . . . WHO REFUSED TO HAVE HIS FEET WASHED

All the major religions of the world are agreed on one basic fact: Man is a sinner and needs to be cleansed. All these faiths — Christianity excepted — are also agreed that cleansing depends upon human merit. Man must *do* something in order to obtain forgiveness. For example, during a visit to an Indian temple, this author was invited by a priest to rub gray ashes into his forehead. He was encouraged to do this because the action would please the god and obtain pardon. Similarly, an elder in a Moslem mosque volunteered information to the effect that forgiveness was not possible unless a sinner fulfilled five basic principles of Moslem law. Within the confines of the synagogue, Jews are taught to keep the commandments, and in many branches of the professedly Christian churches, men are urged to *do* certain things. Salvation is said to be the reward of merit, and unless a man meets the requirements of divine law, salvation must forever be denied.

The teachings of the Lord Jesus Christ were diametrically opposed to this, for He announced that man's greatest efforts would be insufficient. *Unless He cleansed men, they would remain unclean.* This is clearly seen in the account of the Lord's washing the feet of Simon Peter.

The Sublime Saviour

The room was very still as every disciple watched the Saviour. Tragedy seemed to hang in the air, and the idea of a kingdom was swiftly receding. The rugged disciples were beginning to realize that something was wrong. Anxiety clutched at their hearts as they saw the shadows gathering on the Master's face. He had risen from the table, and having girded Himself with a towel, had placed a bowl of water on the floor, and was preparing to wash His followers' feet. Rather reluctantly the first disciple obeyed the Lord's command, and allowed Jesus to take hold of the travel-stained foot. The Lord tenderly washed away the dust, and then repeated the operation with the other foot. Radiantly He looked into the face of His silent follower and then, pushing the bowl along the floor, prepared to wash the feet of the next disciple. The company was truly amazed, but only Simon Peter prepared to give utterance to his feelings.

The Stubborn Simon

"Then cometh he to Simon Peter: and Peter saith unto him, Lord, dost thou wash my feet?" "Yes, Simon, you will not understand the meaning of this now, but soon all will be made clear to you." "Peter saith unto him, Thou shalt never wash my feet." Slowly the Lord sat back on His heels and looked into the face of His determined friend. Peter's statement had electrified the atmosphere, for all the strained emotions of his soul had suddenly found an outlet. The earlier expository notes indicated the two-fold way in which this outburst might be interpreted. Peter was very determined, and had any other than the Lord been in charge of the situation, the position might have been grave. Calmly the Lord continued to watch His outspoken disciple, and then quietly He spoke again.

The Startling Statement

"Very well, Simon Peter; but if I wash thee not, thou hast no part with Me. Friend, all who belong to Me *must be washed* by Me. They cannot cleanse themselves. I must do it for them. I have already told you that what I do you know not now; but you shalt know hereafter. Therefore make your choice now. Submit and be washed, or go your way — you have no part with Me." And in those heart-searching moments, Peter's boisterous determination died within him. Had he been observant, he would have recognized the great satisfaction which suddenly shone in the Master's eyes. It would appear that the Lord succeeded in teaching far more truth through this one action than He had through all His sermons. In one delightful moment, He implanted seed within their hearts which in after days would produce a great harvest of eternal blessing.

The Sensible Surrender

With great grace the Lord washed the feet of Simon Peter and said, "He that is washed needeth not save to wash his feet." And His eyes seemed to add, "When a man has really been cleansed, his chief concern should be that of walking every day in the will of God." Indisputably, neither Peter nor his colleagues understood the full import of the Lord's actions, for they found it so hard to abandon their thoughts of an earthly kingdom. Even after the resurrection they continued to ask, "Lord, wilt thou at this time restore the kingdom to Israel?" They were instructed to return to the city, and there to wait for the fulfilment of the promise relating to the coming of the Holy Spirit. This they did, and when the day of Pentecost arrived, a new illumination flooded their minds. Then they understood why their Lord had insisted upon the cleansing of their feet. They went forth into the city to proclaim a new Gospel; they affirmed that man at his best was still unclean and needed the personal attention of the Son of God. As this realization burst upon the mind of Peter, he went out to preach, and his fiery enunciations gained inspiration from the pre-Calvary scene. He said, "Neither is there salvation in any other: for there is none other name under heaven given among men whereby we must be saved" (Acts 4:12).

SECTION TWO

Expository Notes on Christ's Prediction of the Betrayal

I speak not of you all: I know whom I have chosen: but that the scripture may be fulfilled, He that eateth bread with me hath lifted up his heel against me. Now I tell you before it come, that, when it is come to pass, ye may believe that I am (vv. 18, 19).

This utterance is the natural sequence of verse 10, and should be considered again in the light of chapter 7:70. There is reason to believe that Judas, the son of perdition, was the direct challenge of Satan to Christ. In some senses, the Lord *had* to choose the betrayer to demonstrate that perfection could remain perfection even with a snake in its bosom. See the expository notes on Chapter 6:70. The reference to the fulfilment of Scripture deserves special attention. The citation probably comes from Psalm 41:9: "Yea, mine own familiar friend, in whom I trusted, which did eat of my bread, hath lifted up his heel against me." David's friend was probably the chief counselor, Ahithophel, who because of a grievous dispute forsook his king and even plotted the death of the Lord's anointed. See II Samuel 15:12. Unquestionably, David's first thought in the writing of this psalm was the treachery of his intimate friend, but it is thought-provoking that while the Lord also recognized this fact, He nevertheless expanded the scope of David's message. We find it difficult therefore to escape the conclusion that the overruling providence of God used the deeds and words of men to predict accurately what was ultimately to be fulfilled in the experiences of the Lord Jesus.

John has already stressed the fact that, "having loved his own, he loved them unto the end," and here is further evidence to support that assertion. The Lord reminded His disciples of the fulfilment of the Scriptures even before it came to pass, that when it did take place they would remember His words and believe. He was supplying the evidence beforehand, that at the opportune moment, His words might be remembered and nourish their faith.

> Verily, verily, I say unto you, He that receiveth whomsoever I send receiveth me; and he that receiveth me receiveth him that sent me (v. 20).

In view of the fact that the Lord had only just spoken about the presence of the betrayer, this verse seems to have added significance. It must not be forgotten that Judas had been one of the Twelve, and later one of the seventy whom the Lord sent to preach the good news. It was said that He sent them to preach and heal the sick. It is therefore possible that Judas even performed miracles in the Name of Jesus. Later, when his infamy became apparent to the world, some of his former hearers might have been tempted to reject everything, even his message. And before we condemn these misguided people, let us reflect on the sad fact that their modern counterparts are still with us. Thousands of people have left the church because the preachers sometimes appeared to be false. Had John turned his back on Christ because of the proximity of Judas, the apostle would have been as great a fool as Judas was a sinner. The Lord said, "Whosoever receiveth whomsoever I send, receiveth me." *The message is always greater than the messenger.* "If then the message is from God's Word, reject it not because the messenger proves to be a fraud. What matters it to me whether the postman be black or white, pleasant or unpleasant, so long as he hands me the right letter?" (A. W. Pink).

> When Jesus had thus said, he was troubled in spirit, and testified, and said, Verily, verily, I say unto you, that one of you shall betray me. Then the disciples looked one on another, doubting of whom he spake (vv. 21, 22).

Consider this under three simple but vital headings:

(1) *A Great Pain.* The greatest suffering was caused not by physical infirmities but by burdens which crushed the spirit. There were several occasions when the Lord was troubled and groaned in His spirit. We may never know what it cost the Son of God to identify Himself with sinful man.

(2) *A Great Perception.* The Lord was never taken by surprise. Even from the beginning of His association with the disciple band, He realized the base treachery ultimately to be manifested in the actions of Judas. Nevertheless, this knowledge was never shared with others, never exhibited, either in word or deed throughout the years they lived together.

(3) *A Great Problem.* This was one of the greatest miracles in the New Testament. Even John, who actually reclined on the Master's

bosom, had no knowledge of the betrayer's identity. The announce-ment was disconcerting, for it seemed fantastic that one of their number could do this thing. Their unbelief enhances the wonder of the love which for so long had sheltered a criminal. We shall never know how Christ did this, but even human villainy cannot impair His love for the sinner.

> Now there was leaning on Jesus' bosom one of his disciples, whom Jesus loved. Simon Peter therefore beckoned to him, that he should ask who it should be of whom he spake. He then lying on Jesus' breast saith unto him, Lord, who is it? (vv. 23-25).

The nearness of John to the Lord is both interesting and com-mendable. We read elsewhere that the disciples quarrelled concerning the privilege of sitting on either side of the Master in the Kingdom. Alas, unfortunately, we never read of a similar argument as to who should lean upon the Lord's bosom. Apparently there was no other candidate for the position. John's favorite hymn might have been:

> Nearer still nearer, close to Thy heart;
> Draw me, My Saviour, so precious Thou art.
> Fold me, Oh fold me, close to Thy breast:
> Shelter me safe in that haven of rest.

It was perfectly natural for Simon Peter to whisper to John urging him to seek additional information about the betrayer. Some commentators think Peter should have asked the Lord personally. This may be the case, for it was better to approach Christ directly than to depend upon the ministry of another — however wonderful that other one might be.

> Jesus answered, He it is, to whom I shall give a sop, when I have dipped it. And when he had dipped the sop, he gave it to Judas Iscariot, the son of Simon (v. 26).

Within the social circles of Judaism, the giving of a sop at a feast was always regarded as an act of favor. It represented a special portion which the host was pleased to offer to an honored guest. Perhaps this accounted for the fact that in spite of the clarity of Christ's message, the disciples did not grasp the significance of His action. How could He bestow favor upon a villain? How could any man betray his Master, when the Lord had so signally honored him? Judas Iscariot was always referred to as *"the son of Simon." There* were other men who bore the same name, and wrong identification could mean acute embarrassment. The naming of the child was the responsibility of the parent; the conduct of the growing child became the responsibility of the child himself. The name "Judas" was no indication of the infamy of its bearer.

> And after the sop Satan entered into him. Then said Jesus unto him, That thou doest do quickly (v. 27).

"A paroxysm of mad devilishness hurried him on, as the swine of Gadara rushing into the deep. Jesus' awful words were enough to warn him back; but sin by wilful resistance of light had now become a fixed law of his being. God gives him up to his own sin . . ." (A. R. Fausset). How can finite man fathom the unfathomable depths of this text? The hour had come; what had to be done, would be done. "Judas, you are going to betray Me; all right, do not linger, do it quickly." Even Judas would know the gnawing doubts, the pitiful remorse, the agonizing horrors of a violated conscience. Perhaps in the depths of an evil heart, even he was in distress. This man, in his maddening desire to become rich, opened fully the way to his soul, and unhindered, the evil one took possession of his entire being; Judas was indeed devil-possessed.

> Now no man at the table knew for what intent he spake this unto him. For some thought because Judas had the bag, that Jesus had said unto him, Buy those things that we need for the feast; or, that he should give something to the poor. He then having received the sop went immediately out: and it was night (vv. 28-30).

"It is plain from these words that our Lord and His disciples were in the habit of giving, especially at the time of the great festivals, out of their scanty pittance, something to those more destitute than themselves. Their 'deep poverty abounded unto the riches of their liberality': and by His example He has taught us not merely that it is the duty of those who may have but little to spare, to give of that little to those who have still less, but that religious observances are gracefully connected with deeds of mercy and almsgiving. He joined humility with piety in His practice and doctrine, and in this He has left us an example that we should follow in His steps" (Dr. John Brown).

Accustomed as the disciples were to such almsgiving, it was natural that they should misinterpret the Master's instruction. It was easier to think good than to think evil. Here too is food for thought. Yet Judas knew the meaning of the Saviour's word and went forth to perform his evil deed. "*It was night.*" The last vestiges of the day of grace faded from his horizon, the shadows gave place to the blackness of eternal tragedy. Alas, for Judas, there can never be another dawn.

> Therefore, when he was gone out, Jesus said, Now is the Son of man glorified, and God is glorified in him. If God be glorified in him, God shall also glorify him in himself, and shall straightway glorify him (vv. 31, 32).

Now. Let every Christian read and carefully consider the implication of this small word — NOW. The departure of Judas cleared the way for the glorification of the eternal Son. It was ever thus. Link this verse with John 7:38, 39 and vital truths become obvious.

(1) Evil must depart from the fellowship.

(2) Then, and then alone can Christ be glorified.

(3) Then and then alone can the soul be filled.

(4) Then and then alone can rivers of living water begin to flow through dedicated service.

It was truly remarkable that Christ should view this specific moment as the beginning of the greatest experience He was ever to know. Not at His baptism when the benediction of God made the Jordan valley holy ground; not at the Mount of Transfiguration when the presence of God made the lofty heights a place of heaven; but on the eve of His death, Christ spoke of the glory of God. ". . . Jesus . . . who for the joy that was set before him endured the cross, despising the shame, and is set down at the right hand of the throne of God" (Hebrews 12:2). (For notes on the glorifying of the Father and the Son through the cross, see the homily at the end of chapter 19). Bishop Ryle paraphrases the verses as follows: " 'If God the Father be specially glorified in all His attributes by My death, He shall proceed at once to place special glory on Me, for My personal work, and shall do it without delay, by raising Me from the dead, and placing Me at His own right hand.' It is the same idea that we have more fully expressed in the seventeenth chapter: 'I have glorified thee on the earth; now, O Father, glorify thou me with thine own self.' " (See the expository notes on John 17.)

Little children, yet a little while am I with you. Ye shall seek me: and as I said unto the Jews, Whither I go, ye cannot come (v. 33).

This Scripture must not be confused with the earlier words addressed to the Jewish listeners. The phraseology was identical, but the meaning somewhat changed. Formerly He spoke of His going to the Father, and of that ultimate goal He assured His disciples they also would be able to share the joy of the eternal home (John 14:1-3). Here, however, He refers to His cross, where according to the Scripture, "He would tread the winepress alone." Leviticus 16:17 reveals this was all foreshown in typology: "And there shall be no man in the tabernacle of the congregation when he goeth in to make an atonement in the holy place, until he come out, and have made an atonement for himself, and for his household, and for all the congregation of Israel." Unlike the ancient priest, the Lord was sinless and had no need to make atonement for Himself.

. . . so now I say unto you, A new commandment I give unto you, That ye love one another; as I have loved you, that ye also love one another. By this shall all know that ye are my disciples, if ye have love one to another (vv. 33, 34).

Once again attention is drawn to the important fact that at the beginning of this chapter John introduces his readers to a new theme. Hitherto the Lord brought His message to the Jews, only to see it rejected. Now, in view of His imminent departure, He instructs the disciples for the task of world-evangelism, for the supreme effort of continuing His own work when He had returned whence He came. There appears to be a correct sequence of thought in the events outlined by the apostle. (1) The preachers would need a clear understanding of the message to be preached. (2) Their hearts would need to be cleansed and filled with divine power. The taint of Judas would need to be absent. (3) As they went forth to their task, love would need to be their understanding characteristic. The love of God must be shed abroad in their hearts; their conduct must endorse their teaching. A church without love is a club; a Christian without love is a piece of cold machinery. An informed mind must be supported by a warm heart. The strength of the assembly is assured not by an influx of new members but by the deepening affection of those already there.

HOMILIES

Study No. 48

THE DISCIPLE WHOM JESUS LOVED

This statement indicates that John enjoyed a special place in the affections of the Saviour. The Master loved all His followers, yet for some unrevealed reason an inner circle of comradeship existed within the wider ranks of the disciples: only Peter, James, and John accompanied the Lord on certain missions. Yet it is most interesting to note that even within this inner circle of loyal friends, John occupied a place of pre-eminence. He became known as the disciple whom Jesus loved, and the statement suggests a challenging question. How did John gain this place of distinction in the affairs of his Master?

The Special Place – He leaned upon the Master's bosom (John 13.23)

"Now there was leaning on Jesus' bosom one of the disciples, whom Jesus loved." The Lord's intimation of the coming betrayal shocked His followers, and they found it difficult to believe that one of their number would be a traitor. Spontaneously they cried "Lord, is it I?" But it was left to John, who leaned against the Saviour's breast, to whisper the question, "Lord, who is it?" As mentioned earlier, we read in the gospel record that the disciples quarrelled as to who would be permitted to occupy the seats of honor in the kingdom. Every man aspired to greatness, and the fact that two of their brotherhood had secretly conspired to obtain the places on either side of the throne filled them with disgust. A first-class row seemed to be approaching, when Jesus gently intervened. Yet we do not read anywhere of their quarrelling in regard to the privilege of leaning on Christ's bosom. The disciples possibly considered John's action to be a little effeminate. He saw their frowns of displeasure, but remained indifferent to their scorn. He was not content to remain a yard away from his Lord when he could be near enough to hear the slightest whisper.

The Special Privilege — "Behold thy mother" (John 19:26, 27)

"When Jesus therefore saw his mother, and the disciple standing by, whom he loved, he saith unto his mother, Woman, behold thy son! Then saith he to the disciple, Behold thy mother! And from that hour that disciple took her unto his own home." When Jesus entrusted His dearest earthly possession to the care of John, He conferred upon him the greatest honor. Yet with the honor went a great responsibility, for John was asked to enter into the life of Mary to fill the vacancy caused by the death of Jesus. This was not an easy task; but when John's arm went around Mary's shoulders, it became obvious that he had accepted his Master's challenge. The Lord Jesus knew John was completely truthworthy; His mother would be perfectly safe in the new home. Perhaps John's quiet contemplation on the bosom of Christ prepared him for this great moment. Only those who have leaned on Christ's bosom are fit for the more intimate responsibilities of the kingdom.

The Special Perception — "It is the Lord" (John 21:7)

The pale silvery light of a new dawn was slowly spreading over Galilee's waves when the tired fisherman brought their fishing vessel toward the beach. "Then Jesus saith unto them, Children, have ye any meat? They answered him, No. And he said unto them, Cast the net on the right side of the ship, and ye shall find. They cast therefore, and now they were not able to draw it for the multitude of fishes. Therefore that disciple whom Jesus loved saith unto Peter, It is the Lord." While the remaining disciples struggled with the fish, John calmly looked through the morning haze to recognize his Lord. He had very good eyesight! Neither the mists of the morning nor the storms of life could impair his vision. He occupied such a place of intimacy in the affections of the Lord Jesus that reciprocal love awarded him the great honor mentioned in the Scriptures. He became the disciple whom Jesus loved. There were three reasons why he deserved his reward. (1) When the other disciples thought of a kingdom, John drew nearer to Christ. (2) When they ran for safety, John lingered at the cross to shelter a helpless woman. (3) When they struggled to land a catch of fish, John forgot all earthly gains and rejoiced in the nearness of his Lord.

(Reprinted from *Bible Pinnacles,* page 129.)

Study No. 49

JUDAS . . . WHO GAMBLED AND LOST HIS SOUL

The account of the treachery of Judas Iscariot is the most tragic story in history. It is beyond comprehension that a man who had occupied a position of trust and friendship in the disciple band should ultimately betray his Leader. Many questions have been asked concerning this pathetic episode, but one thing has become evident: the complete story of Judas is summed up in the opening statement of Luke 22:4, "And he went *his* way." It is indeed most doubtful if he ever went Christ's way.

The Way of Glory

"And Jesus ordained twelve, that they should be with him, and that he might send them forth to preach. Simon . . . James . . . and Judas Iscariot" (Mark 3:14-19). The foreknowledge of God does not alter the responsibility of man. Even though Christ knew what would take place, Judas of his own volition deliberately betrayed the Master. To him the call of Christ had been irresistible. It opened vistas of unprecedented possibilities. If this new Leader were to be the Messiah, then the kingdom was at hand, and every man in the nation would have welcomed a place at the side of his King. Eagerly anticipating the splendor of a glorious future, Judas left his friends and followed the Saviour. And there is reason to believe that he worked as hard as anyone else in the days of preaching which followed. This was indeed "his own way," and it is easy to imagine how fervently he proclaimed his message to all and sundry.

The Way of Greed

Many years later, when the apostle John described the criticism made by Judas concerning Mary's gift of ointment, he wrote, "Then saith one of his disciples, Judas Iscariot, Simon's son, which should betray him, Why was not this ointment sold for three hundred pence and given to the poor? This he said, not that he cared for the poor, but because he was a thief and had the bag, and bare what was put therein" (John 12:4-6). There had been times when the disciples were puzzled by the shortage of money. It was inconceivable that one of their number should steal from the common fund; and yet . . . ? Long afterward they remembered and understood. "Judas went *his* way." It was the way of self-pleasing. Probably he argued with himself that his position as treasurer deserved remuneration. He therefore helped himself to money which was not his. Ultimately it was this love of gain which wrecked his soul. As the end of Christ's pilgrimage approached, Judas became increasingly suspicious that something had gone wrong. The promised kingdom seemed to be receding; the Master had grown sad and thoughtful; the enemies were becoming jubilant. Judas noted all these things and realized that Christ's way and his own way were not parallel paths. When the Lord failed to take advantage of the delirious welcome afforded by the crowd as He rode into Jerusalem, Judas knew that tragedy loomed on the horizon.

The Way of Guilt

At an eastern feast, the offering of a sop by the host is recognized as a mark of favor. Almost the last thing Jesus did for Judas was to offer friendship. Judas replied with the traitor-kiss. When the betrayer felt the coins in his hand, he smiled. They were better than nothing! Yes, he was getting out while he was able. *He went his own way.* Poor man! With remorse playing havoc with his conscience; with his coins rudely scattered over the floor; with his hopes and plans completely broken, a poor tormented man, he went out to commit suicide. And of his final destiny there can be no doubt. Jesus prayed and said, ". . . those that thou gavest me I have kept, and none of them is lost but the son of perdition; that the scripture might be fulfilled" (John 17:12). Certain eminent teachers declare that Judas was Satan's imitation of the Son of God. They draw attention to the fact that the same title — "the son of perdition" — is also used of the antichrist (II Thessalonians 2:3). Mention has also been made of the fact that of Judas alone it is said, ". . . from which Judas by transgression fell, that *he might go to his own place*" (Acts 1:25). Here are great mysteries; but one thing is certainly clear. Judas had staked his all; he was a reckless gambler. He lost because he had not the ability to see God's way was better than his own.

SECTION THREE

Expository Notes on Christ's Message to Simon Peter

Simon Peter saith unto him, Lord, whither goest thou? Jesus answered him, Whither I go, thou canst not follow me now: but thou shalt follow me afterwards. Peter said unto him, Lord, why cannot I follow thee now? I will lay down my life for thy sake (vv. 36, 37).

Peter's question is obviously a reference back to the Lord's earlier statement recorded in verse 33. Nevertheless the expanding meaning of the statement is obvious, for while no one can follow Christ to the death of the cross — that is, to make reconciliation for the sins of the people — yet in later days, it would be possible for disciples, emulating the example of the Lord, to remain faithful even unto death. It is generally acknowledged that Peter was crucified upside down as he considered himself unworthy to die as the Lord did. No one would question Peter's sincerity — he meant that he would die for his Lord if that became necessary; however, one's strength may often become weakness when courage begets too much self-confidence. Actually, Peter in his impatience and impetuosity was questioning the wisdom and accuracy of the Master's statement. This is always the precursor of tragedy.

> **Jesus answered him, Wilt thou lay down thy life for my sake? Verily, verily, I say unto thee, The cock shall not crow, till thou hast denied me thrice (v. 38).**

It will be noted that many of the more poignant details of the Lord's prediction and of the collapse of Simon Peter are omitted from John's gospel. Attention is drawn again therefore to the fact that this apostle set out to write those things which the other writers had not included in their memoirs. John was far more concerned with the emphasis to be placed upon the greatness of Christ than he was with the references to Simon's pathetic failure. Consequently this story is confined to the details which magnify the Lord's omniscience. Christ foresaw clearly all that was to take place.

HOMILIES

Study No. 50

CHRIST . . . WHO SAW THE END FROM THE BEGINNING

The Lord foresaw the unique quality of His own decease

Other people might die rather than abandon their faith; indeed some would even be crucified, but no one could do what He was about to do. "Whither I go, ye cannot come."

The Lord foresaw the martyrdom of Simon Peter

". . . thou canst not follow me NOW." "Verily, verily, I say unto thee, When thou wast young, thou girdedst thyself, and walkedst whither thou wouldest: but when thou shalt be old, thou shalt stretch forth thy hands, and another shall gird thee, and carry thee whither thou wouldest not. This spake he, signifying by what death he should glorify God . . ." (John 21:18, 19).

The Lord foresaw the denial of Peter

". . . till thou hast denied me." Boastful and arrogant self-confidence can never deceive the Master. In spite of several failures, this disciple nevertheless reached great heights of victory. He had walked on the water; he had caught the fish with the coin in its mouth; he had made his thrilling confession, "Thou art the Christ." Could such an eminent leader fail? Certainly; the Lord said so, and He knew what He was talking about.

The Lord foresaw the precise nature of the denial

". . . till thou hast denied me *thrice*." This would be no mere slip of the tongue made in a moment of panic. The deed would be repeated until the failure became threefold.

The Lord foresaw the time of the denial

". . . *The cock shall not crow*, till thou hast denied me thrice." Perhaps there was something blessed about this detail. The cock-crow was the harbinger of a new day. Night with its gloom was about to pass away as the rooster welcomed the approaching dawn. Perhaps it was providential that Peter denied at the cock-crow and not at sunset. From the ignominy of shame and the bitterness of defeat, Simon entered a new day, a day made possible by the unfailing love of his incomparable Master.

The Fourteenth Chapter of John

THEME: *The Saviour Holds a Disciples' Press Conference!*

OUTLINE:

    I Christ continues to answer Simon Peter. Verses 1-4.
    II Christ answers Thomas. Verses 5-7.
    III Christ answers Philip. Verses 8-21.
    IV Christ answers Judas. Verses 22-31.

SECTION ONE

Expository Notes on the Continuance of Christ's Message to Peter

Let not your heart be troubled: ye believe in God, believe also in me. (V. 1).

The closing verses of the preceding chapter revealed how the Lord addressed a warning to Simon Peter, and indicated the gravity of Peter's self-assurance. It is not known whether the fourteenth chapter was actually a continuation of that same conversation. Possibly a little time elapsed before the Lord uttered the now famous words, "Let not your heart be troubled," and yet on the other hand, this message could easily have followed the words spoken to Peter. A new tension gripped the hearts of the disciples; the Master had uttered ominous words. Furtively they looked at each other. Judas would betray the Lord; Simon Peter thrice deny the Master — what new villainy would soon be revealed? Their faces were haggard and then, quite suddenly, the Lord smiled and said, "Let not your hearts be troubled." His message was springtime after winter, flowers after barrenness, green pastures after sandy wastes, a radiant dawn after a night of terror. If we consider this chapter to be the continuation of its predecessor, then primarily the words were spoken to Simon Peter. However, throughout Christendom the Church has taken this passage to its heart.

> **In my father's house are many mansions** (dwelling places; homes): if it were not so, I would have told you. I go to prepare a place for you. And if I go and prepare a place for you, I will come again, and receive you unto myself; that where I am, there ye may be also. And whither I go ye know, and the way ye know (vv. 2-4).

The abiding wonders of our eternal home are revealed through various similes within the New Testament. Heaven is called a "Country" in Luke 19:12 and Hebrews 11:16. This probably suggests its expanse, its magnitude, its far reaching greatness. It is called a "kingdom" in Peter 1:11. This suggests the reign of a monarch, orderliness, authority, blessedness under God's rulership. It is also termed a "city" in Hebrews 11 and Revelation 21:1, 2. This undoubtedly suggests citizenship, a population, those who intimately belong to its dwelling places. The fact that the Lord here referred to "my Father's house" suggests love, a family, the joys of a home where the fellowship of the Father is a constant privilege. The Lord Jesus inferred that the preparation of an eternal abiding place was a special task to which He personally intended to devote His attention. It was destined that each disciple would have a dwelling place; that at the appointed time the Son of God would become responsible for the saint's removal from earth to heaven. The angels are said to be ministering spirits sent forth to minister to those who are the heirs of salvation (Hebrews 1:13, 14). Yet — although they are permitted to carry a soul into the bosom of Abraham (Luke 16:22) — Christ alone becomes responsible for escorting the redeemed to the prepared mansion. Had this been untrue, He would have warned them. If things were withheld from the disciples, He had a purpose in withholding the information.

The promise, "I will come again," has been interpreted in a variety of ways.

(1) Some teachers have said it was fulfilled at Pentecost when the Spirit of Truth came to be with the Church. That Christ did indeed come in the person of the Comforter cannot be denied, but to infer that this fulfilled the promise of John 14:3 is a mistake. Even though Christ came at Pentecost, He did not receive *His own unto Himself.*

(2) Some teach that this prediction is fulfilled at the death of a saint. The text, "Yea, though I walk through the valley of the shadow of death, I will fear no evil: for thou art with me; thy rod and thy staff they comfort me" (Psalm 23:4), has been the delight of God's people in all ages. The story of the home call of Stephen in Acts 7:55, 60 provides a glorious example of the Lord's nearness to one about to leave this world.

Nevertheless, we are urged to compare Scripture with Scripture, and while this particular interpretation has merit, it does not fulfill what has been predicted of Christ's return. At the death of a saint, the Lord takes one disciple to the many mansions. When He comes for His Church, the entire Body of Christ will be called to eternal blessedness. "For the Lord himself shall descend from heaven with a shout, with the voice of the archangel, and with the trump of

God: and the dead in Christ shall rise first: Then we which are alive and remain shall be caught up together with them in the clouds to meet the Lord in the air: *and so shall we ever be with the Lord. Wherefore comfort one another with these words*" (I Thessalonians 4:16-18). The student should note that this message to promote the comfort of saints is related to the earlier message, "Let not your heart be troubled." Both Scriptures speak of the Lord's return; both are meant to be a source of comfort. It follows then that while the Lord may indeed come to welcome home the dying saint, the promise does not find complete fulfilment until the graves yield their bodies, until the Church joins the Lord in glory.

It was toward this thrilling climax that Simon Peter was urged to look. Sin may win occasional victories but the final triumph rests with God. When we remember the other words spoken to Simon Peter, it is easy to recognize the superlative wonder of the Lord Jesus Christ. "And the Lord said, Simon, Simon, behold, Satan hath desired to have you, that he may sift you as wheat: But I have prayed for thee, that thy faith fail not: and when thou art converted, strengthen thy brethren" (Luke 22:31, 32). The Lord does not forsake His children each time they stumble and fall. He has covenanted to bring many sons to glory. He is the Master Potter; when the clay is unresponsive, the vessel is broken that it might be made anew. This truth enabled John to write, "Behold, what manner of love the Father hath bestowed upon us, that we should be called the sons of God . . . . Beloved, now are we the sons of God, and it doth not yet appear what we shall be: but we know that when he shall appear we shall be like him; for we shall see him as he is" (I John 3:1, 2).

The Lord probably sighed and said in conclusion, "You know where I am going; you have heard what I shall be doing on your behalf. Remember this in the days to come, and 'Let not your hearts be troubled.' "

HOMILIES

Study No. 51

STOP WORRYING

It is almost superfluous to supply a division of this text, for its message has been meat and drink to the Church in all generations. Nevertheless, for the benefit of young preachers the following homily is suggested:

Worry not about your condemnation — Christ has come

The law was a schoolmaster to bring us to Christ, a schoolmaster who discovered our faults and caused acute discomfort. The knowledge that sin reigned within begat condemnation. Pardon appeared to be beyond our grasp; freedom an impossibility. Then Jesus came.

Worry not about your sins — Christ has died

How can a man escape from the thralldom of evil? How can a soul be liberated from the consequences of sin? The coming of Christ revealed that God cared; the death of Christ revealed He was determined to do more than care. Sympathy is not salvation; a recognition of evil is not necessarily its removal.

Worry not about your decease — for Christ has risen

Death is a universal tyrant. Kings and paupers, saints and sinners, learned and illiterate — all die. The threat of death is a cloud which obliterates the sunshine. Christians alone may be free from fear for, to them, death has died. The risen Lord has ascended, the first fruits of them that slept.

Worry not about your weakness — Christ intercedes

"Be not weary in well doing for in due season ye shall reap if ye faint not." Increasing problems provide a new incentive to pray. "Let us, therefore, come boldly unto the throne of grace, that we may obtain mercy, and find grace to help in time of need" (Hebrews 4:16).

Worry not about your future — Christ is coming again

This is the hope of the church, the guiding star in God's sky. God never supplies December grace in July. With each day comes new strength, with every emergency come fresh supplies of grace. Christians must learn to live a day at a time, remembering that each day might herald the Lord's return. "And every man that hath this hope in him purifieth himself, even as he is pure" (I John 3:3).

SECTION TWO

Expository Notes on Christ's Answer to Thomas

Thomas saith unto him, Lord, we know not whither thou goest; and how can we know the way? Jesus saith unto him, I am the way, the truth, and the life: no man cometh unto the Father but by me (vv. 5, 6).

Throughout the ages Thomas has been known as "the doubting disciple." Yet this man was to be commended, for at least he was honest. Abraham Lincoln once said, "Better to remain silent and be thought a fool, than to speak and remove all doubt." Some men hide their problems, and their secret struggles ruin fellowship. Thomas brought his difficulties to Jesus, for that was the only way to find relief. This man and his colleagues should have been able to answer their own question. Their preconceived ideas demanded the establishment of an earthly kingdom; alas, they could think of nothing else. The idea was now formulating that Christ might be thinking of another city, another earthly paradise in which to set up His throne. "Where is it, Lord? We do not know its location, so how can we know the way to reach it?"

The Lord was very patient. Thomas was more concerned with the location and stressed ". . . whither thou goest"; the Lord emphasized the highway to the location: "I am the way . . . ." It mattered not where any spiritual kingdom was established — in heaven or on earth, at that time or in distant ages; its highway would always be the same. If a man stayed close to the road and traveled in the right direction, his destiny would never be in doubt. "Thomas, you are so concerned about finding, seeing, supporting the kingdom. It will be My task of preparing that place for you. This I told you, Thomas. Your concern should be to find the highway; stay with the highway, and all will be well. You ask where is the way? Thomas, I am the way — the royal highway to blessedness. Stay with Me and you will never be lost!"

The triple-glory of this text constitutes one of the greatest utterances ever to fall from the Saviour's lips. This verse must never be divorced from its context. The Lord Jesus had often repeated that He had been sent from God, that He only spoke the things commanded by God. The Jews attacked His doctrines, criticized His methods, and threatened His life, but He steadily reaffirmed His position. He repeated His claims to deity, He refuted all teaching which did not harmonize with His own, and warned of the eternal tragedy to overtake those who rejected His message. The text now under consideration was another step in the expanding fullness of the Saviour. He was the way, the highway between heaven and earth; He was Jacob's ladder by which a man could ascend to God even as the angels descended to earth. He was the truth, the Word, the expression of the Infinite. The glory of the Father shone in His face; the message of the Father echoed in His tones; the love of the Father overflowed His heart. He was the life — the very life of God, eternal, enduring, divine. This life He offered to men. To possess the Son was to possess life for, "He that hath the Son hath life." "Thomas," He seemed to say, "*these* are the things you need to remember. Do not worry about the kingdom; that will surely be established in the fullness of time. Stay close to me, Thomas, and doubt no more."

If ye had known me, ye should have known my Father also: and from henceforth ye know him, and have seen him (v. 7).

This verse when considered with the closing statement of the preceding verse provides food for thought. The Lord claimed two stupendous things. He was God; to see Him was indeed to see the Father. Within the scope of His ministry had been exhibited all the glories of the Godhead; consequently nothing — nothing could ever be as important as what He said and did. He was not only the Way to God; He was THE ONLY WAY. To miss Him was to miss everything.

This statement is of paramount importance and needs to be stressed in an age when the study of comparative religions occupies the thoughts of innumerable students. An awakening of the moral consciousness in international relations suggests that we search for the good in all men. Therefore, we speak of good Buddhists, virtuous Moslems, refined and educated men of another faith. We seek to find the commendable points for what long was considered alien religions. There are sincere men who spend much time trying to formulate a world-faith acceptable to all nations. Sometimes we are apt to forget that the Lord Jesus said, *"No man cometh unto the Father but by me."* If the charge be made that this is inexcusable arrogance we can only reply that so also was the charge made against Jesus when He first announced His teaching. It was with this in mind that He commanded His disciples to go into all the world to preach the Gospel. The people of other lands were in darkness and danger; they needed the Gospel, and the disciples were commanded to go forth to make disciples of all nations. The giving of tractors, farming implements, schools, colleges, hospitals, medicines, drugs, and a host of other things belongs to our moral obligations as men toward less fortunate members of the human race. The preaching of the Gospel of Christ is even more important, for those we are destined to reach are potential children of God for whom the Lord died. Without food they cannot live; without the Bread of Life they will perish forever.

HOMILIES

Study No. 52

THE ROYAL HIGHWAY

"And an highway shall be there"
Isaiah 35:8
"I am the way"
John 14:6

When the Lord Jesus said, "I am the way, the truth, and the life," He probably remembered the utterance of the prophet Isaiah. "And an highway shall be there, and a way, and it shall be called the way of holiness; the unclean shall not pass over it; but it shall be for those: the wayfaring men, though fools, shall not err therein. No lion shall be there, nor any ravenous beast shall go up thereon, it shall not be found there; but the redeemed shall walk there: and the ransomed of the Lord shall return and come to Zion with songs, and everlasting joy upon their heads: they shall obtain joy and gladness, and sorrow and sighing shall flee away" (Isaiah 35:8-10). The whole of Isaiah chapter 35 is worthy of detailed consideration, for it is filled with the most wonderful prophecies of Christ.

The Special Way

"And a highway shall be there, and a way . . . ." That these two terms should be coupled together is most suggestive. A *way* in olden days was a well-trod pathway, a road used by everyone. A *highway* was a special road often made for and used by a king. Such roads would be made at the king's command and would be reserved for the royal chariots. A modern counterpart would be the great American freeways from which all pedestrians and even bicycles are excluded. Alongside the great freeways of California and New York are lesser roads, leading in the same direction but used by the pedestrians who are forbidden to use the more dangerous highway. The prophet foretold that God would create a special highway, a royal highway which would be open to all travelers.

The Saintly Way

". . . . and it shall be called the way of holiness." That the unclean could not pass over it suggests that nothing that defiled was ever allowed to contaminate the highway. In itself this road would be clean, and tidy, and wholesome. No traveler would be forbidden to use it as long as he conformed to the travel requirements of the country. The unclean were never to be permitted to pass over it. The Royal Builder of the highway would welcome sinners and do for them what no other could do. His precious blood removed their sins.

The Separated Way

". . . the unclean shall not pass over it." The creation of the highway automatically separated people into two communities: those who complied with and those who resisted the regulations. The unclean who sought cleansing would be permitted to travel on the way to glory; the unclean who preferred to remain unclean would travel another road, in another direction, to disaster. Throughout the ministry of the Lord Jesus the separating influence of His message became increasingly apparent. He said those who were not for Him were against Him.

The Simple Way

". . . it shall be for those: the wayfaring men." Even peasants, farm laborers, the simple common folk, would be permitted to use the highway. Academic degrees, social greatness, eminence of any kind would not necessarily be pre-requisites for travelers. Children, tramps, all who would might enter, for in assessing greatness God would be more concerned with purity of heart than social distinction.

The Sure Way

". . . the wayfaring men, though fools, shall not err therein." These men, although they may not have the ability to distinguish themselves in other walks of life, would cover themselves with glory on the road to heaven. God does not always choose the great, the mighty; sometimes He chooses the foolish things of this world to confound the wise.

The Safe Way

"No lion shall be there, nor any ravenous beast shall go up thereon." The lion in ancient days was considered the strongest and most ferocious of all animals. Its presence in any particular vicinity threatened travelers with death. The Royal Highway would be protected by the King's soldiers; enemies would be chased away, so that those who enjoyed the King's favor would know perpetual protection while they traveled in company with the King. "For he shall give his angels charge over thee, to keep thee in all thy ways" (Psalm 91:11).

The Salvation Way

". . . the redeemed shall walk there." Redemption was something known by slaves — those who had been sold into bondage and then emancipated. The REDEEMED shall walk the highway. The Prince of Glory came to earth to save sinners, to set free the captive, to emancipate those who were enslaved. "In whom we have redemption through his blood, the forgiveness of sins, according to the riches of his grace . . ." (Ephesians 1:7).

The Singing Way

"And the ransomed of the Lord shall return, and come to Zion with songs and everlasting joy upon their heads." A happy people is often a singing people; the forgiveness of sin is the forerunner of increasing happiness. The breaking of the chains of captivity is a cause for praise; the opening of the doors of a prison is a prelude to a shout of victory. A rejoicing church sings; heaven itself will be filled with choirs singing the song of Moses and the Lamb (Revelation 5:9).

The Sublime Way

". . . they shall obtain joy and gladness, and sorrow and sighing shall flee away." "And God shall wipe away all tears from their eyes; and there shall be no more death, neither sorrow nor crying, neither shall there be any more pain . . ." (Revelation 21:4). Thus will eternity be welcomed; the travelers on the Royal Highway will have reached their destination; the saints will be HOME. Isaiah looked ahead to the Highway which the creative power of God would make possible; we look back to the Lord Jesus, the fulfilment of every prediction, the joy of His people, the consummation of our deepest hopes.

SECTION THREE

Expository Notes on Christ's Answer to Philip

Philip saith unto Him, Lord, shew us the Father, and its sufficeth us. Jesus saith unto him, Have I been so long time with you, and yet hast thou not known me, Philip? he that hath seen me hath seen the Father; and how sayest thou, Shew us the Father (vv. 8, 9).

Philip had undoubtedly listened to the question asked by Thomas, and had followed with interest every word spoken in reply. The talk about the Father had intrigued him; yet although he stood so near to Truth, he remained so far away. Possibly his thoughts went back to the time when Moses and others were privileged to see manifestations of the Father. If it were possible for such things to be repeated, he wanted to be present. His request revealed he had not understood the words often repeated by the Saviour — "I and the Father are one."

Believest thou not that I am in the Father, and the Father in me? the words that I speak unto you I speak not of myself: but the Father that dwelleth in me, he doeth the works. Believe me that I am in the Father, and the Father in me; or else believe me for the very works' sake. The *Amplified New Testament* renders the last statement: **If you cannot trust me, at least, let these works which I do in my Father's name convince you (vv. 10, 11).**

Compare John 10:38 and reflect on the sad fact that here the Lord had to place His own on a level with unbelieving Pharisees. If His words were unacceptable, then His works might help to convince the doubtful listener. Christ's words and works were always in harmony; either one continually endorsed and supported the other. At Creation He spoke, and it was done; at the tomb of Lazarus He spoke, and the dead came forth. The Lord Jesus was never disobeyed by disease, death, or devils. His authority was never challenged except by those for whom He came to die.

Verily, verily, I say unto you, He that believeth on me, the works that I do shall he do also; and greater works than these shall he do; because I go unto my Father (v. 12).

This is the beginning of a most important section of the chapter. The student must not lose sight of the fact that what is to follow is closely related to the beginning of the account. We may almost consider the aforegoing words as parenthetical; that the Lord momentarily paused to speak certain things to a disciple, but then remembering His initial statement, "Let not your heart be troubled," He proceeded to outline the perfect — that is, the seven reasons why this should be so. This section is among the richest treasures of the Gospel. It is purposed here to study each verse separately, but at the end all seven promises will be considered under one homily.

This verse is a diamond with several facets of truth. "*He that believeth on me,*" like all the other verses using the same phraseology, refers to a man whose heart is filled with dynamic faith. Primarily this was addressed to the disciples, and the promise, "the works that I do, shall he do also" was fulfilled in that the men thus addressed actually did what Jesus did. They opened the eyes of the blind, healed the sick, cast out demons, and raised the dead. There are expositors who infer that this promise was given to all the Church, but the assertion is challenged by some of their colleagues. There is no man on earth today who fully emulates the Lord's example. There are many faith-healers whose claims may be false or true, but it is an irrefutable fact that not even the best, not even the most saintly servant of Christ is raising the dead, cleansing lepers instantaneously, giving sight to the blind, and performing the impossible! The absence of such miracles is blamed on the weakness of the faith of the Church; it is said that if Christians really believed, the old signs and wonders would still be revealed. This may, or may not, be true, but the fact still remains that Christ said: "The works that I do SHALL he do also." He did not say that these works *might* be done IF the disciples had enough faith. He predicted that the miracles WOULD ACTUALLY TAKE PLACE. We are therefore, driven to the conclusion that primarily the promise was given to the men present when He uttered His words.

The importance of miracles was then relegated to minor position, for the Lord said, ". . . greater works than these shall he do . . . ." Can there be any greater miracle than the raising of the dead? Certainly. Let not the student infer that the performance of miracles is not to be expected in the present ministry of the church — that conclusion must be avoided at all costs; nevertheless, there is a place for miracles, and it is certainly not first in the evaluations of God. What may the greater manifestations of divine power be? Before we

try to elucidate these great features, let us remember the words —
BECAUSE I GO TO MY FATHER. The "greater ministry" was to become
a reality *not* because the disciples would have great faith, but rather
because Christ, the Author and Finisher of faith, would be Himself
interceding at God's right hand. Even at the height of individual
success, a blemish might appear in the servant; the faith of the Lord
would be superlative at all times, and it is the knowledge of this
superb fact which inspires the Christian.

The Christian would have a greater message to proclaim. This
would supercede the teachings of Christ simply because there would
be *more of it!* The New Testament minister would be able to proclaim ALL that Christ declared, and then go on to preach about the
outpouring of the Holy Spirit, the manifestations now recorded in
the Acts of the Apostles, the high priestly ministry of the Lord Jesus,
and even the added details of prophetic truth later revealed through
the final revelation given to John on the Isle of Patmos.

The Christian would have a wider audience to reach. The entire
ministry of the Lord was exercised within the narrow confines of a
very small country called Palestine. Today, a modern traveler flying
in a jet plane can travel further in a few hours than Jesus traveled
in all His life. Occasionally, the Saviour spoke to crowds, but for
the most part He addressed audiences which unfortunately would
not even attract some of the popular speakers of our time. He never
left His country on any evangelistic crusade; He was never invited
to any Bible conference; He was not an accredited minister of His
denomination. When judged by the purely normal standards, He
was just an ordinary layman! Yet from His wonderful heart flowed
the rivers of truth to inspire, to cheer, to encourage, to redeem innumerable people. He reached a small country; His followers would
evangelize the entire world. He had to be content to speak to His
own people and occasionally to a handful of Gentiles; His followers
would climb mountains, march through forests, reach lonely islands
of the sea, and make converts in Caesar's household.

The Christian would perform miracles of a different type. For
the most part the Lord Jesus had to be content to perform physical
miracles. He opened the eyes of the man born blind; He cleansed
lepers, and healed a man who had the palsy. He touched bodies,
but sometimes the souls remained out of reach. During the span of
His earthly ministry, the Master never saw a conversion to compare
with that of Saul of Tarsus. Apart from the thief, and possibly Mary
Magdalene, He never saw the power of God transforming the inner
life of men and women. Even His best disciples forsook Him and
fled when danger threatened. Yet within days of Pentecost, Stephen
gladly died for His Lord, and soon afterward the blood of the

martyrs became the seed of the Church. The power of the indwelling Spirit cleansed away the leprosy of sin, banished the blindness of unbelief, restored the ability to make men walk in newness of life, and the power of an invincible ministry raised men to life — men who hitherto had been dead in trespasses and sins. During His sojourn in Palestine, the Lord only succeeded in stirring a small country; afterward, through the ministry of His people, He turned the world upside down.

All this adds meaning to the opening statement of the chapter, "Let not your heart be troubled — do not be upset because I am going away; *because I go to the Father,* your lives will be enriched immeasurably. Your ministry will be more effective, your outlook become more radiant, your influence extend around the world. You will be lifted to heights of blessedness hitherto unknown. *Let not your heart be troubled . . . because I go to my Father."*

> **And whatsoever ye shall ask in my name, that will I do, that the Father may be glorified in the Son. If ye shall ask anything in my name, I will do it (vv. 13, 14).**

This was an entirely new concept of truth; one might almost say that believing prayer in the Name of Christ was born in this discourse. The close interrelationship of Father and Son can never be seen to better advantage. Distance was absolutely meaningless in regard to prayer. While Jesus was with His disciples, they could draw near to ask their petitions. If they had problems, questions, difficulties, all could be placed before their Master. The imminent departure for heaven would change nothing. When He departed He would still remain; while He exercised His ministry at the right hand of the Majesty on high, His ears would remain open to their cry. Prayer would bridge any gap, remove any obstacle, defeat any foe. Nevertheless, it should be considered carefully that the phrase *"in my name"* limits the scope of prayer. Many misguided Christians think that because they ask in Christ's Name, they can ask anything. The reverse is true. It is because they ask IN HIS NAME, they can only ask for certain things. "In His Name" was a divine limitation to prevent stupid requests.

Among the many fine things which A. W. Pink wrote of John's gospel is the following: "What is meant by asking *in the name* of Christ? Certainly it is much more than the mere putting of His name at the end of our prayers, or simply saying, 'Hear me for Jesus' sake.' *First,* it means that we pray in His Person; that is, as standing in His place, as fully identified with Him, asking by virtue of our very union with Himself. When we truly ask in the name of Christ, *He is the real petitioner. Secondly,* it means, therefore, that we plead before God the merits of His Blessed Son. When men use another's name as the authority of their approach, or the ground of their appeal, the one to whom the request is made looks beyond him who presented the petition to the one for whose sake he grants the request. So, in all reverence, we may say when we truly ask in the name of Christ the Father looks past us and sees the Son as the real suppliant. *Thirdly,* it means that we pray only for that which is according to His perfections and what will be for His glory. When we do anything in another's name, it is for him we do it. When we take possession of a property in the name of a society, it is not for any private advantage, but for the society's good. When an officer collects taxes in the name of a government, it is not in order to fill his own pockets. Yet how constantly do we overlook this principle as an obvious condition of acceptable prayer. To pray in Christ's name is to seek what He seeks; to promote what He has at heart . . . . Christ was very far from handing His disciples *a blank check* (as some expressed it), leaving them to fill it in and assuring them that God would honor it because it bore His Son's signature. It is a carnal delusion to suppose that a Christian has only to work himself up to an expectation to suppose that God will hear his prayer and grant what is asked. To apply to God for anything in the name of Christ, the petition must be in keeping with what Christ is. We can only rightly ask God for that which will magnify His Son. To ask in the name of Christ is, therefore, to set aside our own will and bow to the perfect will of God. If only we realized this more, what a check it would be on our ofttimes rash and ill-considered requests. How many of our prayers would never be offered did we but pause to enquire, *Can I present* THIS *in* THAT *Name which is above every name?"*

> Not what I wish, but what I want,
>   O let thy grace supply;
> The good unasked, in mercy grant,
>   The ill, though asked, deny.
>   William Cowper

(For the homily on the power of the Name, see the end of this section.)

If ye love me, keep my commandments. And I will pray the Father, and he shall give you another Comforter, that he may abide with you for ever; even the Spirit of truth; whom the world cannot receive, because it seeth him not, neither knoweth him: but ye know him; for he dwelleth with you, and shall be in you (vv. 15-17).

"If ye love me, keep my commandments." This is the key which unlocks the treasures of heaven. Once again the deity of Christ shines forth, for we never read that Moses the great law-giver commanded Israel to keep *his* commandments. The law of God as expressed through Moses was somewhat negative — "thou shalt not." The other side of the same law as expressed through Christ was positive: "If you keep *my* commandments, YOU WILL LOVE ME, and My intercessory work in heaven will be unhindered; I shall be able to send the Holy Spirit to live in you." This Scripture must be considered in its setting and with its context. True love for Christ accepts His teaching, desires His honor, seeks His will, promotes His wishes, yearns for His nearness. True love promotes prayer, provides a heart free from immoral cobwebs, welcomes the One whose presence makes the heart a temple. The world cannot comprehend these things because the world knows nothing of the love which recognizes spiritual realities.

I will not leave you orphans, (that is, desolate, without a father, bereaved, helpless) **I will come to you (v. 18).**

The Greek word *orphanous* suggests the absence of a father through bereavement. The text should be compared with Isaiah 9:6, ". . . and his name shall be called . . . the everlasting Father . . . ." He was their Father by Creation for He had brought them into being. His removal by death would render them orphans, but He promised this would be remedied by His coming back to them. Could any but God use such language and not exhibit insanity? As the Comforter, Christ promised to return; they would, therefore, continue to know His nearness. Yet at the same time He would be speaking with the Father in heaven — the Father with whom He was ONE. The Father would grant the Son's request and sanction the coming of the Holy Spirit with whom Christ was also ONE. (See comments on verse 36.)

Speaking of the Greek word *parakleetos,* translated "comforter," Dr. J. H. Thayer says it means, "Summoned, called to one's side, especially to one's aid. One who pleads a cause before a judge, a pleader, a counsel for the defense; a legal assistant, an advocate." Thus the Holy Spirit is one who comes to our side, to study our case, to hear our testimony, and then to express this, on our behalf, to Another. The same word is used in I John 2:1 where it is actually translated "advocate." It would seem, therefore, that since we, the accused ones, are unable to appear personally in the divine courtroom, two co-equal Lawyers have undertaken to handle our case. One Great Lawyer stayed near the Judge's seat, ready at any moment to present our defense; the other Great Advocate came down to earth to become more acquainted with the client. His gathered information is relayed back to the courtroom, and thus the client is assured of the very best defense both in heaven and upon earth. The English word *"comforter"* comes from two Latin words: *com* (along side of) and *fortis* (strong).

Consequently, it suggests One with very great strength comes to our side to offer help. An advocate reveals ability in a variety of ways. If his client be distressed, he must console and cheer. If the accused be inexperienced, the Counselor must give reliable advice. If the defendant be a stammerer, the Counselor must speak for him, argue for him, and do all the legal profession demands. Only a few very privileged and wealthy people can be assured of the best legal brains on earth. Nevertheless, the services of heaven's Advocates are offered as a free gift to every sinner on earth.

> Yet a little while, and the world seeth me no more; but ye see me: because I live, ye shall live also. At that day ye shall know that I am in my Father, and ye in me, and I in you. He that hath my commandments, and keepeth them, he it is that loveth me: and he that loveth me shall be loved of my Father, and I will love him, and will manifest myself to him (vv. 19-21).

A more accurate rendering of the opening statement would be: "The world will no longer see me." It was not meant that the world would never again see Him, but that rather He would pass to those realms where only the eye of faith would be able to follow Him. Compare Hebrews 2:9: "But we see Jesus . . . crowned with glory and honor . . . ." It is a revealed fact that some day every man will see Christ and bow the knee and confess that He is Lord to the glory of God the Father. The reference, "at that day," probably referred to the day of Pentecost when the Comforter opened a new day of revelation. Then the divine Spirit witnessed with human spirits that Christ's word was Truth. The ultimate fulfilment of this utterance and many more will not come until that final day when Christ shall be all and in all. Verse 21 endorsed and repeated what had been said earlier, and the promise, "I will manifest myself to him," provided the climax to the seven-fold truth outlined in the following homily.

Finally, it should be remembered that Christ said, ". . . because I live, ye shall live also." He did not speak of His death but of His life. Death was but a shadowy path leading to the sunlight, a temporary eclipse before the spreading radiance of a new day. *"Let not your heart be troubled"* becomes very wonderful when we remember it prefaced a chapter of superlative truth.

HOMILIES

Study No. 53

Seven Stars in a Dark Sky

The storm clouds were gathering; the future was ominous. In spite of many agonizing prayers the Master would soon be taken from them. Their enemies, the hateful priests, were going to triumph;

the cross would be a reality. The Master had broken the bread and dispensed the wine; His lovely voice had actually led them in singing a hymn, but their tones betrayed the despair of their souls. If Israel had been unable to sing the Lord's song in a strange land, how could they be expected to sing the praise of God when their hearts were breaking? They looked at the Lord and were astonished; He was beginning to smile. Tenderness, understanding, yearning, shone in His eyes as He said, "Let not your heart be troubled .... I go ... but I will come again .... I will not leave you comfortless ... orphans ... *because I go unto my Father,* all kinds of things will become possible."

(1) *I will give to you the power to do greater works than these* (verse 12).

(2) *I will answer your prayers* (verses 13, 14).

(3) *I will pray and God shall give you another Comforter* (verse 16).

(4) *I will come to you* (verse 18).

(5) *I will make it possible for you to live also* (verse 19).

(6) *I will love you* (verse 21).

(7) *I will manifest myself to you* (verse 21).

Study No. 54

JOHN . . . WHO BELIEVED IN A PRECIOUS NAME

I John 2:12; John 14:13-14; Acts 3:6; III John 7.

The inhabitants of an isolated village in India were hearing the Gospel for the first time. They were enthralled! Hours later, one of their number went in search of the lady who had preached about Jesus. "What is His Name?" he asked, and when she answered his question, repeating continually, "Jesus . . . Jesus . . . Jesus," the man returned to his people.

> The name of Jesus is so sweet:
> I love its music to repeat;
> It makes my joy. full and complete,
> The precious name of Jesus.

Through His Name . . . Instant Pardon (I John 2:12)

The old apostle sat at his table; before him lay both quill and parchment. Far away, his "little children" were waiting to hear from their beloved pastor. What could he say? He smiled and wrote, "I write unto you . . . because your sins are forgiven you *for his name's sake.*" And if the aged Christian paused to consider his remarkable statement, the entire plan of God's salvation surely appeared before his eyes. Formerly, the acquisition of pardon had seemed to be the work of a lifetime. It required the provision of an offering, the strict observance of religious ritualism, the constant struggle against evil. It was problematical whether any man remained assured of divine forgiveness. And then Jesus appeared to put away sin by the sacrifice of Himself. Faith superceded works, and the Name of Jesus became the passport to new worlds of happiness. Then, through His wondrous Name, a man could obtain in a moment what hitherto had been almost unobtainable.

Through His Name . . . Inspired Prayer (John 14:13, 14; 16:23, 24).

John was reminiscing once more; the completion of his gospel was probably interrupted on many occasions as he paused to recall scenes from the life of his Master. He remembered the day when Jesus revealed the new possibilities of prayer. "Whatsoever ye shall ask the Father *in my name,* he will give it you. Hitherto have ye asked nothing *in my name:* ask, and ye shall receive, that your joy may be full." John agreed; it was true. They had never previously asked God for anything IN THE MASTER'S NAME. This was something entirely new, and revealed (1) the Father's great interest in Jesus; (2) the Master's influence in eternal purposes; (3) the amazing new possibilities of intercession. If this were true, then nothing would be impossible. John smiled; he knew it was true, THE NAME had been a key unlocking the treasury of heaven. The Early Church succeeded because she learned to pray before she began to preach.

Through His Name . . . Increasing Power (Acts 3:16)

To John it only seemed as yesterday when he and Peter "went up together into the temple at the hour of prayer. And a certain man lame from his mother's womb . . . seeing Peter and John about to go into the temple asked an alms." Later, when this beggar had been miraculously healed, and the great crowds clamored for a speech, Peter ably expressed the convictions of the Church: "And his name, THROUGH FAITH IN HIS NAME hath made this man strong." There can be no mistaking the fact that the spearhead of every Christian onslaught upon the citadels of evil was THE NAME OF JESUS. It was the centrality of their teaching; the secret of their power; the reason for the staggering success of their mission. Comparisons are said to be odious, but when the modern church is examined in the light of history, the question is inescapable: What has gone wrong?

> Where is the blessedness we knew
> When first we saw the Lord?
> Where is the soul refreshing view
> Of Jesus and his word?

Through His Name . . . Indomitable Passion (III John 7)

The apostle's ministry was swiftly drawing to a close. Throughout the known world the Gospel had been proclaimed and many churches established. Alas, unfortunate practices were creeping into the assemblies. Diotrophes, for example, was beginning to reveal the priestly, autocratic rule so common in later centuries. He had turned away certain preachers, and this procedure John condemned. These men, FOR HIS NAME'S SAKE, had gone forth to preach the gospel. They should be gladly, gratefully received. Yet, even as he wrote these things, a grim smile came to the apostle's face. This was only a minor difficulty compared with others already overcome. His colleagues had undermined pagan empires, had scoffed at death, and gone to heaven singing. Their sacrifice turned a weak church into a mighty army against which even the gates of hell had not prevailed. They had turned the world upside down, and so can we — if we learn the secret of using —

THE MIGHTY NAME OF JESUS

SECTION FOUR

Expository Notes on Christ's Answer to Judas

Judas saith unto him, not Iscariot, Lord, how is that thou wilt manifest thyself unto us, and not unto the world? Jesus answered and said unto him, If a man love me, he will keep my words: and my Father will love him, and we will come unto him, and make our abode with him (vv. 22, 23).

There is something very attractive about the phrase, "not Iscariot." The matter of identification was a matter of supreme importance to the second Judas; idle gossip, increasing rumors, and the very possession of such a name could lead to acute embarrassment. Not much has been said about this man, and consequently it is difficult to thrill an audience with accounts of his mighty exploits. However, even if John could not say great things about him, the apostle went out of his way to prevent other people saying bad things (Luke 6:16).

Obviously this man had only half-listened to the Master. One particular statement remained in his mind to the exclusion of all else. Had he been an attentive listener, his question would not have been asked; the Lord had already explained why He would not be able to manifest Himself to the world. Verse 21 explains that "having" or "possessing" His commandments inevitably leads to a faithful observance of those commandments. A man may hear the words of Christ and not obey them. A man who has them in his heart, a man who loves the Lord will endeavor by all powers within his grasp to do as Christ desires. This is the clear cut line of demarcation which separates the world from the family of God. An affinity of purpose opens the door for the manifestation of spiritual life and knowledge to the people of God; a closed heart prevents the entry of light and life to those who love darkness rather than light. Judas should have known all this, but like many moderns he listened only in part to what Christ said. The aforegoing verses may be best understood under three headings:

(1) *The Divine Appreciation.* ". . . my Father will love him." Since Christ spoke only those words commanded by the Father, an acceptance of His message was an acceptance of the Father's teachings. Thus to keep the commandments of Christ was a sure way of pleasing God.

(2) *The Divine Approach.* ". . . we (that is, the Father and I) *will come unto him.*" Christ had just announced that He was about to leave the world; now in a special and unique sense He promised to return, with His Father, to be alongside the Christian. He had also indicated that the coming One — the Paraclete — would be the Holy Spirit. Here we have identity of Persons within the Godhead. In one breath, the Lord says that He will send the Holy Spirit; in the next, He promises that He and the Father will return. Thus did He teach clearly the great doctrine of the Holy Trinity, and John is careful to mention these matters, for they were basic reasons for the production of his gospel.

(3) *The Divine Abode.* "We will make our abode with him." That God should again descend to live among His people was amazing; that God should dwell *within* His people was unbelievable (see I Corinthians 3:16).

> He that loveth me not keepeth not my sayings: and the word which ye hear is not mine, but the Father's which sent me. These things have I spoken unto you, being yet present with you (vv. 24, 25).

This was no new doctrine. Repeatedly the Master announced these things, for He realized that in the very near future the Comforter would be able to remind the disciples of that which they had heard. His words were seeds eventually to germinate when the Holy Spirit watered them in the fertile soil of the disciples' minds. Preachers should consider the Master's methods. He did not hesitate to preach the same sermon twice. He announced identical truths two, three, and even four times; but each time He managed to say the same things in a new way. We should never assume that because we have explained a great theme, our audiences have grasped what was said. The value of a sermon is measured not by the immediate response from a congregation but by the depth to which it sinks in the understanding of those who listened.

> But the Comforter, which is the Holy Spirit, whom the Father will send in my name, he shall teach you all things, and bring all things to your remembrance, whatsoever I have said unto you (v. 26).

Care should be exercised in recognizing the close affinity and co-operation between the Lord and the coming Comforter. Christ delivered the message; the Holy Spirit explained it. Sometimes, the Lord was unable to see immediately the desired effects of His preaching. He did not despair; He knew that the Holy Spirit would guarantee the desired results. Healthy seeds do not grow in a moment; sometimes they take weeks to manifest that they are doing what God meant them to do. Sowers — like fisherman — need to develop patience! Pastors should not allow their hearts to become the abode of despair if some sermons appear to fall on deaf ears. God's Word cannot return void.

Peace I leave with you, my peace I give unto you: not as the world giveth, give I unto you. Let not your heart be troubled, neither let it be afraid (v. 27).

That all this belongs to the same discourse — or "Press Conference" — is clear. Verses 1 and 27 contain the same injunction. The Lord was concerned about the worried disciples, and proceeded throughout the discourse to explain various reasons why there was no need to be burdened about the future. He was about to open a highway by which all sinners could reach the many mansions. He outlined the many blessings which would attend their journey to the celestial city. Why then should they be afraid? "Let not your heart be troubled." In view of the fact that the shadow of the cross was already falling across His soul, it was truly remarkable that He was able to exhibit serenity of soul and speak about *His PEACE*. (See the homily at the end of this section.)

Ye have heard how I said unto you, I go away, and come again unto you. If ye loved me, ye would rejoice, because I said, I go unto the Father: for my Father is greater than I (v. 28).

This verse does not teach the inferiority of the Son, and supplies no evidence in support of Unitarian teachings. Verses taken out of their context can be made to mean anything. Because Jesus said, "I am the door," He did not suggest He was made of wood! The Lord Jesus announced His followers should be rejoicing because He was going to the Father, because He was about to ascend into heaven. After thirty years on *a foreign field*, He was going home! Having known the filth of the grimy swamps of sin, the smoke and smog of living where unbelief was so commonplace, He was now to return where the air was pure and sweet, to a city where nothing that defiled was ever given entrance. This verse refers to work, position, earthly association. The Father lived in the scintillating light of holiness. The Lord Jesus had been living among sinners, had touched lepers, and lived with one within whose heart Satan lived. "Throughout this discourse, and in the prayer which follows in chapter 17, the Lord Jesus is represented as the Father's Servant, from whom He had received a commission, and to whom He was to render an account; for whose glory He acted, and under whose authority He spake. But there is another sense, more pertinent, in which the Son was inferior to the Father. In becoming incarnate and tabernacling a- mong men, He had greatly humiliated Himself, by choosing to descend into shame and suffering in this acutest forms. He was now the Son of Man and had no where to lay His head. He who was rich had for our sakes become poor. He was the Man of sorrows, and acquainted with grief. In view of this, Christ was now con- trasting *His situation* with that of the Father in the heavenly sanctuary. The Father was seated upon the throne of highest majesty; the brightness of His glory was uneclipsed; He was surrounded by hosts of holy beings, who worshiped Him with uninterrupted praise. Far different was it with His incarnate Son . . . . Now in going to the Father, the Son would enjoy a vast improvement in situation. It would be gain unspeakable . . . . Therefore, those who loved Him should have rejoiced at the tidings He was going to the Father, because the Father was greater than He — greater both in official status and surrounding circumstances. This was Christ *owning* His place as a Servant, and *magnifying* the One who had sent Him" (A. W. Pink).

> **And now I have told you before it come to pass, that, when it is come to pass, ye might believe. Hereafter I will not talk much with you: for the prince of this world cometh, and hath nothing in me (vv. 29, 30).**

The Lord's ministry was drawing to a conclusion; He had in- structed His disciples carefully, knowing the Holy Spirit would remind them in days to come of all that had been said. Now an enemy loomed upon the horizon. Hell's guerrilla warfare was now to erupt into open conflict; the attack would be led by the infamous prince of evil. Whatever happened the disciples were not to be troubled in heart; they should pay more attention to what they had just heard than to that which they were about to witness. They should be on guard against any sinister doubts whispered by the old enemy; they should guard their souls against any attack. Un- fortunately, they were susceptible and would need to put on the whole armor of God. He, however, was different in that His soul was free from imperfection. Satan had nothing in Christ to which he could look for help. His darts, arrows, suggestions, whispers would be meaningless. He had lost the battle even before he com- menced to fight. The Master's heart was an impregnable city of holiness.

> **But that the world may know that I love the Father; and as the Father gave me commandment, even so I do. Arise, let us go hence (v. 31).**

The instruction was over; school had, for a time, ended. The moment for action had now arrived. The Lord arose. What His Father had commanded, He was ready to do. He had been the Lamb slain from before the foundation of the world; what had been decided in the eternal purposes of God would now be fulfilled on a hill outside the city wall. He was ready. The disciples hardly understood the implications of His message, but they followed Him into the night.

HOMILIES

Study No. 55

STRAWBERRIES IN WINTER

Out-of-season fruit is always a rare commodity. Strawberries in winter or blackberries in the spring will always excite comment; and if prices are not prohibitive, these rarities will always sell. Among the many fruits of the Spirit are love, joy, and peace; but sometimes these have been produced in the most unlikely places at the most unexpected times. Their appearance promotes wonder; their existence under certain conditions creates amazement. It was this fact which astonished the Early Church; they had seen luscious summer fruit in winter. When icy winds had blown upon their Lord, when pre-Calvary conditions had overwhelmed all else with dreariness and woe, the very choicest of heaven's fruit had been found in the words and actions of the Saviour.

My Peace

"Peace I leave with you, my peace I give unto you; not as the world giveth, give I unto you. Let not your heart be troubled, neither let it be afraid" (John 14:27). It seemed incongruous for Christ to speak about His peace when men were planning to murder Him. Treachery of the worst type was about to be exhibited, and even the disciples were soon to demonstrate their unfaithfulness. Alone and in pain, the Lord had every reason to feel bitterness of soul rather than to speak serenely of His undisturbed tranquility. "My peace I give unto you." Anxiety was firmly banished from His mind; hatred did not exist in His heart. Assured that all was well, He calmly walked with God. His soul was an ocean of divine compassion, unruffled by malice; a place of abiding restfulness.

My Love

"As the Father hath loved me, so have I loved you: continue ye in my love" (John 15:8). Constantly the Lord had been challenged by frustration and disappointment. The Pharisees hated Him; the self-confident disciples were about to forsake Him; and Judas would

soon sell his loyalty for pieces of silver. Could any tree produce the
fruit of love in the face of such biting winds of evil? Could Christ
endure such detestable conditions and, at the same time, preserve
the sweet purity of His spirit? Could love overcome hatred even
as peace overcame anxiety? Where sin abounded, grace much more
abounded. Christ loved them all — even Judas Iscariot; and the
words spoken on that occasion seem now to be rays of brilliance
shining from an ancient lighthouse. From the blackness of the past,
the light shines forth to guide us safely into the harbor of the
divine will. Christ said, "If I have loved you, ye ought also to
love one another." A Christian whose love exists only in his theology
is a tinkling cymbal, a sound without music, a desert without life.

My Joy

"These things have I spoken unto you, that my joy might remain
in you, and that your joy might be full" (John 15:11). "The fruit
of the Spirit is . . . joy." Calvary's horizon had already appeared
dark and ominous; the spikes destined to draw blood from the
Master's body had already been forged. The gibbet was lying in
some timberyard awaiting the command which would take it forth
to carry its precious burden. Apparently everything had gone wrong
with God's world, and the road to the green hill was ready for
the blood which would stain its dust. Christ knew that His hour
had come, and calmly welcomed the end. Did I say "the end"?
I was wrong. Let the readers accept my apologies. The Lord went
forth to meet His death knowing it would be a tunnel to a new
era. At the end of the Last Supper He had announced a hymn
and probably pitched the tune. Emotion almost prevented the
disciples from singing their parts, but His resonant, wonderful voice
re-echoed the music of His soul. They wondered how He could be
so buoyant and serene when everything had gone against Him.
Whence came the charm of His manner, the rich cadence of His
tone, the supreme confidence of His bearing? Was He not to be
crucified? Alas, the disciples were short-sighted. They saw the cross;
He saw the throne. "Let us run with patience the race that is set
before us, looking unto Jesus . . . who for the *joy* that was set
before him endured the cross, despising the shame, and is set down
at the right hand of the throne of God" (Hebrews 12:2). His joy
overcame sadness, pain, and death, and secured a deep content
which defied the terrors of crucifixion. This joy He desired to share
with His followers. He said, ". . . that my joy might remain in you,
and that your joy might be full." Love, joy, peace! These were
summer fruits produced in winter. They were rare and very costly.

The Fifteenth Chapter of John

Theme: *Abiding in Christ in an Antagonistic World*

OUTLINE:
I A Great Parable. Verses 1-8.
II A Glorious Partnership. Verses 9-17.
III A Grim Prediction. Verses 18-25.
IV A Gracious Preacher. Verses 26-27.

SECTION ONE

Expository Notes on the Parable of the Vine

I am the true vine, and my Father is the husbandman (v. 1).

It has been generally agreed among the theologians that this discourse was delivered at the conclusion of the Lord's Supper and during the walk toward Gethsemane. The theme might have been suggested either by the light of a moon falling on the great golden vine with which Herod had beautified the temple, or by the vineyards alongside of, or through which, the disciples might have walked. Let us remember that in the previous chapter the Lord was concerned with the worries which beset His followers. He spoke words of comfort, but remembering the great tasks ahead of His followers, He proceeded to outline the prerequisites of fruit-bearing. If these men were to succeed in their unprecedented mission, they would need more than words of solace. To undermine Satan's empire would call for more than a warm feeling of comfort in times of difficulty and sorrow. The demand of the future called for resolution, unwavering courage, and unhindered flow of divine energy from eternal springs of power, a selfless passion to bear lasting fruit in Jesus' Name. If the disciples stood looking for sympathy, they would never succeed in getting anywhere. True peace would only be known when they did what the Lord desired.

Let us then try to visualize the scene as the Master paused on the road to look toward His object lesson. The moonlight possibly played upon the strong, resolute, supporting vine; the branches were heavy with luscious fruit, and the leaves gently sighed with satisfaction as the winds of the night moved them to and fro. The solitudes were rich with the benediction of heaven; the night sky was studded with starry jewels, and the disciples were silent and apprehensive when Jesus said, "I am the true vine, and my Father is the husbandman." There had been, and doubtless there would be, others who would claim this distinction, but He WAS the true vine. He was the One in whom the interest of the Divine Husbandman was centered. God had prepared His body; God had planned, and watched, and waited to see that which He had long desired. His expectations had been fully realized, for the Vine had responded to the divine attention. As the earthly husbandman would be truly delighted with a vine heavily laden with top quality fruit, so the Father was pleased with the Son. Christ "did always those things which pleased God"; how then could the Father be anything else but extremely satisfied with the life and work of Him whom He had sent into the world?

Every branch in me that beareth not fruit he taketh away: and every branch that beareth fruit, he purgeth it, that it may bring forth more fruit. (v. 2).

Care must be taken to remember that Christ was speaking here of fruit-bearing and NOT OF THE POSSESSION OF ETERNAL LIFE. Failure to observe this fact has led to teaching not in harmony with the doctrines of salvation. The warning has been uttered from innumerable pulpits that man is only saved as long as he continues faithful to the claims of Christ, that a lapse into sin could damn his soul. This is wrong. Unfortunately almost every evangelistic crusade brings to light those who have been led astray by this teaching. There are people who repeatedly seek salvation in every gospel meeting. Consequently, in twenty gospel meetings they go forward twenty times. This is not always the result of a weak mind; it is the sign of poor teaching. Everlasting life IS everlasting life. (See homily on John Chapter 10, Section 2.) In this parable the emphasis is upon what we can PRODUCE for Christ, and not what He can GIVE to us.

It is a matter for great regret that the translators of verse 2 overlooked certain very important details. It is most difficult to avoid the conclusion that the widely accepted Authorized Version is wrong in its interpretation. "Every branch in me that beareth not fruit he taketh away: and every branch that beareth fruit, he purgeth it, that it might bring forth more fruit." This verse as it stands suggests severance from the main vine, the result of cutting or pruning by a husbandman who had lost patience with an unproductive branch. But this is not true. The Greek word translated "he taketh away" is *airo*, and according to Dr. J. H. Thayer, this has three meanings. (1) *To raise up.* This is expressed in a variety of ways: *to raise from the ground, to take up stones, or serpents, or a dead body* (John 8:59; Mark 16:18; Acts 20:9). It was used to express *a lifting upward of the hand* (Rev. 10:5); *the eyes* (John 11:41); *the voice,* that is, to speak with loud voice (Luke 17:13). (2) *To take upon one's self and carry what has been raised.* (3) *To carry away what has been raised; that is to move from its place.* The verse should therefore read: "Every branch in me that beareth not fruit, *he lifteth it up.*"

The word translated "purgeth" has been regarded as an act of pruning, cutting, severing, but this is also a mistake. The Greek word is *kathairo,* which primarily means "to cleanse." It was used of trees to express a cleansing from useless shoots, that is, to prune; but it was also used of cleansing the conscience from guilt, and in this setting the use of a pruning knife would hardly be necessary. It will be seen therefore that the root meaning has more to do with "washing" than with cutting.

Therefore we should read the entire text as follows, "Every branch in me that beareth not fruit, he lifteth it up: and every branch that beareth fruit, he cleanseth it, (that is, having lifted it up, he washes away the dirt, and if necessary then, he trims it, prunes it) that it may bring forth more fruit." This message would be fully appreciated in any vineyard where, for various reasons, the vines sometime fall to the ground. The husbandman on his rounds of inspection would see the fallen vine in the dirt, and with loving care would restore it to its rightful place, support it, cleanse it, and do whatever was necessary to repair any damage that had been done. The prevailing thought therefore in this text is *not* an act of judgment, severing a disappointing fruitless branch from the parent stem. Rather we see here the loving patience of a wise husbandman who rejects nothing if there be the slightest chance of restoring a branch to full fruitfulness. The idea that this Scripture supports the teaching of falling from grace is foreign to the theme of the parable God's great mercy does not impair His wisdom. When it becomes necessary to prune the branches, this is done. Let it be remembered, however, that loving wisdom is the hand that holds the knife.

To grasp fully the teaching of this great parable it is now necessary to see the various steps in the procedure and to interpret this in the light of Christ's earlier messages. (1) The husbandman sees a branch fallen to the ground. (2) Gently he lifts it up, and washes away the dirt. (3) He restores it to its former place. (4) If he thinks it necessary, he removes any further hindrance that the harvest be not impaired. According to the teaching of the Saviour, the agent of cleansing was *His own Word* (verse 3). It is most important to understand this operation. The Lord sees a fallen branch, and immediately tries to lift it from the surrounding filth. Then He begins to cleanse it by the application of the Word of Truth. It is the entrance of God's Word that giveth light; it is the application of that same Word to my conduct that begins the pruning of those useless "shoots" hindering the fulfilment of the Lord's desires. It is only when stubbornness of spirit and unresponsiveness in the soul resembles open rebellion that the husbandman is obligated to take more drastic methods. When he has to choose between the health of the entire vine and the immediate reprieve of a consistently unresponsive branch, the end is a foregone conclusion. "If a man abide not in me, he is cast forth as a branch, and is withered . . . ." All this is clearly expressed in the account of Simon Peter's fall and subsequent restoration. Simon had been one of the most fruitful branches in the disciple party. Yet unfortunately he fell and became very contaminated with earth's sin. The Lord saw him, loved him, lifted him, washed him, restored him, and Peter bore more fruit afterward than ever before. There was no need to remove him from the Church, as was commanded in the case of the other offender (Matthew 18:15-17).

When a withered branch threatens other branches and the disease begins to spread to other parts of the vine, the husbandman removes the hindrance from the place of productivity. If another branch can be made to produce a greater yield, the husbandman does what is necessary to obtain the desired results. A man may be a Christian and yet at the same time be disappointing to his Lord. A child may be the son of his parents and yet at the same time cause grief to those who brought him into the world. This strong line of demarcation must be fully recognized. There are carnal Christians; there are also Spirit-filled Christians. To the former at the day of reckoning, the Lord will say, "O foolish Galatians, ye did run well; who hath hindered you?" To the latter, the Lord will say, "Well done, thou good and faithful servant . . . enter thou into the joy of thy lord." A man's presence in heaven is occasioned by the faith that brought him to Christ. The position a man might hold in heaven depends entirely upon the type of service (fruitbearing) rendered between the moment of salvation and the call which takes him into the presence of God. This is explained by Paul in I Corinthians 3. There are stages in fruitbearing: (1) *fruit* (verse 2); (2) *more fruit* (verse 2); (3) *much fruit* (verse 5). God's pruning knife is dedicated to the cause of bringing branches to the peak of production. If the blade appears to be excessively sharp, the human branch should remember "whom the Lord loveth, he chasteneth."

Now ye are clean through the word which I have spoken unto you. Abide in me, and I in you. As the branch cannot bear fruit of itself, except it abide in the vine; no more can ye, except ye abide in me. I am the vine, ye are the branches. He that abideth in me, and I in him, the same bringeth forth much fruit: for without me ye can do nothing (vv. 3-5).

Compare this verse with John 13:10: "Now ye are clean, *but not all.*" The departure of Judas had removed a foul stain from the disciple band. The word of Christ had washed their hearts; they were now acceptable and usable. They could be the instruments by which God would transform the world, but they still needed the power to convince those who refuted their message. Whence came the necessary dynamic? The Lord said, "Abide in me, and I in you." "My going to the Father and the coming of the Comforter to you will make possible an abiding union." Pentecost opened a new era in spiritual experience. Christ planned to devote His entire life to His followers; they should emulate His example and devote their time and talents to Him. When we abide in Christ as a branch abides in the vine, we are utterly dependent upon Him *for He holds us up; supplies life, and reproduces His own particular kind of fruit.* Severed from the vine, the branch falls, dies, and becomes useless. (See the homily at the end of this section.)

Identical truth is taught under a different simile in Zechariah 4, where the prophet spoke of "a candlestick," or lampstand, "all of gold." "And I said, I have looked, and behold a candlestick all of gold, with a bowl upon the top of it, and his seven lamps thereon, and seven pipes to the seven lamps, which are upon the top thereof." Pipes and lampstands suggested open channels through which the oil could flow. This was in keeping with the later message, ". . . This is the word of the Lord unto Zerubbabel, saying, Not by might, nor by power, but by my Spirit, saith the Lord of Hosts" (verse 6). Zechariah spoke of channels through which oil could flow; John 15 mentions open channels through which the life of the Vine might flow. The overflowing life of Christ was the fullness of the Holy Spirit. (See the homily at the end of Section Two, Chapter 7.)

There is a great difference between leaves and fruit. The one looks nice; the other tastes nice. The one provides shade for the birds; the other supplies joy to the husbandman. Even so, the accomplishments of modern man — his training, academic brilliance, beautiful phraseology, elegant pulpit manners, charm, grace, and far reaching fame — may only produce leaves. When to all these commendable qualities is added the power of the Spirit of God, that same man becomes invincible. Leaves are most attractive, but leaves plus fruit are a joy forever.

If a man abide not in me, he is cast forth as a branch, and is withered; and men gather them, and cast them into the fire, and they are burned (v. 6).

A Christian is only of use to Christ as he is fully surrendered to the indwelling Spirit. The production of grapes depends exclusively on the ability of the vine to send its life into the branch. If the flow of life-giving energy be terminated, the vine has no further use for the branch. Christ is only able to produce spiritual fruit in His branches as He is permitted to send life into the disciples. Secret sin grieves the Holy Spirit. The outflow of spiritual usefulness is dependent upon the inflow of spiritual fullness. These two are interrelated, and if the pipeline from the olive tree to the bowl be blocked, the pipeline from the bowl to the lamp must run dry. See the earlier notes on this section. To be useful in the service of God is to enjoy favor; to become a hindrance is to threaten the health of the other branches.

This solemn fact is revealed again in Paul's letter to the Corinthians. The apostle urged self-examination upon all the members of the local church, and suggested that some of the members who were not eligible to partake of the Lord's Supper brought damnation upon themselves. Others, whose actions were not Christ-like, were also inviting disaster by eating and drinking unworthily. "For this cause many are weak and sickly among you, and many sleep" (I Corinthians 11:30). Rather than risk the blessing of the Church, the Lord would prefer to remove, even by death, those who are no longer fit to occupy places of responsibility.

Sometimes one bad slip is sufficient to ruin a brilliant record of service. At Mount Carmel Elijah reached the peak of his ministry, for the people fell on their faces to cry, "The Lord, He is the God; the Lord, He is the God." The fearless prophet was presented with the opportunity to lead thousands of people into a closer relationship with their Maker. Alas, when he became afraid of a woman, his usefulness to that generation terminated. How could he recommend complete faith in God to people who would smile and murmur "Jezebel"? This great branch on Israel's vine became useless, and there is every reason to believe that God took Elijah to heaven when the prophet might have reached the most useful time of his life. In a duel sense his ministry went up in flames!

Moses was the greatest leader Israel ever knew, but one act of indiscretion ruined his testimony and robbed him of the joy of leading Israel into Canaan. Unless the branch abides in the vine, unless the channels be open and clean, the knife of the husbandman *must* be used, not primarily to destroy a disappointing branch but to safeguard the other branches. There is no doctrinal significance in the burning

of the bran e natural procedure with dead wood. To
infer that Christian is to be burned in the fires
of hell is e Bible and betray shallowness of spiritual thinki

If ye y words abide in you, ye shall ask what
ye v done unto you. Herein is my Father
glo nuch fruit; so shall ye be my disciples
(

We must remember Christ was preparing His disciples for
the task of world evangelization. Pagan empires were to be challenged; the evil genius who for so long had wrecked God's world
was to be overcome. Although they were unlearned and illiterate
men, their testimony would confound the world's greatest thinkers,
offset the might of far reaching empires, and bring deliverance to
millions of people. Though some of their number would be fed to
starving lions, though some would die at the stake, other Christians
would continue the work. Ultimate success would be achieved, not
through their scholastic presentation of divine truth, but by the
divine life which flooded their souls. They would be wise to acquire
as much learning as possible, but should remember always this
would be subsidiary to *abiding in Christ*. Their LIFE and not their
LIPS would be the deciding factor in the days and years to come.

If they abode in Him, and if His words filled and thrilled their
hearts, they could ask for anything and their petitions would be
granted. (See the notes on the former chapter.) To ask a petition
in THE NAME OF CHRIST guaranteed the quality of the prayer. It
was not possible to ask in that Name anything out of harmony with
the Name itself. For example, how could a man pray, "Please help
me to find customers for my whisky and narcotics. These things I
ask in the Name of Jesus." To ask in the precious Name was to ask
in the Will of God. If a man abode in Christ, he would be filled
with the life of Christ, and when this happened, his thoughts,
suggestions, and desires, would conform to the divine standard.
Every prayer he offered bore the hallmark of heaven. He asked for
that which God delighted to give. Therefore since his nearness to
his Lord guaranteed he would not ask amiss, the man received everything for which he prayed. It was said of Praying Hyde, "He received
everything for which he asked." This is true fruit-bearing, and this
of necessity must be the standard of true Christianity. ". . . *so shall
ye be my disciples.*"

HOMILIES

Study No. 56

THE THINGS WHICH CHRIST CANNOT DO

One of our popular hymns suggests, "There is nothing that Christ cannot do," and this thought is gladly accepted by the majority of Christians. We love to think that the affairs of daily life are in the hands of an omnipotent God; yet this confidence might be strangely related to fatalism. However comforting the thought may seem to be, the fact remains that there are certain things which He cannot accomplish in the experience of His followers. These truths. are clearly revealed in the parable of the Vine.

The vine cannot produce fruit without the help of a branch

The Lord Jesus said, "I am the vine, ye are the branches: He that abideth in me, and I in him, the same bringeth forth much fruit: for *without me ye can do nothing.*" We have only to change one letter and the final sentence would read *"without me He can do nothing."* And that is true. Unless the vine can have the assistance of the branches, fruit-bearing will be an impossibility. The branch is the expression of the life of the tree, and by its cooperation, the parent tree can fulfil its functions in life. The Saviour declared that what the branch is to the vine, so are we to Him. When He returned to heaven, He commissioned His disciples to go forth into all the world to preach the Gospel; and had they failed in their appointed task the cause of Christ would have been in jeopardy. The Lord Jesus needs men and women through whom to manifest Himself, and should these instruments prove to be unusable, His purposes will be hindered. If there be but one Christian in an office, in a home or in any other sphere, then obviously the Lord will be dependent upon the cooperation of that solitary follower. One of the names given to Christ was THE BRANCH. ". . . Behold the man whose name is The Branch shall grow up out of his place, and he shall build the temple of the Lord . . . he shall bear his glory . . . and shall sit and rule upon his throne . . ." (Zechariah 6:12, 13). What Christ was to God — the expression of His life — we are to Christ. He did not fail His Father; we must not fail our Master.

The Vine Cannot Keep a Branch Healthy Unless it Imparts Life

The unhindered flow of life from the vine to the branch is absolutely essential if the health of the branch is to be maintained. When the life channel becomes blocked, or if for any other reason the sap ceases to flow, decay immediately begins its work of destruction in the branch. Even so the Lord Jesus cannot maintain the life of His people unless He is able to fill them with His Spirit. The command of the Scripture is: "Be filled with the Spirit," and if any earthly hindrance interferes with that process, the health of the Christian is immediately endangered. A simple study of the life of the Lord reveals He was constantly filled with the Holy Spirit. He was born of the Spirit (Luke 1:35). After His baptism in the Jordan, He was full of the Spirit and was led of the Spirit into the wilderness (Luke 4:1). He returned from His temptation in the power of the Spirit (Luke 4:14), and immediately claimed the fulfilment of Isaiah's prediction, for He said, "The Spirit of the Lord is upon me" (verse 18). He resisted all evil, and finally offered Himself through the eternal Spirit (Hebrews 9:14). It is therefore clear that the divine Spirit completely filled the Vine, and unless Christ can likewise fill us, decay will quickly become apparent.

The Vine Cannot Prevent the Useless Branch Becoming a Castaway

"If a man abide not in me, he is cast forth as a branch, and is withered; and men gather them, and cast them into the fire, and they are burned" (John 15:6). If a branch is proved to be useless, nothing can prevent its removal from the sphere of service. We do well to remember that a man's eternal destiny is *not* the theme of this discourse, for Christ had already said that no one could pluck the saint from the hand of His Father. The theme under consideration in this parable is fruit-bearing in the vineyard of God. Every Christian should bear fruit for the Master; but when sin and self ruin fruit-bearing potentialities, God will remove the hindrance to protect others. Disease can easily spread among fruit trees, and with so much at stake, the great Husbandman will resolutely remove all hindrances. The ingathering of the eternal harvest must not be endangered. Even Paul recognized the possibility of becoming a castaway (I Corinthians 9:27). Haunting memories of a lost opportunity are the only clouds that might hide temporarily the glory of the eternal sunshine.

SECTION TWO

*Expository Notes on Christ's Evaluation
of a Deepening Relationship*

As the Father hath loved me, so have I loved you: continue ye in my love. If ye keep my commandments, ye shall abide in my love; even as I have kept my Father's commandments, and abide in his love (vv. 9, 10).

The key words of these verses are *"as"* and *"so."* Probably it was the observance of this commandment which ultimately became responsible for the new name given to the followers of Jesus. At first, they were called "disciples" (*matheetai*). The Greek word signifies they were students or pupils. They followed their teacher as other students followed the ancient philosophers. Wherever the master went, the scholars also went, hoping to glean words of wisdom as they walked together. Following this pattern, the admirers of Jesus followed Him and became *disciples*. At a later date, the citizens of Antioch recognized that this name did not express the true nature of the people who were turning the world upside down. These men were not merely listeners (followers), pupils of Jesus; they had listened so often, and learned so much, they had become *like* their Teacher. They had developed into miniature replicas of their Master. They were — Christians. Therefore, the word *"as"* reveals the measure of Christ's obedience to the will of His Father. Similarly, the word *"so"* exhibits the standard by which we live. What was said of the Branch can be repeated here. What Christ was to His Father, we must be to Him and to each other. He said, *"Continue ye* in my love"; it follows then that they were already *in His love.* His imminent departure to be with God would not necessarily change anything. He would be with them; the old relationship could and should be maintained, for love can cross oceans, climb mountains, laugh at time, and render distance meaningless.

> These things have I spoken unto you, that my joy might remain in you, and that your joy might be full (v. 11).

Obviously "these things" refer to what had already been spoken. Observance of the Master's command opened channels by which His joy would deepen the joy they already knew. As a source of ever increasing satisfaction, the incoming current of happiness would intensify their pleasure, and "their joy would be full." Two homilies accentuate this teaching. (See the homily at the end of Section Four of Chapter 14 and the homily on Chapter 16:23-24, Section Three.)

> This is my commandment, That ye love one another, as I have loved you. Greater love hath no man than this, that a man lay down his life for his friends. Ye are my friends, if ye do whatsoever I command you (vv. 12-14).

When the Master Builder lifts the living stones into their place in the great structure of the Church, love must be the cement binding those stones together. The cold winds of criticism and draughts of backbiting can never penetrate into the sanctuary when the members are knit together in love. Within the fellowship will be the warmth of the Divine Presence; within the hearts of men and women the glow of the Infinite. Life is the supreme treasure of man; to enjoy, preserve, and lengthen its span engages the attention of the greatest scientists and doctors. To sacrifice this inestimable treasure would be inexcusable unless some noble endeavor justified the deed. Love, and love alone can make a man abandon forever the thing he desires most. To die for a friend might be possible; but greater love than this is seldom found within the human breast. *God's love alone is capable of dying for enemies.* "For when we were yet without strength, in due time, Christ died for the ungodly. For scarcely for a righteous man will one die: yet peradventure for a good man some would even dare to die. But God commendeth his love toward us, in that *while we were yet sinners*, Christ died for us" (Romans 5:6-8). It was the expressed will of the Master that this kind of love should be spread abroad in the hearts of God's children; only thus would they be able to love the unlovely; only then would they find the grace to touch the untouchables. There are times when an embrace, a falling tear, a firm handclasp say far more than the most eloquent sermon. Without love, even the most polished servant of Christ is apt to become a tinkling cymbal.

The Lord said, "Ye are my friends, IF — IF YE DO WHATSOEVER I COMMAND YOU." There is a sense in which sometimes a true friend is nearer than a son or daughter. Children can be annoying and antagonistic; a true friend can be closer than a brother. When man becomes a child of God through faith in the Lord Jesus Christ it should not be assumed that automatically he becomes the friend of God. Acceptance into the family of God is governed by faith within the soul; friendship with the Highest is only possible when that same faith controls thoughts, actions, and everything appertaining to the daily conduct of the believer. In a most intimate sense Abraham was a member of God's great family. The Lord called him from Ur of the Chaldees, and the believing man responded and entered Canaan. "BY FAITH Abraham, when he was called to go out into a place which he should after receive for an inheritance, obeyed; and he went out, not knowing whither he went" (Hebrews 11:8). Thus did he — if we may be permitted to use modern terms — become a Christian, a child of God. Yet that was only the beginning of a deep spiritual experience. This same man was later asked to surrender his dearest possession, his son, and when he complied with the requirements of God he earned for himself the rare distinction of becoming the friend of the Almighty. "Art not thou our God, who didst drive out the inhabitants of this land before thy people Israel, and gavest it to the seed of Abraham *thy friend for ever?*" (II Chronicles 20:7). Many centuries after this statement was made, James urged upon the Christians the necessity of faith being wedded to consecrated living, and wrote, "But wilt thou know, O vain man, that faith without works is dead. Was not Abraham our father justified by works, when he had offered Isaac his son upon the altar? Seest thou how faith wrought with his works, and by works was faith made perfect. And the scripture was fulfilled which saith, Abraham believed God, and it was imputed unto him for righteousness: and *he was called the Friend of God*" (James 2:20-23). Acceptance into the family of God is evidence of God's favor in response to faith. Acceptance into the inner circle of divine friendship is the reward for merit. This is not a gift; it has to be earned by meritorious conduct. Therefore said Jesus, "*Ye are my friends —* IF YE DO *whatsoever I command you.*"

> Henceforth I call you not servants; for the servant knoweth not what his lord doeth: but I have called you friends; for all things that I have heard of my Father I have made known unto you (v. 15).

These statements are closely related to the words with which the Lord commenced this series of talks. He had said, "Let not your hearts be troubled." Now He offered encouragement to those He loved. He seemed to be saying, "Cheer up, do you not realize that already you are being promoted? You are not on the fringe of things; you are being co-opted into the council meetings of heaven. What I hear from My Father, I tell to you, that you might know what is to happen. My Father and I are trusting you with our secrets, and relying upon you to put into effect our greatest plans. You are not servants; you are trusted friends. Be of good cheer, therefore, for if My Father does this for you it is sure proof He loves you greatly. Let not your hearts be troubled."

> Ye have not chosen me, but I have chosen you, and ordained you, that ye should go and bring forth fruit, and that your fruit should remain: that whatsoever ye shall ask the Father in my name, he may give it you (v. 16).

Probably the disciples considered this a reference to those days when the Lord found them at the sea shore, but Paul's message to the Ephesians added dignity to the utterance. "Blessed be the God and Father of our Lord Jesus Christ, who hath blessed us with all spiritual blessings in the heavenlies in Christ: According as *he hath chosen us in him before the foundation of the world,* that we should be holy and without blame before him in love" (Ephesians 1:3, 4). The *Amplified New Testament* renders this: ". . . He chose us — *He actually picked us out for Himself, as His own, before the foundation of the world . . . .*" "That we should be holy and *without blame before him in love*" perfectly harmonizes with the Lord's final command in John 15:17: "These things I command you, *that ye love one another.*"

The Saviour was speaking about fruit — fruit that remained.

Yet in carrying this teaching to conclusion, He made no mention of *continuing converts.* These were necessary, but LOVE was cited as the supreme fruit. Even a successful evangelist can be related to a well functioning machine, preaching the same sermons, using the same methods, singing the same songs. Love — increasing, deepening, overflowing love — is the greatest characteristic of a Spirit-filled life. A man may be an ardent lover of truth, and yet his methods and manner can resemble an axe with which he cuts the heads from his listeners. Christ not only spoke about love, He revealed it in all His actions. This MUST be the abiding example of His followers. True ordination comes exclusively from the Lord of the Church. The setting apart of a minister is but a recognition by his colleagues that God has already anointed their brother for service. To refuse to recognize any God-honored ambassador of Christ for no other reason than that he was not produced by a certain college is a breach of the privilege bestowed on the Church by God. *I have chosen you; I have ordained you; I will endorse the prayers offered in My Name.* Thus equipped, the disciples were empowered to go forth to meet the challenge of a pagan world. Yet more important than all their many qualifications was the fact that they had love — love for their Master, and love for the brethren. They were destined to discover it would be better to lose their sermons, their congregations, their possessions, their reputations, their lives than to lose the love of Christ shed abroad in their hearts.

These things I command you that ye love one another (v. 17).

HOMILIES

Study No. 57

THESE IMPORTANT THINGS

The student is invited to consider carefully the words *"these things"* which are found throughout the fifteenth and sixteenth chapters of John's gospel. They appear to be milestones on the road, the land marks on the journey taken by Christ. Reviewing His instructions to the disciples, the Master pin-pointed certain important features, and when considered in their true and proper sequence, much food for thought is forthcoming.

ABIDING IN CHRIST'S PURPOSE

"I am the vine, ye are the branches . . . Abide in me . . . *These things* have I spoken unto you that my joy might remain in you" (John 15: 1, 4, 11). The Lord plans to use His people for the purpose of producing eternal fruit to the glory of God. Surrender to His will, and the carrying out of that purpose lead to increasing joy.

Affection for Christ's People

"These things I command you that ye love one another" (John 15:17). It is not possible to win someone when hatred fills the heart. Love brought Christ from heaven; that same love takes Christians to the end of the earth. Love enabled Him to conquer us; that same love working in us and through us can conquer others. A church filled with love is a happy family; a church without love is an argumentative club.

Acceptance of Christ's Principles

"These things have I spoken unto you that ye should not be offended" (John 16:1). The Lord predicted, "They shall put you out of the synagogues: yea, the time cometh, that whosoever killeth you will think that he doeth God service" (verse 2). The tempter would ask the most sinister question: Why should this be and why should God permit this and that? The Master said, "I have warned you in time. This is the way you must walk. Accept the fact and whatever happens, do not be offended."

Assurance of Christ's Power

"But these things have I told you, that when the time shall come, ye may remember that I told you of them . . ." (John 16:4). The Lord was able to see the end from the beginning. He who had chosen them from the beginning would be with them to the end. All the power of God was in Christ; all the wisdom of God was expressed by Christ. "Remember that I said these things. I know what is coming and thus am able to tell you. The power that enables Me to predict the future is the power that can make all things work together for good to them who are the called according to God's purpose."

Attention to Christ's Promises

"Whatsoever ye shall ask the Father in my name, he will give it you. Hitherto have ye asked nothing in my name; ask, and ye shall receive, that your joy may be full. These things have I spoken unto you in proverbs, but . . ." (John 16:23-25). In the preceding verses, the Lord has indeed spoken in proverbs and used illustrations, but these led to the supreme fact that prayer was soon to become their greatest asset. It was the key to unlock heaven's treasure-house.

Absolute Peace Through Christ's Presence

"These things I have spoken unto you, that in me ye might have peace . . ." (John 16:33). Through all the changing scenes of life — in fair weather and foul, on the mountains and in the valleys — the Comforter would be with them. There was no need for their hearts to be overwhelmed with sorrow. The Lord had a plan, and the power to accomplish His desires rested in His hand. The Lord of heaven would be their constant Friend; He would cheer and guide them and thus was able to say, "In the world ye shall have tribulation: but be of good cheer; I have overcome the world" (16:33).

SECTIONS THREE AND FOUR

*Expository Notes on Christ's Prediction
of an Approaching Storm*

If the world hate you, ye know that it hated me before it hated you. If ye were of the world, the world would love his own: but because ye are not of the world, but I have chosen you out of the world, therefore the world hateth you (vv. 18, 19).

These were solemn words suggesting two Kingdoms diametrically opposed to each other. To have been translated from the kingdom of darkness into the kingdom of His dear Son was sufficient to arouse the hostility of Satan. If the disciples were to be keen, active servants of their Lord, they were to expect opposition. Their message would arouse the anger of the evil one; their ministry would in itself condemn the people to whom they spoke, and as a result, the world would hate them. If they decreased their efforts to evangelize, if they diluted their message, they might retain the friendship of the world. If, on the other hand, they followed their Master, they would need to remember His words, "The servant is not greater than his Lord." There was another occasion when Jesus said, "Woe unto you, when all men shall speak well of you! for so did their fathers to the false prophets" (Luke 6:26).

There was a sense in which this was vitally connected with the world of the first three centuries; there is another which brings the message into the twentieth century. The Early Church was to challenge the might of heathen empires; they were to undermine authorities and repudiate that for which other men had devoted their lives. They were to denounce and condemn everything anti-Christ, and this would bring upon their heads the wrath of emperors. The Christians would be fed to hungry lions and burned at the stake. They would be obligated to die as did the Lord. *The world* referred to that sphere in the grip and control of Satan. From this realm, the Christians could expect no sympathy. Since that first century, things have changed. Now the term, *"the world"* refers to the planet upon which we live, the society in which we move. To infer that every true Christian must essentially be hated by all his fellows would be a mistake. There are many fine people who are not as yet Christians, but who are nevertheless attracted to the cause of Christ by the virtue of those who profess Christ's Name. Not all are evil who are outside; alas, not all are good who are inside the Church. The true Church of Christ has done more for mankind than any other organization on earth. Schools and colleges, homes for orphans and aged people, hospitals, and a thousand other institutions have been erected by money given in Christ's Name. Millions of people recognize this and appreciate what Christianity has done. To say then that all men will hate the Christian would be wrong.

However, while all this is certainly true, there remains a realm in which evil is as deep and as violent as it ever was. There are circles of corruption and vice; there are men whose consciences are depraved and filthy; there are crime barons who handle the narcotic and liquor trades; there are syndicates which do more to damn young lives than can ever be told. There are millionaires who became rich by making other people poor. This is Satan's realm, and any man, minister or layman, who boldly attacks that kingdom encounters increasing opposition. The holiness of God is at war with sin, and sinners who prefer darkness to light, by nature of their likes and dislikes, oppose by every means possible the man whose message denounces their evil trade. When *these men* speak well of the Christian, their plaudits should cast shadows over their friend's soul.

> Remember the word that I said unto you, The servant is not greater than his lord. If they have persecuted me, they will also persecute you; if they have kept my saying, they will keep yours also (v. 20).

"Remember" was one of the great words used by the Lord. Christians are so prone to forget — to forget what He said, to forget His example, to forget to pray. *Remember* should be engraved upon the hearts of God's people! If a young man left his sweetheart waiting on a street corner for hours, his conduct would be inexcusable. Alas, we make our promises to meet Christ at the trysting place, but so often fail to make an appearance. We are too tired, too busy, too interested in the things of earth. The disciples' strength would be conditional upon their remembering to obey the Lord's command. If His words remained in their minds, they would never be far from Him, and this fellowship would enable them to overcome the evil one. These were very vital words for Christians of all generations.

> But all these things will they do unto you for my name's sake, because they know not him that sent me. If I had not come and spoken unto them, they had not had sin: but now they have no cloak for their sin. He that hateth me hateth my Father also (vv. 21-23).

(For the suggestiveness of the phrase, "for my name's sake" see homily at Chapter 14, Section Three.)

If these people had never heard the words of Christ, they would not have been responsible for rejecting the message. God only expects that which is possible from men and women. There are people greatly concerned about the fate of the unevangelized heathen. If salvation be conditional upon personal acceptance of the Lord Jesus Christ, what will happen to souls who die before they even heard the Gospel? There is no great problem in this matter. God cannot expect from anyone that which is impossible. God loves the heathen as much as He loves others; therefore it follows He will know how to act in regard to those who never had an opportunity to love His Son. We should be more concerned over folk *who have heard* the Gospel; they have no cloak for their sin. If such people be within our family, efforts should be redoubled to influence them before they lose their souls.

If I had not done among them the works which none other man did, they had not had sin: but now have they both seen and hated both me and my Father. But this cometh to pass, that the word might be fulfilled that is written in their law, They hated me without a cause (vv. 24, 25).

It was apparent that the people to whom Christ ministered would not have believed whatever He did for them. They heard the greatest sermons ever preached, witnessed the greatest miracles ever performed, saw the greatest Man ever to live on earth, and yet in spite of their enormous privileges, their hearts remained evil. They were not prepared to believe; they preferred to live as they had always done. Nothing could be done for them; their house was therefore "left unto them desolate because they knew not the time of their visitation." They hated Christ without a cause, and will be condemned without an excuse. Let those preachers who proclaim the universality of salvation ponder these verses. When God has done all within His power to reach sinful man, and when the effort has failed, nothing can be done. Righteousness and mercy are co-equal in the Godhead. When mercy is rejected, righteousness demands judgment. The reference to ancient writings seems to be to Psalm 35:19 and Psalm 69:4.

But when the Comforter is come, whom I will send unto you from the Father, even the Spirit of truth, which proceedeth from the Father, he shall testify of me: and ye shall bear witness, because ye have been with me from the beginning (vv. 26, 27).

The Lord predicted the coming of a great storm of persecution and warned of the evil consequences to follow in its wake. Then He said, "BUT — . You will not be alone. Remember this. The

Comforter, the Advocate, the Helper will be alongside you to assist in every moment of need. He will add His testimony to yours; He will endorse what you say. In similar fashion you will add your testimony to His; you will be laborers together WITH God. Therefore, 'Let not your hearts be troubled; ye believe in God, believe also in me.' " Storms may come, but their blasts can never find us alone. Burdens may have to be carried, but God the Comforter will be present to supply the necessary strength. The abiding presence of the Holy Spirit must ever be the secret of successful Christian living.

HOMILIES

Study No. 58

FIVE TURNS IN A HIGHWAY

The little word "but" is one of the most interesting of all Bible words; it represents a turn in a roadway. Dr. Robert Young in his *Analytical Concordance of the Bible* states that in one of its original forms it was used over 2,700 times in the New Testament alone. Another Greek word, also translated "but," was used over 600 times. The word therefore was often upon the Saviour's lips and an elementary study of some of the references reveals great depth of thought, great changes of meaning. With each turn in a road a new range of scenic loveliness comes into view. A straight road through unchanging countryside can be most uninteresting; a road that winds and turns between mountains, waterfalls, rivers, and nature's wonderlands can be exquisitely beautiful if the traveler takes time to consider the changing nature of the country through which he is passing. If life may be considered as a road from earth to heaven, the following verses reveal some of the beauties of the territory through which the Christian journeys.

A New Concept

"For the wages of sin is death; BUT the gift of God is eternal life through Jesus Christ our Lord" (Romans 6:23). From time immemorial, the nation had lived under the shadow of Sinai's law. Sin was a monster in whose clutches, alas, they lived and moved and had their being. The many "thou shalt not's" of the Mosaic commandments enslaved them, and judgment seemed inevitable. The roadway of life had passed in a straight line through forbidding territory for centuries when suddenly it turned to reveal a fresh vista of loveliness. Instead of impending judgment they saw inviting grace. In place of an out-of-reach treasure, they saw a gift from God. This was a new concept, completely unlike anything they had ever known.

A New Communion

". . . ye were without Christ, being aliens . . . BUT now in Christ Jesus ye who sometimes were far off are made nigh by the blood of Christ" (Ephesians 2:12, 13). "We were by nature the children of wrath . . . BUT God . . . hath quickened us" (Ephesians 2:3, 5). Hitherto the Ephesians had been classed as Gentiles — dogs. They were indeed aliens from the commonwealth of Israel. They had no claim upon Jehovah; they had no part in the chosen people. Now a new order had come into being, new scenic wonders created by the hand of God had come within view. Christ had destroyed forever the middle wall of partition, had abolished in His flesh the enmity between Jew and Gentile, "that he might reconcile BOTH unto God in one body by the cross . . ." (Ephesians 2:15, 16). The Church with its fellowship became a reality even ᶜor aliens; the small word BUT introduced travelers to a new revelation of spiritual beauty.

A New Comfort

In spite of the charm of the scenery, the road could be dangerous. The great enemy of God's people would be waiting to harm the travelers to God's city. "And the Lord said, Simon, Simon, behold, Satan hath desired to have you, that he may sift you as wheat: BUT I have prayed for thee . . . ." Christians may travel far along the road of life but they can never journey out of His sight. The Lord foresaw the danger even before Peter heard of it. The Master's intercession won the battle even before Satan attacked the disciple. The Lord's command, "When thou art converted, strengthen thy brethren," reveals the end was never in doubt. The Master is the Unchanging One; as He prayed for Peter, He prays for us. This should offset the challenge of every foe.

A New Companion

". . . therefore the world hateth you . . . BUT when the Comforter is come . . . he shall testify of me . . ." (John 15:19, 26). Along the road to glory, strong enemy contingents may be encountered. Fierce onslaughts may be made upon the elect; the battle will be hard and long, but Christians are never asked to fight alone. As the Captain of the Lord's hosts assisted Joshua (Joshua 5:13-15), the Holy Spirit assists the saints. Through all the changing vicissitudes of the warfare of life, He remains the unseen but present Commander of God's forces. With such a leader, the cause can never be lost.

A New Confidence

"The grass withereth . . . BUT the word of the Lord endureth for ever." This is the strong confidence with which God's people go forth into the world. Though heaven and earth should pass away, the Word of God, unchanging, enduring, continues eternally. Satan may threaten; armies might march against the forces of righteousness, but the gates of hell shall not prevail against the Church of the living God. The promises of God are sure; the purposes of God may be thwarted for a while, but ultimately God's plans will be fulfilled. "And this is the word which by the gospel is preached . . . ." The last turn on this road brings the traveler within sight of the city of God. The things of earth may pass away, BUT — and this is a glorious BUT — "*the word of the Lord endureth for ever.*"

The Sixteenth Chapter of John

THEME: *The Work of the Holy Trinity in the Redemption of Fallen Man*

OUTLINE:

    I. The Saviour and His Preachers. Verses 1-6.
    II. The Holy Spirit and His Power. Verses 7-16.
    III. The Father and His Purposes. Verses 17-33.

SECTIONS ONE AND TWO

Expository Notes on Christ's Five-fold Emphasis of "These Things"

At the end of Section Two of the previous chapter a homily was presented outlining the "these things" spoken by the Lord Jesus. Here we discover a re-emphasis of the earlier teaching. The first six verses of chapter 16 provide a climax to the message already given and an introduction to another discourse concerning the person and work of the Holy Spirit. Five times within six verses John recorded "these things" to stress the Lord's desire to impress upon the disciples certain important facts. The Saviour was about to unfold new revelations of truth, but it seemed vain to proceed further until His followers had learned the lessons already given.

These things have I spoken unto you, that ye should not be offended. They shall put you out of the synagogues: yea, the time cometh, that whosoever killeth you will think that he doeth God service (vv. 1, 2).

To be forewarned is to be forearmed. The Lord did not hesitate to reveal the horrors and dangers soon to come upon His followers. He saw the possibility of their becoming offended by the stigma of the cross. He knew that many professed followers would renounce their faith and return to the ways of darkness. "Having loved his own, he loved them unto the end," and it was this love which enabled them to see clearly that which they would be called upon to endure for His Name's sake. The most fierce opposition would come from religious zealots, those with the misguided belief that they were rendering God a special service by trying to kill them. Saul of Tarsus provided an outstanding example of the accuracy of the Lord's prediction. "And Saul, yet breathing out threatenings and slaughter against the disciples of the Lord, went unto the high priest, and desired of him letters to Damascus to the synagogues, that if he found any of this way, whether they were men or women, he might bring them bound unto Jerusalem" (Acts 9:1, 2). "But Saul shamefully treated and laid waste the church continuously — with cruelty and violence (made havoc of the church) and entering house after house, he dragged out men and women and committed them to prison" (Acts 8:3 *Amplified New Testament*). The word translated "havoc" is *elumaineto* which means to ravage, to devastate, to ruin, to injure. The word has been used to describe a wild boar ravaging the garden — that is, the soil — until the ground bears no resemblance to what it was before. Such then was the result of the persecution of the Church; the wild boar was a religious man who was firmly convinced he did God service. This kind of thing was repeated throughout the Dark Ages, for the most fierce persecutors of the Christians were religious leaders whose fanatical prejudice rendered them incapable of seeing any viewpoint but their own. It has been said that every one of the twelve Apostles, except John, suffered a martyr's death. Their endurance to the end endorsed the Saviour's testimony.

> **And these things will they do unto you, because they have not known the Father nor me. But these things have I told you, that when the time shall come, you may remember that I told you of them (vv. 3, 4).**

To know the Father was to recognize the love which He had for all men; to exhibit bitterness, hatred, malice betrayed the fact that the love of God remained unknown. An acceptance of religious principles was no criterion of true spirituality. When the approaching storm broke over the disciples' heads, it would be well to remember the Lord's words. He who had stilled the storm on Galilee might have stilled or prevented this storm; that He saw its approach and permitted its coming suggested that even the distressing conditions might be an integral part of the divine program. It would be wise in the storm to see not the raging tempest but the Master's hand, to consider not the grave consequences of being overwhelmed but the glorious fact that Christ was equal to the occasion. How great His foresight, His permissive will, His purpose, His power! (1) *His foresight* saw the coming of the tempest. (2) *His permissive will* allowed it to engulf and threaten the safety of those He loved. (3) *His purpose* was obvious. "Therefore they that were scattered abroad went everywhere preaching the word" (Acts 8:4). (4) *His power* demonstrated the ability to save for, in spite of all that emperors did, the Church continued its triumphant ministry.

And these things I said not unto you at the beginning, because I was with you. But now I go my way to him that sent me; and none of you asketh me, Whither goest thou? But because I have said these things unto you, sorrow hath filled your heart. (vv. 4-6).

The Lord has always been mindful not to place upon His children burdens too heavy to be carried. Had he spoken these things earlier, His friends might have broken their hearts. He therefore protected them by preserving His secrets. There were times when He sent them out into the country to preach the Gospel; consequently, there were nights when they lay alone beneath the stars. Had they known the difficulties to be encountered they might have been a prey to needless fears. Now, He tells them these things because the Comforter was about to come, and there would be no more lonely journeys, no more lonely nights. Every doubt and fear could be shared with the Holy Spirit, every burden placed at His feet, every journey undertaken in His company. The former years had been a time of increasing happiness; the Gospel had been preached, the sick healed, the dead raised to life. The thrill of serving Christ brought heaven down to earth, but now, their sun was eclipsed: "Because I have said these things unto you, sorrow hath filled your hearts. If I had told you earlier, your happiness would have been ruined. I tell you now that soon you might know an even greater joy."

Nevertheless I tell you the truth; it is expedient for you that I go away: for if I go not away, the Comforter will not come unto you; but if I depart, I will send him unto you. (v. 7).

The word translated "expedient" is *sumpherei*, which in its primary meaning suggests to bear; to bring together; *to collect in order to help*. Hence, *to help; to be profitable; to be expedient*. The verse could be read therefore: "It is to your advantage that I go away. I shall collect — gather together for your assistance — things you do not now enjoy. It is therefore expedient that I go away." The same root word is found in Acts 19:19, where the text reads: "And many of those who practiced curious arts, *having brought the books* — that is, having collected them and brought them together in one place — burned them before all." The main idea in this text therefore is, that the departure of the Saviour would gather together many things, and through the subsequent coming of the Comforter, these acquired treasures would be presented to the Church. If He did not go to the Father, they would suffer immeasurable loss, as these things would then be unavailable. (See the homily at the end of this section.)

And when he is come, he will reprove the world of sin, and of righteousness, and of judgment: of sin, because they believe not on me; of righteousness, because I go to my Father, and ye see me no more; of judgment, because the prince of this world is judged (vv. 8-11).

This prediction of the Lord's answered two vital questions: (1) How could sorrowful hearts be filled with peace? (2) How could impotent men become invincible? These heartbroken disciples, soon to be scattered were to survive the ordeal ahead, and emerge radiant with happiness to challenge the might of far-flung empires. The entire project seemed fantastic and impossible, and yet the miracles were really performed. Nevertheless, the questions demanded an answer. (1) Their sorrowful hearts would become the temple of the Holy Spirit. As the rising sun banished the darkness of the night, so His coming would drive care from their troubled souls. (2) Their simple words would become the sword of the Lord, for divine strength would be made perfect in their weakness. "Now when they saw the boldness of Peter and John, and perceived that they were unlearned and ignorant men, they marvelled; and they took knowledge of them, that they had been with Jesus" (Acts 4:13). "For ye see your calling, brethren, how that not many wise men after the flesh, not many mighty, not many noble are called. But God hath chosen the foolish things of the world to confound the wise; and God hath chosen the weak things of the world to confound the things which are mighty; and base things of the world, and things which are despised, hath God chosen, yea, and things which are not, to bring to nought things that are: That no flesh should glory in his presence" (I Corinthians 1:26-29).

God's remedy for human insufficiency is the fullness of the Holy Spirit. Divine preaching majors on five vital, basic facts: (1) sin (2) righteousness; (3) judgment; (4) the Scriptures; (5) the Saviour. Preaching without these principles is vain rhetoric. The Holy Spirit was never a soothsayer — He was sent to convict, to trouble, to convince the world of sin.

(1) *Of sin because they believe not on me.* We live in an age when the mention of sin has become unpopular. Men prefer to define it as *undeveloped good.* Crime is said to be indicative of mental illness and not of the depravity of human nature. Governments spend vast sums of money erecting correctional schools, while churches are almost forgotten. Experimental laboratories are found throughout the world; doctors and scientists are seeking new methods of stemming the rising tides of evil, and yet the penitentiaries continue to be crowded, and the streets of certain cities are hardly safe places after dark. The only real method of preventing crime is to change the man who commits it. Dr. Weatherhead wrote of *"the expelling power* of a new affection." An illuminating course of study might change a criminal's thoughts, but if his heart be left unchallenged, as soon as he re-enters the old environment, habits and circumstances combine to pull him into the quicksand of evil. Sin is enmity against

God. We call it by various names, but God calls it SIN — the ugly monster that raised its hand against the Son of the Highest. True preaching never condones sin. The light of God's Word shines into the human heart to reveal, to denounce, to bring to light things displeasing to God. Ministers who shrink from the denunciation of evil are self-employed; God would never own such workmen!

(2) *Of righteousness, because I go to my Father, and ye see me no more.* Righteousness and mercy are co-equal in the divine economy. Mercy loves the sinner, holiness detests the sin. Righteousness is the mediator which brings these two together. There is a sense in which God never forgives sin; sin is evil and must be judged. Forgiveness is directed toward the sinner and not toward his sin. To see these things in their true perspective is to see the entire plan of salvation. It is not the mercy of God that forgives the sinner. Mercy was manifest in the sacrifice of God's only begotten Son. Let it be said reverently, but nevertheless let it be said, that God MUST forgive the guilty when that man comes in the appointed way to Christ. Righteousness demands that he be accepted, for his debt was canceled by the precious blood of Christ. The death of the Son of God made salvation possible; the intelligent faith of a penitent soul makes it an actual fact in the sinner's experience. The wisdom of God devised a plan through which holiness and mercy could unite in rescuing the lost. Holiness stooped to deal with human guilt; mercy stooped to lift the people responsible. Holiness placed man's sin on Christ; mercy placed the Lord's righteousness on sinful man. Holiness wrote man's sinful record in the book of remembrance; mercy canceled the record. The appointed way to this realization was through the cross and resurrection. Jesus said, "Because I go to my Father, and ye see me no more . . . the plans of God must be fulfilled, sin abolished, salvation made possible, your High Priest installed at the right hand of the Majesty on high."

(3) *Of judgment, because the prince of this world is judged.* Sin remains *sin*, wherever it is found. When mercy is rejected, holiness demands justice. The same cross destined to emancipate sinful slaves also condemns the unrepentant. If there be no judgment, why should Christ speak of it? The death of Christ delivered the fatal blow to the kingdom of evil; there Satan was judged, defeated, exposed. The preaching of that message to a sinful world should remind sinners that the path of evil leads to disaster. Through Christ, God called men to repentance; in Christ, He offered them forgiveness; by Christ, they would be eternally condemned if they loved darkness rather than light.

These truths would be expressed continually by the men whose hearts were cleansed and thrilled by the power of the Comforter. His mighty strength would make them invincible; His far-reaching ability would send them to the ends of the earth to establish the kingdom of Christ. "The presence of Christ's Spirit in His Church is so much more desirable than His bodily presence, that it was really expedient for us that He should go away. His corporeal presence could be but in one place at one time, but His Spirit is wherever two or three are gathered in His Name. *Christ's bodily presence draws men's eyes, His Spirit draws their hearts*" (Matthew Henry).

> **I have yet many things to say unto you, but ye cannot bear them now. Howbeit, when he, the Spirit of truth is come, he will guide you into all the truth: for he shall speak not of himself; but whatsoever he shall hear, that shall he speak: and he will shew you things to come (vv. 12, 13).**

Throughout the ministry of the Lord, constant mention was made of the Father. Continually the Lord Jesus bore witness to Him by whom He had been sent. It is of very great importance to notice that throughout the ministry of the Holy Spirit, the same emphasis is placed on the person of the Son. The Holy Spirit never bore witness to the Father. The Lord Jesus said, ". . . for he shall not speak of himself . . . he shall glorify me." God's message for this age is centered in Christ. Sermons without Christ are a waste of time. To enable the disciples to grasp the hidden beauties of the inspired Word of God, the Holy Spirit would become their Teacher, their Professor in God's university. He would take and break the Bread of Life that they might feed upon it. He would explain the mysteries of the divine will that they might understand the greatness of their calling. In times of emergency He would suggest to their minds the words they should utter; in every place they would be able to defend their cause. The Lord indicated there were other things He desired to teach them but they were unable at that time to appreciate all the lessons in God's school. The presence of the Great Teacher would be the guarantee of their ultimate graduation. Then they would not only be able to testify of the past; they would be prophets to speak accurately concerning the end of the age. The Lord's prediction was fulfilled; these men and their converts gave us the New Testament.

> **He shall glorify me: for he shall receive of mine, and shall shew it unto you. All things that the Father hath are mine: therefore said I, that he shall take of mine, and shall shew it unto you. A little while, and ye shall not see me: and again, a little while, and ye shall see me, because I go to the Father (vv. 14-16).**

Once again the members of the Godhead are brought together within the scope of one verse. *"The Father . . . I . . . He."* Never for one moment did the apostle lose sight of his reason for writing this gospel. The Lord had come from the presence of the Father; He was equal with God. This point had not been clearly explained by the other evangelists; John was determined to do what was necessary. "All things that the Father hath are mine." (1) *The Father's eternal status* was Christ's, for the Lord had been with Him from the beginning. (2) *The Father's glory* was His, for He had shared it before the world was (17:5). (3) *The Father's power* was His because Jesus had become the exclusive channel by which heaven was operating upon earth. (4) *The Father's wisdom* was His, for the Lord's voice had also been heard in the eternal council meetings of the Godhead. (5) *The Father's worship* should be given to Him, and consequently He never rebuked any man who fell at His feet to worship. (6) *The Father's possessions* were His for God had given all things into His hands. All these truths supplied added reasons why they should not permit their hearts to be troubled. The Comforter was coming; He would be alongside to help in every time of need. He would be their Teacher and take of the things of Christ to reveal them to the disciples. The future was bright with prospect and hope; they should not be alarmed when the winds of persecution began to blow.

> A little while, and ye shall not see me: and again, a little while, and ye shall see me, because I go to the Father (v. 16).

Observe how the *little while* of the Saviour, to them, sometimes seemed an eternity. The disciples were soon to believe the cross to be utterly devastating; He saw it as "a little while" away from them. After His death, every moment seemed endless; the Lord saw it as a very small and narrow valley through which He would pass to be with them again. Three days compared with the limitless aeons of the ages are as nothing. Christ knew that on His way from the tomb to heaven He would see them again. Four times the Lord referred to His going to the Father (verses 5, 10, 16, 28). The Master might have been excused had He said He was going to His cross. Jesus saw not the valley but the city beyond. "Looking unto Jesus the author and finisher of our faith; who for the joy that was set before him endured the cross, despising the shame, and is set down at the right hand of the throne of God" (Hebrews 12:2).

HOMILIES

Study No. 59

THE BETTER WAY

When the Master told His disciples it was far better that He left them and departed for heaven, it was difficult for His hearers to believe the wisdom of the utterance. Had they been able to see the agony of the crucifixion, the appointed way by which He would make an exit from this world, they would have contradicted His message. Nothing could have been worse than His death, departure, and apparent defeat. They had much to learn, and their lessons were not even begun until the Great Teacher came to continue the work of the Saviour. That it was indeed expedient for Christ to depart was evident from the following:

A greater freedom

"I can best remain with you by leaving you. Imprisoned within a body, I can only be in one place at one time. When I visited My friends in Bethany, I could not be at Sychar's well. If I visited Jerusalem, I had to turn My back on other places. When I sent you to preach in the villages, I could not go with you all. I want to be with you always. Therefore, if I go away with My body, I will return without it. This will enable Me to say, 'Go ye into all the world . . . and lo, I am with you always.' "

A greater intercession

"I can best serve you by being at the seat of all authority. Enthroned at the right hand of the Majesty on high, I shall be able to intercede for you. While I remain on earth, the demands of My ministry limit the time available for prayer. The needs of sinful men occupy My attention for most of the time, and communion is possible only when other people sleep. If I go to My Father, I can remember you always 'and ever live to make intercession for you.' "

A greater revelation

"I can best instruct you by letting another Teacher take My place. I can only help you when you are actually sitting in My presence. When you are miles away, My voice is unable to reach you. Then so much of what I have taught you is quickly forgotten. There are many other things I want you to know, but you are not able to grasp them. The time for your higher education has not arrived, and I must leave. The Holy Spirit will reside in your hearts and minds to remind you of all that I have said. When the time is opportune, He will teach you other things which He heard from My Father."

A greater triumph

"*For three years* I have been with you; the Comforter will be with you forever. *From without,* I have tried to change your ideas and teach you, by way of example, how to live. In some senses My efforts have been hindered, for you, John, are still a Son of Thunder; and you, Peter, are so self-assured that the suggestion of any weakness within your heart stirs resentment. When the Holy Spirit comes, He will influence you *from within.* He will change your nature and create within you a clean heart. The triumph within your souls will be greater than any won through your ministry."

A greater goal

"If I remained with you, death would be your greatest enemy; it would threaten to separate you from Me. If I go away, death will almost be your friend; it will usher you into My Presence. Instead of leaving Me, you will be coming to Me — 'that where I am, there ye may be also.' Down here, I have not had a home; in heaven, the city of God waits to welcome Me. At the end of your earthly journey, I shall be waiting to welcome you home. This fact will help you to live; this truth will help you to die."

A greater message

"Some day when you understand My words, you will say, 'For the preaching of the cross is to them that perish foolishness; but unto us which are saved it is the power of God.' Unless I die and go to My Father, there will be no reconciliation, no atonement, no forgiveness, no hope. Unless I die, there can be no resurrection, and if there be no rising from the dead, what message will you deliver to a sinful world? 'Except a corn of wheat fall into the ground and die, it abideth alone. If it die, it bringeth forth much fruit.' Unless I die, you can never live. If I rise again, you will never die."

SECTION THREE

Expository Notes on the Way Christ Anticipated and Answered a Question

Then said some of his disciples among themselves, What is this that he saith unto us, A little while, and ye shall not see me: and again, a little while and ye shall see me: and, Because I go to the Father? They said therefore, What is this that he saith, A little while? We cannot tell what he saith (vv. 17, 18).

The disciples were obviously puzzled and worried. They had been with Him for years but had not understood His teaching. They listened to much but heard so little. The idea of a Messianic kingdom established within their homeland was so firmly rooted in their minds, it was hard to accept anything contrary to the old idea. That He should even think of leaving them when the kingdom was so near to realization was absurd! They looked at Him and repeated the words He had spoken. What could they mean? The best thing to do when the words of the Lord confused the mind was to sit at His feet and wait expectantly for an explanation.

Now Jesus knew that they were desirous to ask him, and said unto them: Do ye enquire among yourselves of that I said, A little while, and ye shall not see me: and again, a little while, and ye shall see me? Verily, verily, I say unto you, That ye shall weep and lament, but the world shall rejoice: and ye shall be sorrowful, but your sorrow shall be turned into joy (vv. 19, 20).

The Lord knew of their problem; He had watched them without their being aware He was so doing. Sometimes Christians are so concerned over little matters they forget the Lord's eyes are able to read their inmost thoughts. His gracious question revealed the matchless care with which He watched over them. His eyes as searchlights swept along the road ahead to reveal all that would take place. "Ye shall weep and lament, but the world shall rejoice." Nothing takes the Lord by surprise. He knew His followers would be scattered as sheep without a shepherd; He recognized the deep sorrow soon to devastate their hearts; He heard also the laughter of sinners who after His death would consider they had gained their greatest victory. "Your sorrow shall be turned to joy." After the night, comes the dawn; after the storm comes the calm; after the chilling winter comes the cheer and the thrill of springtime.

A woman when she is in travail hath sorrow, because her hour is come: but as soon as she is delivered of the child, she remembereth no more the anguish, for joy that a man is born into the world. And ye now therefore have sorrow: but I will see you again, and your heart shall rejoice, and your joy no man taketh from you (vv. 21, 22).

This was according to Scripture and the facts of life. "Unto the woman the Lord God said, I will greatly multiply thy sorrow and thy conception; in sorrow thou shalt bring forth children . . ." (Genesis 3:16) The fact that Christ should use this illustration and compare it with their own sorrow suggests that in the providence of God something new was about to be born into the world.

There are two possible interpretations of the text. Either *He* was about to give birth to this manchild or they were. There is every possibility that the Lord referred to that new creation, the bringing forth of the Church, the Body of Christ which God planned before the foundation of the world. There was a sense in which the disciples were responsible for this, for when they went forth to preach the Gospel, thousands of listeners responded to their message. At Pentecost the Church was brought to birth.

Much may be said, however, for the other interpretation. The prophet Isaiah foretold clearly that Christ would die. In spite of the fact that the word "travail" was a feminine word referring to childbirth, the prophet said, ". . . *he* shall see *his seed*, he shall prolong his days, and the pleasure of the Lord shall prosper in his hand. He shall see of the *travail of his soul*, and shall be satisfied: by his knowledge shall my righteous servant justify many; for he shall bear their iniquities" (Isaiah 53:10, 11). This utterance was fulfilled when the thief asked for forgiveness. *"When thou shalt make his soul an offering for sin, he shall see his seed . . . ."* It was fulfilled to a lesser degree when, by the operation of the Holy Spirit, the Church was brought to birth at Pentecost. If the latter interpretation be nearer the truth, then the disciples were in sorrow because the One they loved was suffering the acute pangs of labor. The Lord was trying to tell them this ought not to be. They would share His pleasure when the new life came into the world. The darkness of their night of sorrow would be forgotten in the glory of the new day. "And they, continuing daily with one accord in the temple, and breaking bread from house to house, did eat their meat with gladness and singleness of heart. Praising God, and having favor with all people. And the Lord added to the Church daily such as should be saved" (Acts 2:46, 47). It was this joy within the hearts of the disciples which nonplussed the enemies of Christ. The civic and ecclesiastical authorities could take away their liberty, possessions, and even their lives, but the joy of the Church endured through time and into eternity. "No man taketh it from you."

> And in that day ye shall ask me nothing. Verily, verily, I say unto you, Whatsoever ye shall ask the Father in my name, he will give it you. Hitherto have ye asked nothing in my name: ask and ye shall receive, that your joy may be full (vv. 23, 24).

Throughout the Acts of the Apostles we seldom read of the disciples asking questions of anybody. They had been filled with the Holy Spirit and were being led by Him constantly. There was no need to inquire or ask questions; they knew all they needed to know. Their prayers ascended to the throne of God and even before they called, God answered. There can be no doubt whatsoever that the greatest discovery the Early Church ever made was that the power of prayer could accomplish anything. Prayer preceded (1) Pentecost (Acts 1:14); (2) the great revival which swept through the city of Jerusalem (Acts 2:42-47); (3) Peter and John were going to the temple at the hour of prayer when the lame man was healed (Acts 3:1, 2); (4) a prayer meeting in the home of John Mark released the power which brought Peter from the prison (Acts 12:12); (5) a midnight prayer meeting made an earthquake open the doors of the prison in Philippi (Acts 16:25, 26). All these prayers were offered in the Name of Jesus; they were invincible. The Lord was correct when He said, "Hitherto have ye asked nothing in my name." A whole new world was beginning to open before the astonished disciples. Modern Christians might well emulate their example and say, "Lord, teach us how to pray." (For expository notes on "praying in the name of Christ," see earlier chapters. For a study of "the fullness of joy," see the homily at the end of this section.)

These things have I spoken unto you in proverbs: but the time cometh, when I shall no more speak unto you in proverbs, but I shall shew you plainly of the Father (v. 25).

The greatest realm into which Christ could lead a soul was *the knowledge of God.* As a child in kindergarten would be unable to appreciate the teachings of higher grades of education, so the disciples were children in God's school. It had been necessary to give the "sincere milk of the Word"; the time was coming when, growing in grace, they would be able to receive the "strong meat" of increasing revelations. Compare this with Paul's message to the Corinthian church. ". . . Eye hath not seen, nor ear heard, neither have entered into the heart of man, the things which God hath prepared for them that love him. BUT GOD HATH REVEALED THEM UNTO US BY HIS SPIRIT . . ." (I Corinthians 2:9, 10). Paul made it clear that what the greatest intellectual minds of his day were unable to grasp, the uneducated Christians understood perfectly. ". . . *they had been shewn plainly of the Father."*

At that time, you will ask (pray) in My name, and I am not saying that I will ask the Father on your behalf (for it will be unnecessary). For the Father Himself tenderly loves you, because you have loved Me, and have believed that I came out from the Father. *Amplified New Testament* **(vv. 26, 27).**

This great utterance of the Saviour should not be misconstrued. *"He ever liveth to make intercession for us."* There will never be a moment when we shall not be in need of His advocacy before the throne of God. In this text the Lord Jesus taught an even greater truth. Some prayers are not intelligent prayers; some people ask amiss (James 4:3). The Lord's interceding wisdom edits our unwise petitions. If the Lord granted our desires just as we asked, disaster might soon overwhelm us. "He knoweth our frame and remembereth that we are dust." As children, we ask for all kinds of things; as a loving Father He listens to our cry, considers the requests, and gives us what is best. But — and this is a most important BUT — when the Comforter takes control of the Christian, His inspiration begets wiser prayers. "Likewise the Spirit also helpeth our infirmities: for we know not what we should pray for as we ought: but the Spirit himself maketh intercession for us with groanings that cannot be uttered." This text is rendered in the *Amplified New Testament* as follows: "So too, the Holy Spirit comes to our aid, and bears us up in our weakness; for we do not know what prayer to offer, nor how to offer it worthily as we ought, but the Spirit Himself goes to meet our supplication and pleads in our behalf with unspeakable yearnings and groanings too deep for utterance." Therefore, the Lord will not need to separate the unwise requests from the beneficial, for a man praying in the Holy Spirit will be asking for things which please God. Such a man will be greatly loved by the Father; he has truly *believed* . . . such faith can never be denied.

I came forth from the Father, and am come into the world: again, I leave the world, and go to the Father. His disciples said unto him, Lo, now thou speakest plainly, and speakest no proverb. Now are we sure that thou knowest all things, and needest not that any man should ask thee: by this we believe that thou camest forth from God (vv. 28-30).

His words brought a measure of comfort to their hearts, but it was doubtful whether or not they understood the meaning of His words. His declaration that the Father loved them filled them with content but their minds remained in the fog. Indisputably Christ knew this, but He remained serene, for He knew the Holy Spirit, as He had indicated, would complete the work He had begun.

Jesus answered them, Do ye now believe? Behold, the hour cometh, yea is now come, that ye shall be scattered, every man to his own, and shall leave me alone: and yet I am not alone, because the Father is with me (vv. 31, 32).

"Let him that thinketh he standeth, take heed lest he fall." Self-confidence is often the forerunner of disaster. The Lord knew His disciples would forsake Him, but "*having loved his own . . . he loved them to the end.*" A man of lesser stature would have chided them, He saw, sympathized, and remained their greatest Friend. When they were scattered abroad, every man thought only of his own safety. They might have been witnesses at His trial, carried His cross, wiped the blood from His forehead. Alas, unfortunately, they hid themselves and left Him alone. During the hours of His greatest grief He was cheered only by the presence of His Father. The superlative glories of this Christ beggared description.

These things I have spoken unto you, that in me ye might have peace. In the world ye shall have tribulation: but be of good cheer; I have overcome the world (v. 33).

It was almost incomprehensible that the Lord should speak of His peace when the shadow of the cross was already falling across His soul. He had confessed, "Now is my soul troubled," but as the depth of the sea remain undisturbed even when a tempest rages on the surface, so the depth of the Master's life was serene and tranquil even though the fury of hell was about to be unleashed against Him. "I have told you these things, so that in me you may have perfect peace and confidence. In the world you have tribulations, and trials and distress, and frustration: but be of good cheer — take courage, be confident, certain, undaunted — for I have overcome the world. I have deprived it of power to harm; I have conquered it — for you" (*Amplified New Testament*).

(See the homily on "out-of-season fruits" at the end of Section Four, Chapter 14.)

HOMILIES

Study No. 60

THE FULLNESS OF JOY

The apostle John had an infallible formula for happiness. It was a guaranteed cure for melancholia, and promised complete satisfaction to any man or woman who would give it a fair trial. Yet he was unable to claim proprietary rights for his prescription, as he had learned his secrets from Another. He had lived with the Great Physician, and his opportunities for study had not been neglected.

Abiding in Christ

"Abide in me, and I in you. As the branch cannot bear fruit of itself, except it abide in the vine; no more can ye, except ye abide in me . . . . These things have I spoken unto you, that my joy might remain in you, *and that your joy might be full*" (John 5:4, 11). Supreme happiness only becomes possible for the Christian when he learns to abide in his Lord. Should anything prevent the flow of life from the Lord to His child — from the vine to the branch — spiritual tragedy will undoubtedly follow. The health of the branch is dependant upon clean channels through which the life-giving sap may flow. And in like manner this is true of the relationship between Christ and His followers. Thus and thus alone can the peak of happiness be reached. It is this close union with Christ which engenders happiness; it is proximity to Him which begets *the fullness of joy*.

Communing with Christ

"Verily, verily, I say unto you, Whatsoever ye shall ask the Father in my name, he will give it you. Hitherto have ye asked nothing in my name: ask, and ye shall receive, *that your joy may be full*" (John 16:23, 24). This constituted the new teaching on prayer. Through the medium of Christ, the disciples could talk with God and confidently expect to receive from Him definite answers to their petitions. When humble fishermen found in the Lord Jesus the authority and means whereby to approach the throne of grace, they quickly discovered that language was inadequate to express the joy resulting from a real answer to prayer.

Studying the words of Christ

"And now come I to thee; and these things I speak in the world, *that they might have my joy fulfilled in themselves*. I have given them thy word . . ." (John 17:13, 14). The immortal prayer of Christ reveals many truths, but this is one of the greatest. We may never know how often Jesus secretly prayed in the mountains, for

He constantly sought the place of communion. Yet in the Garden of Gethsemane the Lord ordained that His prayer should be made public in order that the disciples might have access to His words. He desired that they should be acquainted with His statements, for through this medium abundant joy would reach their hearts. His gracious words are now recorded in a book which is a source of real happiness to every devout reader.

Walking with Christ

"That which we have seen and heard declare we unto you, that ye also may have fellowship with us: and truly our fellowship is with the Father, and with his Son Jesus Christ. And these things write we unto you, *that your joy may be full* . . . . Walk in the light" (I John 1:3, 7). It remains one of the greatest miracles of our faith that through His death and resurrection the Saviour has become omnipresent to His people. He has said, "I will never leave you." And if this be true we are thereby provided with the opportunity of walking with Him in blessed fellowship. The road of life need never be lonely. Every path can be an Emmaus road, on which our hearts may burn as we listen to His word. It is doubtful whether any measure of happiness can supercede the blessedness — the fullness of joy made possible by keeping in step with Christ.

Talking about Christ

"Having many things to write unto you, I would not write with paper and ink: but I trust to come unto you, and speak face to face, *that our joy may be full*" (II John 12). This is a fitting climax for all that has gone before. If we enjoy the preliminary stages, we cannot refrain from talking about the Lord Jesus Christ. It is easy for us to imagine John sitting with the "elect lady and her children," and as they conversed about the Saviour, their faces shone with holy delight. It is a cause for deep regret that so many Christians talk so little about the One whom they profess to love. The weather, the political outlook, the sporting results, business affairs, and matters of health are all matters for daily discussion. John preferred to speak often of Jesus, for he had long since discovered this to be the chief secret of continuing happiness. He loved to write . . . *"that your joy might be full."*

The Seventeenth Chapter of John

THEME: *The Lord's Prayer*

OUTLINE:

      I. Christ Commences His Prayer . . .
           He prays for Himself. Verses 1-5.
     II. Christ Continues His Prayer . . .
           He prays for His followers. Verses 6-24.
    III. Christ Concludes His Prayer.
           He makes a promise. Verses 25, 26.

Introduction to Chapter Seventeen

This is one of the greatest passages of the Bible. If the gospel of John may be likened to a mountain range, this chapter represents one of its highest peaks. Here we see breath-taking views of eternal beauties which cannot be viewed from any other place. John leads us slowly to those lofty places from which we gaze back to the very beginning when Christ lived with His Father in the remote realms of eternal ages. We are hushed as we hear again the Saviour's words, "O Father, glorify thou me with thine own self, with the glory which I had with thee before the world was." From this lofty eminence we look at the awe-inspiring cosmos: above us, in outer space, are millions, trillions of starry planets; out there in the unknown may be innumerable undiscovered suns and moons, and yet before any of this came into being, the Lord was. John points forward to that other eternity, when things as we now know them will have changed, when the smoke and grime of earth will belong to the past, when the glory of God shall fill the earth as the waters cover the sea. We wonder what it means as we hear the Lord say again, "Father, I will that they also, whom thou hast given me, be with me where I am, that they may behold my glory . . . ." It all seems too good to be true. The Christian, by faith, has often seen the Lord; then, however, faith will be lost in sight for we shall see Him as He is. The eternal city will not be the distant goal; it will be around us. The streets of gold not something of which we sing, but something over which we shall walk. The Lamb of God will not be our unseen Master, but the Lord into whose presence we shall be able to go. The seventeenth chapter of John's gospel is the lofty eminence from which these amazing wonders may be viewed. This mountain peak is truly holy ground from which we are able to trace the path as it winds among the lowlands, the green pastures in which we rested, the still waters which slaked our spiritual thirst, the rough places where conflicts were fought and won. The Lord's prayer lifts us to heaven's look-out where all things are made clear. There is no prayer equal to this prayed by the Lord.

It will be remembered that in the two previous chapters the Lord instructed His followers about the value of believing prayer. He repeated His words that if they truly prayed in His Name, the Father would grant their requests; He even reminded them that hitherto they had not asked anything in His Name. It was fitting that such discourses should be followed by this prayer. Having told them they should pray, He proceeded to provide the greatest example they would ever know. Having talked about prayer, HE PRAYED. Every student should note carefully the following facts. First, the Saviour prayed for Himself, and then for His followers. When He prayed for Himself, He asked for one thing; when He interceded for His followers, His prayer was sevenfold. In praying for Himself, He was utterly selfless; He asked for something only because that gift could be returned to the glory of His Father. When He asked the seven things for His followers, He did so that their joy might be increased. Ultimately detailed studies of the Lord's prayer will be presented, but meanwhile the seven requests are enumerated.

1. ". . . Holy Father, keep through thine own name those whom thou hast given me, *that they may be one,* as we are" (verse 11).
2. "And now come I to thee . . . *that they might have my joy . . .*" (verse 13).
3. "I pray . . . *that thou shouldest keep them from the evil one*" (verse 15).
4. ". . . *that they might be sanctified . . .*" (verse 19).
5. ". . . *that they may be made perfect . . .*" (verse 23).
6. "Father, I will that *they . . . be with me where I am . . .*" (verse 24).
7. ". . . *that they may behold my glory . . .*" (verse 24).

These represent the seven stages on the road to eternal happiness. Together, they form the perfect prayer, for there is nothing superficial, nothing trivial. Each of these petitions was in accord with the sovereign will of God; each carried the imprint of holy commendation. To pray thus would be to pray in the Name of Jesus, for so He prayed. With these thoughts in mind, let us proceed to the study of the text.

Expository Notes on the Beginning of the Lord's Prayer

These words spake Jesus, and lifted up his eyes to heaven, and said, Father, the hour is come; glorify thy Son, that thy Son also may glorify thee (v. 1).

The five verses which comprise this section teach five things concerning the Saviour: (1) *how selfless;* (2) *how strong;* (3) *how sure;* (4) *how satisfied;* (5) *how sublime.* Let us consider them in that order. ". . . glorify thy Son, that thy Son also may glorify thee." The Lord was utterly selfless in asking for this benediction. He desired it for one reason; that it might be returned to glorify Him whom Christ delighted to honor. Had the Master's request ceased earlier, men might have wondered if the Lord desired earthly fame, increasing popularity, a terrestrial kingdom. That He revealed the increasing desire to honor His Father shows His absolute devotion to the cause He came to serve. So many of our prayers are selfish; we ask for many things, but seldom mean what we say when we add, "Grant us these things *according to Thy will.*" Negative answers to prayers beget frowns upon our faces. This reference takes us back to chapter 12:23, 24. "The hour" mentioned frequently in the fourth gospel referred to that moment when the Son of God would offer Himself, the Just for the unjust; the time when Satan's power would appear to engulf the Holy One. It is truly significant that Christ did not ask for power to die, for a lightening of the load He was expected to carry. Neither did He ask for encouragement in any shape or form. He was not alarmed by the cross with its suffering; He saw only a means of glorifying God. If what had to be done was done successfully, if He fulfilled the plans made in eternity, heaven would resound with the praise of His Father. An unspeakable yearning of soul was exhibited when He fervently looked toward heaven; His soul was made bare when He said, "Father, do this for Me that I might be able to do more for Thee."

As thou hast given him power over all flesh, that he should give eternal life to as many as thou hast given him (v. 2).

The term "flesh" has a three-fold meaning within the New Testament. (1) It is used of mankind; that is, to signify the presence of human beings: "I will pour out my Spirit on all flesh" (Acts 2:17). (2) It is used to express our physical frame; that is, the tissue which covers our bones: ". . . for a spirit hath not flesh and bones" (Luke 24:39). It is used also to express our lower nature, the carnal side of life which, unfortunately, is ever present within the Christian: ". . . they that are in the flesh, cannot please God" (Romans 8:8). Whether one or all of these features may be included in the direct applications of this text is something for each student to decide. Probably it included all, for absolute authority was given to Christ. As we shall consider in the study of chapter 18, the Lord's power was sufficient to overwhelm the entire party of men who came to arrest Him. Christ possessed also the spiritual authority which enabled Him to dispense the Bread of Life. He gave eternal life to all who believed in His Name. This conception of the eternal greatness of Christ enabled Tennyson to write:

"STRONG *Son of God, Immortal Love.*"

And this is life eternal, that they might know thee the only true God, and Jesus Christ, whom thou hast sent (v. 3).

This was an entirely new concept of truth. The knowledge of God was something previously reserved for the elect, the favored among the race. The high priest, on the day of atonement, was permitted to enter into the Holiest of Holies, there to catch a fleeting glimpse of the mercy seat, but ordinary citizens were never given that privilege. Moses had climbed into the solitudes to listen and commune with God. To him had been granted the honor of getting a glimpse of God's back as the Infinite moved through the lofty valley. Yet Moses was alone when this happened, and the benediction of the hilltop never came on any other man. The scholastic rabbis knew something of the Holy Writings; they even knew something about God; but to know God as a Father, to seek and enjoy His presence, to fall at His feet in humble adoration, to share His home, and gaze into His face – to KNOW God was something existing only in the realms of fancy. Even eternal life was a vague out-of-reach treasure which all men desired, but so few ever hoped to possess. The coming to earth of the Son of God completely shattered their preconceived notions. Eternal life was not a reward at the end of a meritorious life; it was a gift to undeserving sinners. This boundless invaluable treasure was not a new dispensation of grace from an eternal judge but a gift from their Friend, Jesus of Nazareth. To know Him was to know God; to enjoy the smile of His favor was to receive life – everlasting life. The laws of Moses, the traditions of the Fathers, success and defeat, effort and failure, all these were subservient to the one predominant thing: Christ had come. Life everlasting had already begun; they had learned to love the Saviour.

I have glorified thee on the earth: I have finished the work which thou gavest me to do (v. 4).

It was easy for the Lord to draw near to God; there was no blemish to mar His approach. No earth-born cloud could arise to hide Him from His Father's eyes. A lifetime had been lived in complete dedication to the purposes of heaven. God had been glorified in all the words and deeds of the Son; nothing had been overlooked; the work was finished. The perfect Son was able to present the perfect prayer because His valiant conduct on the battle fields of life had gained the right of audience with the Almighty. It is difficult for us to appreciate all that is included in this simple, yet tremendous utterance of the Master. Throughout His arduous ministry, He had never sought glory for Himself. He claimed equality with God only because sinful men challenged His doctrines. He indicated He came from God only because they constantly affirmed He emerged from a poor home in Nazareth. The claims to supernatural grandeur were made only to enhance the glory of God. The Lord never stole the limelight, and even when crowds of people waited to sing praises, He withdrew to the hillside to meet God. Christ had been utterly selfless. Although He was the strong Son of God, Jesus remained the humblest of the sons of men. Now the hour — the greatest hour was about to strike; He was ready.

And now, O Father, glorify thou me with thine own self with the glory which I had with thee before the world was (v. 5).

The Lord Jesus only asked one request for Himself; and this was repeated, for He knew exactly what He wanted. ". . . before the world was." Before stars twinkled in any sky, waves beat out their force on any beach, birds sang in any bush, leaves rustled on any branch, rivers flowed from any hills, before man even walked the earth, in the limitless reaches of eternity, God was there. Man is now beginning to explore the fringes of the vast absorbing world above us. Rockets are forcing their way upward; electronic devices are being sent into orbit; scientists bend over the drawing boards; technicians work day and night, and brave young astronauts courageously face the future. Man knows that in outer space exist innumerable spheres far bigger than the planet upon which he lives. Undiscovered realms of celestial beauty beckon him to attempt the apparently impossible. He may see each night the same stars which Abraham saw. The same moon that shines upon modern industrial cities shone upon Eden. Yet to the eternal One, time is nothing. God placed stars in the sky as we place pictures on a wall. He did in a moment what man has been unable to do in milleniums.

Before time began, God was. When time ceases, God will be. Back, far back, back in eternity, the Triune God lived and moved, and had Their being. They existed in realms undefiled by iniquity. The air breathed was Holiness; the words spoken were Praise; when They smiled, Glory transfigured the universe. Christ knew all this for He had been there. Time and necessity had made changes. He had descended to earth on a special mission. That mission was nearing completion and the Son was about to return whence He came. The prospect was thrilling, the outlook sublime. He saw not the night of suffering but the dawn of resurrection. He heard not the sneers of sinners but the acclamation of the angels. He was going Home. O joy! "Father, glorify thou Me, not with crowns and jewels; not with earthly honors, but surround Me again with the intrinsic glory and wonder of Thine own dear Presence. Let me breathe again that old atmosphere, and know the intimate fellowship which inhabited eternity '. . . . the glory which I had with thee before the world was.' "

Thus did Jesus begin His prayer. We bow our heads. This was the eternal Son, the Master, our Redeemer.

SECTION TWO

Expository Notes on Christ's Seven-fold
Prayer for the Disciples

I have manifested thy name unto the men which thou gavest me out of the world: thine they were, and thou gavest them me; and they have kept thy word. Now they have known that all things whatsoever thou hast given me are of thee. For I have given unto them the words which thou gavest me; and they have received them, and have known surely that I came out from thee, and they have believed that thou didst send me (vv. 6-8).

Matthew Henry wrote of this whole prayer: "(1) *It was a prayer after a sermon;* when He had spoken from God to them, He turned to speak to God for them. Those we preach to, we must pray for. The word preached should be prayed over for God *gives the increase.* (2) *It was a prayer after sacrament.* He closed the solemnity with this prayer, that God would preserve the good impressions of the ordinance upon them. (3) *It was a family prayer.* Christ's disciples were His family, and, to set a good example before masters of families, He blessed His household, and prayed for them . . . . (4) *It was a parting prayer.* When we and our friends are parting, it is good to part with prayer (Acts 20:36). (5) *It was a prayer which was a preface to His sacrifice* which He was about to offer. Christ prayed then as a priest offering sacrifice, in the virtue of which all prayers were to be made. (6) *It was a prayer which was a specimen of His intercession,* which He ever lives to make for us within the veil."

The key words of the preceding verses are ". . . the men which thou gavest me out of the world: thine they were, and thou gavest them me." Christ recognized, as men never could, the strong underlying predestinating influences of election. God was the supreme Ruler of the universe; His was absolute power. These men were His *by right of creation* for all things owed their existence to the creative powers of the Almighty. They were *morally* and *legally* His property. Their imperfections had offended the law of heaven; their being sinners forfeited whatever right they might have had. As a slave unable to pay his debts becomes the property of the landowner, so these men, unable to cancel their debt to God, automatically became His to do with as He thought fit. He could place them in prison; He could demand their lawful execution; He could exact any fit retribution — instead God gave them to Christ, that they might be transformed by the power of the Gospel. When the men accepted the words of Christ and believed the message, evidence was supplied that once again God had been omniscient.

I pray for them: I pray not for the world, but for them which thou hast given me; for they are thine. And all mine are thine, and thine are mine; and I am glorified in them (vv. 9, 10).

We are reminded that the unity of the Divine Family was ever before the Son of God. God and He were co-equal; their possessions were mutually owned. What God possessed by creation was given to the Son; what the Son won by redemption was surrendered gladly to the Father. Prayer has ever been a mystery; why Christ should plead for the protection of the disciples when they were loved by the Father seemed inscrutable. It would appear that God would care for His own without having to be asked so to do. Forces are at work in the universe of which we know nothing. We may, however, be sure that Christ would not have prayed if prayer had been unnecessary. He believed that prayer could liberate power from heaven; He realized the release of this dynamic was made possible by earnest supplication; therefore He prayed. If we do not understand clearly all the intricacies of this exercise, let us, however, pray, for prayer performs miracles.

The First Request

THE UNITY OF THE CHURCH

And now I am no more in the world, but these are in the world, and I come to thee. Holy Father, keep through thine own name those whom thou hast given me, that they may be one as we are. While I was with them in the world, I kept them in thy name: those that thou gavest me I have kept, and none of them is lost, but the son of perdition; that the scripture might be fulfilled (vv. 11, 12).

The disciples were men with varying temperaments. James and John were men with explosive spirits. Their impetuosity carried them away; their anger earned the title, "The sons of thunder." Peter might have belonged to their family circle. Thomas, however, was a different type of fellow; often he looked at the shadows and failed to see the sunshine. It was easier to doubt than believe. Andrew was not a brilliant preacher but he became an untiring worker. Judas was a sly, mischievous thief. Naturally there were moments when these men did not agree on certain questions; on one occasion they quarrelled because some members of the family discovered others were trying to book special seats at the coronation of the Messiah! What a tragedy would have followed if one of the irate disciples had forsaken the others in order to start a new movement with similar aims. This might have been done, for the Saviour's ministry had brought together first twelve, then seventy, then five hundred brethren. Had John criticized Judas and gone out to begin a new denomination, his action would have deserved the greatest condemnation.

Throughout the years of His public ministry, the Lord somehow managed to preserve the unity of His little band of followers. As their good Shepherd He had faithfully led them into green pastures and beside still waters; now, He was worried. Wolves had already appeared on the horizon; false shepherds would soon issue their challenge; His sheep were in danger. "I am no more in the world." He was certainly upon earth, but He was not speaking as a man among men. The glory of the High Priest was already shining upon His countenance. His prayer was being offered as if He were already seated at the right hand of the Majesty on High. "Father, as their intercessor before the throne, I beseech thee to remember them, for they are still in the place of danger; they are indeed in the world. Soon their faith will be tried to breaking point; their courage might falter; their tears run and their blood flow. Holy Father, hold them; keep them, that they may be one as we are one."

Present-day conditions in Christendom have become frightening. In spite of the constant intercession of the ascended Lord, the Church has been split in all directions. If this could happen when He prayed, what might have happened had He abandoned His task? Unfortunately the Church has suffered because men thought more of their own pride than of the cause of Christ. There have been those who loved to have the pre-eminence among saints; when their own brand of doctrine was not accepted as the exclusive teaching of the assembly, they left to begin a new cause. Thereafter, instead of exalting the Lord, they denounced their former brethren, and their crossfire provided entertainment for worldly observers. "These Christians — see how they fight each other!" Fore-seeing these dangers, Paul recommended two things: (1) "I therefore, the prisoner of the Lord, beseech you . . . keep the unity of the Spirit in the bond of peace." (2) "Till we all come in the unity of the faith, and of the knowledge of the Son of God, unto a perfect man, unto the measure of the stature of the fullness of Christ" (Ephesians 4:1, 3, 13). Paul admitted a difference of theological doctrine but denounced carnal criticism. There are times when all Christians need to emphasize what they believe to be true, but there can never be any justification for wholesale condemnation of other brethren who also believe in the finished work of the Son of God. When Christians argue over one percent of doctrine, when at the same time they could be having fellowship in the other 99 percent, their action dishonors the Lord. Strife, backbiting, enmity, and carnality are as displeasing to God as the rejection of Christ. Some people who reject Christ know no better; Christians who profess to sit at Christ's feet have no excuse for the brutality with which they decapitate their brethren. There is reason to believe that if Christ returned to minister on earth as He did long ago, He would begin by denouncing many of the religious leaders. It is not sufficient to be sound in doctrine; righteousness demands Christians be sound in heart. The letter of the word killeth; it is the Spirit that giveth life. One of the last commands given by Christ to His followers was, "Love one another." Certain evangelical people find it far easier to love the heathen than to observe the Lord's command and love their brethren. Christ prayed for the unity of the Church, and this petition preceded all others, for He knew it to be the predominant need of His followers. (For information on Judas, see the expository notes on preceding chapters of John's gospel.)

The Second Request

THE HAPPINESS OF THE CHURCH

And now come I to thee; and these things I speak in the world, that they might have my joy fulfilled in themselves. I have given them thy word and the world hath hated them, because they are not of the world, even as I am not of the world (vv. 13, 14).

These words might have been prayed in secret; the Lord could have waited until He was actually at the Father's right hand before He expressed this great desire. The Master preferred to pray where the disciples could hear what was being said. He desired to teach them that true prayer was not merely a means of gaining assistance for some special project, a means to a desired end. Communion with God was an incentive to increasing happiness. To speak with God was to be in touch with God; to be near God meant His influence could reach our level; "the skin of our faces" could shine with the light of an indwelling holiness. The disciples had been accustomed to bringing their problems to the Master. This would soon become impossible as He was about to return to heaven. What then could they do in emergency when the future presented problems incapable of solution? The answer was expressed in one great word — PRAYER. Christ had instructed them in the noble art of intercession; now He demonstrated what it meant to pray.

They should not be too surprised when the world unleashed diabolic attacks, nor discouraged if the path of life appeared stony and steep. The joy of the Christian depended upon the unfailing faithfulness of the Lord Jesus. In fair weather and foul, He would continue as their great High Priest before the throne of grace. They could reach Him at any time; they had a private line to His Office! It was necessary to remember His words and consider what had been spoken. When the Holy Spirit came, He would stimulate memory and guide them into the truth. Their joys and sorrows, successes and failures, problems, questions, hopes, longings, and everything else could then be relayed to heaven, where, in the presence of the Father, all things would be considered. They belonged to a Royal Society; the enmity of the world could be ignored. The sneers and jeers would come from people who knew nothing of the superlative happiness of the children of God. We must remember this followed His initial request. True happiness would be impossible unless the brethren lived together in unity. ". . . there the Lord commandeth the blessing." "Therefore, if thou bring thy gift to the altar, and there rememberest that thy brother hath ought against thee; leave there thy gift before the altar, and go thy way; *first be reconciled to thy brother*, and then come and offer thy gift" (Matthew 5:23, 24). Happiness is a plant; it grows best in the soil of peace!

The Third Request

THE PROTECTION OF THE CHURCH

I pray not that thou shouldest take them out of the world, but thou shouldest keep them from the evil one. They are not of the world even as I am not of the world (vv. 15, 16).

" 'I pray not that they may be speedily removed by death: If the world be vexatious to them, the readiest way to secure them would be to hasten them out of it. Send chariots and horses of fire to fetch them to heaven.' Christ would not pray so for His disciples. Because He came to conquer those intemperate passions which make men impatient of life, it is His will that we take up our cross, and not outrun it. Because He had work for them to do in the world, the world could ill spare them. In pity therefore to this dark world,

Christ would not have these lights removed out of it, especially for the sake of those in the world *that were to believe in Him through their word.* They must each in his own order die a martyr, but not until they had finished their testimony. The taking of good people out of the world is a thing by no means to be desired. Though Christ loves His disciples, He does not presently send for them to heaven, but leaves them for some time in this world that they might be ripened for heaven. Many good people are spared to live, because they can ill be spared to die" (Matthew Henry).

There are times when it is easier to die than to live. Death, however painful, represents a way of escape, and a Christian overwhelmed by difficulties might be tempted to desire that quick way home. The idea is foreign to the nature of God. When He desires the presence of a saint in heaven, He has the power to translate that person to glory; there are times when to suffer with Him is infinitely better than to reign with Him. In any case, one is the forerunner of the other. Any man who runs away from the hard task can hardly be trusted with the easy tasks.

The dangers awaiting the disciples were varied. There was *the danger of persecution;* Satan would endeavor to stifle their testimony in death. Yet not all the devil's attacks would be so crude and obvious as that of open persecution. There would be *the danger of becoming weary in well-doing.* To labor for a long time without any visible signs of success can be a most disheartening business. Despondency can be a cloud to blot out the sunshine. Satan is always quick to take advantage of such circumstances; his voice whispers, "What is the use, you are getting nowhere. Give it all up." There would be *the danger* of backsliding. "Because iniquity shall abound the love of many shall wax cold." Demas, for example, would love the world and forsake his old friend, Paul. In this way the testimony could be ruined; the preachers might begin to flirt with the world. There would be the danger of *becoming spiritual autocrats;* men who loved to have the pre-eminence among the brethren. Then the trusted ambassadors would be more concerned with making a name for themselves than with the project of extending the kingdom of God. Unfortunately, Diotrephes provided an infamous example of this papal authority that denied religious freedom even to those within whose hearts burned the holy flame (III John 9). There would be *the danger arising from the evil scheming of Satan's followers.* Lies might be told, lies that would make a net to entangle the innocent. Thus even when the preacher remained above reproach before God, people might refuse to listen to his testimony because of the falsehoods already heard about him. Satan had many arrows in his quiver, many poison darts in his possession. The disciples were not sufficiently strong to negotiate the many dangerous turns in the road ahead; they needed help. "Father, keep them from the evil one. Preserve them in the midst of that antagonistic world, for they do not belong to it; their citizenship is in heaven."

The Fourth Request

THE SANCTIFICATION OF THE CHURCH

Sanctify them through thy truth: thy word is truth. As thou hast sent me into the world, even so have I also sent them into the world. And for their sakes I sanctify myself, that they also might be sanctified through the truth. Neither pray I for these alone, but for them also which shall believe on me through their words. That they all may be one; as thou Father art in me, and I in thee, that they also may be one in us, that the world may believe that thou hast sent me (vv. 17-21).

The Greek word translated "sanctify" is *agiasmos;* it was only used by Biblical and ecclesiastical writers. Its root meanings are those of *consecration; setting apart for holy service; purification;* that is, cleansing, being preserved in a fit state for the special and holy administrations. It did not signify sinless perfection, for had this indeed been the case, there would have been no need for the Saviour to sanctify Himself. As used in this prayer of Christ, the word seems to have an expanding meaning in regard to the disciples. The Saviour had just confessed that the men given to Him from the world were not of the world; the world would hate them. He prayed, "As they are not of the world, let them be separated unto the kingdom of God; may no defilement nor taint of evil be upon them; let all those things be cleansed away (Hebrews 9:13; 13:12). Then, O Father, keep them clean through thy word. Let them grow in grace until the very likeness of God begins to dwell in their hearts – until they become holy."

Throughout the Old Testament writings this was the overruling thought in all things pertaining to the ministry of the Tabernacle. When vessels were sanctified, they were cleansed, set apart, and used exclusively for special and holy service. "And Moses took of the anointing oil, and of the blood which was upon the altar, and sprinkled it upon Aaron, *and upon his garments,* and upon his sons, and *upon his sons' garments* with him; and sanctified Aaron and his garments, and his sons and his sons' garments with him" (Leviticus 8:30). "And Moses sprinkled thereof upon the altar seven times, and anointed the altar and all its vessels, both the laver and its foot, *to sanctify them"* (Leviticus 8:11). It will be seen therefore that the act of sanctifying meant a very definite setting aside of something made fit for specialized service. The holy vessels were never used for mundane tasks in the homes of Israel. They belonged to the House of God, and remained ready to do the will of God.

Christ had been singularly set apart; He was entirely consecrated and ready to do whatever the Father desired. Now in this act of prayer, Christ was rededicating Himself to a new task. Through the death of the cross, He was to become the great High Priest of His people; therefore, He renewed His vows, and set Himself apart on the altar of service, to be able to live and make intercession for those who trusted Him. He desired the disciples to emulate His example and in their own right to be set apart for the service of the Highest. As He had been sent, He was now sending them. They had identical commissions and tasks. The Lord came into the world to preach the Gospel; they were going out with the same message. He resisted evil in order to be sanctified for His task; they ought to follow in His footsteps. "Sanctify them through thy truth." The medium of cleansing was the Word of God. "The entrance of thy word giveth light." Therefore, having revealed the imperfections within the Christian, the Word of God began its cleansing, purifying ministry. Compliance with the commands of God led to a clean temple and the fullness of the Holy Spirit.

When the Lord prayed for all who would believe through the preaching of the disciples, He included every convert won from that day until now. He envisaged the complete Church in many lands. When He asked that all these followers might be *one*, His utterance became an indictment on the Church of the twentieth century. He had already prayed for the unity of the Church; the repetition of the request revealed how important He considered this to be. Sanctification was not possible in a disrupted Church; holiness was an illusion when discord wrecked the assembly. ". . . that they also may be one in us: THAT THE WORLD MIGHT BELIEVE THAT THOU HAST SENT ME." There has never been any greater deterrent to the progress of the Gospel than quarrelsome people within the Church. The world knows nothing about the finer points of doctrine. The deity of Christ; the inspiration of the Bible; the various interpretations of prophecy; whether Christ comes before, during, or after the tribulation are all matters of which they have no understanding. The world only knows that in the church on the corner of the street are people who profess to be Christians. When these people fight and separate to form rival groups, the people of the world sneer and turn away from the Church, the message, and even the Saviour. Some people moan because of their inability to attract sinners into the evangelistic meetings of their church, but they forget it was their own stupidity which drove the sinners away. If Christians practised the will of God as often as they preached about it, they would turn the world upside down.

The Fifth Request

THE PERFECTION OF THE CHURCH

And the glory which thou gavest me I have given them; that they may be one, even as we are one: I in them, and thou in me, that they may be made perfect in one; and that the world may know that thou hast sent me, and hast loved them, as thou hast loved me (vv. 22, 23).

Once again the Lord coupled together *the unity of the Church* and *the successful evangelization of the lost.* When the Master went out of His way to repeat anything, that particular theme lay very close to His heart. Christians should ponder long over the various requests made known through the Lord's prayer. Lest we forget, let it be repeated that having taught to His followers the necessity for prayer, the Lord now showed them how best they could pray. This was the greatest prayer ever offered to God; it was meant to be the example for prayers of all people in all ages.

Within the sentence, "that they may be made perfect in one," the word translated "perfect" is *teteleiomenei.* It comes from the verb *teleioo,* which means *to carry through completely; to accomplish; to bring to an end.* Here then is something in advance of the act of sanctification. The former is carried through to a successful conclusion when the taint of sin is banished forever, when the Christian becomes Christ-like. That the apostle John firmly believed this would become an accomplished fact is clear from I John 3:1-3. "Behold, what manner of love the Father hath bestowed upon us, that we should be called the sons of God: therefore the world knoweth us not because it knew him not. Beloved, now are we the sons of God, and it doth not yet appear what we shall be; but we know that, when he shall appear, *we shall be like him;* for we shall see him as he is. And every man that hath this hope in him purifieth himself even as he is pure." Probably this was one of the greatest undertakings in the entire plan of God. It becomes increasingly evident why it was expedient for the Saviour to go away; without the indwelling of the Holy Spirit, moral imperfections would never be removed. He came to teach men to live, and the first essential in the art of living was to die daily (Galatians 2:20). Unless this could be accomplished, heaven remained a mirage on distant horizons.

". . . that the world may know that thou hast sent me, *and hast loved them, as thou hast loved me.*" Perfection of soul shines through the eyes, finds expression in word and deed, and is the only infallible way of impressing those to whom we try to minister. Unbelievers are affected more by what we are than by what we say. Consequently our testimony must be endorsed by consecrated living; our lives can be thrillingly eloquent even though our tongues be stammering.

The Sixth Request

THE HOME-GOING OF THE CHURCH

Father, I will that they also, whom thou hast given me, be with me where I am (v. 24).

This was an ordered, planned prayer. There was nothing haphazard about it. The Lord knew what He desired, and His petitions were expressed in an ordered way before the throne of the Almighty. True prayer supplies work for God. So many prayers offered in our churches provide a news bulletin for the Father — a long list of occurrences with which He is already familiar. Many sincere people quote texts as though to convince God He should be doing something extra to vindicate what He promised. God does not need to be reminded of His promises; they are written on His heart. God has not to be coerced, persuaded against His will to aid His children. He is more anxious to help than they are to ask. When the Saviour prayed, His requests were ordered, definite, precise, and when the prayer was concluded, the entire life, work, progress, and ultimate destiny of the believers had been placed into the hand of God. This, and only this, is true prayer. There are certain non-conformist leaders who detest the written prayers of their conformist brethren; they denounce those who seem to be unable to talk face to face with their Heavenly Father. This is a cause for regret. Any man at prayer is upon holy ground; it is not for others to criticize but to join him. *It is better to read, and mean what is read, than to speak and say nothing.* The Saviour did not read His prayer, but the fact that He planned it for an ordered sequence of thought became obvious even as He prayed. The successive stages of the Christian pilgrimage were all clearly defined. When the saints have been made perfect — that is, made ready to inhabit the many mansions — the power of God takes them home. "If I go and prepare a place for you, I will come again, and receive you unto myself; that where I am, ye may be also."

The Seventh Request

THE REWARD OF THE CHURCH

. . . that they may behold my glory, which thou hast given me: for thou lovedst me before the foundation of the world (v. 24).

This is the ultimate achievement of the saints. To love and own Him as Saviour; to work for Him in the seeking of others

and the resultant extension of the kingdom; to read the Word of
God and discover the riches of our inheritance in Him; all this is
as nothing when compared with the supreme joy of seeing His face.
"And they sung a new song, saying, Thou art worthy . . . . for thou
wast slain, and hast redeemed us to God by thy blood out of every
kindred, and tongue, and people, and nation; and hast made us unto
our God kings and priests: and we shall reign on the earth. And I
beheld, and I heard the voice of many angels round about the
throne, and the living ones, and the elders: and the number of
them was ten thousand times ten thousand, and thousands of thousands; saying with a loud voice, Worthy is the Lamb . . ." (Revelation 5:9-12). "And I saw a new heaven and a new earth . . . .
And I saw no temple therein: for the Lord God Almighty and the
Lamb are the temple of it. And the city had no need of the sun,
neither of the moon to shine in it: for the glory of God did lighten
it, *and the Lamb is the light thereof*" (Revelation 21:1, 22, 23).
Thus did the Lord complete His sevenfold request on behalf of
His followers. Christ's prayer covered the entire history of the
Church and gave promise of the fact that He who had begun a
good work within His people would complete it. If the seven
petitions may be likened unto milestones along the Christian road,
then it was obvious that at one glance He saw the entire highway
as it reached into the distance. Now from His throne in heaven
it is easier still to see that road, and to watch each phase of the
journey as it unfolds in the experience of the travelers. His continuous intercession for His children guarantees, that in due course,
those who commence at the Cross will finish at the throne.

> After the toil and the heat of the day,
>   After my troubles are past,
> After the sorrows are taken away,
>   I shall see Jesus at last.
> After the shadows of evening shall fall,
>   After my anchor is cast,
> After I list to my Saviour's last call,
>   I shall see Jesus at last.
>   He will be waiting for me,
>   Jesus so kind and true.
>   On His beautiful throne,
>   He will welcome me Home:
>   After the day is through.

Expository Notes on the Conclusion of Christ's Prayer

O righteous Father, the world hath not known thee, but I have known thee, and these have known that thou hast sent me. And I have declared unto them thy name, and will declare it: that the love wherewith thou hast loved me may be in them and I in them (vv. 25, 26).

It is worthy of intense consideration that almost as soon as the Saviour had presented His petition, He ceased praying. He said what He desired to say, and then stopped. Long prayers can be tedious when they say nothing. The conclusion of this intercession may be divided into three simple headings:

(1) *A Great Partnership.* Through the miracle of redeeming grace, the Father, the Saviour, and the Church have been bound together in the common bundle of life. Through the Son, the Father has been able to reach the Church; through the Saviour, the Church was able to recognize the Father. "He in us, and we in him, and all of us in each other."

(2) *A Great Promise.* "And I have declared unto them thy name, and *will declare it* . . . ." The work of instruction which He had commenced, would be continued as He spoke to them through the Comforter. They had enrolled in God's school and had been proficient in the early grades. He was attracted to His students and planned to stay with them as they progressed. He intended to become personally responsible for their graduation. The work of introducing them to the deeper things of spiritual education would become increasingly exciting as He continued the tuition.

(3) *A Great Purpose.* ". . . that *the love wherewith thou hast loved me may be in them,* and I in them." The Teacher's secret was out! He not only intended to teach them; He planned to transform them. He planned not only to place additional facts into their minds; He determined to put divine love in their hearts. Thus would He gain for Himself an abiding place in their affections; thus would He make their souls His home.

To repeat an earlier statement: this was the greatest prayer ever prayed. The seventeenth chapter of John's gospel is holy ground; there the Christian should kneel, consider, and worship. If this is prayer, every church member should repeat earnestly, "Lord, teach me how to pray."

HOMILIES

The main homily on John 17 is to be found in the seven-fold petition of the Master as outlined in the expository notes. The following details are offered as a further incentive to constructive thought.

Study No. 61

CHRIST AND THE SECRET OF HIS MINISTRY

The Lord Jesus was by far the busiest of all God's servants. Throughout each day of His ministry, endless lines of people waited to see Him, touch Him, hear Him. Time for quiet reflection was almost impossible to find, for when the congregations dispersed, the disciples remained with their problems. Perhaps one of the unmentioned temptations of Christ was that of Satan's attempt to make the Lord irritable and impatient. There were many subtle pitfalls along the Master's pathway, but each one was safely offset by the fact that HE MADE THE TIME FOR COMMUNION.

The Morning Watch

"And in the morning, rising up a great while before day, he went out, and departed into a solitary place, and there prayed" (Mark 1:35). With each new day came fresh demands upon His resources. Decisions had to be made, people met, messages delivered; and all the time Satan would be waiting for the chance to upset the Son of God. If ever man had reason to be tired, to stay just a little longer in the warmth of His bed, Jesus had. He was truly human, and shared the feelings and desires which we know. Yet when the need demanded that He rise early, He resisted every inclination to stay. During the morning watch, He replenished His store of power; through the day His inspiration never decreased.

The Evening Benediction

"And when he had sent them away, he departed into a mountain to pray. And when even was come, the ship was in the midst of the sea, and he alone on the land . . ." (Mark 6:46, 47). The busy day was over; the crowds had been persuaded to retire. Tomorrow would be another day! When most preachers would have gone to bed, Christ climbed the hillside. The day had been a success; He desired to return thanks. How could He place His head on a pillow until He had first placed His cheek on the Father's bosom? When the storm broke, the shrieking winds reminded Him of the chilling fears harassing the hearts of His children. When He rescued the disciples, the smile on His face told of the serenity in His heart.

The Solitary Vigil

"But so much the more went there a fame abroad of him; and great multitudes came together to hear, and to be healed by him of their infirmities. And he withdrew himself into the wilderness, and prayed" (Luke 5:15, 16). Success often begets danger; the plaudits of the crowds sometimes create discords in the soul. There are times when even one's best friend can be a hindrance. There are times when audible prayers are necessary, but to pray aloud when others are listening is not always good. It therefore becomes essential to find the secret place where the heart can be expressed, where the tears can flow. A man may attend a public prayer meeting because he is expected so to do. When he climbs the mountain to be alone with God, his action reveals hunger for eternal realities.

The Exacting Warfare

"And it came to pass in those days, that he went out into a mountain to pray, *and continued all night in prayer* to God" (Luke 6:12). Big battles are not won easily; large concentrations of enemy troops are not dispersed in a moment. At the graveside of Lazarus and at His baptism in the Jordan, the Lord prayed brief but intense prayers; in the solitudes of the hillside, He continued in prayer for hours. Sometimes the answer to prayer is obtained instantaneously; at other times it is not (Daniel 10:2, 12). To pray momentarily and leave a job unfinished is a waste of effort; to pray, and to pray through to victory is to indicate that another great lesson in God's school has been fully mastered.

> Prayer is the soul's sincere desire,
>   Uttered or unexpressed:
> The motion of a hidden fire
>   That trembles in the breast.
> Prayer is the simplest form of speech,
>   That infant lips can try.
> Prayer the sublimest strains that reach
>   The Majesty on high.

The Eighteenth Chapter of John

Theme: *Christ Is Brought to Trial*

OUTLINE:

    I. Power disarms the Crowd. Verses 1-11.
    II. Peter disowns the Christ. Verses 12-27.
    III. Pilate dishonors his Calling. Verses 28-40.

SECTION ONE

Expository Notes on the Events in the Garden of Gethsemane

The eighteenth chapter of John's gospel opens a new and final section of the narrative. After the first introductory chapter, the apostle devoted eleven chapters to the descriptive account of the Lord's ministry in the world. Events, scenes, conversations, miracles were faithfully retold to provide a backdrop for the second section, chapters 13-17, in which the Lord was revealed as the watchful, kindly Master preparing His followers for the difficulties of the future. Having ministered to a lost world and instructed His own how to reach that world with the Gospel, the Lord now turned His face toward His greatest task. From time to time He had warned His disciples He would be delivered into the hands of sinful men and would be crucified; now, the hour had come when His predictions would be fulfilled.

The other evangelists described the crucifixion, but an examination of their record reveals John's account to be completely different from any other. It should be remembered that this apostle was one of the disciples permitted to accompany Christ into the garden; he saw what most of the others were unable to see. Therefore, had he so desired, John could have given an eye-witness account of the fierce conflict which took place beneath the olive trees. Yet he omitted these details as if they were of minor importance. Some writers think he did this because contemporary authors had already said all that was necessary. There is reason to believe we must search further for a satisfactory explanation. John was determined to emphasize that God had been manifest in the flesh, the Eternal Word had tabernacled among men, and throughout his gospel John continually produced evidence to support his theme. He spoke not of the tears and agony of Christ, but of the supernatural power which swept the enemies from their feet. John remembered the dynamic which overwhelmed those who came to crucify the Son of God. These details belonged exclusively to the fourth gospel; this was John's privilege. He was not writing of a King, a Servant, nor a perfect Man. John saw the Incarnate Word, and after fifty years, his memory had not suffered; his eyes had not grown dim.

> When Jesus had spoken these words, he went forth with his disciples over the brook Cedron, where was a garden, into the which he entered, and his disciples (v. 1).

"These words" obviously refer to the discourse just completed. Having told His followers all they needed to know, the Lord wasted no time; He had a task to perform; His hour had come. "Cedron" or, as the Hebrew spells it, "Kidron" means *dark waters.* It was often called "the black brook," either because it ran through a dark valley or because its waters were stained by filth from the city. Whenever a spiritual awakening came to Israel, the repentant kings smashed their idols at the brook Cedron, and the filth of the uncleanness was swept away in its waters. It was to this historic stream that Christ made His way on the night when He thought of the removal of the world's iniquity. ". . . where was a garden . . . ." Students might like to consider the outstanding gardens of Scripture. (See the homily at the end of this section.)

> And Judas also, which betrayed him, knew the place: for Jesus ofttimes resorted thither with his disciples. Judas then, having received a band of men and officers from the chief priests and Pharisees, cometh thither with lanterns and torches and weapons (vv. 2, 3).

It was both pathetic and ironic that Judas should choose this secret place in which to exhibit the treachery in his soul. This was a favorite hide-away of the Lord; when the strain and tension of His ministry threatened to overwhelm Him, He retired for a while to the stillness of this hallowed garden. There in the silences He knelt to pray. There, He placed His hand into the hand of God and became refreshed. Often Judas had watched his Leader but unfortunately, although he saw so much, he learned so little.

The Greek word translated "band" is *speiran,* and according to Dr. J. H. Thayer, this signified the *"tenth part of a legion, that is, about six hundred men."* This, then, was a military operation and not a casual arrest by an officer of the law. The representatives of the high priest had secured official support from the governor and prepared for any resistance which might be forthcoming, this large company of soldiers and officials went forth in search of the Lord. The movement of so many troops through the city would inevitably attract inquisitive sightseers and probably a thousand people went into Gethsemane to look for Jesus. They were prepared for every emergency. If the fugitive hid, they had lanterns to seek His hiding place; if His followers resisted, they had weapons with which to subdue any rebellion. They were so strong! so foolish! so blind.

Jesus therefore, knowing all things that should come upon him, went forth, and said unto them, Whom seek ye? (v. 4).

The Lord was never taken by surprise; He knew all things that should come upon Him but, instead of running away, He calmly went to meet the enemy. From the inner recesses of that secluded spot, He had first gone to awaken His sleeping disciples; then together they had rejoined the other disciples, and now as a compact band, they stood before the crowd. He knew why they had come. He knew also that they would take Him; yet deep within His heart lay the desire to make another effort to lead them into the Truth. His question introduced the greatest demonstration of supernatural might they ever witnessed.

They answer him, Jesus of Nazareth. Jesus saith unto them, I AM. And Judas also, which betrayed him, stood with them. As soon then as he had said unto them, I AM, they went backward, and fell to the ground (vv. 5, 6).

It is hard to understand how a man who had been seated with Christ and the other disciples should within a matter of hours be found among the Lord's enemies. Satan had surely entered into the heart of Judas. From the lofty heights of spiritual exaltation he had fallen into the abyss of selfishness and shame. The lips which had moved in the preaching of the message were soon to present the traitor-kiss; the hands which had been lifted in blessing over the heads of suppliants were soon to hold blood money. *"Judas stood with them."* Then, suddenly, irresistible power swept them from their feet. They rolled, staggered, fell; and in the awful silence which followed even the six hundred soldiers lay flat upon the ground. Some of the torches were surely blown out; the lanterns were overturned; the men bewildered. Christ, regal, dignified, invincible, looked at the men and sadly smiled. Once again, the inner glory of His divine nature had broken through the frail barrier of flesh to demonstrate the invincibility of His power. He might have killed them, but He preferred to spare them in the hope that someday they might see, and believe, and repent. This is but another of the I AM's found throughout the gospel of John. How foolish they were even *to think* they could take Him; how blind and stupid *to try again* when He permitted them to regain their feet.

> Then asked he them again, Whom seek ye? And they said, Jesus of Nazareth. Jesus answered, I have told you that I am: if therefore ye seek me, let these go their way. That the saying might be fulfilled which he spake, Of them which thou gavest me have I lost none (vv. 7-9).

The Lord had now quietly withdrawn His power. His attempt to open their eyes had failed for they were still intent on His capture; hate had blinded their eyes to every manifestation of truth. In the hour of His greatest need, Christ thought of His own, and asked that they might be permitted to escape. *His intercession saved their honor, their lives, their future ministry.* The closing part of this verse referred to 17:12.

> Then Simon Peter having a sword drew it, and smote the high priest's servant, and cut off his right ear. The servant's name was Malchus. Then said Jesus unto Peter, Put up thy sword into the sheath: the cup which my Father hath given me, shall I not drink it? (vv. 10, 11).

"Christ's being bound was very significant. Before the men bound Him, He had bound Himself to the work and the office of a Mediator. He was already bound to the horns of the altar with the cords of His own love to man and duty to His Father. Guilt is a bond on the soul by which we are bound under the power of Satan. Christ, to free us from these bonds, submitted Himself to be bound for us. To His bonds we owe our liberty. Thus the Son maketh us free. Christ was bound, that He might bind us to duty and obedience. His bonds for us are *bonds upon us,* by which we are forever obliged to love and serve Him. Christ's bonds for us were designed to make our bonds for Him easy to us, to sanctify and sweeten them; these enabled Paul and Silas to sing in the stocks" (Matthew Henry).

Peter can hardly be blamed for his inability to recognize the hand of God working amid the unpleasant events of that night. His impetuosity in acting without the expressed permission of his leader may be understood but not condoned. A good soldier is a man under authority; rash action on the part of an unauthorized individual can lose a campaign. Probably Peter struck with the determination to slay the first man to lay hands on the Master. Mercifully, he misjudged his aim, for the servant lost his ear and not his head. "We may add that the *life* of Malchus was safe while Christ was there, for none ever died in His presence" (A. W. Pink). When Christ returned good for evil; when the servant was healed by the power of the One he had come to take, the man was provided with memories which in after days haunted him. If he ever told his story in the high priest's palace, we may be sure the Holy Spirit used the testimony to convict every hearer. The Lord had said,

"Ye have heard that it hath been said, Thou shalt love thy neighbor, and hate thine enemy. But I say unto you love your enemies, bless them that curse you, do good to them that hate you, and pray for them which despitefully use you, and persecute you" (Matthew 5:43, 44). The words written in Luke 22:50, 51 supply overwhelming evidence that the Lord practised what He preached. John omits the details to be found in the synoptic gospels; he was more concerned with the predominant fact that what was taking place had been planned in the eternal counsels of heaven.

The statement, "The cup which my Father hath given me," seems to be most thought-provoking. A cup suggests limitations. The experience through which the Son was about to pass would indeed be grievous but it would end; the cup would soon be empty. Christ saw not the bitterness of the cross; He saw and recognized the Father's will. The sweetness of being in true accord with God provided the antidote to the agony of any suffering to be endured. This was the way the Father had planned; any other would have been unthinkable.

HOMILIES

Study No. 62

THREE GARDENS WHICH TELL THEIR OWN STORIES

"And the Lord planted a garden eastward in Eden." I wish I could have seen that garden. Alas, I was born too late! Did it possess long winding paths, and were there enchanting borders of multicolored flowers? Were there shady corners where Adam sat listening to the songs of the birds? Were some of the flowering trees aflame with the Creator's art? And did the gentle breezes of evening produce music of exquisite sweetness as they played among the leaves? Yes, I wish I could have seen that garden, for it has been said, "One is nearer to God in a garden than anywhere else on earth." A garden is a mirror reflecting a world. There, we find enemies; there, we find friends. Within the confines of a garden stalks the shadow of death; but in that same shadow may be found promise of glorious resurrection. The gardens of the Bible have a wonderful story to tell.

The Garden of Tragedy . . . death commencing (Genesis 2:8)

It was all over, and poor Adam hardly knew where he was or what he was doing. Tears probably blinded his eyes, and a cloud on the sun sent shadows scurrying across the lawn. The time would now come when newly turned earth would announce an addition to the Creator's design. The day would eventually

dawn when a grave would be found in God's wonderful world, and
for a while the birds would cease to sing. Yes, it was now a certainty
that some day human blood would stain the good earth: for Adam
had sinned! Forever he would remember the sinister whisper which
had said, "Ye shall not surely die." He frowned. Death was an
unpleasant word. How could he die, when he had only just commenced to live? He shuddered as another cloud passed across
his soul. He had not died physically; but his innocence, his purity,
his joy had ceased to exist. Germs had invaded his soul, and the
grave which someday would spoil God's countryside would only
be the forerunner of myriads more. Evil had lifted an ugly head;
storm clouds loomed on the horizon; and when Adam was required
to leave his lovely home, he realized he had lost more than would
ever be regained.

The Garden of Testing . . . death challenged   (John 18:1)

Someone had planted another garden. It was still and serene,
for night had covered it with a shadowy mantle. There is reason
to believe that the moon shone from the heavens, for men that
night were able to see things at which even the angels veiled their
faces. The Prince of heaven, a Knight in the shining armor of
purity, had come to challenge the monster which from Eden had
stalked through God's great world. Everywhere a trail of anguish
had been left behind this raging enemy. Homes had been plunged
into sorrow; hearts had been ruthlessly broken; young lives had
been snapped as if they had been but tender twigs, and death had
reigned supreme. The monster had been invincible, for its greatest
ally had its fifth column in every challenging heart. Now the tyrant
was to meet his match; this was destined to be a night of nights.
There is hardly need to repeat what has been told elsewhere. It
is sufficient to say that although the Lord was hurt in the struggle,
He succeeded in giving to His greatest enemy a fatal blow.

The Garden of Triumph . . . death conquered   (John 19:41)

The golden face of the sun was slowly appearing above the
distant horizon; rays of scintillating brilliance were fast dispelling
the shadows of the night. The silent garden was waking from sleep.
Calm, dignified, radiant, an angel guarded the mouth of the sepulcher.
His eyes were pools of happiness; the joy of the eternal shone
from his face. When he saw the woman approaching, he smiled;
he had great news to announce. "Be not affrighted; Ye seek Jesus
of Nazareth, which was crucified: he is risen; he is not here; Behold
the place where they laid him . . ." (Mark 16:6). I should love to
have been in that garden. At the appointed time the stone was
rolled away, and the King of Glory came forth triumphantly. Death

had been vanquished — Eden's monster had been overcome, hope had been born anew. Now, forever, God's children would be able to sing, "O death, where is thy sting? O grave, where is thy victory?" It has been written that someday God will make a new world — and perhaps He will plant a new garden — "and there shall be no more death" (Revelation 21:4).

(Reprinted from *Bible Highways*, page 1.)

Study No. 63

CHRIST . . . AND HIS TANTALIZING INCONSISTENCY!

It was not always easy to understand the actions and teachings of the Lord Jesus, and there were many occasions when the disciples were nonplussed. Extreme weariness was evident when He lay asleep in the storm-tossed boat, yet within minutes Omnipotence hushed the raging seas. At one moment the disciples felt they had a very human Brother and Leader, the next they gasped with astonishment and cried, "What manner of man is this?" The strangest contrast of this kind is found in John's gospel.

An Unexpected Collapse

The silence of the garden had been rudely shattered by the excited clamoring of a fanatical mob. Led by the traitor Judas, the people had come to arrest the Nazarene. There was to be no mistake this time! Feelings of antagonism had been roused to intensity; the meddlesome Carpenter was to be removed before Passover. Like hunting dogs eager for the kill, the rabble pressed forward as their lanterns turned the garden into a bewitched fairyland. "Jesus therefore, knowing all things which should come upon him, went forth, and said unto them, Whom seek ye? They answered him, Jesus of Nazareth. Jesus saith unto them, I AM. And Judas also, which betrayed him, stood with them. As soon then as he had said unto them, I AM, they went backward and fell to the ground." And amid all the astounding events of that dread week, this surely must rank as the greatest. It was distractingly humiliating to have one's face pressed into the dust before Him whom they desired to capture. How easy it is to believe that when Christ shall be manifested in glory, every knee will bow, and every tongue will confess that He is Lord.

A Unique Challenge

What was the cause of this amazing collapse? There can only be one answer. Invisible power, irresistible dynamic swept them off their feet when Jesus said, "I AM." It will be seen that the word "he" has been printed in italics. It was placed there by the translators in order — as they thought — to make the passage readable. They erred, for the Scripture would have been its own interpreter.

I AM is God's name. When Moses asked the Lord, saying, ". . . when I come unto the children of Israel, and shall say unto them, The God of your fathers has sent me unto you; and they shall say to me, What is his name? what shall I say unto them?" God answered him, saying, "I AM THAT I AM: and he said, Thus shalt thou say unto the children of Israel I AM hath sent me unto you" (Exodus 3:13, 14). God is the eternally present; and this was the name given by Christ in the Garden of Gethsemane. It represented His claim to deity; and the power which overcame the crowd more than endorsed the word of His great challenge.

An Unopposed Capture

When His question was repeated, the dazed men slowly regained their feet and hesitantly answered that they sought the Nazarene. Within a few moments they were binding the Lord Jesus with ropes brought specially for the job; but the arrogance of those men had been severely jolted. It was unnatural for Omnipotence to be overcome by men who only minutes before had been paralyzed by two of His words. The confused scene needs an explanation. If the disciples ran for their lives, at least we can appreciate their stupefaction when they saw their glorious Leader submitting in such a perplexing manner. We sympathize with Simon Peter, whose impetuosity severed the ear of Malchus. The Master's quiet rebuke demoralized His followers, and feeling the cause was lost, they turned to flee. The mob took Jesus away, and even the angels wept — or did they? Perhaps they were too amazed.

An Undisguised Concern

Some things stand out in bold relief. It is quite obvious that had Christ desired to resist aggression, He could easily have done so. That He permitted the enemies to lead Him away suggests He preferred to go with them. Yet before He finally capitulated the Lord made a request which was instantly granted. "If therefore ye seek me, *let these go their way.*" In that grim hour of danger, He sacrificed Himself that His followers might be protected. "Having loved his own . . . he loved them unto the end." It is not too much to say that Christ's intercession saved the men who thought He had failed them. What would the savage crowd have done to Simon Peter when one of their comrades stood disfigured and bleeding? "He ever liveth to make intercession for us." It was true then — it is true now. What a wonderful Saviour.

(Reprinted from *Bible Treasures*, page 121.)

SECTION TWO

Expository Notes on Christ's Appearance Before the High Priest

Then the band, and the captain, and the officers of the Jews took Jesus and bound him, and led him away to Annas first; for he was father-in-law to Caiaphas, who was the high priest that same year. Now Caiaphas was he, who gave counsel to the Jews, that it was expedient that one man should die for the people (vv. 12-14).

It is almost beyond comprehension that the troops with their commander proceeded to arrest the Saviour. We might be excused for thinking they would have been afraid to place hands upon the Blessed One; instead they shackled Him. "We believe it was to this the Saviour referred when, speaking by the Spirit of prophecy, He declared, 'Many bulls have compassed me: strong bulls of Bashan have beset me round. They gaped upon me with their mouths, as a ravening and roaring lion . . . . dogs have compassed me, the assembly of the wicked have enclosed me.' We doubt not that they bound Him with heavy chains, for of him who furnishes perhaps the fullest type of Christ it is written, 'Joseph was sold for a servant: whose feet they hurt with fetters: he was laid in iron' (Psalm 105:17, 18). Is not the antitype of this suggested in Isaiah 53:5, where we are told not only that he was 'wounded for our transgressions' but 'bruised for our iniquities'! Did not this take place when they bound His wrists and ankles with handcuffs and fetters!" (A. W. Pink).

It is significant that Jesus was neither dragged nor driven. The overwhelmingly ostentatious display of military might was neither useful nor necessary to take Christ; He was "brought as a lamb to the slaughter, and as a sheep before her shearers is dumb, so he openeth not his mouth" (Isaiah 53:7). Bishop Ryle was very correct when he wrote, "One thing is very clear: the love of Christ for sinners is a 'love that passeth knowledge.' To suffer for those who are in some sense worthy of our affection, is suffering that we can understand. To submit to ill-treatment quietly, when we have no power to resist, ·is submission that is both graceful and wise. *But to suffer voluntarily*, when we have power to prevent it, and to suffer for a world of unbelieving and ungodly sinners, unasked and unthanked — this a line of conduct which passes man's understanding. Never let us forget that *this* is the peculiar beauty of Christ's sufferings . . . . He was led away captive, and dragged before the high priest's bar, not because He could not help Himself, but because He had set His heart on saving sinners . . . ."

Certain problems have been occasioned by the fact that two high priests seem to have been in office at the same time. The Mosaic law directed that the office of high priest was a life long privilege. Once a man had been anointed for such high service, he continued as the national intercessor until death terminated his ministry. (See Exodus 40:15 and Numbers 35:25). The Roman occupation of Palestine introduced many changes, some of which were unpopular with the Jewish people. It seems that the Romans appointed a new high priest every year. In this way they could be certain to have in office a man who readily cooperated with the civic authorities. Annas was the real high priest; Caiaphas was the civic head, the puppet of the Roman authorities who pulled the strings. However, there can be no doubt that Annas was the greater authority in matters relating to the ecclesiastical life of the nation. Some writers think the crowd first went to Annas because his was the nearer of the priests' homes. These are details which are not of extreme importance. The fact remains that the people were so determined to bring an accusation against the Lord, so intent on His condemnation, that they left no stone unturned in the endeavor to secure a conviction.

Gethesemane was at the foot of the Mount of Olives and on the east side of Jerusalem. The journey undertaken that night would take Christ through the sheepgate, and it was through this gate all animals destined for sacrifice in the temple were obligated to pass. Unfortunately the rabble did not know prophecy was being fulfilled in their actions. They were bringing the Lamb of God to the sacrifice; unwittingly they were cogs in the machinery helping to produce salvation for a benighted world of sinners. Reference has already been made to the infamous prediction made by the high priest. (See the expository notes on Chapter 11:49-52.)

> And Simon Peter followed Jesus, and so did another disciple: that disciple was known unto the high priest, and went in with Jesus into the palace of the high priest (v. 15).

Throughout the fourth gospel reference is made to "that other disciple *whom Jesus loved*" (13:23; 19:26; 20:2; 21:7; 21:20). Most commentators agree this statement refers to the author of the fourth gospel — John. ". . . whom Jesus loved" is omitted from this verse. John was a fisherman from Galilee; later he was classed as an ignorant unlearned man. It is not easy, therefore, to see him as an intimate member of a priestly family far away in Jerusalem. The fact that John was indeed a Galilean would have made him suspicious in the eyes of Christ's enemies. Simon Peter was challenged on this very point; yet the unnamed disciple was permitted to pass unmolested. It should also be remembered that later the high priest did not know either Peter or John (Acts 4:13); therefore, it cannot be concluded that the "other disciple" known to the ecclesiastical ruler was the writer of this gospel. That there were other "secret disciples" known to the high priest cannot be denied. John 19:38 suggests that both Joseph of Arimathea and Nicodemus belonged to this category. There might have been others.

> But Peter stood at the door without. Then went out that other disciple, which was known unto the high priest, and spake unto her that kept the door, and brought in Peter. Then saith the damsel that kept the door unto Peter, Art not thou also one of this man's disciples? He saith, I am not (vv. 16, 17).

A tangled web was being woven around Peter. It should not be assumed altogether that the girl's intentions were wicked. She did not use harsh words concerning the captive; her insinuations did not carry the imprint of evil. Had she delivered a filthy accusation against the Lord, had her eyes flashed and her hands moved in denunciation, Peter might have retaliated with flaming words of defense. Unfortunately, whereas he was braced against the storm, he had no defense against the quiet and almost inoffensive remark of a servant girl. Satan is a master tactician; he knows our weak points, and he exploits them in a truly devastating manner. Almost before he knew what was taking place, Simon Peter was slipping, and as has happened so often, one mistake led to the next and finally, a distracted man, he stumbled into the night to break his heart. (See the important homily at the end of this section.)

> And the servants and officers stood there, who had made a fire of coals; for it was cold: and they warmed themselves: and Peter stood with them, and warmed himself (v. 18).

"The apostle stood among the crowd of His Master's enemies, and warmed himself like one of them. Apparently he had nothing of which to think but his own bodily comfort, while his Lord stood in a distant part of the hall, cold and a prisoner. Who can doubt that Peter, in his miserable cowardice, wished to appear one of the party who hated Christ, and sought to conceal his real character by doing as they did? And who can doubt that while he warmed his hands, he felt cold, wretched, and comfortless in his own soul?" (Bishop Ryle). The proud, boastful, self-reliant Peter was now in grave danger. Cold and shivering, he sought warmth in the company of unbelievers; the joy of fellowship with his beloved Master was now a thing of the past. "He stayed to warm himself; but those that warm themselves with evil doers grow cold toward good people and good things. Those that are fond of the devil's fireside are in danger of the devil's fire" (Matthew Henry).

> The high priest then asked Jesus of his disciples, and of his doctrine. Jesus answered him, I spake openly to the world: I ever taught in the synagogue, and in the temple, whither the Jews always resort; and in secret have I said nothing. Why askest thou me? ask them which heard me, what I have said unto them: behold, they knew what I said (vv. 19-21).

This must forever remain the strangest trial ever to be held in a court of law. No charge was brought against the prisoner; no witnesses were produced in support of the accusations. No counsel for the defense was forthcoming, and no evidence for the defense was ever permitted to be expressed. The accused was pronounced guilty even before He was heard; the trial terminated before it began! Having arraigned Him, it became necessary to intimidate the Prisoner in the hope that in some unguarded moment His unpremeditated statements might provide a basis on which to build the case for the prosecution. This was indeed the forerunner of the hateful inquisitions destined to become infamous in later centuries. The Lord was acutely aware of the evil genius of the questioner; His calm, dignified answer revealed the naked superficiality of Israel's hierarchy. Christ knew that they had already rejected His testimony; what use or good purpose would be served by repeating what had often been said? "If you hear not my testimony, call the people and let them testify. Even your own servants can testify of my doctrines; so why ask me?" The statement, ". . . *and in secret have I said nothing,*" was singularly interesting, for the Lord was appropriating to Himself something which belonged exclusively to God. "For thus saith the Lord that created the heavens; God himself that formed the earth and made it; he hath established it, he created it not a void, he formed it to be inhabited: I am the Lord and there is none else. *I have not spoken in secret, in a dark place of the earth* . . . . I the Lord speak righteousness, I declare things that are right" (Isaiah 45:19). Once again readers are reminded that this was in keeping with the central theme of the fourth gospel. Christ was God.

And when he had thus spoken, one of the officers which stood by struck Jesus with the palm of his hand, saying, Answerest thou the high priest so? Jesus answered him, If I have spoken evil, bear witness of the evil; but if well, why smitest thou me? (vv. 22, 23).

The New English Bible renders the text, ". . . one of the police struck him on the face." J. B. Phillips in his *New Testament in Modern English* renders it: "As he said this, one of those present, an officer, slapped Jesus with his open hand, remarking, 'Is that the way for you to answer the high priest?' " There appears to be insufficient evidence to ascertain without doubt that the officer hit Christ with his open hand. The Greek word used here is *rapisma* and, according to Dr. Thayer, its primary usage is to express *a blow with a rod, or a staff, or a scourge.* In a secondary capacity it expresses *a blow with the flat of the hand, a slap in the face, a box on the ear.* There exists the possibility that the officer used a rod or a scourge to punish the prisoner. Such procedure in a court of law was detestable, unpardonable, and without precedent. When the presiding judge or magistrate failed to denounce the action, he revealed the hypocrisy of the entire proceedings. If such things happened today, the judge would never again be permitted to sit on the bench. Yet in all these details it is possible to see the unfolding of the plans of God, the unerring accuracy of the sacred record. Five centuries before the Advent of Christ, Micah predicted, "Now gather thyself in troops: he hath laid seige against us: they shall smite the judge of Israel *with a rod upon the cheek*" (Micah 5:1).

The calm, dignified reply given by Christ to the man who struck Him revealed He was in possession of His soul. At a later date, a similar thing happened to Paul, but immediately flaming words of resentment sprang to the apostle's lips. "And the high priest Ananias commanded them that stood by him to smite him on the mouth. Then said Paul unto him, God shall smite thee, thou whited wall: for sittest thou to judge me after the law, and commandest me to be smitten contrary to the law? And they that sood by said, Revilest thou God's high priest? Then said Paul, I wist not, brethren, that he was the high priest: for it is written, Thou shalt not speak evil of the ruler of thy people" (Acts 23:2-5). Paul was exceedingly gracious in correcting a mistake; the Lord had no need to recant or withdraw any words — He was perfect in all His ways.

Now Annas had sent him bound unto Caiaphas the high priest (v. 24).

The word "had" should be omitted; it is not justified by the original Greek. J. B. Phillips renders the text perfectly: "*Then* Annas sent him, with his hands still tied, to the High Priest Caiaphas." Annas was beginning to be embarrassed. The prisoner was liable to damage the priest's prestige; it would be better to get rid of Him, to place the responsibility on another's shoulders. When he removed his prisoner, he increased his own guilt.

And Simon Peter stood and warmed himself. They said therefore unto him, Art thou not also one of his disciples? He denied it, and said, I am not (v. 25).

"Peter probably thought he might be bound with his Master before the high priest, and had he done so, he would probably have stood faithful. But the Devil who was sifting him had a much finer sieve than that through which to run him. He brought him to no formal trial where he could gird himself for a special effort. The whole trial was over before he knew he was being tried. So do most of our real trials come; in a business transaction that turns up with others in the day's work, in the few minutes talk or the evening's intercourse with friends. Here it is discovered whether we are so truly Christ's friends that we cannot forget Him nor disguise the fact that we are His. In these battles which we must all encounter, we receive no formal challenge which gives us time to choose our ground and our weapons. A sudden blow is dealt us from which we can be saved only by habitually wearing a coat of mail sufficient to turn it, a coat of mail we can carry into all companies" (Marcus Dodds).

> One of the servants of the high priest, being his kinsman whose ear Peter cut off, saith, Did not I see thee in the garden with him? Peter then denied again: and immediately the cock crew (vv. 26, 27).

Peter's rash action in the garden had not passed unnoticed; it was now producing unpleasant repercussions. Suddenly the disciple's heart was filled with dread. He was recognized not only as a follower of Christ, but as a militant enemy of the people who addressed him. The consciousness of acute danger shattered his ego, and to hide his fear, he began to curse. When the cock sent its shrill challenge to greet the approaching day, the solemn fact was announced that the mighty had fallen; the impregnable had been vanquished. Poor Peter! Had he obeyed the Master's command, "Watch and pray lest ye enter into temptation," this might never have happened. He had been so sure, so self-confident, so boastful. Alas, he had yet to learn that a man is never as tall as when he is prostrate before God; the way to reach the stars is to kneel.

HOMILIES

Study No. 64

Simon Peter . . . Who Sat at Two Fires
(Luke 22:55 and John 21:9)

During the night in which our Lord was betrayed, two men passed through a doorway into the darkness of the city. One man turned and walked into the bitterness of eternal remorse; the other walked into the arms of God. At that doorway Judas and Simon Peter parted forever. The Lord has set forth in detail the account of Peter's great tragedy, and since his path of sorrow is so clearly defined, let us consider it.

The Downward Path to Calamity

Peter should have known better, for the Lord had said unto him, "Simon, Simon, behold, Satan hath desired to have you, that he may sift you as wheat"; but in self-confidence the disciple replied, "Lord, I am ready to go with thee, both into prison, and to death." Almost immediately he began to drift from Christ.

(1) *And Peter followed afar off.* This was his first mistake. When a Christian begins to backslide, the beginning of the trouble can always be traced to this cause. The loss of intimate communion leads to disaster.

(2) *And Peter warmed himself at the fire* (Mark 14:67). This was his second mistake. Following in the distance, he became cold and was attracted to the fire — the enemy's fire. There appeared to be little harm in his actions, but real danger lurked in the company gathered there. And this story is very true to present day life. When a Christian becomes cold in heart the fires of worldliness always provide a source of attraction. It is a time of supreme danger.

(3) *And Peter sat down among them* (Luke 22:55). Any plan concerning an early departure was forgotten. He intended to stay and enjoy fellowship around the fire. This was his greatest mistake. Something was certainly wrong when a disciple of Christ felt at ease among the Master's enemies.

(4) *And Peter denied his Lord — "I know him not."* We are told that Simon Peter denied thrice, yet strange to relate, the denials were not identical. The first denial concerned his allegiance to Christ. It is always thus.

(5) *And Peter denied his association with the disciples* — the Church. To the accusation, "Thou art also of THEM," he replied, "Man, I am not." Satan is never content with a first denial. He endeavors to bring the backslider away from the fellowship of the saints, for otherwise the man may recover.

(6) *And Peter began to curse and swear* (Mark 14:71). When he was accused of speaking with a different dialect, he used their type of expression and so overcame their final objections. His sin appeared to sever all his connections with Christ, and he seemed completely lost. He stumbled through the doorway into the darkness of the street, *but took the right turn.*

The Upward Path to Christ

"And the Lord turned and looked upon Peter, and Peter remembered the word of the Lord . . . and Peter went out, and wept bitterly" (Luke 22:61, 62). Somewhere in the city he broke his heart.

(1) *The risen Lord sent a special invitation asking Peter to return.* When Mary came to the tomb she was met by an angel who said, "Go your way, tell his disciples AND PETER that he goeth before you into Galilee: there shall ye see him, as he said" (Mark 16:7). We must remember that in spite of his great mistake, Peter was still a disciple. Special mention was made of his name, for this was a great effort to bring back a wanderer.

(2) *The risen Lord personally sought for Simon.* When the

Emmaus travelers returned to announce the resurrection of Christ, they heard the disciples saying, "The Lord is risen indeed, *and hath appeared unto Simon*" (Luke 24:35). Paul also cited this great appearance, for obviously it was known to all the Church (I Corinthians 15:5). The Lord probably knew of Peter's shame and reluctance to accept the invitation, and therefore went forth in search of him. What they said to each other has remained a great secret. It is better that way.

(3) *The Lord publicly gave a new commission to His restored follower.* The scene which took place at the edge of the Sea of Galilee has now become famous (John 21). At another fire, Peter made his three-fold confession and received his thrilling commission. His service on the day of Pentecost, and throughout the following years, demonstrated how complete had been his recovery. We are able to understand why he wrote, "Unto you therefore which believe, *he* is precious" (I Peter 2:7).

SECTION THREE

Expository Notes on Christ's Appearance Before Pilate

Then led they Jesus from Caiaphas unto the hall of judgment: and it was early; and they themselves went not into the judgment, lest they should be defiled: but that they might eat the passover (v. 28).

It was specifically required by Mosaic law that all people to observe the passover should be free from defilement. The judgment hall belonged to the Gentiles and therefore was out of bounds on the eve of the great Feast. These men were about to commit the greatest sin on earth, yet they feared lest they might become defiled. They were about to murder the Son of God, and yet desired to be fit to enter the house of God. They fervently wished to remember how the blood of a lamb was shed in Egypt and yet, at the same time, were desirous of shedding Christ's blood on a hill outside their city wall. Religion without reality is a sham, a fake, a tragedy. It is folly to worship God on Sunday if we crucify Christ on Monday. A man may be exceedingly ritualistic, but the profession of Christianity does not guarantee reality in the experience of the formal worshipers. The people who crucified the Lord were among the most religious folk in the world. *Bonar* correctly said, "Christ and ritualism are opposed to each other as light is to darkness. The true Cross in which Paul gloried, and the cross in which modern ceremonialists glory, have no resemblance to each other. The Cross and the crucifix cannot agree. Either ritualism will banish Christ, or Christ will banish ritualism."

Pilate then went out unto them, and said, What accusation bring
ye against this man? They answered and said unto him, If he were
not a malefactor, we would not have delivered him unto thee
(vv. 29, 30).

The Greek word *kakopoios* is translated "malefactor." It is com-
prised of two words wedded together: *Kakos* and *poios* which together
mean *one with an evil nature; a wrong doer; one whose inner nature
begets outward crime.* Acts 25:16 reveals that Roman law required
three basic things: (1) A definite charge had to be placed against
the accused; (2) The accused and the accuser were to be brought
face to face; (3) The accused should be given the opportunity to
speak for himself. Speaking in his own defense, Paul said, "It is not
the manner of the Romans to deliver any man to die, before that he
which is accused *have the accusers face to face, and have license to
answer for himself concerning the crime laid against him.*" Pilate in
observing these basic principles of Roman law was justified in asking
what manner of accusation was being brought against Jesus. Momentarily, the accusers were at a loss to know how to answer, for they did
not have any specific charge to make. To them, it was sufficient that
they desired His death. Their great Sanhedrin had passed sentence;
that was enough! The governor should not meddle. They had supplied the jury; he was but the figurehead to enunciate the sentence of
death. The inference that the prisoner must be an evil man was
dastardly. He whose nature was said to be evil had gathered children
into His arms, touched the untouchables, given hope to the hopeless,
healed the sick, raised the dead, and had been the nations's greatest
Benefactor. Throughout the three and a half years of His unprecedented, thrilling ministry, thousands of people called Him "Blessed."
Now the ruler said *His inner corruption begat crime.*

Then said Pilate unto them, Take ye him, and judge him according
to your law. The Jews therefore said unto him, It is not lawful
for us to put any man to death (v. 31).

Poor Pilate. He struggled in vain to avoid the responsibility
being thrust upon him. The Jews were correct in their assertion
even though they were condemned by their actions. The Sanhedrin
possessed ecclesiastical authority but the carrying out of a death
sentence had to be referred to the Roman overlords. Palestine had
been occupied; they were not masters of their own house. Nevertheless, within weeks, these same people encouraged the stoning of
Stephen, and were directly responsible for sending Saul of Tarsus
on his murderous mission.

Attention is drawn to the fulfillment of a very special prediction.
Centuries earlier, Jacob analyzed his sons. When he spoke of Judah,
he said, "The sceptre shall not depart from Judah, nor a lawgiver from

between his feet, *until Shiloh come;* and unto him shall be the gathering of the people" (Genesis 49:10). When the Jewish leaders announced that absolute authority was no longer their prerogative, they unwittingly confessed the scepter and lawgiver were no longer supreme in Israel. The nation had been subjugated to a foreign dynasty. The patriarch announced this could never happen UNTIL SHILOH HAD COME. They did not realize that Shiloh was even then standing in their midst.

> **That the saying of Jesus might be fulfilled, which he spake, signifying what death he should die (v. 32).**

It will be remembered that often the Lord told His followers He would go to the city of Jerusalem and be delivered into the hands of sinful men to be crucified. John remembered those solemn predictions and emphasized that in all the unpleasant details of the crucifixion the unfailing, unswerving purpose of God was being fulfilled.

> **Then Pilate entered into the judgment hall again and called Jesus, and said unto him, Art thou the king of the Jews? Jesus answered him, Sayest thou this thing of thyself, or did others tell it thee of me? (Is that your own idea or have others suggested it to you — *New English Bible.*) Pilate answered, Am I a Jew? Thine own nation and the chief priests have delivered thee unto me: what hast thou done? (vv. 33-35).**

When Pilate announced his intention to liberate the accused, the legal advisors of Israel conceived their most diabolical scheme. Treason was an unforgivable offense in domains of the Caesars. A man guilty of this crime was commanded to commit suicide in his bath. This unpretentious exit saved much expense, and to a measure, preserved the honor of the accused. A few well told lies announcing the honorable governor had succumbed to the rigors of his duty, that he had died in the faithful service of the Emperor, preserved the good name of the deceased's family. If, however, the accused fled, the legions of Rome extended a long arm to bring him back to Rome where he would be executed without mercy. Knowing all this, the crafty Jews said, ". . . if thou let this man go, thou art not Caesar's friend: whosoever maketh himself a king speaketh against Caesar" (John 19:12). Indisputably this fear lurked in the back of Pilate's mind throughout the entire trial of Jesus. If he opposed the Jews he could lose much. Unfortunately, he did not realize that if he supported and appeased them, he would lose much more.

The thoughts and fears of the governor found expression when Pilate asked Jesus directly if He were truly a King. With unerring accuracy the Lord exposed the feelings of His judge. Possibly Pilate was somewhat embarrassed by the quiet dignity, the compelling personality, the moral and spiritual strength of the prisoner. With a shrug of the shoulders and a quick outburst of feelings, he replied, "Am I a Jew, that I should think such thoughts. I ask because your own leaders brought you into my court and are even now awaiting my verdict." How strange that a Roman judge had to inquire from the prisoner what wrong had been done. The counsel for the prosecution failed to produce a charge; the judge now hoped the prisoner would help the court out of its dilemma! This was tantamount to a federal court judge looking at a criminal to say, "Son, we have no charge against you but please be a good fellow and tell us what you have done so that we can decide quickly how many years you should spend in the penitentiary."

"So you are a king, are you?" returned Pilate. "Indeed I am a king," Jesus replied; "the reason for my birth, and the reason for my coming into the world is to witness to the truth. Every man who loves truth recognizes my voice" *The New Testament in Modern English* by J. B. Phillips (v. 37).

There was nothing vague nor indecisive about the Master's reply:

Certainly, I am a king (*Amplified New Testament*). Yet, My kingdom is not of this world: if my kingdom were of this world, then would my servants fight that I should not be delivered unto the Jews: but now is my kingdom not from hence. Pilate therefore said unto him, Art thou a king then? Jesus answered him, Thou sayest that I am a king (v. 36).

The translation in the Authorized Version is not good. As the translations already quoted indicate, the Lord's reply was easily understood; it was definite, decisive, clear. He was a King, but not just another potentate of the earth. His kingdom was founded upon eternal principles of righteousness. His armies included innumerable angels, but His greatest weapon was TRUTH. Truth contradicts and corrects evil; truth assures all subjects of justice; truth, the very truth of God's Word makes the crooked straight, the rough places plain, and prepares sinners for an abiding place in the presence of a glorified Lord.

Pilate said unto him, What is truth? And when he had said this, he went out again unto the Jews, and saith unto them, I find in him no fault. But ye have a custom, that I should release unto you one at the passover; will ye therefore that I release unto you the King of the Jews? (v. 38, 39).

Was Pilate sceptical — or anxious — or doubtful? Who can answer authoratively? This man whose learning was probably matched by the weakness of his vacillitating nature could have been saying, "I have heard much; I have seen much. Philosophers have lectured in my presence, and all claim to know the truth. I have heard so much, I have learned so little. When all is said and done, what is truth?" Yet we must recognize one important detail. Pilate was not angry with Christ, for he went out immediately to suggest the release of the accused. "If he found no fault in him, he was bound in conscience to discharge him. But he was willing to trim the matter, and please all sides, being governed more by worldly wisdom than by the rules of equity" (Matthew Henry). It was as if he said, "Let us assume the man is guilty"; it was as though he thought "the crowd that wishes to make him king, will acclaim my wisdom and accept a compromise." Probably he hoped they would recognize in him the counterpart of their great ancestor Solomon. The idea of pardoning a criminal at the time of Passover was not new. Long before in Egypt God had spared a guilty nation; they re-echoed the sentiments of Jehovah when they emulated His example and spared one worthy of death. Unfortunately, there was a restricting limit on Israel's mercy; they preferred to release a bandit who might pilfer their pockets rather than liberate One whose words would jolt their conscience.

Then cried they all again, saying, Not this man, but Barabbas. Now Barabbas was a robber (a bandit) (v. 40).

The word signifies a plunderer, a man without conscience who, to gain his ends, might even commit murder. The word used here is *leestees*, and is somewhat different from the other Greek word *kleptees*, which means to come unexpectedly as a thief, to pilfer, to steal (Matthew 24:43). The Jewish choice was ominous; instead of the gracious, gentle, thrilling ministry of the Healer, they chose a murderer, a plunderer, a villain. Their subsequent history demonstrated that sometimes it is possible to choose in haste and suffer forever.

HOMILIES

Study No. 65

PILATE . . . WHOSE WIFE HAD A DREAM (Matthew 27:46)

The scene was set for the greatest drama in history. At the gates of the governor's palace, an insistent mob clamored for attention. The feast day was at hand, and before it commenced, dirty work had to be done — and done quickly. As the sun arose to send its golden beams across the darkened sky, the shouts of the people echoed along the cobbled streets. Awakened thus from his sleep, Pilate went forth to the trial of Jesus ignorant of the fact that his own soul would also be tried that day. Losing his balance on the slippery slope of indecision and compromise, the judge began to fall and every passing hour brought him closer to disaster. How wonderful to recall that in those moments, God sufficiently loved this sinner to plan a final attempt to save him. In common with all other aspects of redeeming love, this was beyond comprehension.

How Great Was the Grace of God

Pilate's wife lay deep in slumber; she had not yet risen from her bed. Outside, her husband endeavored to outwit the bigoted people who were beginning to blackmail him, and silently Christ stood listening. The woman stirred uneasily; she was restless. God had stooped to touch her slumbering eyes, and as she slept, she dreamed — of Jesus. Suddenly, awaking with a start, she remembered that Pilate had gone to be the judge of the Prophet.

Trembling with premonition of disaster, she wrote her urgent message, "Have thou nothing to do with that just man: for I have suffered many things this day in a dream because of him." If Pilate had taken her advice, his soul might have been saved. Had he not been so devoid of true understanding, he would have recognized this dream to be a medium of grace. God never ceases His attempt at rescue while there is still a chance to succeed.

How Great Was the Goodness of a Woman

Possibly the governor dismissed this appeal as an intrusion into his own affairs. His wife should mind her own business! How could she understand the intricacies of this difficult case? These Jews had threatened to tell Caesar, and if a charge of treason should be brought against him, his future would be ruined. He had nothing to lose in crucifying the prisoner; he had nothing to gain in resisting these arrogant Jews. Let her mind her own affairs! She did not understand.

Ah, but she did. If misfortune overtook her husband, she could not escape; irrevocably her life was linked with his. She knew more. She knew that death was not the greatest of all tragedies. It was far better to die in honor than to live in shame. "Husband," she would have cried, "do that which is right. This Man is just; therefore stand by him whatever the cost." Pilate should have been very proud of his noble partner. A good woman is the greatest jewel outside of heaven; a bad woman is the vilest creature outside of hell.

How Great Was the Guilt of Man

Rudely brushing aside both the grace of God and the entreaties of his gracious lady, Pilate washed his hands before the multitude, saying, "I am innocent of the blood of this just person." Then, in contradiction to his verdict, he sent Jesus forth to be scourged and crucified. He had washed his hands, but had never touched the soiled places of his soul. To save himself, he sacrificed his Prisoner and his honor. Yet we are told that within seven years of his deed, a broken destitute man removed from high office by the governor of Syria, alone and unwanted by Caesar, Pilate went out into the darkness of the night to hang himself. His body was found by a workman.

Poor, guilty man; I feel sorry for him. He met the Saviour and refused to love Him. And now it is dark — exceedingly dark.

The Nineteenth Chapter of John

THEME: *The Crucifixion of Christ*

OUTLINE:

      I. A King Is Condemned. Verses 1-16.
     II. A King Is Crucified. Verses 17-37.
   III. A King Is Carried. Verses 38-42.

SECTION ONE

Expository Notes on the Closing Scene of Christ's Trial

Then Pilate therefore took Jesus, and scourged him (v. 1).

The reader of the New Testament cannot fail to notice the continued consistency with which Pilate sought to release his prisoner. The governor used every method to get the Jews to drop their capital charge but, alas, failed to persuade them. Simon Peter later declared, "The God of Abraham, and of Isaac, and of Jacob, the God of our fathers, hath glorified his Son Jesus; whom ye delivered up, and denied him in the presence of Pilate, *when he was determined to let him go*" (Acts 3:13). Yet, in spite of the increasing desire of the governor, the overruling purposes of God thwarted his every effort. Ultimately the Apostles saw this great truth in bold relief for they prayed and said, "For of a truth, against thy holy Child Jesus, whom thou hast anointed, both Herod, and Pontius Pilate, with Gentiles, and the people of Israel, were gathered together, *for to do whatsoever thy hand and thy counsel determined before to be done*" (Acts 4:27, 28). God saw the end from the beginning, and while Pilate remained responsible for his own actions, all was clearly revealed in the foreknowledge of the Almighty. "It pleased the Lord to bruise him" (Isaiah 53:10). Therefore, no power on earth could have prevented the death of the Lord Jesus.

Suddenly, Pilate seemed to hope that his tormentors might be satisfied if they saw the horrible flogging of their victim. He therefore commanded Jesus to be scourged. J. C. Ryle says, "The cruel injury inflicted on our Lord's body was probably far more severe than an English reader might suppose. It was a punishment which among the Romans, generally preceded crucifixion, and was sometimes so painful that the sufferer died under it. It was often a scourging with rods and not always with cords, as painters and sculptors represent. Josephus . . . particularly mentions that malefactors were scourged and tormented in every way before they were put to death. Smith's *Dictionary of the Bible* says that under the Roman mode of scourging. 'The culprit was stripped, stretched with cords or thongs on a frame, and beaten with rods.' "

The Roman scourgings were exceedingly severe and not limited, as among Jews, to forty stripes (Deuteronomy 25:1-3). When the Roman Emperor Constantine became a Christian, he abolished crucifixion. Cicero stated, "The very name (crucifixion) ought to be excluded, not merely from the body but from the thought, eyes, and ears of Roman citizens." If Pilate followed the general procedure, then the Lord was stripped of His garments, stretched on a frame, and mercilessly thrashed with thongs which bit into His flesh. The agony endured must have been excruciating, and we can only bow our heads in wonder when we consider that while this beating was administered, He still possessed the power which had previously paralyzed His enemies.

And the soldiers platted a crown of thorns and put it on his head, and they put on him a purple robe, and said, Hail, King of the Jews! and they smote him with their hands (vv. 2, 3).

See the earlier notes for the meaning of the Greek word *rapisma* (p. 380). These blows were more than mere slaps with an open hand: they could have been solid punches or even blows rained upon Him by rods or whips. There was great significance in the fact that men crowned Christ with thorns. When God first made the world, there were no thorns nor thistles. These were introduced later when sin marred God's handiwork. From time immemorial thorns have been the emblems of sin; unwittingly, the soldiers crowned the Saviour with the emblems of a world's iniquity. The purple robe had ever been the symbol of royalty, but within the writings of the prophets purple and scarlet were also indicative of sin and sacrifice. The picture presented in John 19 was that of a King bearing the sins of many. (See Isaiah 53:11.)

A. W. Pink in one of his brilliant expositions declared, "Christ was on the point of making atonement for sin, therefore sin must be revealed in all its enormity. (I) *Sin is lawlessness,* therefore did Pilate scourge the innocent One. (II) *Sin is transgression,* therefore did Pilate set aside all the principles and statutes of Roman jurisprudence. (III) *Sin is iniquity* (injustice), therefore did these soldiers smite that One who had never harmed a living creature. (IV) *Sin is rebellion against God,* therefore did Jew and Gentile alike maltreat the Son of God. (V) *Sin is an offense,* therefore did they outrage every dictate of conscience and propriety. (VI) *Sin is coming short of the glory of God,* therefore did they heap ignominy upon His Son. (VII) *Sin is defilement, uncleanness,* therefore did they cover His face with vile spittle." The Lord's hand had dispensed healing; their hands struck blows. His voice had spoken words of cheer; they reviled Him. His holy soul overflowed with love and mercy; they were embittered, murderous, despicable.

> How greatly Jesus must have loved them
> To bear their sin
> In His body on the tree.

Pilate therefore went forth again, and saith unto them, Behold, I bring him forth to you, that ye may know that I find no fault in him. Then came Jesus forth, wearing the crown of thorns, and the purple robe. And Pilate saith unto them, Behold the man! (vv. 4, 5).

Let it be considered that the Prisoner made no attempt either to remove His crown by lowering His head, nor the robe by endeavoring to shake it from His shoulders. Since these things were indicative of the purpose which brought Him into the world, He gladly bore His burden to the end. "He who knew no sin was made sin for us." It is not without significance that God provided a sevenfold witness to the perfection of His Son. Since *seven* is the number of completion, all students should give careful consideration to the following facts: (1) *The traitor Judas* said, "I have sinned in that I have betrayed the INNOCENT blood" (Matthew 27:4). (2) *The Judge, Pontius Pilate,* said, I find NO FAULT in him" (John 18:4). (3) *Herod,* as reported by Pilate, said, ". . . nothing worthy of death is done unto him." Literally this reads, "Nothing BLAMEABLE is found in him" (Luke 23:15). (4) *Pilate's wife,* after dreaming about the Lord said, "Have thou nothing to do with that JUST man: for I have suffered many things this day in a dream because of him" (Matthew 27:19). (5) The *dying thief* said, "We receive the due reward of our deeds, but this man hath done NOTHING AMISS" (Luke 23:41). (6) The *Roman centurion* glorified God and said, "This was a RIGHTEOUS man" (Luke 23:47). (7) *Other people standing close to the cross* exclaimed, "Truly, this was the SON OF GOD" (Matthew 27:54).

Probably when the governor presented Christ to the multitude he hoped they would relent and be content to let the prisoner go. He had not fully realized the avowed intention of the Jewish rulers. They were determined that Jesus should die. The sight must have been appalling, for Christ had been thrashed unmercifully. His back and face were lacerated; blood oozed from many wounds. Yet with unmistakable dignity He stood before His enemies and even Pilate became conscious of an indefinable something which revealed the majestic wonder of this amazing Carpenter. Preachers might like to compare, contrast, and preach about three trenchant statements:

(1) Behold the Man (John 19:5);
(2) Behold your King (John 19:14);
(3) Behold the Lamb of God (John 1:29).

When the chief priests therefore and officers saw him, they cried out, saying, Crucify, crucify. Pilate saith unto them, Take ye him, and crucify him: for I find no fault in him. The Jews answered him, We have a law, and by our law he ought to die, because he made himself the Son of God. (vv. 6, 7).

It was incongruous that they should appeal to their law when at the same instant they were flagrantly disobeying its commandments. The penalty for blasphemy was *stoning* and not crucifixion. Compare I Kings 21:13. They were eager to obtain an indictment, and fearing Jesus might gain a last minute reprieve, they charged Him with blasphemy. Pilate had little, if any, interest in an alien faith. Jewish customs, traditions, and religious practices were of no concern to him. Yet there was something about the new accusation which troubled his mind.

When Pilate heard that saying, he was the more afraid; and went again into the judgment hall, and saith unto Jesus, Whence art thou? But Jesus gave him no answer (vv. 8, 9).

It is most difficult to believe the governor feared the Jews. He possessed either the power to do as they required, or the ability to overcome any opposition which might arise spontaneously on the floor of the assembly. Of what, of whom then was he suddenly afraid? There can only be one logical answer. He was afraid of Jesus. It was hardly possible to be scared of one who had just been flogged by his soldiers — the threat lay in the possibilities of the new accusation. If this Man had indeed claimed to be the Son of God, a new angle had been presented on behalf of the prosecution. Could it be possible that this prisoner was indeed what He had claimed? Pilate recognized the dangers of passing sentence on a Jewish patriot; now a new terror began to envelop his mind. It was one thing to sentence a Jew; it was another to sentence the Son of God! A. W. Pink says, "Whence art thou? . . . It is clear that Pilate was not asking about His human origin, for he had already sent Christ as a 'Galilean' to Herod (Luke 23:6). Was this then a question of idle curiosity? No, the 'more afraid' of the previous verse shows otherwise. Was it that Pilate was now deeply exercised and anxiously seeking for light? No, for his outburst of scornful pride in the verse that follows conflicts with such a view. What, then? First, we think that Pilate was genuinely puzzled and perplexed. A Man altogether unique he clearly perceived Christ to be.

But was He *more* than man? The deepening fear of his conscience made him uneasy. Supposing that after all, this One were from heaven. That such a thought crossed his mind at this stage we fully believe, and this leads to the second motive which prompted his question. Pilate hoped that here was a way out of his difficulty. If Christ were really from heaven, then obviously he could not think of crucifying Him. He therefore has Christ led back into the judgment hall and says, 'Tell me privately your real origin and history so that I may know what line to take up with thine enemies.' " (For the "Silences of Jesus," see the homily at the end of Section One, Chapter 4).

> **Then said Pilate unto him, Speakest thou not unto me? knowest thou not that I have power to crucify thee, and have power to release thee? Jesus answered, Thou couldest have no power at all against me, except it were given from above: therefore he that delivered me unto thee hath the greater sin (vv. 10, 11).**

Roman arrogance began to assert itself, for Pilate was a man accustomed to absolute obedience. Many prisoners had probably cringed and begged for mercy at his feet; it was startling and even disconcerting that the normal practice should be broken. Even if the prisoner were the Son of God, he, Pontius Pilate, was still the appointed representative of the Caesars. Jesus might be the representative of a heavenly kingdom, but he at least acted on behalf of the greatest earthly authority. The prisoner should remember, too, that since Pilate was judge, in his hands lay the destiny of all present. "I have power to crucify thee, and have power to release thee" was only relatively true, yet it *was* true. The governor's testimony produced his own indictment. Pilate saw Jesus in the shadow of Caesar's throne; Christ saw the governor in the shadow of God's throne. The Lord Jesus was a Man of supreme confidence. When the mob rushed Him to the edge of the cliff in Nazareth, He allowed them to do so knowing that at the opportune time He would walk through their midst untouched. When Peter drew a sword in Gethsemane, the Lord announced His ability to summon angels to His assistance. As occasion demanded, Jesus walked on the sea, performed miracles, and defied the hostility of men who threatened to kill Him. Yet nowhere is His confidence revealed to better advantage than in Pilate's hall. "Thou couldest have no power at all against Me — unless My Father permitted it." When Christ indicated the greater sin of the priests, He also revealed the "great" sin of the man who was violating every principle of justice.

> **And from thenceforth Pilate sought to release him: but the Jews cried out saying, If thou let this man go, thou art not Caesar's friend: whosoever maketh himself a king speaketh against Caesar (v. 12).**

With every passing moment Pilate was being driven into a corner. He had determined to secure the acquittal of Jesus, but now the cost of this action was becoming increasingly apparent. The crowd had already chosen between Christ and Barabbas; now he had to choose between Christ and himself. "Most men like Pilate have a day of grace, and an open door put before them. If they refuse to enter in; if they choose their own sinful way, the door is often shut, and never opened again. There is such a thing as a day of visitation when Christ speaks to men. If they will not hear His voice, and open the door of their hearts, they are often left alone . . . . It was so with Pharaoh, Saul, and Ahab. Pilate's case was similar. He had his opportunity and did not choose to use it. He preferred to please the Jews at the expense of his conscience, and to do what he knew was wrong. We see the consequence — 'Jesus gave him no answer' " (Bishop Ryle). (See also the earlier notes regarding Roman laws and treason, p. 386.)

When Pilate therefore heard that saying, he brought Jesus forth, and sat down in the judgment seat, in a place that is called the Pavement, but in the Hebrew, Gabbatha. And it was the preparation of the passover, and about the sixth hour: he saith unto the Jews, Behold your King! (vv. 13, 14).

The historian Josephus confirms that near to Pilate's palace was a pavement (Antiquities, 15:8; paragraph 5) and it was upon this pavement Pilate's judgment seat was placed. There, with due ceremony and disdain, a frustrated governor hit back at the Jewish leaders, and all the while the King of heaven stood silently watching. The exact time at which these events took place seems to be a little confusing. Some of the ancient manuscripts place the time at the third hour, which appears to agree with the account given by Mark 15:25. Dr. Scofield says, "John used the Roman, Mark used the Hebrew computation of time." Some expositors find difficulty in the passage, "And it was the preparation of the passover," but this becomes plain when students remember that the Passover supper was not a part of the feast *which followed it.* "The supper was a memorial of the redemption of the first-born in Israel on the night BEFORE the Exodus; the feast was the anniversary of their actual escape from the thraldom of Pharaoh. 'In the fourteenth day of the first month is the passover of the Lord, and in the fifteenth day of this same month is the feast' " (Sir Robert Anderson). It will be seen, therefore, that there are no contradictions in the relative events described by John in the fourth gospel. The supper had been eaten the night before these events; the fast was still to come.

But they cried out, Away with him, away with him, crucify him. Pilate saith unto them, Shall I crucify your king? The chief priests answered, We have no king but Caesar. Then delivered he him therefore unto them to be crucified. And they took Jesus and led him away (vv. 15, 16).

It is extremely doubtful whether any more blatant hypocrisy can be found in Scripture. It was common and irrefutable knowledge that all Jews hated the Caesars. Inherent in every Jew was the yearning that someday Messiah would come to drive out the accursed legions of the foreign dictator. Yet in the hour of Christ's agony, these people hypocritically confessed allegiance to a man they loathed. When Caesar, a few decades later, destroyed their nation and temple, the Jews had only themselves to blame. When men and nations reject the Son of God, the repercussions of their actions are destined to be everlasting. "The ways of transgressors" are hard; this was never more apparent than in the year 70 A.D. when the smoke of a blazing sanctuary blackened the heavens. Israel had cried, "His blood be on us and on our children!" Their request was granted.

HOMILIES

Study No. 66

THE CROWNS OF THE SAVIOUR

This is a most interesting study, for there are three places in Holy Scripture where the Lord is said to be crowned. When viewed together, these texts provide a comprehensive picture of the purposes of God in man's salvation. We find in John 19:2 that Jesus of Nazareth was crowned with thorns; and that revelation sums up the Christ of yesterday. He is the source of all true happiness. Hebrews 2:9 reveals that Christ is now crowned in heaven, where at the right hand of His Father He intercedes on behalf of all His people. That truly expresses the Christ of today, and suggests the source of unfailing help. The last picture is described in Revelation 19:12 where the apostle John declares, "And on his head were many crowns." This expresses all the teaching concerning the Christ of the future. The statement, "We see Jesus . . . crowned," can be an enthralling text.

Jesus . . . crowned with thorns (John 19:2).

"And the soldiers platted a crown of thorns, and put it on his head, and they put on him a purple robe, and said, Hail, King of the Jews." The irresponsible actions of these men were almost prophetic. Actuated by thoughts of brutal persecution, they thought only of the fierce pleasure which their Victim would provide. In order to express the hidden meanings of divine revelation, no action would have been better suited to the moment. As mentioned before, thorns were never meant to be a part of God's world, and only appeared when sin marred God's handiwork. They were the emblems of sin. In their blind and wilful ignorance the soldiers crowned Jesus with the evidence of a world's guilt. Their actions were indeed prophetic and within a short space of time, God fulfilled their prediction. He took — not the emblems of sin, but sin itself, and made it to rest upon the head of His beloved Son. "The Lord hath laid on him the iniquity of us all." Therein lies the secret of man's happiness.

Jesus . . . crowned with glory and honor (Hebrews 2:9)

"But now we see not yet all things put under him. But we see Jesus, who was made a little lower than the angels . . . crowned with glory and honour." The Christ of yesterday may appear to be a wonderful Saviour, but if the Gospel contains nothing more, it can be of little use to present day men and women. The writer to the Hebrews continues the story and describes how the Lord Jesus ascended to the right hand of the Majesty on high, to be crowned with glory. The eternal Father said, "Sit on my right hand until I make thine enemies thy footstool," and while all the assembled hosts of heaven watched, He crowned the Lord Jesus with glory and honor. The epistle to the Hebrews teaches that Christ ever liveth to make intercession for us, and we may draw near in full assurance of faith and find grace to help us in time of need. If the reconciliation accomplished at the cross brings happiness, the intercession at God's right hand brings help to all who believe.

Jesus . . . crowned with many crowns (Revelation 19:12)

"And I saw heaven opened, and behold a white horse; and he that sat upon him was called Faithful and True . . . . His eyes were as a flame of fire and on his head were many crowns . . . . And he was clothed with a vesture dipped in blood: and his name is called the Word of God . . . . And he had on his vesture and on his thigh a name written, King of Kings and Lord of Lords." From his island prison, the apostle John saw "the things to be hereafter" and his soul-thrilling vision revealed that in the closing moments of time the Lord Jesus would return to earth to reign among His people. The kingdoms of the world would be His domain, and "the tabernacle of God shall be among men." The hymnist has conjectured that the accumulation of crowns expresses the fact that the saints will have already presented their rewards to their Saviour. John undoubtedly thought of the kingdoms to become the possession of Christ. Yet the supreme fact seems to be that the eternal home of all who love the

Saviour will be found in those days. The Christ of the future transcends all else, and every true Christian exclaims: "Even so, come, Lord Jesus."

SECTION TWO

Expository Notes on the Crucifixion of the Son of God

And he bearing his cross went forth into a place called the place of a skull, which is called in the Hebrew Golgotha: where they crucified him, and two others with him, on either side one, and Jesus in the midst (vv. 17, 18).

J. B. Phillips calls the place of execution "Skull Hill." It was not a mountain but a small rounded hill in the side of which were darkened depressions resembling the eyes and mouth of a skull. The Hebrew or Jewish name was "Golgotha"; the Gentile, or Latin, "Calvary." Its remarkable resemblance to a skull automatically made it the place of death — sinister, saddening, depressing. It was to this small hill that Jesus was led, that there in the place of death, the Lord of Life might give to death its death blow.

This entire passage of John's gospel is rich with prophetic fulfilment. Almost every detail of the crucifixion had been clearly and unmistakably foretold by the prophets, and in pursuing his predominant theme, John traced every fulfilment and remembered to remind his readers that everything was foreordained by God. The method to be used in the murder of God's Son was indicated by the psalmist, for in Psalm 22:16 the Holy Spirit declared of the Coming One, "For dogs have compassed me: the assembly of the wicked have inclosed me: *they pierced my hands and my feet.*" The Jews executed criminals by *stoning them* and not by crucifixion. The prophet Isaiah added details to the prophetic picture by saying, ". . . he hath poured out his soul unto death: and he was numbered with the transgressors . . ." (Isaiah 53:12). Even the conversion of the thief found a place in the prophetic utterances for Isaiah said, ". . . when thou shalt make his soul an offering for sin, HE SHALL SEE HIS SEED: he shall prolong his days, and the pleasure of the Lord shall prosper in his hand" (Isaiah 53:10).

The statement, ". . . and Jesus in the midst," appears to be singularly attractive for this was in keeping with His character. Students will find great interest in the "in the midst's" of the New Testament. There are at least seven wonderful Scriptures which, when placed together, supply stimulation for thought.

(1) As a Boy, Jesus was IN THE MIDST of the doctors, both hearing and asking them questions (Luke 2:46).

(2) As a Redeemer, Christ was IN THE MIDST of the thieves (John 19:8).

(3) As the risen Lord, He was IN THE MIDST of His disciples (John 20:19).

(4) As the Head of the Church, He was IN THE MIDST of the lampstands (Revelation 1:13).

(5) As the omnipresent Saviour, He promised to be IN THE MIDST of the two's and three's gathered in His name (Matthew 18:20).

(6) As the ascended Prince of Glory, He was IN THE MIDST of the heavenly hosts (Revelation 5:6).

(7) As the Lamb, He was described as being IN THE MIDST of the throne of God (Revelation 7:17).

Christ was always in the midst of His people and as such was accessible in every emergency of life.

> And Pilate wrote a title, and put it on the cross. And the writing was JESUS OF NAZARETH THE KING OF THE JEWS. This title then read many of the Jews: for the place where Jesus was crucified was nigh unto the city: and it was written in Hebrew, and Greek, and Latin (vv. 19, 20).

According to the prediction of Isaiah 52:14, the face of the Lord Jesus was marred beyond recognition. Excruciating agony had left its awful mark on the countenance of the Son of God, but any difficulty of identification was removed when Pilate affixed the title to the cross. Many theologians have speculated as to the exact reason why the governor acted as he did. Probably although he had heard Christ's words about the eternal kingdom, his chief reason for nailing the identification to the cross was that by so doing he annoyed the Jewish leaders. They had coerced him into sentencing the prisoner; they had charged Jesus as having made Himself a king; the governor therefore decided to strike at their pride by announcing to everybody that the nation had lost its royal Leader. The fact that he proclaimed the kingship of Christ in three languages guaranteed the whole world would understand the message. Hebrew was the language of the Jews; Greek, the tongue of the educated world; Latin, the language of the Romans, the language of law. Whether or not Pilate fully understood the implication of his message is extremely doubtful, but as A. W. Pink said, "In each of these realms, Christ is KING. In the religious world, He is the final revelation of the true God (Hebrews 1:2; John 14:9). In science, He is the Force behind all things. 'By him all things consist' (Colossians 1:17). In jurisprudence, He is supreme, the Law-giver and Law-administrator (I Corinthians 9:21)."

> Then said the chief priests of the Jews to Pilate, Write not, The King of the Jews; but that he said, I am king of the Jews. Pilate answered, What I have written I have written (vv. 21, 22).

The reaction of the rulers was immediate. The governor's announcement reflected on the dignity of the nation, and at the same time uttered an indictment against the men who were supposedly the counselors of the Jewish people. Pilate, piqued and secretly infuriated because these people had forced his hand, was elated that he had roused their ire, and deepened their annoyance when he refused to remove the identification tablet. The Almighty was guiding in the affairs of men, for the governor accurately expressed what was already in the mind of God. One wonders if these great words helped illumine the mind of the dying thief who said, "Lord remember me when thou comest into *thy kingdom.*"

> Then the soldiers, when they had crucified Jesus, took his garments, and made four parts, to every soldier a part; and also his coat: now the coat was without seam, woven from the top throughout. They said therefore among themselves, Let us not rend it, but cast lots for it, whose it shall be. Thus was the scripture fulfilled which saith, They parted my raiment among them, and for my vesture they did cast lots. These things therefore the soldiers did (vv. 23, 24).

It was the custom of the East that an executioner could claim the deceased man's clothing. It would appear that the same custom prevailed at the cross, for no objection was made when the soldiers proceeded to divide the Master's garments. Jesus had been stripped naked prior to execution and while the spikes were being driven into His body, the bundle of clothing had lain a few yards away. Now that the prisoner was securely fastened to the tree, the soldiers relaxed and proceeded to divide their treasure. The coat appeared to be a garment of worth; to rend it would be to spoil it. If all had a piece, no one would have anything. The men sat down; the dice were produced, and there in the shadow of the cross, they gambled for a garment. Unfortunately, they remained ignorant of the Christ who was able to give them the robe of righteousness. (See homily at the end of this section.)

Once again John was careful to indicate that this had been foretold by the prophet (see Psalm 22:18).

> Now there stood by the cross of Jesus his mother, and his mother's sister Mary, the wife Cleophas, and Mary Magdalene (v. 25).

This is a text which should be greatly beloved by all women. It probably represents the greatest thing ever done by their sex, for when most of the disciples were conspicuous by their absence, these three wonderful women were present to offer comfort to Him whose heart was breaking. (See the homily at the end of this Section.)

> When Jesus therefore saw his mother, and the disciple standing by, whom he loved, he saith unto his mother, Woman, behold thy son! Then saith he to the disciple, Behold thy mother! And from that hour that disciple took her unto his own home (vv. 26, 27).

It is a well-known fact that the Lord spoke seven times from the cross, but John only mentions three of the utterances. This is the first of the three, and deserves attention. The Lord was perfect. While He attended to the affairs of God, He still remembered the woman who brought Him into the world. It has been said that some Christians are so heavenly minded they are of no earthly use! The Lord provided the perfect example for His followers. While he gave considered attention to all the prophetic utterances and assured Himself that all the predictions were being fulfilled, He remembered to provide for His widowed mother. It was as if He said to John, "My mother will be losing a son today. Tonight there will be an emptiness within her soul. John, if you would like to please Me, enter into her life *and take My place.* Be to her another Jesus. And John, endeavor to do this task well, that soon my mother will exclaim, 'John, I only have to shut my eyes and listen to your voice, and I could almost believe He was back with me again.' John, be another Jesus for My mother." The same type of message was delivered to Mary, and as John's arm slowly went around her shoulders, the Master knew He had not spoken in vain. (See the homily at the end of Section Two, Chapter 13.)

The term "Woman" was not a harsh term; it was used often during the Lord's ministry. To address a woman thus exhibited esteem and respect and this should be remembered as the text is considered. From this Scripture it has been argued that Mary could not have had other children, otherwise, Christ had never committed her, a widow, to John. But the Word of God plainly declares that she DID have other children. 'Is not his mother called Mary? and his brethren, James and Joses, and Simon, and Judas? and his sisters, are they not all with us?' (Matthew 13:55, 56). The same Word of God also shows us that *they* were, at that time, ill-fitted to be Mary's companions and guardians. 'I am become *a stranger* unto my brethren, *and an alien unto my mother's children*' (Psalm 69:8). These were the Saviour's own words. How then could *they* take the Saviour's place, and be unto Mary what He had been? We surely need no stronger proof than we have here, that Mary, the mother of Jesus, was never meant to be honored as divine, or be prayed to, worshiped, and trusted as the friend and patroness of sinners. Common sense points out that she who needed the care and protection of another, was never likely to help men and women to heaven, or to be in any sense a mediator between God and man" (Bishop Ryle).

After this, Jesus knowing all things were now accomplished, that the scripture might be fulfilled, saith, I thirst. Now there was set a vessel full of vinegar; and they filled a sponge with vinegar, and put it upon hyssop, and put it to his mouth (vv. 28, 29).

It should not be imagined that Jesus was hanging in some kind of semiconscious state upon the cross. He was in complete possession of all His faculties. His mind, as keen as ever, scanned the entire range of prophetic utterance, and remembering an unfulfilled Scripture, proceeded forthwith to do what was necessary. The record of fulfilment had to be completed before the triumphant words, "It is finished," rang from His lips. The Holy Spirit had inspired David to say, "They gave me also gall for my meat; and in my thirst, they gave me vinegar to drink" (Psalm 69:21). The vinegar was probably some kind of sour wine, but this text should not be confused with the other drink which Christ refused. Matthew 27:34 says, "They gave Him vinegar to drink mingled with gall; and when he had tasted thereof, he would not drink." This was a mixture given to victims in order to deaden their pain. When Christ tasted it, He refused to drink the liquid as He was determined to remain conscious to the end. Only thus could be demonstrated His superiority over all circumstances; only thus could He be sure that all would be fulfilled according to the will of God. Crucifixion always begat extreme thirst, and this enables us to understand to some measure at least the poignancy of Psalm 22:15: "My strength is dried up like a potsherd; and *my tongue cleaveth to my jaws;* and thou hast brought me into the dust of death." There exists the possibility that one of the soldiers had become deeply impressed by what he had seen, and taking pity on the Crucified, dipped the sponge into the sour wine and lifted it to the lips of the Saviour. It is a comforting thought that not all who stood at the cross had hearts filled with bitterness.

When Jesus therefore had received the vinegar, he said, It is finished: and he bowed his head, and gave up his spirit (v. 30).

The triumphant utterance, "IT IS FINISHED," is but one word in the Greek testament *tetelestai.* Coming from the root word, *teleo,* it means *to bring to a close, to complete, to finish perfectly.* Probably it is beyond the capabilities of finite man to appreciate and express all this meant to Christ. Everything which He had helped to plan in the ageless counsels of infinity; all the patterns, desires, yearnings of God had been brought to culmination. All the types and prophetic utterances had been fulfilled. Reconciliation for sins, the overthrow of the kingdom of Satan; all that had to be done in order to make salvation possible had been completely accomplished. The victory was gained, the battle was over. The verse declares that Christ then bowed His head and surrendered His spirit. Even the order of action suggests dignity. Dying people generally breathe their last before their heads fall forward. A semiconscious person would have drooping head. The details of the passing of Christ are thrilling. (1) He remembered an unfulfilled prediction. (2) He proceeded to make its fulfilment absolute. (3) He announced the completion of God's great work. (4) He uttered His cry of triumph. (5) Peacefully He lowered His head. (6) He dismissed His spirit.

DID EVER MAN DIE AS HE DIED?

" 'It is finished.' The root Greek word here, *teleo*, is variously translated in the New Testament. A reference to some of its alternative renditions in other passages will enable us the better to discern the fullness and finality of the term here used by the Saviour. In Matthew 11:1 *teleo* is translated as follows: 'When Jesus had *made an end of* commanding his twelve disciples . . .' In Matthew 17:24 it is rendered, 'They that received tribute money came to Peter and said, Doth not your Master *pay* tribute?' In Luke 2:39 it is translated, 'And when they had *performed* all things according to the law of the Lord . . . .' In Luke 18:31 it is rendered, 'All things that are written by the prophets concerning the Son of man shall be *accomplished!*' Putting these together we learn the scope of Christ's utterance. 'It is finished.' He cried — It is 'made an end of,' it is 'paid,' it is 'performed,' it is 'accomplished.' What was 'made an end of'? — our sins, our guilt. What was 'paid'? — the price of our redemption. What was 'performed'? — the utmost requirements of God's law. What was 'accomplished'? — the work which the Father had given Him to do. What was 'finished'? — the making of atonement!" (A. W. Pink).

> The Jews therefore, because it was the preparation, that the bodies should not remain upon the cross on the sabbath day, (for that sabbath day was an high day,) besought Pilate that their legs might be broken, and that they might be taken away (v. 31).

The day on which the Saviour was crucified was one of Israel's "high days"; it was also on the eve of the regular Sabbath, and coincided with the beginning of the feast of unleavened bread. In the estimation of all Jewry this time was held as sacred, and defilement in any shape or form could not be tolerated. Crucifixion was notoriously slow in its process and victims had been known to linger for several days before they succumbed to exposure and pain. The arms of the victim were spiked to the cross-beam, but on the upright part of the gibbet was a small ledge upon which the feet rested, and to which they were fastened. This was the only support other than the nails through the palms of the hands. The crucified always suffered extreme agony, but at such moments when the pain became unbearable, a measure of relief was obtained by the victim easing the weight on the nails by pressing as best he was able on the small supporting ledge beneath the feet. When it became necessary to hasten the death of the crucified, the Romans used an iron bar or mallet with which they broke the victim's legs. They literally smashed the bones so that no weight could be placed on the feet. Thus, the body sagged entirely upon the nails, and the resultant pressure ultimately ruptured the heart. When this permission was given, the soldiers were commanded to do what was necessary, and for a while it almost appeared as if one prophecy would escape fulfilment. "He keepeth all his bones: not one of them is broken."

Then came the soldiers, and brake the legs of the first, and of the other that was crucified with him. But when they came to Jesus, and saw that he was dead already, they brake not his legs; but one of the soldiers with a spear pierced his side, and forthwith came there out blood and water (vv. 32-34).

When Pilate received into audience Joseph of Arimathea and heard that Jesus was dead, he found it difficult to believe the news. Not until the centurion corroborated the message did he believe the end had indeed come. The soldiers disobeyed a command when they did not break the legs of Christ. They probably thought the action totally unnecessary since the Carpenter was dead. Had they obeyed their officer's command, the Word of God would have been violated. It may be well said that God would not have permitted the breaking of the legs of Jesus. From time immemorial the Hebrews had observed the Passover rites, and one of the most important parts of the ritual was that not a single bone of the lamb had to be broken. "They shall leave none of it unto the morning, *nor break any bone of it* . . ." (Numbers 9:12). During the centuries, the priests had faithfully observed the commandment without ever understanding its significance. Now, on a green hill outside the city wall, the type was being fulfilled in all its strange simplicity. There was added significance in the unbroken body. The church, the Eve out of His side, was to be called "The Body of Christ." Hurt she may be but severed — never.

Matthew Henry has an illuminating paragraph concerning the piercing of the Master's side. "The opening of His side was significant. When we would protest our sincerity, we wish there were a window in our hearts, that the thoughts and intents of them might be visible to all. Through this window, opened in Christ's side, you may look into His heart, and see love flaming there, love strong as death. The blood and water that flowed out of it were significant. They signified the two great benefits which all believers partake of through Christ — blood for atonement, water for purification. Guilt contracted must be expiated by blood; stains contracted must be done away by *the water of purification*. These two must always go together. Christ has joined them together, and we must not think to put them asunder. They flowed from the pierced side of our Redeemer. They signified the two great ordinances of baptism and the Lord's supper. It is not the water in the font that will be to us the washing of regeneration, but the water out of the side of Christ; not the blood of the grape that will refresh the soul, but the blood out of the side of Christ." (See also the homily at the end of this section.)

> And he that saw it bare record, and his record is true; and he knoweth that he saith true, that ye might believe. For these things were done, that the scripture should be fulfilled, A bone of him shall not be broken. And again another scripture saith, They shall look on him whom they pierced (vv. 35-37).

John thus autographs his writing. From time to time, men have denied his authorship of the fourth gospel, but a very elementary comparison of the gospel and the epistles of John reveals an affinity of purpose and expression which removes all doubt except for minds where preconceived ideas defy intelligence. The same might be said of all who ridicule and criticize the sacred Scriptures. Men who should have known better have declared the Old Testament to be a collection of ancient legends, fables, stories. Students have been taught that the historicity of the Old Testament narratives is open to question, and unfortunately some have paid more attention to their tutors than to God. Practically every detail of the Lord's crucifixion was accurately foretold centuries before He came to earth. If these amazing records were produced by overwrought minds or collected by an ancient storyteller, then the unfailing fulfilment of their predictions would suggest the Bible to be an even greater miracle than it is.

HOMILIES

Study No. 67

THE SOLDIERS WHO CRUCIFIED JESUS

Somewhere near the city of Jerusalem was a military camp, the most dangerous garrison in the entire Roman Empire. Its soldiers were not unaware of the greatness of their peril, for they had already tasted of the bitterness of the people whose land they occupied. Each night they talked around their camp fires, and the advent of Jesus into the life of the nation provided the most disturbing of all their themes. It was said He could even walk on the sea, that He could raise the dead. If such a man were to lead Israel, there could be serious trouble. As the feast time approached, every soldier looked to his weapons. Then came the most startling news of all.

The enemy had rejected their king, and were now clamoring for His elimination. On the most fateful day in history, the soldiers went out to superintend the death of Jesus; and in the shadow of the cross their own individuality was soon displayed.

The Indifferent Man

"Then the soldiers, when they had crucified Jesus . . . took his coat . . . and said, Let us not rend it, but cast lots for it, whose it shall be" (John 19:23, 24). Some unknown person, possibly a woman, had woven a coat without a seam and had presented it to her Lord. The soldiers coveted this treasure, and turning their backs on the cross, cast lots for the garment. They were so interested in the prospect of material gain that they had no thought for Christ. Thus they foreran the materialists of today. There are folk who live for the sole purpose of increasing their wealth, and alas, they are so poor they have nothing but money! Surely, the only true test of wealth is to take away all material possessions, and afterward to ascertain what a man has left. True riches consist in abiding peace, rest of heart, and in the abundance of friends who remain true even in the hour of adversity. The soldiers were so shortsighted that they were unable to see beyond this opportunity of getting something for nothing.

The Incensed Man

"But when they came to Jesus, and saw that he was dead already, they brake not his legs; but one of the soldiers with a spear pierced his side" (John 19:33, 34). This represents one of the most callous acts of humanity, and we can only speculate as to the cause of the man's bitterness. The would-be persecutor actually thrust his spear into a dead body. It seems that he wanted to hurt Jesus and was disgruntled because he had arrived too late to do as he had planned. Why was he so bitter? Perhaps he had had dealings with unscrupulous Jews, and in arrogant self-righteousness had classed all of that race in the same category. To him, Jesus was just another Jew — someone he hated. And are there not such people still living? Are there not multitudes who, having met a few hypocrites, vehemently scorn the Gospel and reject the Saviour? In many cases man's sense of justice has been warped by the prejudice and bitterness of his heart.

The Inspired Man

"And the centurion which stood over against him . . . said, Truly this was the Son of God" (Mark 15:39). "Ah, wise man, the more I look at you, the more I like you. You heard the Lord asking the Father to forgive sinners; you listened to the request of the dying thief, and probably marveled at the amazing response made by Jesus. I have always wondered if you were the same officer who earlier insisted that there was no necessity for Christ to enter a simple abode. He had only to speak the word, and the miracle would be accomplished. Some day in heaven, I think I shall want to ask you that question. You were right, you know; He was the Son of God."

It is night time, and the three men are back in camp. The first proudly displays his winnings — a coat. The second bitterly nurses his grievance. The third, with a strange peace filling his heart, remembers the words of the Crucified. I see them so clearly now; but I wonder which I resemble most?

Study No. 68

THE THREE MARYS WHO LINGERED AT THE CROSS

"Now there stood by the cross of Jesus his mother, and his mother's sister Mary, the wife of Cleophas, and Mary Magdalene" (John 19:25). If I were a woman, this would be one of my favorite texts. When most of the disciples had forsaken Christ, three women lingered in His presence. They were all named Mary. If we could link this verse with I Corinthians 13:13, where the triple attributes of faith, hope, and love are mentioned, then we might be able to present each of these women with a surname. A little examination reveals that they traveled to the cross along different pathways.

Mary Faith — His Mother

The story of Joseph's wife is among the loveliest stories in the world. Faced with the physical impossibility of Christ's conception, she believed and said, "Be it unto me according to thy word," and in joyful anticipation sang, "My soul doth magnify the Lord." His subsequent coming, and the cumulative testimony of the shepherds, the wise men, the prophet Simeon, and the prophetess Anna, only increased the wonderment of her heart. Later, she heard the Boy Jesus name God as His Father; and by the time He was thirty she had sufficiently grown in faith to be able confidently to expect His first miracle (John 2:5). She had no doubt, for she had come to realize the extent of His power. Alas, her faith was soon to suffer. The Pharisees came asking about His age and accusing Him of blasphemy. Mary gathered together her other children and went seeking Him. It is said that His kinsmen thought He was beside Himself, and would have taken Him home (Mark 3:21, 31). Then came the cross, and any remaining thought of His divinity disappeared. Mary went away, and as far as we know never returned until the news of the resurrection electrified everybody.

Mary Hope — The Wife of Cleophas

The entire background of this woman's experience is different. She was the wife of a disciple who is also mentioned in the account of the walk to Emmaus. Possibly in common with many other people, she had rallied to His cause firmly believing Him to be the promised Messiah. Each miracle added fuel to the fires of her hopes; but as with the first Mary, the tragedy of the cross devastated her soul. It is more than likely that she was the unknown companion accompanying Cleophas back to the home in Emmaus, and their testimony to the Stranger was most illuminating. They said, "We trusted it had been he which should have redeemed Israel." Such hopes would have perished but for the resurrection.

Mary Love — Magdalene

If Magdalene is to have a surname, it must be LOVE. She had known the misery of being possessed by devils, and then Jesus had brought heaven to her soul. The memory of His unsurpassed kindness and power thrilled her as every day, with other women, she followed ministering to Him. She also had faith, and fervently hoped He would be the Messiah; yet underneath lay something greater. She loved Him. Had he failed? Had he been a blasphemer? People said so, but their opinions made no difference. She had loved Him in life; she loved Him in death, and perhaps that is the reason why she was the only one of the three Marys to return on the morning of the resurrection. Primarily she did not return to worship the risen Lord; she came because she still loved the dead Jesus. "And now abideth faith, hope, love, these three: but the greatest of these is love." Perhaps we may be permitted to say, "And now abideth Mary Faith, Mary Hope, Mary Love, these three: but the greatest of these is Mary Love." There is a faith — a mental assent — that cannot survive a Calvary. There is a hope — that can be submerged by disappointment. But love is unchanging; it is eternal, it is like God. Such love brought the Saviour down to us; such love alone can take us up to Him.

> Let me love Thee, Saviour,
> Take my heart forever:
> Nothing but thy favor
> My soul can satisfy.

Expository Notes on the Funeral of Christ

And after this Joseph of Arimathea, being a disciple of Jesus, but secretly for fear of the Jews, besought Pilate that he might take away the body of Jesus: And Pilate "granted permission." He came therefore and took the body of Jesus (v. 38).

Students might wish to compare this account with the other funerals of the Bible. There is much food for thought in the study. When God buried Moses, no other attended the final rites. When the body of John Baptist was placed to rest, only his disciples gathered around the grave. At the interment of the Son of God were two people — the men who carried His body. We are told that a few women looked on from a distance, but possibly even the angels veiled their faces as Joseph and Nicodemus gently carried their precious burden to the grave. There were no undertakers, no friends, family, neighbors; only two bearers were present.

Pilate was probably intrigued by Joseph's request for the body. It seemed incongruous that one of the honorable counselors should make this request when his colleagues were directly responsible for the death of Jesus. Such a burial might lead to exciting repercussions. This is the story of the triumph of light over darkness, courage over cowardice, faith over doubt. Years earlier, Nicodemus had visited the Saviour and conversed with Him about matters related to the establishment of the kingdom (John 3); later he uttered half-hearted words of defense in the Sanhedrin only to see his effort smothered in a virulent attack by the other people present (John 7). When it was too late to fall in adoration at the Lord's feet, both Joseph and Nicodemus boldly expressed their love for the Master. It should be remembered that they buried a DEAD CHRIST; they had no idea that soon the city would be electrified by the news of His glorious resurrection. They sought permission to take His body to burial firmly believing that within a matter of hours they might themselves become the object of scorn.

Arimathea, *"a city of the Jews,"* has been identified as Ramah, Samuel's birthplace, called Armathaim in the Septuagint. Other writers associate the place with Ramleh, a place on the road from Jaffa to Jerusalem. It was said to be six or seven miles from the chief city and if this were correct, then Joseph had no difficulty in being present at the meetings addressed by the Lord Jesus. He was an honorable counselor, a good man, and just (see Luke 23:51). When he and Nicodemus united in the determination to bury Christ's body, the world was provided with the New Testament equivalent of the friendship which existed between David and Jonathan. These two secret disciples did what even Peter and John apparently did not think of doing. The costly spices brought by the ruler of the Jews were meant to adorn the body and thus make it fragrant for interment. Isaiah foresaw this event seven hundred years earlier for he wrote: "And he made his grave with the wicked, and *with the rich in his death . . .*" (Isaiah 53:9). That Christ would occupy the tomb of a wealthy man seemed altogether beyond the bounds of possibility. The Lord had neither friends, property, nor money. Three graves, or possibly even one common grave would have been prepared by the authorities and plans were made to bury the deceased victims as quickly as possible after death had taken place. The sudden intervention of Joseph was not an accident; his thoughtful deed had been written on the heart of God from all eternity.

> And there came also Nicodemus, which at the first came to Jesus by night, and brought a mixture of myrrh and aloes, about a hundred pound weight. Then took they the body of Jesus, and wound it in linen clothes with the spices, as the manner of the Jews is to bury (vv. 39, 40).

A. R. Fausset in his *Bible Encyclopedia and Dictionary* says of the aloes, "The more precious kind grows in Cochin China and Siam and is not exported, being worth its weight in gold. The perfume is from the oil thickening into resin within the trunk . . . . It is used for perfuming garments (Psalms 45:8) and beds (Proverbs 7:17). It is the image of all that is lovely, fragrant, and incorruptible (Numbers 24:6; Song of Solomon 4:14). It was used by Nicodemus, along with myrrh, 100 pounds in all, to enwrap amidst linen the sacred body of Jesus." It will be readily understood that Nicodemus did not bring an inexpensive collection of perfumes; he probably brought to the burial of Christ some of his greatest treasures. He who had been a secret disciple for so long was now determined to give to the Lord the best of his possessions. He reminds us of Mary who also brought her box of very precious perfume.

Fausset also says, "The Jews entombed, if possible, or else interred their dead; the rabbins alleging as a reason, 'Dust thou art, and unto dust shalt thou return' (Genesis 3:19). Even enemies received burial (I Kings 11:15). *The law ordained the same treatment for a malefactor* (Deuteronomy 21:23). 'And if a man have committed a sin worthy of death, and he be to be put to death, and thou shalt hang him on a tree: *his body shall not remain all night upon the tree,* but thou shalt in any wise bury him that day; (for he that is hanged is accursed of God) . . . .' A cave was the usual tomb as Palestine abounds in caves . . . . Kings and prophets alone were buried within the walls of towns. A strong family feeling led the Israelites to desire burial in the same tomb as their forefathers . . . . To be excluded from the family burying place, as Uzziah and Manasseh were, was deemed an indignity (II Chronicles 26:23 and 33:20). To give a place in one's own sepulchre was a special honor; as the children of Heth offered Abraham and as Jehoiada was buried among the kings (Genesis 23:6, II Chronicles 24:16). So Joseph of Arimathea could not have done a greater honor to our crucified Lord's body than giving it a place in his own new tomb, fulfilling the prophecy of Isaiah 53:9" (*Fausett's Bible Encyclopedia* — page 104).

> Now in the place where he was crucified there was a garden; and in the garden a new sepulchre, wherein was never man yet laid. There laid they Jesus therefore because of the Jew's preparation day; for the sepulchre was nigh at hand.

These wonderful men gently washed the Master's body, wrapped it in clean linen, added their costly perfumes, combed His hair, and reverently placed the Lord upon the slab in the garden tomb. Surging love mingled with overflowing emotions as they performed their task; they were burying the Lord of Glory. Although they did not know it, they too were swiftly becoming immortal.

HOMILIES

See "Two Men Who Triumphed Gloriously in the End," Chapter 3, Section One

See "The Incomparable Christ," Chapter 7, Section Three

See "The Three Gardens," Chapter 18, Section One

The Twentieth Chapter of John

THEME: *The Resurrection of the Lord Jesus Christ*

OUTLINE:
    I. The Empty Tomb. Verses 1-10.
    II. The Exciting Testimony. Verses 11-20.
    III. The Exasperating Thomas. Verses 21-31.

SECTION ONE

Expository Notes on the Coming of the Disciples to the Tomb

The first day of the week cometh Mary Magdalene early, when it was yet dark, unto the sepulchre, and seeth the stone taken away from the sepulchre. Then she runneth and cometh to Simon Peter, and to the other disciple, whom Jesus loved, and saith unto them, They have taken away the Lord out of the sepulchre, and we know not where they have laid him (vv. 1, 2).

"The resurrection of Christ was more than hinted at in the first divine promise and prophecy (Genesis 3:15). If Christ was to bruise the serpent's head AFTER His own heel had been bruised by the enemy, then must He rise from the dead. The passing of the ark through the waters of judgment on to the cleansed earth, foreshadowed this same great event (I Peter 3:21). The deliverance of Isaac from the altar, after he had been given up to death three days before (see Genesis 22:4), is interpreted by the Holy Spirit as a receiving of Him back, in figure, from the dead (Hebrews 11:19). The crossing of the Red Sea by Israel on dry ground, three days after the slaying of the paschal lamb, was a type of Christians being raised together with Christ. The emergence of Jonah after three days and nights in the belly of the fish forecast the Saviour's deliverance from the tomb on the third day. Prophecy was equally explicit: 'Therefore my heart is glad, and my glory rejoiceth: my flesh also shall rest in hope. For thou wilt not leave my soul in hades; neither wilt thou suffer thine Holy One to see corruption. Thou wilt show me the path of life' (Psalm 16:9-11). *We cannot make too much of the death of Christ, but we can make too little of His resurrection*" (A. W. Pink).

Many and varied are the verses connected with the story and

doctrines of the resurrection but some deserve special attention. "Therefore we are buried with him by baptism into death: that like as Christ was raised up from the dead *by the glory of the Father,* even so, we also should walk in newness of life" (Romans 6:4). "Therefore doth my Father love me, because *I lay down my life,* that I MIGHT TAKE IT AGAIN" (John 10:17). "But if the *Spirit* of him that raised up Jesus from the dead dwell in you, he that raised up Christ from the dead shall also quicken your mortal bodies by his Spirit that dwelleth in you" (Romans 8:11). A careful comparison of these texts enables the student to appreciate the fact that all three Members of the divine family shared in the triumph of the resurrection. That which was planned by the Trinity was carried out systematically when each Member played His part.

John appears to be very explicit in affirming that Mary came to the sepulcher *when it was yet dark.* This and the corresponding verses of Matthew and Mark make exciting reading. (See the homily at the end of this section.) Her coming into the streets at this early hour was not without some measure of danger. While the passover feast represented one of the sacred times in Israel, the fact remained that a crowd sometimes drew a crowd, and among the multitudes would be many unscrupulous men whose morals left much to be desired. Accommodation was taxed to the limit, and many visitors would probably be sleeping in the shadows of the wall. Women who walked the streets at night were known to be of questionable repute; Mary, in coming to the tomb at such an early hour, exhibited a bravery which should not be forgotten in the wonder of the resurrection story.

At first sight there appear to be contradictions in the various versions, but the problems are quickly resolved when the Scriptures are placed side by side. Possibly Mary was the first woman to arrive at the sepulcher, but was quickly followed by the other Marys. Magdalene saw that the stone had been removed, and hastily jumping to the wrong conclusions rushed to tell Peter and John the disturbing tidings. Meanwhile, the other women drew near to the tomb, and heard the angelic announcement. There is no discrepancy in the account. Mary would have been there at an even earlier hour but ceremonial law prevented her associating with death in any shape or form until curfews were over. Some theologians have speculated as to the reason for the woman's haste to tell *Peter and John.* Why did she single out these men and not the others? Perhaps their homes were nearer; maybe, her first thought was to tell Mary, the Lord's mother, for after all she would be the one most intimately concerned with the disappearance of her Son's body. If this were the case, she would need to visit John's home, for this disciple had taken Mary to "*his own home*." Finally, Peter and John had already asserted their leadership of the small band of disciples. Their dominant personalities made them natural choices for any position of authority now that the Master had gone. The woman's electrifying announcement that someone had violated the sanctity of a tomb demanded action. If her testimony were true, the robber should be apprehended immediately.

Peter therefore went forth, and that other disciple, and came to the sepulchre. So they ran both together; and the other disciple did outrun Peter, and came first to the sepulchre (vv. 3, 4).

Both men were excited and a little anxious, but John — who was probably much younger than Peter — outdistanced the older man and arrived first at the tomb. It will be remembered that John lived much longer than Peter, and therefore the assumption is safe that he was the younger man.

And he stooping down, and looking in, saw the linen clothes lying; yet went he not in. Then cometh Simon Peter following him, and went into the sepulchre, and seeth the linen clothes lie. And the napkin that was about his head, not lying with the linen clothes, but wrapped together in a place by itself. Then went in that other disciple which came first to the sepulchre, and he saw, and believed (vv. 5-8).

Peter and John were very different in temperament, outlook, and thought. Both had been possessed of fiery natures, and John particularly was notorious as "a son of thunder." Yet John, by proximity to Christ, had absorbed something of the meditative loveliness of his Master. Anxiety and youthful energy brought him to the sepulcher; reverence and deep devotion stopped him at the sepulcher; and then worship, faith, and keen perception enabled him to see what less observant men would have missed. John was careful to indicate that they saw not the emptiness of the tomb but the linen clothes and the napkin *wrapped together in a place by itself.* A. T. Pierson wrote, "'Wrapped together' fails to convey the true significance. The original means *rolled up*, and suggests that these clothes were lying in their original convolutions, as they had been tightly rolled up around our Lord's dead body. In 19:44 it is recorded how they tightly wound — bound about — that body in the linen clothes; how tightly and rigidly may be inferred from the necessity of loosing Lazarus, even after miraculous power had raised up the dead body and given it life (11:44). This explains 20:8 — '*and John saw and believed.*' There was nothing in the mere fact of an empty tomb to compel belief in a miraculous resurrection; but when John saw, on the floor of the sepulchre, the long linen wrappings that had been so tightly wound about the body and head lying undisturbed in their original convolutions, he knew that nothing but a miracle could have made it possible."

With loving care Joseph and Nicodemus had placed the Master's body on the slab within the rocky tomb, but at the appointed moment the Lord's body — glorified, transformed — rose through the wrappings and these in turn fell flat. Even the napkin by which the head had been circled and enclosed was in its special place. Neither friend nor foe could have arranged those garments in their meticulous order; the clothing itself bore testimony to the mighty hand of God. "And the angel answered and said unto the women, Fear not ye: for I know that ye seek Jesus, which was crucified. He is not here: for He is risen, as He said. Come, *see* that Peter looked into the grave and wondered; his friend looked and *believed*. That one simple detail reflected the entire world.

For as yet they knew not the scripture, that he must rise again from the dead. Then the disciples went away again unto their own home (vv. 9, 10).

John was particularly honest in making bare his soul. "They knew not the scripture" suggests they had never truly listened to the Lord's predictions concerning His death and resurrection. They had been so desirous of an earthly kingdom that their selfish wishes superceded the teaching of Christ. They heard so much, but learned so little; nonplussed, thoughtful, they returned to their home, but John had already seen the glimmering of a new day. He knew not the Scripture, but the witness within his heart testified to the resurrection of the Master. Something phenomenal had taken place; a miracle had been performed within the tomb. It is truly suggestive that they did not go in search of information regarding the identity of possible thieves. Had they believed an infamous robbery had taken place, they would have hastened to the authorities to lodge a complaint, or visited the gardener's home to ask if people had been permitted to visit the area of the tomb. This they did not do; the Lord's body was still absent, but Peter and John made no attempt whatever to locate it. This surely must rank as another piece of evidence to support the assertion that Christ rose from the dead.

HOMILIES

Study No. 69

MAGDALENE . . . WHO WALKED TOWARD THE SUNRISE

Someone has said, "Little is much when God is in it," and every mention of Easter reminds one of the old proverb. There are several significant details about this thrilling resurrection story but the most intriguing of all is the time factor of Magdalene's visit to the sepulcher. If we could sit in conference with the three authors, Matthew, Mark, and John, we should be greatly interested as they discussed their viewpoint. They apparently disagreed about the time of Mary's memorable visit to the tomb.

Let John Tell Us

"Yes, Brother, we would like to hear your version." The apostle smiles and points to his message in chapter 20:1. "The first day of the week cometh Mary Magdalene early, *when it was yet dark,* unto the sepulchre, and seeth the stone taken away from the sepulchre." With his quiet clear voice of authority he declares, "She came when it was still dark," and his fathomless eyes seem to suggest this was true in a dual sense. The darkness of the city compared with the darkness of her soul. Her Friend and Master had been crucified, and by one cruel stroke of misfortune all her hopes had perished. Life could never be the same now that Christ was dead. She had awaited the passing of the Sabbath, but so great was her desire to be near the tomb, she came when it was still dark. Possibly all kinds of doubts and objections arose within her mind, but she came nevertheless. She had no idea that the Lord would be alive; to her, alas, Christ had gone forever. Yet even a dead Christ was better than none at all. His tomb would forever be holy ground; with anxious devoted heart she hurried to Joseph's sepulcher.

Let Matthew Tell Us

We imagine Matthew's discreet little cough as he rises to tell his story. "My brother John, you are right and yet you are wrong. It was dark both within and without her soul, but another detail should be added to the account. Listen . . ." and Matthew carefully points to his own record (28:1): "'In the end of the sabbath, *as it began to dawn* toward the first day of the week, came Mary Magdalene . . . . to see the sepulchre.' My brother John, it is true to say that she came when it was dark — IT WAS DARK: but as she continued toward the tomb, the shadows of the night commenced to flee. Signs of the approaching day were beginning to become visible. You will agree that this also became true of her deepest feelings. She did not know about the Lord's resurrection. He was dead, and with Him her joys had also been buried. Yet some urge took her to the tomb, and this proved to be one of the greatest events in her life. Yes, it is true for us all — the darkness disappears when we draw near to Christ. We may sit at home wondering how the stone may be removed; we may ask innumerable questions concerning many things. The wisest and best thing to do is draw near to Christ. Life teaches many wonderful lessons, but not the least is that clouds disintegrate and disappear as they draw nearer to the sun."

Let Mark Tell Us

Mark is smiling; he is the youngest of the three. He has often talked with Simon Peter, and seems sure of his facts. "Brethren, listen and I will read from my writings at 16:2. 'And very early in the morning the first day of the week, they came unto the sepulchre *at the rising of the sun.*' I am sorry, gentlemen, if I seem to disagree with you. No, do not misunderstand me; I am not suggesting that you are wrong. Perhaps it was dark when our sister commenced her journey and, brother Matthew, maybe it did begin to dawn as she drew nearer to the tomb; but I am quite certain that the sun was rising as she came to the sepulchre. My brethren, a new day had begun." We seem to hear his deep chuckle as he continued, "Of course, a new day had begun. The Sun of Righteousness had arisen with healing in His wings; and may everlasting glory be to His holy Name."

Let Us Tell Them

Are they startled to see people of a later age intruding upon the privacy of their conversation? Let us take courage. Are they not our older brethren? "Matthew, Mark, and John, we are pleased to meet you. Your writings have often inspired us. We have been greatly interested in your animated conversation; but we desire to repeat one of our proverbs — 'Little is much when God is in it.' The little differences in the time factor of your story thrilled us. Don't you realize that it took the three of you to write our story? We also knew what it meant to pass along the road leading from darkness into the light of a new day. We also found a risen Lord, and have never ceased praising Him. Indeed, this sums up the whole of the Christian experience. One might sit at home for years, wondering, asking, debating all kinds of recurring questions. We knew the urge that brought us from doubt to assurance, from darkness to light. We came, some of us even in despair, only to find that in Christ our Risen Lord lay the glory of the new day of experience. Because He lives, we shall live also."

SECTION TWO

Expository Notes on Mary's Meeting With Christ

But Mary stood without at the sepulchre weeping: and as she wept, she stooped down, and looked into the sepulchre, and seeth two angels in white, sitting, the one at the head, and the other at the feet, where the body of Jesus had lain (vv. 11, 12).

". . . the disciples went away again unto their own home. But Mary stood without at the sepulchre . . . ." The contrast is strange, provocative, wonderful. How could Mary go anywhere? She had no direction in which to travel. Her Lord was missing; the world had grown empty; where could she go? Much has been written about the order of the appearances made by Christ after His resurrection. Probably Pink's list is as good as any. "So far as our present light reveals, the Saviour made *eleven* appearances between His resurrection and ascension. First, to Mary Magdalene alone (John 20:14). Second, to certain women returning from the sepulcher (Matthew 28:9, 10). Third, to Simon Peter (Luke 24:34). Fourth, to the two disciples going to Emmaus (Luke 24:13). Fifth, to the ten apostles in the upper room (John 20:19). Sixth, to the eleven apostles in the upper room (John 20:26-29). Seventh, to seven disciples fishing at the sea of Tiberias (John 21). Eighth, to the eleven apostles and possibly other disciples with them (Matthew 28:16). Ninth, to above five hundred brethren at once (I Corinthians 15:7). Tenth, to James (I Corinthians 15:7). Eleventh, to the eleven apostles, and possibly other disciples on the Mount of Olives at His ascension (Acts 1). His twelfth appearance, after His ascension, was to Stephen (Acts 7). His thirteenth, to Saul on the way to Damascus (Acts 9). His fourteenth, to John on Patmos (Revelation 1). And this was the last — how profoundly significant. The *final* appearance was *His fourteenth.* The factors of fourteen are seven and two; seven being the number of perfection, and two of witness. *Thus we have His own perfect witness to His triumph over the tomb."*

Mary's tears revealed the overflowing sorrow of her soul; unfortunately, sometimes our needless sorrow blinds us to the glories of Easter day. Luke says the women saw two men; John calls the men angels. We have here a glimpse of the agelessness of eternal beings. The angels were created long before Adam, and therefore were older than four thousand years. Yet, according to Mark 16:5, the heavenly messenger was still *a young man.* Age will be outlawed in the everlasting kingdom, for there people never grow old. Bishop Andrews made many fine comments concerning the resurrection story and not the least of these was the following: "We

learn that between the angels there was no striving for places.
He that sat at the feet was as well content with his place as he that
sat at the head; we should learn from their example. With us, both
angels would have been at the *head,* and never one at the *feet.* With
us, none would have been at the feet; *we must be head-angels all!"*

> And they say unto her, Woman, why weepest thou? whom seekest
> thou? She saith unto them, Because they have taken away my
> Lord, and I know not where they have laid him. And when she
> had thus said, she turned herself back and saw Jesus standing,
> and knew not that it was Jesus (vv. 13, 14).

A thrill had gone throughout heaven; probably the angelic hosts
watched as the Lord rose from the encircling garments, and probably
too, they sang together at this introduction of a new age of redeeming glory. When some of their number were commissioned to go
down to the tomb to announce the glad news, God supplied fresh
evidence that the angels are ". . . ministering spirits, sent forth to
minister for them who shall be heirs of salvation" (Hebrews 1:14).
The angels must have been present even when Peter and John visited
the tomb, but alas, the men were too intent on other things; their
eyes "were holden" so that they did not see what the women saw.
This suggests that often we also are accompanied by God's messengers. Our inability to see them does not change the fact that
they are there. "For he shall give his angels charge over thee, to
keep thee in all thy ways. They shall bear thee up in their hands,
lest thou dash thy foot against a stone" (Psalm 91:11, 12). It is well
to remember that Christ is never far from those who seek Him, and
even though He may pass unrecognized, this sublime fact should
comfort all whose hearts are heavy with grief.

> Jesus saith unto her, Woman, why weepest thou? whom seekest
> thou? She, supposing him to be the gardener, saith unto him,
> Sir, if thou have borne him hence, tell me where thou hast laid
> him, and I will take him away. Jesus saith unto her, Mary. She
> turned herself, and saith unto him, Rabboni; which is to say,
> Master (vv. 15, 16).

There is something wonderfully attractive about Mary's avowed
intention. She never paused to ask how she would be able to carry
a body, nor where she would take it. Her only thought was to find
and be near Him again. He belonged to her; where was He? How
could she go home with Simon and John? How could she sit list-
lessly when somewhere lay the form of her Beloved? With exquisite
grace and indescribable charm, the Master called her by name,
and she knew His voice. She stared; she wiped the tears from her
eyes, and as glad relief flooded her soul, she fell on her knees before

Him. Mary asked the question of the supposed gardener, and without waiting to receive an answer, turned again toward the tomb, the center of her problems. The enunciation of her name, in the same old way, by the same well-known voice, filled her soul with jubilation. *She turned herself back;* joyously looked into His radiant face; and then falling on her knees allowed her body to surge forward as though she would embrace His feet in reverent wonder.

Jesus saith unto her, Touch me not; for I am not yet ascended to my Father: but go to my brethren, and say unto them, I ascend unto my Father, and your Father; and to my God, and your God (v. 17).

A comparison of this text with others in the synoptic records suggests that in her impetuosity, she might even have partially succeeded in her attempt to embrace His feet (compare Matthew 28:9). However, nothing can change the fact that Christ's command introduced a new phase of teaching in the ministry of the Saviour. His words presented an entirely new command, for never before had He told anyone to stay away from Him. The key word in His ministry had been COME, and His chief lament that people would not come. Yet on the morning of the resurrection He forbade Mary to touch Him. Later, He invited Thomas saying, "Reach hither thy finger, and behold my hands; and reach hither thy hand, and thrust it into my side: and be not faithless, but believing" (verse 27). Students should be careful to note that between the interviews with Mary and Thomas, the Lord made a visit to heaven. The reason for the command to Mary was made clear: "Touch me not; FOR I AM NOT YET ASCENDED to my Father." By this statement the Lord could not have meant the ascension from the Mount of Olives. Had this been the thought in His mind, of necessity He would have been obligated to issue a similar command to Thomas. He invited Thomas to thrust a hand into the wound because *by that time He had already been to the Father and had returned safely.* (See the homily at the end of this section.)

It is not without significance that Christ did not say, ". . . unto my God and your God; unto my Father and your Father." Throughout Old Testament ages, "God" had been the name by which Israel thought of the Almighty; the term "Father" had remained almost unknown. When the Lord taught His disciples to pray, saying, "Our Father . . ." this had been something new to them. Yet now, when redemptive work had been gloriously completed, the term "Father" becomes predominant. Under Moses and the law, men were told to remember God; in Christ and through the merits of His precious blood, sinners may draw near to a Heavenly Father.

Mary Magdalene came and told the disciples that she had seen the Lord, and that he had spoken these things unto her (v. 18).

The first human preacher of the resurrection was a woman; she rushed to tell doubtful men the thrilling message of Christ. In this she acted correctly for Christ had so commanded. There are some who would silence the testimony of women, proclaiming that the work of preaching is something exclusively reserved for men. Those same people should remember that if everything depended upon men the kingdom might have perished long ago. It would be better if women asked whether or not they were capable of remaining silent! Can any woman — or man for that matter — meet the risen Lord and remain mute? If Mary had *not* witnessed to those men, she would have disobeyed and dishonored her Lord, and probably her soul would have burst! There were four other women who would have — who probably did — agree most heartily with Magdalene. They were the daughters of Philip the evangelist; they had listened to their father so often, they probably knew some of his sermons by heart. When opportunity presented itself, the girls did a little preaching in their own right. It is not said that Philip ever rebuked them, nor that he remonstrated with Luke for advertising the presence of four disobedient, headstrong, talkative girls! (see Acts 21:8, 9).

Then the same day at evening, being the first day of the week, when the doors were shut where the disciples were assembled for fear of the Jews, came Jesus and stood in the midst, and saith unto them, Peace be unto you. And when he had so said, he shewed unto them his hands and his side. Then were the disciples glad when they saw the Lord (vv. 19, 20).

At the beginning of that memorable day, the Lord instructed Mary not to touch Him as He had not yet ascended to His Father; at the close of the day, He was back among His disciples, and as we shall see later, the restriction was no longer operative. The Lord had made His all-important visit to heaven, and in the presence of God registered a certain dynamic claim. When His mission was successfully accomplished, He returned to those on whose behalf He had made the journey. (See the homily at the end of this section.) The Lord had no need to knock upon the closed and barred door; His resurrection body had been freed from the restraints and limitations known throughout His lifetime. He did not chide them on their unfaithfulness nor scold them for hardness of heart. (1) *What peace* — the very peace of God; (2) *what prints* — the print of nails; (3) *what pleasure* — it thrilled their hearts and enabled them in after days to challenge the might of heathen kingdoms.

HOMILIES

Study No. 70

MARY MAGDALENE . . . WHO WAS TOLD TO KEEP HER DISTANCE
(John 20:17)

The Lord Jesus Christ did and said many strange things, and every day promised new and exciting experiences to the men who followed Him. Yet even they must have been greatly surprised when they heard of His command to the beloved Magdalene. It was Easter Sunday morning when the faithful woman went down to the tomb. she asked one whom she supposed to be the gardener, if he had taken away the body; and while she awaited an answer, she suddenly recognized her Lord's voice. Instinctively she fell at His feet to worship Him; but as she reached out her hands, He said, "Touch me not; for I am not yet ascended to my Father." It seems that later she was permitted to touch Him, but the initial command brought an entirely new note into the teaching of Jesus.

The New Command

The key message of Christ's ministry had been, "Come unto me . . . and I will give you rest." When the leper fell at His feet, the Saviour stretched forth a hand and *touched* him. Just one week after meeting Magdalene, He invited Thomas to place a finger into the mark of the nail; and, to say the least, His denial to Magdalene seems as strange as His invitation to Thomas seems unfair. Why did Christ tell the woman to keep her distance? The text obviously supplies the answer. "I am not yet ascended to my Father." There is a three-fold newness of relationship here, and we do well to notice it. (1) *A new relationship between man and Christ.* Something had happened to Jesus, for whereas He had formerly invited people to draw near, now he forbade His disciple to touch Him. *Calvary had changed the Saviour's attitude.* (2) *A new relationship between Christ and God.* On that Easter day neither communion in the mount nor the promise of an imminent departure for heaven would suffice. It had become immediately necessary to present Himself before the Almighty. Why? (3) *A new relationship between God and man.* The Fatherhood of God takes the pre-eminent place in the gospel. "I ascend unto MY FATHER and YOUR FATHER, and to my God and your God." Therefore it is clear that the first thing Jesus did on that memorable day was to ascend into the immediate presence of God.

The New Credentials

When an ambassador has been appointed to a foreign court, his first duty is that of presenting his credentials to the reigning sovereign. Until these have been accepted, he has no authority to represent his people in that land. The same thought is expressed in the Old Testament teaching concerning the high priesthood of Israel. Before the priest could represent the people, he himself had to be accepted by God. Then the blood of the offering would be sprinkled on the mercy seat and the appointed man could act on behalf of his nation. The epistle to the Hebrews clearly reveals that Christ is now our accepted High Priest. His death at Calvary fulfilled every type concerning the blood of the lamb, and the only thing that remained to be accomplished was the presentation of His credentials before the throne of God. Therefore on that Easter day the scene in heaven beggared description, for all the angelic host watched the eternal Son presenting before His Father the evidence of His sufferings.

The New Challenge

"Then the same day at evening . . . came Jesus and stood in the midst, and saith unto them, Peace be unto you. And when he had so said, he shewed unto them his hands and his side. Then were the disciples glad when they saw the Lord." It was as though He said, "Can you see these wounds in my hands and my side? They were the credentials which I presented on your behalf in heaven. My Father accepted them; will you?" Thomas was not present at that meeting, but all his doubts were banished eight days later when the Saviour said, "Thomas, reach hither thy finger, and behold my hands; and reach hither thy hand, and thrust it into my side: and be not faithless, but believing." This constituted the new challenge. Here we have blessing in triplicate. The disciples looked at the Lord and discovered a new *peace*. "Peace be unto you." They recognized the way of *pardon*. "He shewed unto them his hands." They experienced *pleasure*. "Then were the disciples glad when they saw the Lord." They knew that Christ had died for them; they were sure He also would intercede for them; what more could any man desire?

> Oh, the peace the Saviour gives,
> Peace I never knew before:
> And the way has brighter grown,
> Since I learned to trust Him more.

(Reprinted from *Bible Treasures*, page 137).

Expository Notes on Christ's Dealings With Thomas

Then said Jesus to them again, Peace be unto you: as my Father hath sent me, even so send I you. And when he had said this, he breathed on them, and saith unto them, Receive ye the Holy Spirit. Whose soever sins ye remit, they are remitted unto them; and whose soever sins ye retain, they are retained (vv. 21-23).

"Luke tells us that He said, 'Behold my hands and my feet, that it is I myself: HANDLE ME, and see' (Luke 24:39). It was most appropriate that *this* word should be recorded in the third gospel, which portrays Him as the Son of man; and it was most suitable to omit this detail in the gospel which speaks of His divine dignity and glory. Observe here, 'He shewed unto them his hands and *his side*.' Luke says, 'his hands and *his feet*.' This variation is also significant. Here, His word in John would presuppose His 'feet,' for they, in common with His hands, bore the imprint of the nails. But there was a special reason for mentioning His *side* here — see 19:34: through His pierced side a way was opened to His *heart*, the seat of the affections. *In John we see Him as the Son of God, and God is love"* (A. W. Pink).

When the Lord repeated the message, "Peace be unto you," He not only impressed the truth upon their consciousness; He assured them of something most necessary as they prepared to fulfil their commission. *"As the Father hath sent me, even so send I you."* In some senses, their mission was to be as important as His. He was sent to make salvation for sinners possible; He was now sending them, for without the proclamation of the message, even the triumph of the cross would fall short of that which God intended. How can men be saved unless they hear the Gospel? And how can preachers proclaim the message unless there is a message to proclaim? God and redeemed men were inextricably united in the endeavor to evangelize humanity. A mere handful of apparently impotent people would capture the world for Christ; the very idea seemed fantastic and ludicrous, and yet it was true. There would be innumerable conflicts and very much pain, but the commission carried the strength to succeed. The reiteration of His words, "Peace be unto you," was destined to remain in their minds forever. Even sixty or more years later, John remembered quite clearly that He had repeated His message.

And when he had said this, he breathed on them and saith unto them, Receive ye the Holy Spirit. It is well to remember that at the beginning of time, God breathed into Adam the breath of life. Before the first Adam could embark upon the ministry which God gave to him — that of tending the garden and replenishing the earth — he needed the life and power which made the task possible. Even so, before the disciples could fulfil the wishes of the Master, before they could go forth to evangelize the world, they also needed spiritual strength to triumph. Therefore Christ breathed upon them, and the Holy Spirit at that moment began to reside in their hearts. Many ministers state the Holy Spirit never indwelt men until Pentecost, but this is wrong. At Pentecost they were signally anointed with power for service; prior to this they were filled for holiness. *The battles within must first be won, otherwise campaigns without will fail before they begin.* The Scriptures which describe those events between the "breathing of the Holy Spirit" and the day of Pentecost make thrilling reading. When the Lord Jesus ascended into heaven, His watching disciples did not groan and feel utterly deserted — they actually worshiped Him and returned to Jerusalem with increasing joy. Even Peter, so slow to understand, so quick to make mistakes, was beginning to understand the teachings of the Old Testament. Surely the Holy Spirit was already guiding the impetuous man into the proper understanding of the Word of Truth (see Acts 1:15-22).

Much error has been taught in regard to the supposed transmission of the ability to forgive sins. The text has been quoted as the Biblical justification for apostolic succession and the privileges said to be vested in the Roman priesthood. In regard to this point, Bishop Ryle has well said, "The meaning of these words, I believe, may be paraphrased thus: 'I confer on you the power of declaring and pronouncing authoritatively whose sins are forgiven, and whose sins are not forgiven. I bestow on you the office of pronouncing who are pardoned and who are not, just as the Jewish high priest pronounced who were clean and who were not clean in cases of leprosy.'"

There is no real difficulty in this message of Christ. Is it an unwarranted assumption of power when a teacher tells a class that two and two make four? Is it inexcusable when a builder tells an apprentice that if he conforms to certain building laws, the result will be a house? The death and resurrection of Christ had produced the Gospel of the grace of God; a new message of unlimited charm could now be preached to sinners. This message declared that if a man would believe in and respond to the claims of Christ, forgiveness of sin would become an actual experience. Pardon was no longer the anticipated result of meritorious living. The forgiveness of sin was a gift instantaneously received by those who conformed to divine requirements. It was completely unthinkable that God could ever violate His promises; what He stated would infallibly come to pass. Therefore, knowing as they did the message, acquainted as they were with the requirements made by God, these commissioned men were able to recognize those whose hearts were toward the Saviour. If a man trusted Christ, the Apostles were authorized to tell him at once that his sins were forgiven. Similarly when a man rejected the Lord Jesus, the same Apostles were justified in affirming that his sins remained. They were able to do this, *not because they had special powers invested in them, but because they themselves had the utmost confidence that Christ would honor His own promise.* By the same standard *every minister* with the same discernment may say to a convert, "Thy sins are forgiven thee." This does not mean that he personally can forgive sins, but that he knows the thing has happened. Even if he did not utter the formula, it would make no difference — *the job would have been done anyway.* The Roman perversion of this great text has brought untold sorrow to millions of people; for centuries it enslaved and misdirected the Church of God. This doctrine was never meant to be a fund raiser for new ecclesiastical projects nor a weapon with which to terrorize superstitious people. The doctrine of the forgiveness of sins, as announced to the disciples and afterward proclaimed by them, was the harbinger of great joy. Forgiveness is *free;* it is the gift of God.

> But Thomas, one of the twelve, called Didymus, was not with them when Jesus came. The other disciples therefore said unto him, We have seen the Lord. But he said unto them, Except I shall see in his hands the print of the nails, and put my finger into the print of the nails, and thrust my hand into his side, I will not believe (vv, 24, 25).

Thomas was one of those men who possessed a gloomy disposition; it was easier far to be sad than to laugh. If Thomas were lost in a forest, he would probably sit down and die rather than take the path that might lead him deeper into distress. Yet he was not a coward, and it should always be remembered that he was willing to accompany Christ to death rather than to live alone. (See the expository notes on chapter 11:16.) It is easy for us to understand that despondency had dwarfed all else in the mind of Thomas. The tragedy of the cross had overwhelmed him; he almost wished he were dead. It is noteworthy that while the other disciples securely fastened the door of their apartment, lest the Jews should find and put them to death, Thomas deliberately went into the city. If he were caught and executed, what did he care? His Master was dead; was there any reason why he should live? When Thomas was about, the sky was generally overcast, but in the most delightful way the sun usually managed to shine through the mists.

> And after eight days again his disciples were within, and Thomas with them: then came Jesus, the doors being shut, and stood in the midst, and said, Peace be unto you. Then saith he to Thomas, Reach hither thy finger, and behold my hands; and reach hither thy hand, and thrust it into my side: and be not faithless, but believing (vv. 26, 27).

That the Lord invited Thomas to thrust his hand into his side suggests the wound must have been large. The Master's side had surely been ripped open. Only thus would the passage of a hand have been possible. It should also be remembered that this is the only place in the Testament where Christ was actually addressed as GOD. The man who knew so well how to descend into the valley of despondency was also an expert climber. He who lived in the gloom of the valley appreciated the sun-lit summit of Christian experience.

> And Thomas answered and said unto him, My Lord and My God. Jesus saith unto him, Thomas, because thou hast seen me, thou hast believed: blessed are they that have not seen, and yet have believed (vv. 28, 29).

It will be remembered that at the cross the soldiers said, "Let us see him come down from the cross, and we will believe." Yet in Bethany, the Lord said to Martha, "Said I not unto thee, if thou wouldest believe, thou shouldest see the glory of God." Faith sees the invisible and reaches the unreachable!

> And many other signs truly did Jesus in the presence of his disciples, which are not written in this book: But these are written, that ye might believe that Jesus is the Christ, the Son of God; and that believing ye might have life through his name (vv. 30, 31).

The reference to the "other signs" does not of necessity imply things of which we have no knowledge. John did not set out to write *everything* that might be written about the Lord Jesus; the Gospel was never meant to be a complete life story of the Master. John endeavored to write those things pertinent to his theme. There were other manifestations of the risen Lord which he omitted, probably because he knew other brethren had already written the details. For example, Luke told of the walk to Emmaus, and Matthew of the great missionary commission that was destined to take them into all the world (Luke 24 and Matthew 28). To repeat with emphasis what has been said, John had no desire to write a biography of the Lord; he was far more concerned to supply sufficient details to lead men into a saving knowledge of Christ the Son of God. Happy is that man who uses His life to extol the virtue of his Master.

HOMILIES

Study No. 71

THE RESURRECTION OF JESUS . . .
THE MESSAGE THAT CHANGED THE WORLD
(I Corinthians 15)

The preaching of the resurrection of the Lord Jesus was easily the greatest bombshell ever to explode in the ancient world. So completely unexpected and catastrophic to Jewish policy, it was destined to have far reaching repercussions. Immediately the Jewish world was divided into two sections, and the division has continued to this day. The leaders of the nation declared the body of the Lord Jesus had been stolen; the Apostles maintained Christ had risen from the dead and that they had seen Him. If, in the final analysis, death overcame Jesus, then His ministry ended in defeat. We are, therefore, obliged to face the issue — either Christ rose again, or He remained in His tomb. In true Pauline fashion, let us consider a few propositions.

If Christ be risen — Death is not the end

Perhaps the greatest enemy of mankind is death, for all human endeavor seems destined to terminate in a grave. The leading thinkers, the most brilliant of mortals, and all the sons of men walk along pathways which inevitably lead to a tomb. And ever since this ugly specter came to darken man's outlook, he has asked the question — "If a man die, shall he live again?" (Job 14:14). Even prior to the proclamation of the gospel message, the Jewish nation was divided on the subject. The Pharisees believed in the survival of the soul; the Sadducees declared that death terminated existence. Death is the fog barrier clouding distant horizons, and all people speculate as to what lies beyond the reach of mortal vision. If Christ rose again, then our greatest question is answered. Death cannot be the end.

If Christ be risen — He is the world's greatest Teacher

This is so because He accurately foretold the event. Constantly He warned His disciples that He would be delivered into the hands of sinful men, would be crucified, and after three days would rise again. That they forgot His message does not alter the fact that He predicted what was to take place. A striking comparison is provided in the case of one of Britain's leading spiritualists who declared that in proof of his faith he would return after death to attend a special meeting to be convened in London. The meeting was held, and a great audience thronged the auditorium; yet, to the disappointment of all, the famous prophet failed to appear. If Christ rose again in fulfilment of His promise, He alone of all the world's teachers was able to accomplish such a miracle.

If Christ be risen — That is the secret of New Testament dynamic

Almost as great as the resurrection itself was the complete transformation in the disciples. Men who had fled from Gethsemane in order to save their lives, suddenly acquired a new power which enabled them to scorn the threat of death. Many of these early Christians were thrown to hungry lions; others were burned at the stake, and "they held not their lives dear unto them." They challenged the power of heathen dynasties, and in their own life blood established the creed of their new faith. The resuscitation of their waning hopes and the subsequent evangelizing of the world demand that some explanation be given for this outstanding miracle. If Christ be risen, the problem is immediately solved.

If Christ be risen — He is still accessible to sinners

If Christ rose again to hide Himself in eternal remoteness, His action was entirely foreign to all that He previously taught, and completely lacking in wisdom. The Saviour never desired the life of a hermit, and constantly sought the presence of those who needed His help. If that same Saviour be risen again from the dead, it is certain that He can still be found by all who seek Him. If this were not true, the gospel story would have an anti-climax that would make it the laughing stock of the world. Critics would undoubtedly pinpoint the initial word of these propositions. They would ask how a seeker could be sure of the fact. The answer is very simple. Christ said, "Come unto me, all ye that labour and are heavy laden, and I will give you rest." Millions of men and women have accepted His invitation; and on the simple evidence that a dead Christ could do nothing, inward peace eloquently testifies to the reality of a risen Lord.

The Twenty-first Chapter of John

THEME: *Simon Peter Meets the Risen Lord*

OUTLINE:

    I. Peter's New Concern. Verses 1-11.
    II. Peter's New Commission. Verses 12-19.
    III. Peter's New Constraint. Verses 20-23.
    IV. Conclusion. Verses 24-25.

SECTION ONE

Expository Notes on Peter's Fishing Expedition

I think John must have loved Simon Peter; the closing chapter of the fourth gospel was almost dedicated to the memory of this time-honored disciple. He and John had much in common, and not even the passing of decades could impair the apostle's memory of the fiery disciple whose deeds were destined to live forever. As John prepared to lay aside his pen, as his masterly account drew to conclusion, Simon Peter was second only to Christ and it was a foregone conclusion they would be drawn close together on the final pages of the manuscript. Twelve times John mentions Peter by name, and there is reason to believe that this chapter presents the greatest picture ever produced of the big fisherman.

> After these things Jesus shewed himself again to the disciples at the Sea of Tiberias; and on this wise shewed he himself. There were together Simon Peter, and Thomas called Didymus, and Nathaniel of Cana in Galilee, and the sons of Zebedee, and two other of his disciples (vv. 1, 2).

"The Sea of Tiberias" was another name for the Sea of Galilee (John 6:1), and it was to this place the small band of disciples went. In view of the fact that Matthew 28:16 says, "Then the eleven disciples went away into Galilee, into *a mountain* WHERE JESUS HAD APPOINTED THEM," the question has arisen, "What were the seven disciples doing on the beach?" Another has asked, "Why were there only seven disciples when many more had heard the command?" Much discussion has centered in these problems. *Pink* thinks this was an act of disobedience, a needless manifestation of an impetuous nature. The ever-boisterous Simon was not content to await the

Master's coming; he must needs go down to the sea to fish. Others think that since the mountain and the sea were so close together, the opportunity to fish enabled them to obtain food; they were hungry; the events of recent days had kept them moving and hunger necessitated their obtaining supplies from some source. Let us be content in the assumption that possibly both these elements were present when Peter announced his intention of going fishing. It might have been that the other disciples preferred to remain on the hillside. If they had not arrived in Galilee as yet, we do not know what occasioned their delay. The identity of the "two other disciples" has not been revealed. Perhaps the vacancy in the list of names was left that we could sign the record!

Simon Peter saith unto them, I go a fishing. They say unto him, We also go with thee. They went forth, and entered in a ship immediately; and that night they caught nothing (v. 3).

Peter was never a man to sit still. He was a man of action; to remain motionless was unthinkable. Let us not condemn him; while it is quite wrong to be running around in circles when the Lord has commanded one to wait, nevertheless, those early days needed men of action, men who seeing the difficulties would never rest until Christ's banner flew proudly over areas where sin had reigned. Peter and later Paul were Christians of this caliber and the church of God will always be in their debt. Some people think the scarcity of fish reflected the impatience and carnality of the fishermen, but this is only a point of view. It is wiser to say the men caught nothing because God so ordained it. Even the greatest fisherman waits in vain if God prevents the fish from cooperating. There was much more at stake that night than the appeasing of men's hunger. At the opportune moment, the Lord would supply breakfast; first, He desired to feed their souls with the Bread of Life, to give to them a new lesson — how to become fishers of men.

But when the morning was come, Jesus stood on the shore: but the disciples knew not that it was Jesus (v. 4).

It will be remembered that Christ after His resurrection chose occasionally to withhold the power of recognition from His followers; that is, He came in disguise to teach great truth. It is a wonderful thing for the eyes of the downcast to fill with glad surprise. It is even more wonderful after a night of fruitless toil when men suddenly discover their uselessness was foreordained by God to help achieve unprecedented victories. Even the darkest night has a glimmer of radiance when mariners believe Christ awaits them on the shores whither they journey (See Mark 16:12).

Then Jesus saith unto them, Children, have ye any meat? They answered him, No. And he said unto them, Cast the net on the right side of the ship, and ye shall find. They cast therefore, and now they were not able to draw it for the multitude of fishes (vv. 5, 6).

Probably Christ seemed to be one of the fish merchants who came to the beach in order to buy directly from the fishermen. When His question echoed across the bay, Peter probably replied, "We haven't any. Tomorrow, we may have some." The Saviour's answer, "Cast your net on the right side of the ship," presents problems. It is hard to understand how experienced men who had been to the recognized fishing grounds, men who had failed to catch one fish, should suddenly respond to a Stranger's invitation to throw their nets into shallow water. Let no reader misunderstand these remarks. The author firmly believes that Christ, the Son of God, could have prepared many fish just as He prepared a great fish to intercept Jonah's flight from God (Jonah 1:17). Nevertheless, Christ's ability to do this would not explain the fishermen's readiness to obey an apparently senseless command. It is probable that from His vantage point on the beach the Master saw the movements of a shoal of fish swimming around the bay. His echoing command, "Cast the net on the right side of the ship, and ye shall find," made the fishermen look in that direction, and instantly they saw what He saw. Their frenzied endeavor to get the net over the side resulted in a great haul of fish. The indolence and bitter disappointment of the preceding hours were completely banished as they struggled to land their catch. If this assumption be correct, if Christ had indeed seen the direction in which the fish were swimming and realized they would pass on the *right* side of the ship, it is easily understood why He spoke as He did. Sometimes we look for His hand in the miraculous events of life. It is wiser and better to see His guidance in the ordinary episodes of daily routine, to see and appreciate His nearness when we think He is far away. We need to detect the unfolding of His plans in the little things of life, in the disappointments and failures by which we are surrounded constantly.

> **Therefore that disciple whom Jesus loved saith unto Peter, It is the Lord. Now when Simon Peter heard that it was the Lord, he girt his fisher's coat unto him, (for he was naked,) and did cast himself into the sea. And the other disciples came in a little ship; (for they were not far from land, but as it were two hundred cubits (about one hundred yards) dragging the net with fishes (vv. 7, 8).**

"How characteristic of the two apostles are the features which appear in these two simple incidents. John contemplates and divines; Peter acts and springs forward. 'It will not fail to be noticed,' says *Reuss*, 'that Peter has need to be instructed by John;' which means that by this detail the author seeks to elevate John above Peter. But in all that follows, everything tends on the contrary to give Peter the rank. What results from this is simply that the story tends to characterize the two principal apostles by their different gifts, as they afterward showed themselves throughout their whole career — Peter, the man of missionary activity; John of contemplative knowledge. The garment called *ependutees* is an intermediate one — it is the *blouse* of the workman. After having taken it off, Peter was really naked except for the *subligaculum* — the apron — required for decency . . . . the Greek usage of the word *gummos*, 'naked,' authorizes this sense. The Greek word for 'he girded himself' includes the two ideas of *putting on* the garment and *fastening it*." (F. L. Godet).

Peter's impetuosity aroused an intense desire to get to Christ quickly. He forsook the boat and left his colleagues to struggle with the net. Sometimes an unwarranted excitement makes us forgetful of duty. Faith without works is dead, and the man whose forgetfulness increases the burdens of other people will hardly be able to win those tired souls for Christ. Peter might have been better employed helping to land the fish rather than floundering around in the tide. The fishermen *dragged* the net close to shore, probably believing they would have a better chance of landing the fish in shallow water.

> As soon then as they were come to land, they saw a fire of coals there, and fish laid thereon, and bread. Jesus saith unto them, Bring of the fish which ye have now caught. Simon Peter went up, and drew the net to land full of great fishes, an hundred and fifty and three: and for all there were so many, yet was not the net broken (vv. 9-11).

Had the Master caught the fish with His own line? Did the Lord Jesus kindle a fire, cook the fish, and carve the bread? These are questions all would like to ask. The breakfast on the beach was destined to become immortal in the memory of those present. The Lord was Host, Cook, Waiter, Friend, Teacher, and in every role proved Himself to be an expert. Had Christ desired, He could have caught sufficient fish to meet every requirement; to Him it was easy to catch a multitude of fishes as it was to take one. He was content to supply the first helping of the meal. Afterward He asked for additional supplies in order to teach that in fishing for men He and the disciples would need to work in close harmony. "We are labourers together *with God*." (1) He is quite able to catch His own fish. (2) He instructs His followers, how, where, and when to cast their nets. (3) As they were destined to share what He had caught, He also desired to share what they had caught. Either ministered to the other. This is the ultimate in Christian experience. Possibly Peter's hurried swim to shore left him stranded and embarrassed on the beach; the Master's request provided the excuse to work off a little more of his energy. (For the contrast between the fishing experiences, see the homily at the end of this section.)

A. W. Pink has an interesting comment on this part of the story. "Peter drew the net to land: how remarkable is this in view of what is said in chapter 21:6. 'They were not able to draw it for the multitude of fishes.' Surely this indicates another important lesson in connection with service. What six men had been unable to do in their own strength, one man now did when he went to his work from the feet of Christ. Peter was weaker than gossamer thread when he followed his Lord afar off; but in His presence . . . power came upon him." Peter was concerned about his future, his appetite, and his occupation. When he said, "I go a fishing," he expressed all that was in his mind. Then a new concern begat exuberance and excitement; he dived into the sea and swam for the shore, only to feel strange and perhaps a little ill at ease as he stood alone with his Master. He who had failed so badly, desperately wanted to please the Lord, and this concern added strength to his arms as he hurried to pull the net ashore. John remembered it all, and probably smiled as he wrote his story. Peter, in spite of many faults, was a likable man. John liked him and so do we.

HOMILIES

Study No. 72

Students should compare and contrast the fishing stories recorded in Luke 5 and John 21. They are so alike, and have so much in common, that both contribute to each other.

PETER . . . WHO HAD THE SHOCK OF HIS LIFE!

Simon Peter's second meeting with Christ was momentous. "And it came to pass, that, as the people pressed upon Christ to hear the word of God, he stood by the lake of Gennesaret, and saw two ships standing by the lake; but the fishermen were gone out of them and were washing their nets. And he entered into one of the ships, which was Simon's, and prayed him that he would thrust out a little from the land. And he sat down, and taught the people out of the ship" (Luke 5:1-3). This was to become a day of shocks for Simon Peter.

Peter Listening

Gently, the small ship rose and fell on the bosom of the sea; and slowly with skill born of long practice, the fisherman moved his oars backward and forward. The stillness was broken only by the musical waves on the beach, the creaking of the oars in the oarlocks, and the sweet notes of the Teacher's voice. Sometimes He lifted His hand to add emphasis to a part of His message; sometimes His voice lowered to a whisper; but even then His audience, seated on the rising beachhead, heard every word. And time stood still! The people could have listened forever. The oars gently dipped in the water; the boat rose and fell; the Teacher contentedly sat in the stern. Charming eloquence, challenging thought, compassionate entreaty, irresistible winsomeness — these were the characteristics of His message, and as Simon listened he almost forgot he was controlling the floating pulpit. His movements were automatic.

Peter Learning

A subdued murmur arose from the congregation; the service had ended. People were beginning to stand, and smiles of appreciation were on many faces. The Preacher was turning around on His seat in the stern — "Thank you very much, Mr. Fisherman." His eyes were alight with pleasure. "Now launch out into the deep and let down your nets for a draught. I always like to compensate people who help Me in My work, and your willingness to lend Me this boat meant a great deal to Me. Let us move into deeper water and let down the NETS." And poor Simon frowned. The Teacher was so appreciative but — "Master, we have toiled all the night and have taken nothing: nevertheless, at thy word, I will let down the NET" (verses 4, 5). Surely the Lord had difficulty in hiding His smile, for He knew Simon was due for a shock. The ship was heading for deep water. ONE NET was made ready and allowed to trail as Andrew rode the boat around in a wide arc. And Jesus watched the entire operation. How delightful! "And when they had done this, they enclosed a great multitude of fishes: and their NET brake." "O Simon Peter, what a shame! Your good net is breaking. I told you to put down the NETS." Silvery wonders were still coming up from the deep; the bottoms of the boats were covered; the piles of flopping fish were getting larger — "And they came and filled both the ships, so that they began to sink," "Quick, brother Andrew, I'm getting wet; bale water, throw the fish out, row back to the shore."

Peter Languishing

"When Simon Peter saw it, he fell down at Jesus' knees saying, Depart from me for I am a sinful man, O Lord. For he was astonished and all that were with him, at the draught of the fishes which they had taken" (verse 9). Poor Peter! He had lost his morning; he had lost some of his remarkable catch; he had damaged his net; his self-confidence had been shattered. The sermon had weakened his resistance; the fish destroyed it. This was indeed the Christ, and as Simon looked into the face of the Master his knees gave way, and he cried, "I am a sinful man, O Lord." And Christ gravely watched him. It had taken a great deal of careful planning, much patience, a sermon, a sinking ship, and a shoal of fish to bring Peter to his knees. *Some legs are very stiff!*

Peter Leaving

"And Jesus said unto Simon, Fear not; from henceforth thou shalt catch men. And when they had brought their ships to land, they forsook all, and followed him" (verses 10, 11). Their business went into voluntary liquidation. Did they stay long enough to dispose of their fish? What happened to the boat? What did their families say when they went off on what appeared to be a wild goose chase? Peter and his companions never regretted their decision. At Pentecost their net enclosed an exceedingly great multitude of fishes — even three thousand, "and for all there were so many, yet was not the net broken." This was the glorious fulfilment of an old promise. "Fear not; from henceforth thou shalt catch men."

(Reprinted from *Bible Treasures,* page 93.)

It will be remembered that when the Lord told Peter to cast out the NETS, one net was unable to hold the catch. Yet in after days when the Master instructed His followers to cast the NET on the right side of the ship, even though 153 LARGE fish crowded into it, yet the net did not break. A man is both wise and safe to do exactly as Christ commands.

SECTION TWO

Expository Notes About the Breakfast on the Beach

Jesus saith unto them, Come and dine. And none of the disciples asked him, Who art thou? knowing that it was the Lord. Jesus then cometh and taketh bread, and giveth them, and fish likewise. This is now the third time that Jesus shewed himself to his disciples, after that he was risen from the dead (vv. 12-14).

There is one notable omission about this feast. When formerly the Master sat at the table with the disciples, before they commenced to eat He gave thanks. "And Jesus took the loaves; and when he had given thanks, he distributed to the disciples . . ." (John 6:11). It is not said that He followed this example when they breakfasted together on the beach. If He did, John did not record the fact; if He did not, there could be hidden treasure in the omission. As the perfect God-Man among men, He was ever mindful of setting a good example. When He fed His disciples at the early morning

breakfast, He appeared not as the perfect Man but as their Redeemer, their risen Lord. He had no need to return thanks — HE
WAS ADMINISTERING SOMETHING DIRECT TO THEIR HUNGRY SOULS. The
diet was identical with that of former days; it was the most suitable, the most sensible for fishermen. If John had written how Christ
prepared some other kind of meal, the critics of all ages would have
pronounced the gospel fraudulent. The silence which prevailed
throughout the meal was born not of unbelief but of deep reverence,
recognition, and profound respect. This was the Lord; this was
their Master.

> So when they had dined, Jesus saith to Simon Peter, son of Jonas,
> lovest thou me more than these? He saith unto him, Yea, Lord;
> thou knowest that I love thee. He saith unto him, Feed my lambs
> (v. 15).

"When Christ entered into this discourse with Peter — it was
after they had dined — He foresaw that what He had to say to Peter
would give him some uneasiness. Peter was conscious that he had
incurred the Master's displeasure, and could expect no other than
to be upbraided with his ingratitude. Twice, if not thrice, he had
seen his Master since His resurrection, and Christ said not a word
to him about it. We may suppose Peter to be full of doubts upon what
terms he stood with his Master; sometimes hoping the best, yet not
without some fear. But now at length his Master puts him out of his
pain" (Matthew Henry).

There can be no doubt that Christ carefully planned this entire
episode. John 18:18 speaks about the *fire of coals* at which Peter
denied the Lord; John recalled how the Master had kindled a similar fire. At first there was no need for the Saviour to say anything;
the fire was searing Peter's conscience. Formerly, the disciple sat
with the Lord's enemies; here he sat with the Lord's people. There
he hungered and there was no food for a disciple's soul; here he
sat at the Lord's own table. There his burning words of denial left
a scar on his soul; here, his confession of love thrilled those who
listened.

(1) Much interesting comment has been made regarding the
meaning of *"more than these."* Some have thought Christ was asking
if Peter's love superceded the love of the other brethren. "Simon,
do you love Me more than John and the others love Me?" It is
problematical whether this supplies the correct interpretation as the
question might have caused resentment in the hearts of the others
had Peter's answer been in the affirmative.

(2) Others think Christ's question could be expressed: "Simon,
do you love Me more than you love these brethren?" This question

would have been easier to answer; it would not be an offense to the others to reply, "Yes, Lord, I do."

(3) "Than *these* . . . ." A few commentators suggest Christ was pointing toward the unconsumed fish, that He was saying, "Simon, so quickly and so easily you went fishing. Simon, do you love Me more than you love to fish; that is, Simon, could you continue to leave your occupation and everything else, just to follow Me and do My will?" It is not wise to be dogmatic about the relative values of these suggestions; the important feature is that Christ must have pre-eminence in *all* things. We cannot ask Him to be second in any project.

The Greek words used in the passage to express "love" are not identical. The Lord asked, "Simon, do you LOVE Me with that deep devotion that a son would have for a father. Simon, do you really LOVE ME?" But Peter was unable to forget the shame of his former failure, and replied, "Lord, I am very, very fond of Thee. You are my Friend, and within my heart is great affection for You." It should be understood that he said this, not because he did not truly love the Christ, but *rather because he was learning to love himself less.* The resultant commission to feed the lambs of Christ's flock did much to restore his confidence. It should be noticed that Peter was told to feed LAMBS. Sheep should be able to feed themselves!

> He saith to him again the second time, Simon, son of Jonas, lovest thou me? He saith unto him, Yea, Lord, thou knowest that I love thee. He saith unto him, Feed my sheep. He saith unto him the third time, Simon, son of Jonas, lovest thou me? Peter was grieved because he said unto him the third time, Lovest thou me? And he said unto him, Lord, thou knowest all things; thou knowest that I love thee. Jesus saith unto him, Feed my sheep. (vv. 16, 17).

When the Lord asked the question the third time, He graciously used Peter's word, *phileis me*: "hast thou affection for me?" It is noteworthy that when our faith is too small to reach His level of sublimity, grace brings Him down to our level; otherwise we should die in despair. Three times Peter denied his Lord; three times the Master urged him to confess. Overwhelming fellowship with Christ is the only antidote for the haunting memories of past failure. (1) If Christ could give this commission to Peter, then the disciple's lapse had been pardoned. (2) If Christ could trust even the lambs of the flock to Simon's care, then the Great Shepherd had confidence in Peter even though the disciple had none in himself. (3) If the mature sheep were to be led into green pastures and beside still waters, then even Peter could expect help from the One whose far reaching mercy had brought these sheep into the fellowship of the fold. Simon Peter received three things: (1) *Pardon for his soul.* The Master had not cast him off. (2) *Peace for his mind.* Christ still trusted him. (3)

Power for his service. The protection of the sheep necessitated the continuing interest of the Good Shepherd.

HOMILIES

See "The Three-fold Invitation of Jesus" at the end of Section Three, Chapter 1.

SECTIONS THREE AND FOUR

Expository Notes on an Unfounded Rumor

Verily, verily, I say unto thee, When thou wast young, thou girdest thyself, and walkedst whither thou wouldest: but when thou shalt be old, thou shalt stretch forth thy hands, and another shall gird thee, and carry thee whither thou wouldest not. This spake he, signifying by what death he should glorify God (vv. 18, 19).

Peter had confessed, "Lord, thou knowest all things"; here was the evidence that he had spoken correctly. As a youth, he had enjoyed natural freedom; soon he would be bound and imprisoned. Formerly he controlled his own actions; finally death would come to offend every natural instinct. Yet even in this Peter would know the superb joy of glorifying God. Truly, the Lord Jesus knew everything. He saw the end from the beginning; He was the Living Word. The apostle remained faithful to the day of martyrdom, when like his Lord he was crucified. As the last surviving apostle, John saw this in bold relief, and was able to write: "This spake he, signifying by what death he should glorify God."

And when he had spoken this, he saith unto him, Follow me (v. 19).

This was a reiteration of the old invitation and command. Originally, the Lord said, "Follow me, and I will make you fishers of men" (Matthew 4:19). Since that day there had been joys and sorrows, successes and defeats. Peter had changed on innumerable occasions; the Lord had been the same "yesterday, and today, and forever." Man's unfaithfulness cannot change the faithfulness of God. "Peter, the command is still the same: Follow me."

Then Peter, turning about, seeth the disciple whom Jesus loved following; which also leaned on his breast at supper, and said, Lord, which is he that betrayeth thee? Peter seeing him saith to Jesus, Lord, and what shall this man do? Jesus saith unto him, If I will that he tarry till I come, what is that to thee? follow thou me (vv. 20-22).

Peter was still Peter. He provided a living example of the old saying, "God brought Israel out of Egypt in one night; it took Him forty years to bring Egypt out of Israel." To bring a man into the kingdom of God is relatively easy when compared with the task of making that same man like Christ (See I John 3:1-3.) The Master's gentle rebuke reminded Peter, and still reminds us, that it is better by far to keep our eyes on Christ than to inquire into the affairs of other Christians — especially when those affairs are not strictly our concern. (See the homily at the end of this section and at the end of Section Two, chapter 13.)

> Then went this saying abroad among the brethren, that that disciple should not die: yet Jesus said not unto him, He shall not die; but, If I will that he tarry till I come, what is that to thee? (v. 23).

There was something very fitting about the triumphant way in which the apostle prepared to conclude his memoirs. He spoke not primarily about death, but of the return of Christ. It was John's great hope that one day the Lord Jesus would return in glory! To this he looked; for this joyous event he labored. If the Lord were indeed the Son of God, and if He loved the Church as was proclaimed near and far, then nothing could keep them apart. John considered this to be the greatest message ever told. Men who wasted time on the propagation of silly rumors should lean upon the Master's bosom; there, stupidity would be banished; there, wisdom would be born.

> This is the disciple which testifieth of these things, and wrote these things: and we know that his testimony is true. And there are also many other things, which Jesus did, the which, if they should be written every one, I suppose that even the world itself could not contain the books that should be written. Amen (vv. 24, 25).

John concluded his gospel with a majestic utterance. He had done his best to witness to the inexpressible glory of the Eternal Word; alas, he had only touched the fringe of things. The apostle had enjoyed describing the shallows of God's far reaching sea; unfortunately, he felt incompetent to express the inexhaustible wonders of God's fathomless ocean of infinite worth. He, John, had written many things; contemporary writers had written other things, but the subject remained virtually untouched. Was this the fanciful expression of an overwrought tired mind? No, John was probably very correct in his utterance. The Word was Jesus; and Jesus was the Word, Who, from the beginning, had been with God. In very deed and truth, this Christ had done many other things, wonderful things which were beyond the expressive powers of the world's best writers. Even now the world is filled with volumes about Jesus, but if all were known that might be known probably there would be no room anywhere for any other books; and possibly very few authors would even think about writing them. If Christ fills eternity, it would be a simple matter to fill a planet.

HOMILIES

Study No. 73

PETER . . . WHO WAS TOLD TO MIND HIS OWN BUSINESS

The nature of Simon Peter might have been described under three heads: (1) *He was very impulsive.* His fellow disciples hardly knew what to expect from the big fisherman, for while they soberly considered the pros and cons of a matter, their colleague enthusiastically pronounced a verdict. (2) *He was very inquisitive.* He was susceptible to the opinions of other people, and more often than not this led to trouble. (3) *He was very inflammable*, very temperamental. He could be alternately joyful and sad; inspired and carnal. Yet in spite of that fact, we all like Simon Peter.

A Dangerous Concern

The seaside breakfast had ended, and the disciples were watching the silvery waves move along the beach. Surging emotions filled their souls, for they realized that the Stranger who had awaited the incoming boat was the Lord. It was wonderful to see Him as He gracefully sat watching the hungry men eating the meal He Himself had prepared. Tenderly He had spoken to Peter, and the thrice asked question, "Lovest thou me," had stirred them deeply. Their colleague had been moved almost to tears, for the denials of an earlier occasion were still present in his mind. Then, after a while, Peter looked at John and said to Christ, "Lord, and what shall this man do? You tell me that when I am old another shall gird me and carry me whither I would not. Well, what about John? What will happen to him?" And the Lord answered, "If I will that he tarry till I come, what is that to thee? Simon Peter, your greatest mistake is that you are often looking at and thinking of other people. Do you remember how I sent you to take money from the mouth of the fish? You were upset then because other people's opinions overshadowed your outlook. Do you remember how you denied knowledge of Me? That happened because you permitted other people to influence you. Peter, be less concerned about other folk, and think more of your Master."

A Delightful Correction

"What is that to thee? If I be the Lord, and you are My servant, your chief aim should be to do My will. If I decide that John should linger till I return, that is no business of yours, is it? Simon Peter, if you are to feed My lambs, and shepherd My sheep, you will need to look constantly to Me. The days ahead will be difficult, and if you lose sight of your Master, anything can happen.

Therefore, do not be unduly inquisitive concerning John. Attend to your own affairs." Thus did Christ correct His disciple, and we all realize how necessary this had become. Even in after days Simon still permitted the opinions of others to sway his actions and on one occasion Paul rebuked him because he compromised with the exponents of circumcision. Peter was always getting into trouble because he had not mastered the art of minding his own business (see Galatians 2:11-16).

A Definite Command

"Follow thou me." When Peter heard this command, his thoughts probably went back to the morning when the Lord first called him, when after borrowing Peter's boat, Christ said, "Follow me, and I will make you to become a fisher of men." Now, another commission had been given. He had been told to shepherd the flock of God. "Simon, follow me, for only thus will you succeed."

(1) *The Follow-Me of Enlightenment.* The Christian pathway is beset with many dangers, and problems will arise to confound those who are not prepared for the emergencies of the way. "Follow Me, and you will learn of Me."

(2) *The Follow-Me of Endeavor.* To follow Christ means to emulate His example. It means more than accompanying Him. When a soldier follows an officer into battle, he does so to help his leader in the conflict ahead. To follow Christ means to fight for Him.

(3) *The Follow-Me of Endurance.* "But when thou shalt be old, thou shalt stretch forth thy hands, and another shall gird thee, and carry thee whither thou wouldest not. This spake he, signifying by what death he should glorify God." Tradition asserts that Peter was crucified for his faith, that at his own request he was crucified head downward, as he considered himself unworthy to die as did his Lord. Thus the fearful disciple who failed before the taunts of a servant girl eventually reached unprecedented heights of personal loyalty. He followed His Lord to a cross; he was faithful unto death.

Some theologians think that John originally terminated his memoirs at the end of chapter 20, that the final chapter was an afterthought, added at a later date. This might be true, but the consensus of opinion joyfully endorses the apostle's decision to add his postscript. Simon Peter's story belongs to all. At the beginning of the gospel, John reveals the power of the Lord in creation; at the end he tells of the grace of the Lord in redemption. He who placed the stars in the sky also placed sinners in the Kingdom of God. He was the Son of God, the King of Israel —

OUR MASTER

INDEX OF HOMILIES